AMERICAN BABYLON

POLITICS AND SOCIETY IN TWENTIETH-CENTURY AMERICA

Series Editors
William Chafe, Gary Gerstle, Linda Gordon, and Julian Zelizer

A list of titles in this series appears at the back of the book

AMERICAN BABYLON

RACE AND THE STRUGGLE FOR POSTWAR OAKLAND

Robert O. Self

PRINCETON UNIVERSITY PRESS   PRINCETON AND OXFORD

Library of Congress Cataloging-in-Publication Data

Self, Robert O., 1968–
American Babylon: race and the struggle for postwar Oakland/
Robert O. Self.
p. cm. — (Politics and society in twentieth-century America)
Includes bibliographical references and index.
ISBN 0-691-07026-1
1. Oakland Region (Calif.)—Race relations. 2. Oakland Region
(Calif.)—Politics and government—20th century. 3. Oakland Region
(Calif.)—Economic conditions—20th century. 4. African Americans—
Civil rights—California—Oakland Region—History—20th century.
5. Black power—California—Oakland Region—History—20th
century. 6. Property tax—Political aspects—California—Oakland
Region—History—20th century. 7. Homeowners—California—Oakland
Region—Political activity. 8. Social classes—California—Oakland
Region—History—20th century. 9. City and town life—California—
Oakland Region—History—20th century. 10. Suburban life—California—
Oakland Region—History—20th century. I. Title. II. Series.

F869.O2S455 2003
979.4'6600496073—dc21   2003040461

British Library Cataloging-in-Publication Data is available

This book has been composed in Sabon

Printed on acid-free paper. ∞

www.pupress.princeton.edu

Printed in the United States of America

10 9 8 7

ISBN-13: 978-0-691-07026-1 (cloth)

ISBN-10: 0-691-07026-1 (cloth)

ISBN-13: 978-0-691-12486-5 (pbk.)

ISBN-10: 0-691-12486-8 (pbk.)

For Mom and Dad and Jennifer

_____

Contents

Illustrations ————————————————————————

MAPS

Acknowledgments _____

THE INSPIRATION AND SUPPORT of colleagues, friends, and family made this book possible. There are not enough pages here to thank them properly or enough time to express the depth of my gratitude. James Gregory and Richard White shepherded the project from the beginning with grace and patient attention. Jim has exerted a steady, critical, indispensable influence on my thinking and writing. Richard has been a brilliant editor and sage advisor and continues to push me toward big ideas. His scholarly standards and intellectual vision have marked out new territory for a generation of Americanists who have worked with him. Thomas Sugrue expressed faith in the project early and has done more to assist in its realization than I had a right to expect. His advice and readings of the manuscript have been indispensable. All three have been extraordinary mentors and good friends, and I owe them an enormous debt.

Colleagues at the University of Michigan, including Paul Anderson, Charlie Bright, John Carson, Fred Cooper, Beate Dignas, Geoff Eley, Kevin Gaines, Val Kivelson, Michele Mitchell, Maria Montoya, Gina Morantz-Sanchez, Rebecca Scott, Maris Vinovskis, and Penny Von Eschen made Ann Arbor a wonderful place to write and teach and offered support at critical junctures. I would especially like to thank Matthew Countryman, Scott Kurashige, and Matthew Lassiter for conversations about our shared research interests, as well as timely critical readings, that immeasurably improved the book. A special thank you to Earl Lewis for supporting this project as both historian and dean. Colleagues in the Michigan Society of Fellows, especially James Boyd White (director), Sharad Chari, Oz Frankel, Thomas Guglielmo, Carla Mazzio, Alka Patel, Monica Prasad, Daniel Rothenberg, Adam Smith, and Peter Wilf read drafts of several chapters, gave thoughtful comments, and warmly encouraged me. I owe a special, unpayable debt to Tiff Holmes. Thank you all.

Thank you to Phil Ethington, who read the manuscript at a crucial early stage and offered both insightful criticism and encouragement. For conversations and generously shared insights and readings that shaped the book in important ways, I am particularly grateful to Linda Nash, Becky Nicolaides, and Wendell Pritchett. For reading parts of the manuscript and for unselfish and timely help along the way, I would like to thank Kate Brown, Clay Carson, George Chauncey, John Findlay, Roberta Gold, James Grossman, Arnold Hirsch, Thomas Holt, William Issel, Peniel Joseph, Michael Katz, Gretchen Lemke-Santangelo, Carl Nightingale, George Sanchez, Amanda Seligman, Heather Thompson, Andy Wiese, and Charles

Wollenberg. Joe William Trotter and Tera Hunter at the Center for Afro-American Urban Studies and the Economy at Carnegie Mellon University hosted a conference on African Americans in the postindustrial city in October 2001 that brought together an incredibly stimulating group. Thanks to them and to Ronald Bayor, Venus Green, Karl Johnson, Kenneth Kusmer, Charles Payne, Richard Pierce, and Joel Tarr. Martha Biondi encountered this book late in its evolution and gave it critical attention and showed great care for its realization. Her scholarly and intellectual example have been enormously important. At Princeton University Press, Thomas LeBien showed great patience and skill with the manuscript and made this book what it is. My deep gratitude extends as well to Brigitta van Rheinberg, who did wonderful work as editor when she inherited the book. Finally, many thanks to the people of Oakland and the East Bay who took the time to speak with me. Special thanks to Paul Cobb, Norvel Smith, and David Hilliard. To all of the above, your collaboration was essential. The mistakes remain my own.

The good graces of many people and institutions made the research for the book possible. The staff of the Institute for Governmental Studies at the University of California at Berkeley, especially Terry Dean, Ron Heckart, and Marc Levin, deserve enormous credit for providing the material that lies behind the book. Many thanks to the staff of the Bancroft Library, also at Berkeley; Bill Sturm of the Oakland History Room, Oakland Public Library; Robert Haynes and Veronica Lee of the African American Museum and Library at Oakland; Ron Riesterer and the staff of the library at the *Oakland Tribune*; the staff of the history department at the Oakland Museum of California; Susan Sherwood at the Labor Archives and Research Center, San Francisco State University; Gene Vrana at the International Longshoremen's and Warehousemen's Union Library in San Francisco; the staff of the Stanford University Archives; the Ford Foundation; and the staffs of the municipal libraries of San Leandro, Fremont, and Milpitas. Grants from the National Science Foundation, the U.S. Department of Housing and Urban Development, the American Philosophical Society, the graduate school at the University of Michigan, and the history department and graduate school at the University of Washington made the research and writing financially possible. Finally, I am grateful to Onno Brouwer, Trisha Wagner, and Erik Rundell at the University of Wisconsin Cartography Lab for their wonderful maps.

I could not have imagined undertaking this project without the support of family and friends. Grateful cannot begin to describe how I feel. My parents, Jim and Elise, have given beyond measure. Their example, especially of what familial love and commitment can be, has been a constant source of strength throughout this project and my life. Jennifer has been a gift as a sister, and as a woman she is, simply, incredible. Lise Nelson inspired and encouraged. I owe her a great deal. In Seattle, Kate and Devin Malkin, Ivan and Suzie Miller, Linda Becker, Janet Stecker, and the residents of Bob the House and Honn House made life there special, as did fellow historians Kathy Morse, Bonnie Christensen, and Margaret Paton Walsh. In San Francisco, Maggie Miller and Bill Christmas, and later Eamon, gave me far more than a place to crash. In Berkeley, Edie and Neill Rodman opened their home to me innumerable times. Thank you one and all, and to new friends and colleagues in Milwaukee and Chicago as well. All of you are deeply embedded in these pages.

Abbreviations

AFDC	Aid to Families with Dependent Children
AFL	American Federation of Labor
AME	African Methodist Episcopal Church
ANC	Aid to Needy Children
BART	Bay Area Rapid Transit
BUMP	Blacks United Mobilizing for Progress
CAP	Community Action Program
CEP	Concentrated Employment Program
CETA	Comprehensive Employment and Training Act
CHP	Committee for Home Protection
CIO	Congress of Industrial Organizations
CME	Christian Methodist Episcopal Church
COINTELPRO	Counterintelligence Programs
CORE	Congress of Racial Equality
COUP	Community Organization United for Progress
CP	Communist Party
CRC	Civil Rights Congress
CRCC	Civil Rights Coordinating Committee
CREA	California Real Estate Association
CSO	Community Services Organization
EBDC	East Bay Democratic Club
EDA	Economic Development Administration
EEOC	Equal Employment Opportunity Commission
FEPC	Fair Employment Practices Commission
FHA	Federal Housing Administration
HOLC	Home Owners Loan Corporation
HUD	Department of Housing and Urban Development
ILWU	International Longshoremen's and Warehousemen's Union
JOBART	Justice on Bay Area Rapid Transit
MAPA	Mexican American Political Association
MCSU	Marine Cooks and Stewards Union
MDTA	Manpower Development and Training Act
MOAP	Metropolitan Oakland Area Program
NAACP	National Association for the Advancement of Colored People
NALC	Negro American Labor Council
NAM	National Association of Manufacturers

NAREB	National Association of Real Estate Boards
NCDH	National Committee against Discrimination in Housing
OCCUR	Oakland Citizens Committee for Urban Renewal
OEDC	Oakland Economic Development Council
OEDCI	Oakland Economic Development Council Incorporated
OEO	Office of Economic Opportunity
OVL	Oakland Voters League
RAM	Revolutionary Action Movement
RMA	Retail Merchants Association
SASSO	Southern Alameda County Spanish Speaking Organization
SDS	Students for a Democratic Society
SNCC	Student Nonviolent Coordinating Committee
SSUC	Spanish Speaking Unity Council
UAW	United Automobile Workers
UOD	United for Oakland Committee
VA	Veterans Administration
WOPC	West Oakland Planning Committee

AMERICAN BABYLON

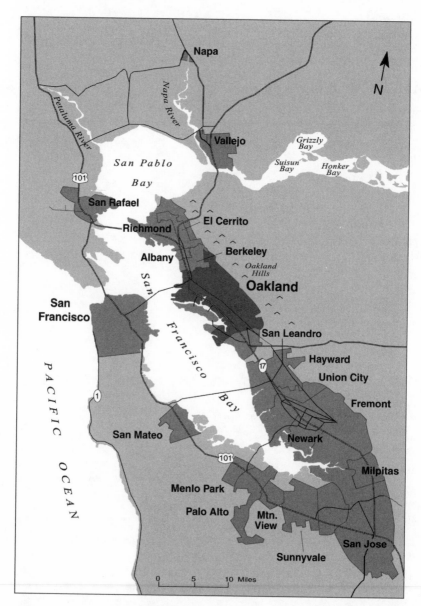

Map 1.1. The San Francisco Bay Area in the 1960s. Note the horizontal diffusion of urbanized development along the East Bay, from Richmond in the north to San Jose in the south. Oakland was not the urban "center" of the Bay Area, but postwar boosters hoped that it would become an East Bay rival to San Francisco with its own set of dependent suburban satellites. Cartography Lab, University of Wisconsin.

Introduction

THE MOST SIGNIFICANT political, economic, and spatial transformation in the postwar United States was the overdevelopment of suburbs and the underdevelopment of cities. As ostensible signifiers of this transformation, "white flight" and "urban decline" mask volatile and protracted social and political struggles over land, taxes, jobs, and public policy in the thirty years between 1945 and the late 1970s. Such struggles dominated postwar Oakland, California, and its nearby suburbs, ultimately giving rise to two of the nation's most controversial political ideologies: a black power politics of community defense and empowerment and a neopopulist conservative homeowner politics among whites. In 1945 boosters in Oakland envisioned their metropolis in the tradition of California urbanism as a verdant, interconnected garden that combined suburban growth and urban vitality. Thirty years later the Black Panther Party and other African American activists viewed Oakland as an exploited colony that was controlled from the suburban perimeter. The postwar garden had become, in their view, an "urban plantation." At the same time, suburban homeowners worked to monopolize and segregate the assets of postwar prosperity, efforts that culminated in 1978's Proposition 13, the nation's first and most influential tax limitation measure. As the home of both the Black Panther Party and the tax revolt, California's story is postwar America's story—black and white, urban and suburban, rebellion and backlash—narratives that are inextricably linked and demand to be told as one.[1]

Histories of the postwar United States typically tell separate stories. Civil rights was the great freedom movement. Suburbanization was driven by affluence and "white flight." Urban history was characterized by deindustrialization and ghetto formation. These stories stand side by side, but we are left with a surprisingly impoverished analytical language for thinking of them relationally. To consider them in relation is not just to recover their deep connections but to rethink the stories themselves. Civil rights in places like Oakland was a vibrant and dynamic dimension of postwar metropolitanization that cannot be reduced to an epilogue of the southern movement. Furthermore, the tropes of crisis, ghetto formation, and black violence that have guided postwar urban historiography can lead us to overlook the essential fact that African Americans as a whole constituted the group in national life most deeply engaged in challenging urban decline and imagining remedies to the urban crisis. Black communities nationwide were not merely the victims of the "second ghetto." They articulated and pushed for political and economic alternatives. For their part, suburban whites did not merely or only "flee" the city. They were drawn into suburban city building by material and ideological incentives. The metaphor of flight, though accurate in many respects, shifts focus away from the complicated political production of suburban communities in place. Furthermore, it fails to capture the essential political-economic issue in suburban development: taxation and its relationship to the provisioning of a welfare state and the distribution of social costs. Telling urban and suburban histories together moves us beyond generalizations like "white flight" and "black power" to the specific context in which each was embedded. Telling them together demonstrates the centrality of metropolitan history to postwar American history.[2]

The politics that produced segregation and the politics that fought it are the story of this book. In Oakland and the East Bay, as the tax revolt and black power evolved together, in tension, they faced off over how the region's assets and prosperity would be distributed. Suburban city building drew homeowners, almost exclusively white and Anglo, into political battles to shape their new communities. In conflicts over land, taxes, and housing, a combination of federal policy, homeowner self-interest, and the real estate industry's profit-driven embrace of racial exclusivity encouraged suburban residents to take narrow views of their social responsibility. When black Oaklanders undertook the postwar struggle for racial equality, they challenged the inequities of this suburban city building and accompanying signs of urban underdevelopment: residential segregation, job discrimination, urban renewal, and deindustrialization. Over time, those challenges grew increasingly urgent and militant, precipitating among many East Bay African Americans a break with liberal assumptions and strategies in favor of community empowerment. African American–led political movements thus interpenetrated with a suburban politics focused on homeownership, taxes, and a retreat from connections to a larger social collective. These critical postwar developments were not abstractions of national politics. They were grounded in urban space, in the particular metropolitan distribution of wealth, opportunity, and resources of the second half of the twentieth century.[3]

In these local contexts, the struggle for the postwar city began with the challenges facing working-class movements in the 1940s and ended with the challenges facing black-led political movements in the 1970s. Thirty years apart, organized labor and African American activists stood at center stage in setting an urban reform agenda for their generation. In the 1940s Oakland labor's political leaders called for a social democratic city, with union wages, inexpensive health care, affordable housing with low taxes, and public transportation available for all. Their program made mention of civil rights, but African Americans were implicitly junior partners, and there was little critique of white privilege. Thirty years later African American radicals and reformers, first in contest, then in alliance, called for a remarkably similar social democratic city with renewed demands for racial equality. But much had changed since the 1940s, and once in positions of authority black leaders faced a new set of problems: entrenched poverty, deindustrialization, a weak urban tax base and a strong suburban one, and all of the social consequences of four decades of segregated development. They had to contend with the failure of the postwar political economy of growth liberalism to deliver either social mobility or economic security to black Americans as a whole.[4]

Even as cities and suburbs became battlegrounds over racial segregation and economic power in local places like the East Bay in these years, metropolitan spatial development and the national state shaped one another. "We are not engaged in a local or provincial issue," Oakland NAACP President Clinton White explained. After World War II the federal government moved aggressively to define urban and suburban forms, a remarkable turnaround from the minimalist state urban policy of the first half of the century. An enormous array of federal programs, agencies, subsidies, and incentives now played as important a role in metropolitan development as private corporations and municipal governments. Local politics in places like Oakland and the East Bay thus ultimately became contests over the nature and expression of the American welfare state, in both New Deal and Great Society variants. Across the postwar United States, as cities were remade by two of the most extensive internal migrations in the nation's history—the migration of southern African Americans to the cities of the Northeast, Midwest, and West and the mass suburbanization of whites—the federal government did not stand idly by. It gave contour and direction to these migrations. Its housing policies helped to develop some places and underdevelop others. Programs like urban renewal subsidized the accumulation of wealth and other resources among some groups—primarily white property holders—and denied those subsidies and protections to other groups—primarily African Americans. Further, in the remapping of postwar American capitalism, the commerce and manufacturing that drove consumption grew increasingly mobile, while the nation as a whole gradually shifted toward a service economy. In this process, too, the federal state exerted a heavier hand than at any other time in the nation's history.[5]

The focus of this book thus moves from contests over how to distribute the benefits of postwar economic growth and metropolitan expansion in the 1940s to contests over how to distribute the costs of the same in the 1970s. It involves more than a transition from an era of possibility to an era of limits, however. Oakland and the East Bay embodied what was at stake in California politics between the end of World War II and the late 1970s: the distribution of the assets and debts of postwar affluence, the triumph of growth liberalism and the vast inequalities it created and left unresolved, the possibilities of a welfare state and the retrenchment of the tax revolt. Places like Oakland gave the nation a new politics after World War II. But in the end, power in the postwar metropolis was not evenly distributed. The tax revolt placed debilitating limits on struggling cities like Oakland at the exact historical moment when African Americans achieved their greatest political successes.

Oakland is a horizontal city where the single family home dominates the landscape. It slopes upward from the eastern shore of San Francisco Bay on former tidal flats across a gently ascending rise to a series of hills separating the city from neighboring interior valleys. By the 1920s real estate interests had carved the city into long, narrow strips that marked neighborhoods by income and elevation—flatlands, foothills, and hills—and embedded a class regime literally into the physical terrain (map 1.2). Stretching from the smoke-stack factories of the industrial bay shore inland toward the foothills, block after block of workers' cottages and California bungalows gave Oakland a distinctly proletarian feel at midcentury. In the flatland neighborhoods of West Oakland, the city's densest and oldest district, the lifeblood of community and politics was the railroad and the docks. Thousands of white railroad operators, firefighters, and craftspeople; black laborers, Pullman porters, redcaps, and dining car waiters; black and white teamsters, and longshore and warehouse workers had settled in West Oakland by the 1940s. Like many urban neighborhoods in midcentury America, West Oakland was a mixture of industry, commerce, and residence where factory employment was close at hand for both men and women. Neighborhood stores, barber shops, restaurants, taverns, laundries, and other businesses provided hundreds of additional jobs and needed local services. With its industrial, commercial, and residential districts close and abutting, West Oakland was, in the words of one resident, a "city within a city."

In the workplaces and communities of midcentury West Oakland, African American residents forged a distinct laborite culture that blended class politics with civil rights. Based in the Brotherhood of Sleeping Car Porters and other black railroad unions, as well as the left wing of the International Longshoremen's and Warehousemen's Union (ILWU) on the docks and the Marine Cooks and Stewards Union (MCSU) on the ships, this culture extended its influence broadly through the East Bay. It was by no means universal and never enjoyed the endorsement of the majority of whites. But it nonetheless flowered in the working-class districts of the Oakland flatlands—and north into Berkeley—nurturing through the dark days of Cold War anticommunism a social and political milieu in which antiracism and progressive ideas, debate, and struggle were the order of

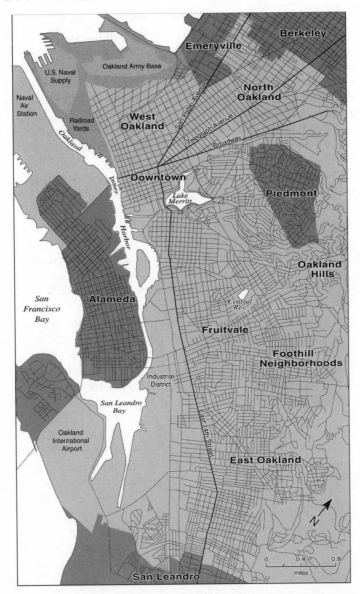

Map 1.2. Oakland neighborhoods after World War II. West Oakland, Fruitvale, and East Oakland made up what was commonly called the "flatlands," which extended north into Berkeley. The city of Piedmont, an elite, upper-class bedroom community, was entirely surrounded by Oakland. The incorporated cities of Alameda, Emeryville, and San Leandro are also featured. Cartography Lab, University of Wisconsin.

the day. In this milieu, Pullman porters joined with University of California law graduates in Democratic political clubs. African American women, many of them daughters of southern Jim Crow, engaged in an activist homeowner politics that subverted the prescriptions of postwar white domestic femininity. And calls for black economic rights and a broader welfare state for all California workers defined the political agenda. This culture extended its reach across time. Black longshoremen, veterans of the brutal class wars on the docks in the 1930s, articulated an internationalism that would, in the 1960s, influence Oaklanders Huey Newton and Bobby Seale as they founded the Black Panther Party. Black leaders from the railroad unions established political strategies in the 1940s that would guide a generation of activists in the late 1960s and early 1970s. From one decade to the next across the second half of the century, these neighborhoods were home to a rich range of laborite, community, civil rights, and eventually black liberation politics.[6]

West Oakland had predominantly crowded and worn turn-of-the-century housing. East Oakland, alternately, an expansive set of neighborhoods running the length of the southeastern two-thirds of the city, boasted tracts of newer California bungalows and ranch-style homes. As Oakland's industry spread along the flatlands here in the first half of the century, home-builders created suburblike neighborhoods within relatively easy distance of local factories. Chevrolet, General Motors, Willys-Overland, Fisher Body, Durant Motor Co., Faegol Motors, and the Star Motor Company made East Oakland the center of automobile production in Northern California by the 1930s. It was home as well to numerous machine shops, canneries, cotton-processing plants, tire and rubber companies, steel-casting plants, and light assembly shops. East Oakland also produced wood products, wire and cable, phonographs, office machines, and farm implements. Merchants followed this industrial expansion, taking advantage of the consumer market created by a burgeoning residential population located far from the downtown retail center. By the end of World War II, East Oakland stretched for seven miles southeast of downtown. Its neighborhoods, commercial strips, and factory districts looked and felt like the thriving garden metropolis imagined in Oakland's booster literature. "It's an amazing new West," an Oakland broadsheet declared in 1946, "and the Metropolitan Oakland Area, California is at its very heart!"[7]

In East Oakland, and other similar neighborhoods, another political tradition developed in the postwar years. Skilled workers joined with merchants and other small business interests, all largely white, in a diffuse populism that counterposed "the public" against big business and downtown property owners. Adherents of this midcentury populism were vehemently pro-union, resistant to high taxes, and wedded to the ambition of suburban homeownership that the "amazing New West" promised. In the 1940s these politics embraced a commonsense notion of what constituted a "fair share" for "working people" on a range of economic matters from wages to taxes and leisure. These politics, which emerged at the same time in nearby suburban cities like San Leandro and Milpitas, led in multiple directions. In one of those directions lay an individualist conception of property rights that buttressed calls for low taxes throughout the postwar period and provided the ideological grounding for the emergence of the so-called tax revolt of the late 1970s. Oakland and the East Bay thus incubated two of California's most important postwar political traditions: a broad liberal one that sought expansions of the social wage and racial equality; and an equally broad populist-conservative one that celebrated private rights and understood liberalism's limits through property and homeownership. These two visions clashed at key moments in California's postwar history. This book is about those clashes. It is also about the fierce contests within and challenges to these broad paradigmatic American political ideologies.[8]

Working-class Oakland lived and labored in the flatlands. In contrast, the city's professional, middle, and upper classes resided in the hillside districts, or in the "foothills" along the edge of the flatlands. The hills featured sweeping views of the entire San Francisco Bay region, a status perch for the city's professionals, bankers, and employers. "High above the turmoil of traffic and the hustle of business," a 1930s promotional piece rhapsodized, "are homes tucked away among the tree-covered slopes." Piedmont, a foothill city entirely surrounded by Oakland, was (and still is) a refuge of middle-class and elite withdrawal from the hum of the streets. Ten minutes by automobile from downtown, it nonetheless felt entirely removed from the din of industrial Oakland, nestled among eucalyptus trees along curving streets with verdant yards and gardens. Since the 1920s the city's political class had resided here, including Oakland's civic patriarchy, the Knowland family, owners of the *Oakland Tribune* and players in local and national politics. Beyond Piedmont, in the Oakland Hills proper, were smaller communities of professionals, wealthy merchants, and a few industrialists. In between the hills and flatlands lay a third ecology of residence, foothill neighborhoods of detached single-family homes draped over a terrain of alternately rising and falling slopes. A mish-mash of white-collar civil servants, merchants, professionals, and other skilled working-class people owned homes here. Overwhelmingly native born and Protestant, they attended the many churches nearby and shopped in the commercial district along MacArthur Boulevard, which runs the length of the city from downtown to far East Oakland.[9]

In the hill neighborhoods, too, ideological and material interests competed to shape people's outlook. Piedmont was home not just to the city's elite bankers, lawyers, and property owners, but to a fiercely antistatist conservatism wedged in the far right of the state's Republican Party. In particular, Joseph R. Knowland and his son, William F. Knowland, battled progressives within the state Republican apparatus and worked to push the party to the right in the 1930s and 1940s. Dedicated enemies of organized labor, the welfare state, and radical politics of all varieties, the Knowlands helped to set the political tone for many of the city's other downtown property owners, their patrons and guardians, and those with a vested interest in downtown as a site of capital accumulation. At the same time, in other hillside neighborhoods, especially Montclair northwest of Piedmont, a strikingly different tradition had emerged by midcentury. Liberal professionals and civil servants from both the progressive wing of the Republican Party and the center of the Democratic Party pushed for some of the same reforms sought by organized labor: neighborhood improvements and a more open city government on the local level and a modest welfare state at the federal and California state level. Long frustrated with the conservative Republican cronies who ran Oakland, they were interested in opening channels of political opportunity for their class and, more broadly, in improving the lives of the city's residents through political alliances with organized labor. Over the postwar decades, both of these hillside political outlooks and the class interests they represented would factor enormously in the struggle for Oakland.

This book tells a story in three parts. Part I traces visions of the postwar city—those of urban trade unionists, African American leaders and activists, and first-generation suburbanites—and the contests to realize those visions. At the end of World War II, men and women in California's East Bay invested in the promise of a postwar industrial garden. The garden embodied the optimism of growth liberalism. Cites and suburbs alike were to bloom and prosper, with workers and their families lifted into the middle class by high wages, the easy accessibility of homeownership, and a new state activism at both federal and local levels. The postwar economy, centered on the single-family home and its consumption needs, would draw urban and suburban worlds into a productive, mutually beneficial relationship. More than a metaphor, the garden came to represent a concrete political and spatial formation: class harmony in pastoral cities where factories and homes existed in unobtrusive balance; homeowner democracy in both city and suburb, literally "*home* rule" in the words of one suburbanite; and an endless horizon of upward social mobility with a plentiful supply of good jobs and inexpensive new homes. African Americans and whites, workers and employers, urbanites and suburbanites, renters and homeowners agreed on the garden's allure but imagined the distribution of its costs and rewards differently. Those differences were the mainspring of politics.

The industrial garden metaphor guided urban development and planning after 1945, but it was no postwar invention. Its antecedents extended into nineteenth-century English urban social criticism and French Utopianism. In the first half of the twentieth century, the "garden city" movement emerged on both sides of the Atlantic in the writings of Ebenezer Howard and Lewis Mumford and in the practical demonstrations of places like Letchworth, England, and a host of American suburbs. An alternative to both city and country, garden cities were meant to occupy the mean between civilization's opposites by combining factories, dwellings, commerce, greenbelts, and services into a single entity—"all the advantages of the most energetic and active town life, with all the beauty and delight of the country," to borrow Howard's formulation. Much of urban history has focused on the garden metaphor's application to suburbs, but urban modernism, especially midcentury American versions, drew heavily on its formula as well. To date, however, histories of urban space and modernist city planning, on the one hand, and histories of politics and social struggle, on the other, have not been brought together; they remain strangely apart. Part of my contribution here is to suggest how joining them produces a richer history of both place and nation.[10]

Part II begins with Oakland planners, developers, and capitalists turning to the instruments and technologies of postwar urban design to remake their city. In the 1950s and 1960s they hoped to restore property values by redeveloping land, clearing slums, constructing highways and rapid transit, and mechanizing the port—a broad engineering of new urban forms. They sought to revive the city, and downtown in particular, as a site of capital accumulation. At the same time, African Americans sought a different sort of urban renaissance, one shaped by the goals of economic opportunity for the growing black community: jobs, development, and neighborhood investment. The two visions clashed, as the reengineering of Oakland, coupled with structural economic changes, further disadvantaged the city's black working class. To resolve the tension between divergent views of the city, liberal reformers focused on remaking citizens, reconstructing people themselves through a variety of measures, from juvenile delinquency programs to the War on Poverty. Instead of a resolution, a new politics was born—a struggle over control of urban resources in the late 1950s and 1960s that dominated and convulsed the city like nothing since the organized labor campaigns of the 1930s.

In Part III the story's denouement comes in a series of revolts and restorations. The industrial garden was deemed a failure even by those who a generation earlier had invested so much in its promise. But its demise was interpreted very differently in Oakland and nearby suburbs. For black leaders and activists, the new postwar metropolis in California and its political economy undergirded by segregation had failed to deliver upward mobility to the majority of black workers. This realization spawned revolts in Oakland, led by African American community activists and the Black Panther Party. Together, they articulated a radical critique of the whole of metropolitan development since World War II and implicated liberalism in continued black poverty. In contrast, in nearby suburbs, perceptions of the industrial garden's failure there spawned a new activist conservatism, led by homeowning taxpayers. They reacted to the mounting costs of California's rapid postwar development by attacking and limiting the liberal state. Homeowners embraced tax reform for an enormous variety of reasons, but they nonetheless produced a dramatic convergence of political ideology around an antistatist, property-owning individualism that would have enormous consequences for California and the nation. By 1978 Oakland civic authority had passed into the hands of the black bourgeoisie, and Proposition 13 had signaled the emergence of a new suburban order. The book ends on this profoundly ambivalent note. Despite the industrial garden's failure, a new generation of urban and suburban Californians believed that they could revive and reinvent its promise, albeit from vastly different points of view, ideological grounding, and spatial location.

This book proceeds on two levels and may be thought of as a guide to two interconnected dimensions of the postwar city. The first is political culture: how political contest is shaped, framed, and understood. The second is metropolitan space: how and where urbanization creates markets, property, and communities. I briefly take up each in what follows. In terms of political culture, this book primarily follows two stories: the trajectory of the postwar black struggle, in all of its diverse forms, and the politics of suburban city building, in all of its equally diverse forms. Both shaped political culture in Oakland and the East Bay but also in California as a whole.

Born within the liberal and radical milieus of the New Deal era, African American politics in Oakland evolved into various forms of neighborhood-based reform and Maoist and nationalist revolutionary movements in the 1960s and 1970s. The historiography and much of the social science theorizing of the post–World War II black liberation struggle draw on the southern experience. Indeed, the southern civil rights movement has been rendered so completely as *the* paradigmatic postwar black struggle that most historical surveys make little mention of the North and West outside of a brief discussion of black power and offer no framework in which to understand the northern and Pacific Coast dimensions of African American politics and social movements. One collection of readings even includes a section entitled "The North Has Problems Too," an opaque reference to the North's status as a secondary site of struggle.

Attention to the South is richly deserved, but an overreliance on the southern story has shaped national understandings of black politics and given them a spurious twist: as triumphant civil rights "moved north" after 1965, the movement foundered on the shores of urban rebellions and black nationalism. North and South have come to represent the inverted histories that we tell about African American liberation politics in the second half of the twentieth century. The South is "the movement." The North is the foil. The South is nonviolent. The North is violent. The South is paradigmatic, the North an aberration.[11]

Rewriting the history of postwar African American social movements and politics in the North and West requires a richer, deeper, and necessarily more complicated story in which northern and Pacific Coast cities are not places where civil rights organizing stalled or failed in some absolute sense, but places where the postwar black rights movement took unique forms and trajectories and experienced its own successes and setbacks, where African Americans pushed to dismantle the segregation embedded in urban industrial and postindustrial capitalism, and where a dynamic black political culture nurtured multiple strategies and ideologies of resistance, accommodation, and liberation. These places deserve to be understood as more than either derivative of or antithetical to the southern movement. Collapsing African American politics into such a narrative flattens twentieth-century U.S. history. This is not to suggest that northern and western African American history should be disconnected from southern history. Rather, it is to argue that we must connect the building of African American political capacity and social organizing to the longer sweep of northern and western urban history and political economy. And in doing so, we must think beyond a triumphalist southern story and a declensional northern one.[12]

Narratives of civil rights that begin in Montgomery, or in *Brown v. Board of Education*, and end in Birmingham perpetuate a southern exceptionalism that obscures decades-long African American organizing in the postwar North and West. In cities like New York, Philadelphia, Chicago, Cleveland, and Oakland, African Americans worked first within New Deal liberalism and later outside of it to reform the labor and housing markets from which they had been excluded. Much of the modern civil rights movement, and its emphasis on *economic* rights, in the United States was dedicated to a critique of and confrontation with the two-tired welfare state instantiated in the New Deal—especially its segregationist housing policies, its lack of fair employment and full employment provisions, its exclusion of hundreds of thousands of black workers from the protections of labor laws, and its deeply biased forms of social insurance, including what is now called "welfare." This required a massive engagement with the major institutions of the nation—especially the state, finance and real estate capital, and industrial employers of all sizes—that coincided with and was propelled by the largest internal black migration in American history: the movement of four million African Americans from South to North and West. Moreover, the New Deal state's intimate involvement in urban policy meant that the federal government, municipal politics, and metropolitan development converged during these decades to a degree unprecedented in the nation's history. This made the federal government an adversary as often as an ally. In this sense, the postwar black struggle in America represented one of the world's most sustained and militant engagements with the modern state apparatus.[13]

Oakland provides an excellent vantage from which to launch an inquiry into this history. Best known as the birthplace of the Black Panther Party in 1966 and as a national fulcrum of black radicalism throughout the late 1960s, Oakland was also a major seat of African American influence in California politics beginning in the late 1940s and the home of an extensive tradition of black social advocacy and organizing. Indeed, the generation of black activists before the Panthers developed strategies, alliances, and sources of power that profoundly shaped the political terrain of race in both the East Bay and California as a whole. Recovering the story of that generation, men and women who achieved none of the national media exposure and fame of the Panthers and faced little of the state-sponsored harassment and investigations, allows us to appreciate both the surprising continuities as well as the jarring divergences between the activists of the 1940s and 1950s and those of the 1960s and 1970s. Understanding the broader patterns of African American political organizing in Oakland and California in the postwar decades brings into focus a neglected chapter in the black liberation struggle and confirms a trajectory of struggle that depends neither on the traditional markers of the southern movement nor on the conflation of violence, protest, and nationalism that have hampered thorough understandings of black power and black radicalism. The long postwar black liberation movement in the East Bay featured a fluid political environment in which philosophies and strategies competed with and interpenetrated one another. Above all, in the decades after World War II, civil rights in Oakland stood less for *civil* rights than for economic rights, the foundation on which black American political demands had rested since the 1930s.[14]

The postwar city, and especially segregation and deindustrialization, has recently garnered substantial attention among American historians. Joining an earlier urban historical literature on ghetto formation has been an emergent scholarship on the urban crisis. Both historiographical literatures emphasize the hardening of racial segregation in the urban nation after World War II and the brakes placed on racial liberalism by northern whites in conjunction with federal urban policy in the postwar decades. Extending explorations and critiques begun by, among others, W.E.B. DuBois, St. Clair Drake, and Charles Abrams, this new scholarship has offered an important and thoroughly historicized understanding of the relationship between economic restructuring, poverty, race, and the industrial city. But the standard narrative still marginalizes rather than emphasizes African American politics and self-activity. In our understandable zeal to document the limits whites have placed on liberalism, it is too often overlooked that black Americans too imagined the city and its possibilities, reacted to urban decline and decay, and fashioned politics and social movements with the ambition of making their neighborhoods and cities better places to live. Whether they succeeded or failed, their efforts require serious attention and reflection.[15]

African American activists in Oakland, San Francisco, and Los Angeles fought to secure a place for black communities within the shifting patterns of metropolitan geography and economy that accompanied the vast spatial transformation of midcentury urban America. They engaged the processes and institutions responsible for the second ghetto and the urban crisis as no other group in California. Industrial restructuring, redevelopment and urban renewal, highway and rapid transit construction, and suburban city building together became the pivots around which black politics turned. These issues were not merely the backdrop to the black liberation struggle. Through them the movement itself was constituted. In Oakland in particular, the political discourse and strategies of the long postwar African American rights movement stressed the failure of urban and metropolitan political economy to secure the promise of democracy and opportunity—they stressed the failure of the postwar metropolis and modernism itself. In this sense, the movement, including liberal, radical, and nationalist variants, was not primarily a response to southern mobilization, but a parallel development that sought to redistribute economic and political power within the increasingly divided metropolis. When local, state, and federal political efforts had failed to do this, when liberalism came up wanting, many African Americans turned to black power and radical liberation politics.[16]

Liberalism is too plastic a concept to leave without a definition. It can alternately mean progrowth politics or regulatory politics; racial equality or white racial privilege masking as colorblindness. Its meanings change over the course of the twentieth century and vary according to who is deploying the term. In part the usefulness of the term resides in its generality. I have made every effort to clarify the meaning of the term in each chapter's context. But broadly, liberalism as it came to be constituted in the American polity between the end of World War II and the late 1970s meant four things: (1) New Deal liberalism, its institutions, and its commitment to a modified welfare state; (2) moderate market regulation in the interests of the middle and working classes, largely white, in the context of continued economic growth; (3) racial liberalism, that is, racially equal opportunity in social and political life, as well as some state intervention to achieve an "equal playing field"; and (4) individualism, the belief that society and politics, as well as reforms and government policies, should be organized around individual people rather than groups or classes. As we will see, there were deep contradictions within liberalism itself; how can a state policy both be liberal and promote racial apartheid? These contradictions are made abundantly clear in what follows. Indeed, the contradictions within liberalism are among my primary topics.[17]

By the late 1960s, many African American radicals and nationalists referred to the United States as Babylon. It was often an elusive metaphor, but it captured the profound cynicism engendered by decades of liberal failure as well as the remarkably optimistic belief in rebirth, in beginning again. In 1969 the Black Panther Party warned that fundamental change must come to the nation, lest it "perish like Babylon," the biblical city that fell under the weight of its own corruption and imperial ambitions. Babylon as both place and concept passed into the lexicon of radical black politics in the late 1960s, borrowed from African American religious traditions as well as from the Jamaican Rastafarians for whom Babylon denoted Western capitalism and imperialism. In the hands of the Panthers, Babylon acquired a new rhetorical provocativeness, as when the party imagined that "in the concrete inner city jungles of Babylon" men and women would join together "to cast aside their personal goals and aspirations, and begin to work unselfishly together." Babylon stood both for the inevitability of imperialism's demise and for the possibility that something might be erected in its place, something better, more democratic. "The people of Babylon" could, through struggle, throw off oppression and create a new day. For the Panthers and other black radicals, the industrial garden of midcentury had become Babylon—a false city that had to be remade to stave off collapse.[18]

Babylon provides a powerful metaphor, like the industrial garden, through which to think about a particular moment in postwar American urban history. Indeed, Babylon reminds us that black power, and contests over its meaning and implications, is a fundamental part of the political history of urban America. Facing a national crisis of unprecedented dimensions— following decades of segregation and industrial restructuring—African American radicals and liberals alike responded politically. Black communities were not solely victims of an "urban crisis"; they were burdened with, and engaged in, conceiving remedies. In Babylon, black power advocates found an *urban* referent—albeit one that stretched deep into the history of the black church—through which to conceive the plight of the black nation. This book self-consciously embraces the term, not because it was an ideal, unproblematic or even always transparent analogy, but because it evokes the essential realities of the postwar American city: poverty amidst wealth, national economic growth with urban decline, and the hardening of apartheid within the liberal state. The journey through those seeming paradoxes inevitably takes us to the connections between the city and political power and to three decades of intense contest over the uses, value, and nature of urban space.[19]

Past East Oakland, across the city line, lay southern Alameda County — in the 1940s an enormous expanse of small towns, orchards, ranches, open farmland, and tidal flats. Here was the region's suburban future. The flatlands widen considerably south of Oakland, stretching across a great breadth from the bay to the inland hills. Between the hills and the water, only San Leandro and Hayward existed as incorporated cities in the 1940s. San Leandro, directly across the city line from Oakland, combined truck farming, a few industrial assembly plants, and food processing into a viable economic base. Close enough to Oakland to serve as a bedroom community for commuters, San Leandro would come to play a crucial role in the regional struggle to shape residential and industrial politics after the war. In addition to San Leandro and Hayward — a slightly larger, though otherwise similar, city — southern Alameda County was home to ethnic Mexican *colonias*: unincorporated residential districts of laborers, merchants, and a few professionals, all of them attached to the rural economy and its cycles of fruit and vegetable harvest, processing, and canning. The bulk of the land there, however, tens of thousands of acres, was dedicated to ranches, farms, orchards, and small commercial settlements, uses that would fade ever more quickly and irrevocably as the postwar years went by. But, as Oakland's Chamber of Commerce put it in the late 1930s, "cattle still graze over the slopes."

To understand what happened to this suburban East Bay landscape after 1945, we must dig deep into local planning and politics and keep in view both the broad structure of U.S. capitalism and the federal state and the particularities and contingencies of place. For here lies a second site of political culture examined in this book: the political culture of property and homeownership cultivated in California's hothouse of boosterism, populism, and individualism. Postwar suburbanization was as much a product of local planning and politics as of national macroeconomic processes and broad patterns of capital mobility. Indeed, to take up suburbanization as primarily a function of the national mobility of capital is to miss the extraordinary diversity of suburban forms and the importance of local issues and markets in their emergence. In Oakland, planners and boosters after World War II promoted a regional, metropolitan distribution of industrial investment and growth, campaigning nationally for factories, warehouses, and other facilities for the city's suburban periphery. This initially benefited but ironically ultimately undermined Oakland itself. At the same time, economic incentives within emerging suburban communities—San Leandro, Hayward, Union City, Fremont, and Milpitas especially—gave rise to a homeowner politics that embraced industrial growth, linked racial segregation with high property values, and secured the bourgeois amenities of "garden living" through the property taxes paid by corporate industrial property owners. Both efforts contributed to industrial decentralization in California's East Bay in the 1950s and produced new metropolitan locations of residential and industrial capital.[20]

Recovering East Bay suburban history means mapping how capital and politics create space. It means charting a history of how places are produced. This account of the East Bay investigates the intersection of political and spatial histories in the processes of city building. Across the breadth of these decades, white suburbanites did not "flee" Oakland. They were drawn to suburban communities by the powerful economic and cultural incentives behind city building: new housing markets subsidized by the federal government; low taxes underwritten by relocating industry; and the assurance that a new home, spacious yard, and garage signaled their full assimilation into American life and its celebration of modernity and consumption. From their first encounter with the home mortgage market, through dozens upon dozens of relationships, from the handshake over a home sale to the capital mobility that brought new industries to their cities, suburbanites participated in a process of market creation. That process generated expectations: homeowners came to expect, and later demand, low property taxes; they came to expect and rationalize racial segregation; and they came to accept as natural the conflation of whiteness and property ownership with upward social mobility. To secure those expectations, suburban homeowners were not shy about entering electoral politics over the course of the postwar decades to assert their property "rights" and to contain the benefits of suburbanization within city boundaries. Lifted into the middle class by the federal welfare state, white residents of southern Alameda County fought the extension of those same benefits to African Americans.[21]

The story of East Bay suburbanization thus chronicles the interaction between large forces at work in the region and nation, especially the mobility of industrial and residential capital, and the local strategic opportunism of homeowners, real estate developers, and other property-oriented interests, who sought to maximize the profitability of various kinds of markets. This local opportunism was itself a synthesis of two venerable traditions within American political culture: low-tax fiscal conservatism and booster promotion. That synthesis evolved into one of the most powerful political movements of the second half of the twentieth century in California and ultimately the nation. Its adherents, legion by the 1960s, came from virtually every economic station, united by their status and interests as homeowners. Indeed, postwar suburbanization had the effect of creating a proto-class, the members of which might have had dissimilar political loyalties (as well as different incomes, jobs, etc.) but could be united on the single issue of property taxation. Postwar suburbanization helped to instantiate, in place, a tax-conscious voting bloc. That bloc competed with advocates of liberalism and radicalism to define the direction of the state in the postwar decades. Suburban city building in the East Bay in the 1950s and 1960s, as in the nation, called forth a contentious debate about the relationship between public and private resources that set the stage for the transformation of the physical American landscape and the terrain of national politics.[22]

This story of politics and political culture is intertwined with another important postwar story—the modernization of urban space. Thus, the second dimension and narrative trajectory of the book follows the history of space. It is more than a matter of neighborhood demographics and the movement of industry. Space is about the processes through which markets, property, communities, and even class and race are constituted within capitalist urbanization. Space as both a metaphor and an analytical hinge can be abstract. But space as historically constituted is quite concrete—recall, for instance, the aforementioned apartheid, urban redevelopment, suburban factories, black power politics in Oakland, and tax revolt politics in the suburbs. To make the specificity clear, I offer here a brief typology of how space as a category of analysis is deployed in the book. I use it in three overlapping but distinct ways: space as property, space as social imagination, and space as political scale.

I place space before the reader not because it is the sole or even the most important dimension of the story, but because it offers a critical context for understanding the history of Oakland, the East Bay, and the nation in this period. People, communities, and institutions did not compete for resources for abstract goals and purposes. They competed to put those resources to use to create particular and concrete places. We cannot separate historical actors from their spatial relationships. Class and race are lived through the fabric of urban life and space. Civil rights, black power, and tax reform political movements did not call for rights in abstract terms and ill-defined places. They called for very specific things in relation to very specific places. Space is not the whole story, but it would be a strange and incoherent one without it.[23]

The most obvious spatial element in any city is its built environment: office buildings, factories, dense neighborhoods, parks, and schools. These are the physical markers of cities that distinguish them from other types of places. But office buildings and factories are not simply buildings; they are also *money*—a form of capital that is, for a time, fixed in space as property. Capitalism drives the creation of fixed spaces. But nearly as quickly as that fixed space is created, capitalism creates extraordinary pressures either to abandon existing cities or to remake them in altogether new ways. Here lies the source of the tensions of development and redevelopment that we have come to associate with urban life. The physical features of a city, though seemingly fixed, are always being "redeveloped." This is the reality of the city in the capitalist marketplace. But the residents and workers within cities are never simply the docile subjects of capitalism. They protest, they strike, they vote. Ultimately, urban politics is one of the principal ways the costs and benefits created by capitalism are distributed across both space and social groups. Contests over that distribution, and its rippling effects, produced the central drama in the making and remaking of Oakland and the East Bay in the postwar decades.[24]

Property can be conceived of as space that produces capital. Boundaries drawn around property—in the form of corporate city limits, racial red lines, zoning codes, or highway rights-of-way, for instance—signal where to invest and where not to invest. They constitute a grammar of local development. At the core of urban politics lie tensions and contests over the role of property in civic life, over the distribution of the property tax burden, and over the buying and selling of property. At the same time, space is *more than* just property. Capitalism values different spaces differently. Once those values are in place, embedded in property, that powerfully determines all kinds of aspects of social life. The effects of property are far-reaching; they extend well beyond the marketplace. They structure all kinds of interactions—from where one can buy a home to where politics is organized, from how police interact with neighborhoods to where children go to school. The struggle for the postwar city was over no less than the power to control and organize space and the leverage to wring opportunity out of the American industrial metropolis during its disruptive postwar cycles of development and redevelopment.

Space is also a primary component of social imagination. Spatial analogies are imaginative maps through which people organize and record what cities mean. Jane Jacobs was interested in such maps when she offered her reading of dense Manhattan streets. George Chauncey has creatively uncovered the maps of gay New Yorkers in bath houses, street cruising, and nightlife in early twentieth-century Manhattan. St. Clair Drake and Horace Cayton found such maps in the ethnic and racial geography of Chicago's South side in *Black Metropolis*. In Oakland there are maps as well. One, the industrial garden, helps to organize the first three chapters of this book. First and foremost a booster paradigm of growth and opportunity, the garden became an open-ended metaphor with appeal across the social spectrum. By the late 1960s, the garden had become, in the words of one African American community organizer, a "plantation." In this view, the city of opportunity had become an internal colony. The difference between a garden and a plantation, between an open, connected city and a colony, between a neighborhood and a ghetto, between the pastoral and the imperial, is paramount. These differences tell us a great deal about what is at stake in the struggle for the city. The shift from garden and pastoral metaphors to plantation and colonial metaphors follows the narrative of politics throughout this book. We should not conflate ideas and rhetoric with the lived experience of citizens, or with the more concrete realities of zoning codes, property values, and tax rates. But neither should we settle for the banality that the "reality" of a city belies the representations of planners and boosters and the prejudices of residents. Urban life constantly confounds such easy dichotomies.[25]

Finally, space organizes political scale. We can think of American electoral politics as a series of linked arenas that ascend from the household through the neighborhood, the district or ward, the city, county, state, and ultimately to the federal government. At each scale there are levers of power that control certain dimensions of public life. Zoning ordinances are decided at the city level. Public housing has historically been a federal project administered through municipalities. Labor law lies within state and federal jurisdiction. And so on. The scale at which politics happen—including both formal electoral politics and *politics* more broadly—matters enormously. The urban political terrain is far more than an extension of national party politics, as the homeowner mobilizations of the 1970s so clearly demonstrate. City governments exert critical control over local economic development, which creates patterns of local political struggle absent at the federal level. But there are equally important "city limits," limits to what cities can do because they are both trapped in the capitalist marketplace and subject to policies and decisions made at other levels of power. One of the stickiest paradoxes of urban and suburban history is the extraordinary power of local political arenas, on the one hand, and the vast reach of federal power across jurisdiction and distance, especially after World War II, on the other. Where political projects are mobilized, as well as the sorts of spaces they attempt to control, are highly significant yet frequently overlooked dimensions of struggle and strategy. Particularly in the postwar decades, when an activist federal government partnered with cities in an array of different projects, cities competed with one another for investment and an elusive tax base. In short, location matters, for politics as much as for property values, for race as well as class.

The temptation is to tell the history of this period solely in terms of urban decline. But Oakland is hardly representative of unidirectional demise. A journalist described Oakland in the 1960s as "a familiar kind of industrial city: high-rise office buildings and apartments downtown, plasticine shopping centers on the fringe, and slowly decaying wooden houses in between." The city never fully made it as an industrial capital. Despite the tremendous wartime growth of its shipbuilding, food processing, and automobile industries, Oaklanders entered the postwar period much as they had left the 1930s, anxious that the city's relatively small industrial base would disappear. While cities like Detroit, Chicago, and Los Angeles employed hundreds of thousands of manufacturing workers at various peaks between the 1920s and 1950s, Oakland never employed more than fifty or sixty thousand. When deindustrialization felled Detroit, it cut down a mighty giant. It wreaked havoc on Oakland as well, but Oakland has virtually always been on the make, selling itself to outside capital as often as hosting it. To tell the story of Oakland as one solely of industrial decline is to miss the larger truth that there was hardly a golden industrial past from which the city slipped. The postwar period is less a tragic story of deindustrialization tearing asunder a once mighty industrial empire than the story of a struggling medium-sized city, first in industrial America, then, beginning sometime in the 1960s, increasingly in postindustrial America. For better or worse, it has been a hard road.

Oakland embodied the seeming contradictions of the postwar American metropolis. It was characterized by poverty amidst wealth; racial apartheid at the heart of liberalism; and high unemployment in periods of economic growth. Because of these conditions, it has much to tell us about politics and space in late twentieth-century America. Oakland was thus typical in ways that allow it to stand for the urban nation in this period. But its typicality should not obscure the very different histories of other postwar American cities. Oakland was and is far less segregated than Chicago, Milwaukee, or Philadelphia. Oakland was not a Fordist giant like Detroit. Political systems in other cities—especially Chicago, New York, and Philadelphia—incorporated a large black electorate much earlier than in Oakland because of their ward-based electoral systems. Oakland's relationship to San Francisco makes it more like Newark and Camden than like Washington, DC, or Atlanta. The East Bay suburbs were more industrial than many across the nation. And so on. Only additional comparative scholarship on these questions will shed greater light on Oakland's relative representativeness. What we may say without caveat, however, is that the story of Oakland and the East Bay that I recount here forms no straightforward arc, no simple tale of hope giving way to disillusionment. Neither is it a triumphalist one of discrimination yielding over time to inclusion. These sorts of bald opposites are of little use. It is an American story precisely because it is unfinished. Its endings continue to be contested, its meanings alive with contemporary political significance.

Part One

URBAN AND SUBURBAN POLITICS
AND THE CALIFORNIA DREAM,
1945–1964

1

Industrial Garden

WHEN THE CENTURY'S most violent and bloody war came to a close in 1945, for whom in the United States had victory been secured? Americans, the *Saturday Evening Post* wrote, "are fighting for a glorious future of mass employment, mass production, and mass distribution and ownership." A coming abundance was predicted, too, by Eric Johnston, president of the U.S. Chamber of Commerce, who wrote in *America Unlimited* of a "utopia of production" in the postwar age. Like many American opinionmakers, the *Post* and Johnston imagined an ascendant white American middle class unprecedented in size, wealth, and security—in their eyes the war's beneficiaries. For organized labor's part, wartime cooperation in the tripartite state had won trade unions unparalleled access to national levers of power and convinced many that thicker bread and fatter butter could be had within the new postwar order. Labor's enemies remained legion, however, many lying in wait for the end of patriotic cooperation and the resumption of political and shopfloor struggles. For African Americans, however, an economy of abundance that excluded them seemed poor reward for wartime patriotism and sacrifice. The Double-V campaign—victory over racism abroad and at home—had come to symbolize the fusion of national duty and criticism of national hypocrisy within 1940s black politics. The war changed the nation forever, but it left unresolved, indeed it raised with renewed imperative, questions of class power and racial equality in the American polity.[1]

As postwar celebration and peacetime reconversion proceeded amid nationalist cheers and civic ceremony in California's East Bay in late 1945, three groups who had gained by the war—business, labor, and African Americans—pulled the city of Oakland in divergent directions. The war's economic bounty had empowered the city's business leaders, encouraging them to pursue plans for aggressive metropolitan economic growth. The war had also emboldened Oakland's strong trade unions, united by the Alameda County Central Labor Council, to set standards for local wages and to extend unionization to new workers as wartime wage and price controls lapsed. Swelled to three times its prewar size by migration, the city's African American community sought economic and political power and an end to the region's notorious Jim Crow employment and housing practices. Though by no means entirely unified or undifferentiated, each of these three groups hoped above all to fashion a postwar political culture on its own terms that could remake Oakland and translate its conception of progress into concrete material gains. Calls for wartime unity during the first five years of the decade had neither reconciled competing class interests nor bridged racial divides, in Oakland or the nation.

In 1945 Oakland's business leaders embraced a vast program of vigorous regional economic development that was supposed to harmonize class relations and prevent a return of economic depression. It was the class vision of a regional commercial and property-owning elite. Oakland's trade union movement, led by American Federation of Labor (AFL) unions, similarly favored growth but did not intend to give business and industrial capital a free hand. In 1946 unions staged a citywide general strike to defend their power to control local wages and working conditions. Neither business nor labor in the main spoke to the concerns of African Americans. Trade union and NAACP leaders within Oakland's African American community sought to end racial discrimination in East Bay labor markets, a barrier to equality for which the city's businesses and white unions were responsible. In 1945, just as the war was ending, African American activists brought the city's bus and rail transportation company, the Key System, before the federal government's wartime Fair Employment Practices Commission (FEPC). Civil rights advocates hoped that the Key System suit would act as a wedge to open the entire local economy to black workers.

Each effort drew on distinct economic and political priorities in an attempt to shape the relationship between markets and place. Each constituted a different assumption about progress, the appropriate mean between the social production of the economy and the lives and ambitions of people. Whether or not Oakland would become the center of a thriving industrial metropolis attractive to investors, the city's unions would control the local labor market, and African Americans would succeed in opening that labor market depended on the political, ideological, and imaginative production of place. Answers would emerge slowly over several decades of contention. Nevertheless, in these efforts of 1945 and 1946 are powerful glimpses that reveal the dilemmas of postwar America to be less about abstract issues of rights than about the entangled demands of class and racial identity, state and municipal power, and capital accumulation expressed in concrete relationships among people, markets, and local places like Oakland, its neighborhoods, and outlying suburbs. They were about the desire to rationalize space for social ends.[2]

This chapter sets the stage for our exploration of urban social movements, politics, and place by introducing midcentury Oakland and the East Bay from the perspectives of the downtown business community, organized labor, and African American neighborhoods. Oakland embodied the combination of human energy, political convulsion, and economic expansion that made American cities in the 1940s epilogues to one era and prologues to another. The epic class battles that had so marked cities in the first four decades of the century had ebbed, and the liberal modernism of the New Deal state seemed to promise an end to the urban tensions of the 1930s. The unprecedented prosperity that attended the war, and the centrality of cities to wartime production, represented the consolidation of urban manufacturing power embodied in American industrial cities since the late nineteenth century. Nonetheless, the war had interrupted, but not altered, the decline of urban America that had begun in 1929, the end of a long period of central-city vitality dating to the late nineteenth century. Other forces marked beginnings. The war brought millions of rural Americans from across the country—the largest share, both African American and white, from the South—to northern and Pacific Coast cities. These cities would occupy a pivotal place in the postwar national debate over the meaning of race. That debate would take place within an urban-suburban system undergoing epochal shifts and facing unprecedented strain. As industrial decentralization accelerated, as national capital investment and population shifted to the West, especially California, Oakland in 1945 stood at the axis of the transformative forces swirling across the American urban landscape.[3]

Envisioning a Metropolitan Oakland

In the decade between 1945 and 1955, the Oakland Chamber of Commerce married boosterism to regional planning in its Metropolitan Oakland Area Program (MOAP). No mere "second city" in San Francisco's shadow, Oakland was to become the center of a dynamic metropolis. The MOAP outlined a set of relationships and social harmonies thought to ensure postwar economic development: suburban industry tied to downtown Oakland and the port, universal homeownership in both city and suburb, an absence of industrial strife, and booming West Coast markets. Oakland's business establishment, operating through the activist Chamber of Commerce, envisioned and then set out to create, both physically and imaginatively, a metropolitan Oakland. Inaugurated in 1935, the campaign borrowed from California iconography but reconfigured booster images around manufacturing rather than earlier promotional incarnations like agriculture, real estate, and tourism. Neighborhoods and factories, workers and managers, homes and highways were to coexist in a delicate balance that brought the machine (industry) into harmony with the garden (single-family home). It was a model of postwar urban/suburban imagining, with deep roots in nineteenth-century American culture: the industrial garden. By the late 1940s, the MOAP was the major promotional vehicle for the industrialization of the East Bay corridor with huge annual national advertising campaigns and a Washington, DC, lobbyist. Through the MOAP the city would campaign relentlessly for the attention of American capital.[4]

Much more than a booster dreamscape, the MOAP represented the response of Oakland's business class to an acute crisis in downtown as a site of capital accumulation. On Oakland's major commercial and retail thoroughfares along Broadway as well as Washington, Franklin, and Webster streets in the central business district, property values declined more than 50 percent between 1925 and 1955. Anxiety about the profitability of downtowns was shared by local business leaders across the nation. American downtowns as a whole reached their pinnacle of profitability in the first decades of the twentieth century but had been in steep decline since. Decentralization, especially the growth of chain stores and the flourishing of business districts in outlying areas, took firm hold of metropolitan regions throughout the country, inaugurating a decades-long central-city crisis that would build across midcentury until the much-heralded "death" of downtowns in the 1960s. Downtown merchants and their political spokespeople often behaved like civic patriarchs, but they were not all-powerful. Indeed, by the 1940s they were a class with sinking fortunes, struggling to maintain the profitability of their property holdings in a business climate that no longer favored central business districts. The sharp decline in downtown's generation of both private revenue (profit) and public revenue (taxes) called for a response—the MOAP.[5]

Oakland's experience with industrial expansion in the interwar years had convinced postwar business and civic leaders that if East Bay cities were to be engines of growth, they must be sold to Midwest and East Coast owners of capital. Oakland had accumulated much of its modest industry during the 1910s and 1920s. In those decades, city boosters, the Chamber of Commerce, investors, and local entrepreneurs assembled in Oakland and the nearby suburban communities of Berkeley, Richmond, Emeryville, and San Leandro an industrial base of small factories, machine shops, and manufacturing facilities, most of them branch plants of eastern companies. Early on, chemical, electrical, wood, and paint products, and the manufacture of machine tools, predominated, along with one of the nation's largest canning and packing industries, which processed fruits from Oakland's agricultural hinterland in southern Alameda County and the Central Valley. After World War I the East Bay acquired numerous automobile and truck manufacturing plants, including Chevrolet and General Motors, the Durant Motor Company, Willys, Faegeol, and Caterpillar Tractor (boosters dubbed Oakland "the Detroit of the West," even as promoters in

Southern California claimed the same title), as well as a major shipbuilding
and ship-repair firm, the Moore Dry Dock Company. The city's port facilities and two transcontinental railroads made Oakland a major center of
shipping and transportation as well.[6]

World War II reshaped the economic landscape of the region and influenced postwar MOAP strategies. A major center of shipbuilding,
troop transportation, food processing, and naval supply during the
global conflict, Oakland and the East Bay occupied a crucial niche in California's industrial "arsenal of democracy." The war stimulated and gave
contour to the local economy in three critical ways. First, shipbuilding in
Oakland, Richmond, Alameda, and Vallejo triggered growth in Oakland's numerous subsidiary industries, adding tens of millions of dollars
annually to the economy. The Pacific Coast led the nation in shipbuilding
by 1943, with the East Bay's share a phenomenal 35 percent. Second, the
"gold rush" of federal contracts throughout the East Bay corridor, from
Vallejo and Richmond south to San Leandro and Alameda, deepened an
industrial metropolitanization already underway. Third, the wartime
jobs boom brought half a million migrants to the Bay Area during the
first half of the 1940s, an enormous expansion of the regional consumer
market. Since the 1920s the Oakland Chamber of Commerce, the Downtown Property Owners Association, and the Oakland Real Estate Association had dreamed of a "greater East Bay" economy with Oakland at its
center. World War II seemed to make that dream a reality. But Oakland's
cautious business class did not take postwar prosperity for granted.
Building a prosperous industrial landscape in the postwar decades, they
believed, required winning intense competition with other Bay Area and
California cities for markets, industries, and investment. Metropolitanization through the MOAP was their formula: an economically integrated set of cities to the north and south of Oakland, a multicentered expanse of industry and residence held together by highways, rail lines, and
the centrifugal force of Oakland's downtown. It was suburbanization re-
cast as urbanization.[7]

A tight-knit, though fractious, coalition oversaw postwar economic
development and planning in Oakland. The publisher of the *Oakland
Tribune* and longtime Chamber of Commerce torchbearer, Joseph R.
Knowland, led this group. Knowland was one of a handful of powerful
Republican Party stalwarts in the state's major cities who oversaw local
civic affairs with paternalist conservatism. Like *Los Angeles Times* publisher Harry Chandler, railroad heir and banker William Henry Crocker,
and *San Francisco Chronicle* publisher Michael De Young, Knowland established himself in politics and civic promotion by leveraging the power
of the newspaper in an era when the printed word dominated political
campaigns and city boosting. But Knowland did not control Oakland's

business and industrial establishment single-handedly. Henry Kaiser, leading architect of West Coast war production with his shipbuilding and steel empire, maintained company headquarters in Oakland and took a keen interest in local planning. The downtown retail industry, led by R. H. Biggs of Capwell's and Irving Kahn, owner of Kahn's Department Store and president of the Downtown Property Owners Association, formed an important bloc. The Moore Dry Dock Company, second to Kaiser in Bay Area shipbuilding during the war, the Bechtel Company, and a handful of small manufacturers, bankers, and real estate interests influenced postwar economic planning. Though significant conflicts developed within Oakland's commercial and industrial class in the years following the war, for the most part a consensus existed. Rather than fight decentralization, Oakland would attempt to turn it to advantage. Expanded metropolitan development would benefit everyone as long as the "center," Oakland, held.[8]

In promoting "metropolitan Oakland," business interests sought to resolve the instability of capital. Boosters and developers know by calculation what often eludes the person on the street: capital moves through and shapes local places in concrete ways. Residential capital makes homes and neighborhoods. Industrial capital makes factories, goods, and jobs. Both generate public capital in the form of property taxes, which in turn make schools, roads, fire departments, and so on. These flows of capital on which cities rise and fall are governed by an elaborate system of rules: the taxes, zoning codes, transportation and labor costs, land prices, and rents on which investors and the owners of capital figure returns. The geography of these relationships was not abstract to Oakland's economic elite. The concrete spaces that capital could produce— West Oakland's booming wartime shipyards, for instance, or East Oakland's mini Detroit, a flourishing set of neighborhoods between Seminary Avenue and the San Leandro boundary where General Motors and Fisher Body plants employed thousands of workers—translated economic abstractions into a physical and social landscape. Such a translation, on a broader scale, was the objective of the MOAP.[9]

To attract the eastern and midwestern capital necessary to extend wartime industrial growth into the postwar decades, it was crucial to make California and the East Bay look like a good investment. The linchpin of the pitch was the East Bay's elaborate and idealized industrial garden: a mixture of single-family California ranch-style and bungalow homes, small factories, and larger industrial plants in a coordinated middle landscape that joined economic progress and social stability. The region, boasted the Chamber, possessed "a most unusual combination of city, suburban, and country life, closely associated with, yet distinct from, business, factory, and shipping." During the decade between 1945 and

1955, the Oakland Chamber of Commerce and the Alameda County Board of Supervisors invested heavily in national MOAP advertising, placing promotional material in business trade journals, real estate magazines, popular weeklies, and major urban dailies. The Chamber promoted an industrial corridor spanning the East Bay from Richmond in the north to the unincorporated areas of Alameda County in the south. With "Oakland at its very heart," this expansive metropolitan region offered prospective investors "new high-income western markets," a "huge new labor supply," and "enormous industrial developments." And it offered easy connections to the Pacific Rim economies, where "countries are hungry for goods," and to the greater American West, where railroad rates from Oakland to the "eleven Western states" were comparable to those from Chicago and Los Angeles.[10]

The principal concern of Chamber promoters was extending the manufacturing capacity of Oakland and the East Bay. They envisioned a series of medium- and small-sized factories, branch plants of eastern and midwestern concerns, in a "diversified industrial economy" that relied on skilled and semiskilled labor. Fearing a repeat of the economic disaster of the Depression, Chamber promoters called for a "balanced industrial economy that makes for stability even in times of stress." This "smokestack" recruitment strategy was typical of midcentury civic imagineers in second-tier industrial cities across the nation, who understood economic development as a set of progressions and multipliers in which industrial growth stimulated transportation and service-sector growth, and ultimately retail and wholesaling growth. Downtown vitality lay at the end of this causal chain. Oakland boosters did not abandon the nineteenth-century industrial city and its logic of production. They imagined its modernization. All that remained was the investment to make it happen.[11]

In its conception of metropolitan space, the MOAP dissolved class tensions in the homogenous world of small property holders. The Chamber's imagery celebrated a garden-city model of neighborhood development and industrialization. Homes were literally "gardens" into which factories, while accessible by automobile, did not intrude. "Homes for industrial workers are unrivaled," a 1945 Metropolitan Oakland advertisement declared, while "factories employ more than 400 persons," and "workmen find happiness in their garden-set homes . . . their children are healthy in the mild, equable climate." For a postwar nation worried about the return of depression and open class hostilities, the sell was enticing. In the East Bay, MOAP literature noted, "employer and employee alike may have a garden-set home, with patio and vegetable garden, within easy distance of factory or office." The garden image allowed boosters to play against western stereotypes. Gone was the unstable frontier. In its place one could find "conscientious workers who look toward a secure future

Page 21

Factories . . .
employ more than 40,000
persons with an annual industrial payroll in excess of
forty-two million dollars . . .

Workmen . . .
find happiness in their
garden-set homes . . . their
children are healthy in the
mild, equable climate . . .

Figure 1.1. The Metropolitan Oakland Area Program advertised nationally in the late 1940s and early 1950s. The MOAP's industrial garden imagery was designed to appeal both to workers and, more consequentially, to industrialists and potential investors. The key to postwar progress, according to MOAP boosters, was a combination of affluence, class harmony, and the "happiness" produced by "garden-set" homes. Courtesy of the Bancroft Library, University of California, Berkeley.

rather than the boomtown excitement and high-pay but short-lived jobs of less stable areas." The garden had tamed a volatile western economy and replaced class antagonism with cooperative neighborliness. With workers and employers living in harmony in garden communities, the Chamber offered investors a permanent industrial infrastructure, large new markets, and easy metropolitan mobility, the best that a modernized California had to offer.[12]

The MOAP's industrial garden invoked a gendered social order that would have been familiar and comfortable to investors. Workers were male, their labor skilled, productive, and rewarding. Women were pictured fulfilling their duty in an industrial economy: taking charge of children and consumption. The social comprehensiveness of the MOAP was startling in this regard. Boosters and planners began with broad patterns of political economy, from capital mobility to the transportation of goods and the organization of an entire metropolitan industrial interface. But they concluded their narrative of progress inside the private home, the axis of the modernist American economic project where marital conviviality, the happiness of work*men*, and the accumulation of consumer goods suggested an epochal social fulfillment tied to transformations in the physical spaces of the region. An impoverished representation of the actual social order, this imagining was a telling expression of the interpenetration in midcentury American culture of ideas about capital, class, gender, and space. And, it anticipated how the *home*—as property, as a site of consumption, and as a political identity—would come to dominate postwar politics and urbanization.[13]

The stable, ordered landscape of property-holding workers envisioned in the MOAP was embedded in the community-planning theory and class anxieties of the first half of the century. In the constant growth of industry from Oakland outward into suburban districts, the MOAP foresaw not a middle-class hinterland of white-collar commuters, but a series of industrial and mixed-class residential communities. This understanding of metropolitan development was inspired by the modernist urban planning of Clarence Stein, Lewis Mumford, and others associated with the Regional Planning Association of America. Believing in the social coherence and spatial logic of the neighborhood, these urban theorists emphasized the decentralization of industry and residence in discrete units within a balanced metropolitan area. Industrial and residential districts were distinct from one another, but their close proximity was an intentional and definitive element of suburbanization. At the same time, the possibility that homeownership could be made available to an ever larger number of workers—through a combination of mass-produced tract developments and the conversion of inexpensive peripheral agricultural land—promised a more stable class order. Both government and private developers saw the ownership of property as the key to ensuring a long-term bourgeois ideological consensus. In this sense, planners and boosters understood geography as more than a backdrop to social relations. They and other city-builders believed that class and place were mutually constituting elements of the social order. Each was produced in part through the other.[14]

Between the 1920s and the 1940s, a variety of arguments for democratizing the U.S. housing market—the housing market among whites— had emerged to shape the ideological assumptions underlying the MOAP. Herbert Hoover was among the most aggressive advocates of mass-production techniques in the construction industry. The latter, he believed, were necessary to ensure "permanent prosperity" in macroeconomic terms, as well as to promote the consumption that gave the individual homeowner "a constructive aim in life" in which "he and his family live a finer life and enjoy more of the comforts and cultivating influences of our modern civilization." Even before the Depression made reviving the home construction industry a national priority, Hoover argued that a housing market more accessible to large numbers of working-class Americans could become an economic engine on a par with the automobile industry, one recently revolutionized by Henry Ford. By 1934, when Congress passed the first of several New Deal housing bills, it was widely believed that reconstructing the housing industry would stimulate production by encouraging a home-centered consumption—of building materials, but also of home appliances, electric energy, and the financial services necessary to home purchase. By the early 1950s, when mass-production pioneers like William Levitt, Henry Kaiser, and Fritz Burns had begun to build vast subdivisions of affordable homes, homeownership was understood to promote class consensus, political stability, and economic growth—an ideological formation of enormous consequence for both postwar government policy and metropolitan political economy.[15]

Half booster crusade, half regional plan, the MOAP revealed the ambitions of Oakland's business and political class for the postwar East Bay. At the same time, the MOAP represented Oaklanders' conviction, long a familiar part of development in the western United States, that cities must be sold. The almost comedic clamor for attention and the relentless hawking of so-called natural advantages can seem quaint in retrospect. But in 1940s' California they were serious business for cities on the make. Just forty miles from Oakland's southern boundary, San Jose and Santa Clara County launched their own version of the MOAP in the postwar years, on their way to accumulating the suburban factories, industrial parks, and civic infrastructure that would lay the foundation for the making of "Silicon Valley" in the 1960s and 1970s. San Francisco had announced its own impressive regional economic agenda by the mid-1940s, which included a multicounty mass transit system, a redeveloped downtown, and a tourist-centered waterfront. And since the 1920s Los Angeles had proven to be the state's industrial titan with its own elaborate booster promotions. In this fierce intercity competition for investment, Oakland could little afford to watch from the sidelines.[16]

Despite its seeming coherence, the Metropolitan Oakland Area Program stands as one of the most ironic expressions of the midcentury American downtown dilemma: to save downtown from the pernicious effects of decentralization, boosters promoted decentralization. The MOAP signaled the dedication of Oakland's business class to the territorial expansion of industry and residence along the greater East Bay corridor, but it did not advocate abandoning Oakland proper in favor of suburban development. The Chamber, influenced by Knowland's downtown-advertising-dependent

Tribune, wanted the best of both worlds: continued development and property value increases in Oakland as well as booming suburbs. This was revealed both in planning documents and in postwar bond elections. In 1935 the City Council had adopted zoning ordinances that designated a long shelf of land along Oakland's southwestern boundary, almost all of the city's waterfront acreage, for industry. During the 1930s and early 1940s, Chamber promoters emphasized to investors the availability of prime industrial land in this area. By 1945 a healthy 24 percent of the city's land was zoned industrial, but the Oakland City Planning Commission noted "a scarcity of sites for large manufacturing and industrial establishments in the city." Hence the logic of suburban development. Simultaneously, however, the Chamber and the City Council supported public bond measures for capital improvements in Oakland, and the City Planning Commission, working closely with business leaders on the Postwar Planning Committee, adopted a program of capital investment designed to keep Oakland's downtown the center of East Bay retail, commerce, and entertainment.[17]

The actual residents and workers of Oakland figured unevenly in the MOAP vision. In its initial advertisements in the early 1930s the Chamber had boasted in a doubly revealing passage that the city's "supply of predominately white labor" operated "on a 90 percent open shop basis." And, as the MOAP's depiction of "garden living" for workers revealed, the Chamber was anxious to portray the city's class relations as congenial and unproblematic. While not factually inaccurate, the MOAP's rhetoric muted class conflict by idealizing skilled workers, marginalizing unions, and racializing the city's workforce. In recognition of the state Chamber's partial accommodation to union strength in the late 1930s, the remarkable gains made by labor unions during the war, and the influence of racial liberalism during the conflict with fascism, postwar MOAP advertisements reversed themselves and highlighted the strong presence of organized labor in Alameda County and abandoned the racialized language. As a counterweight, however, in the late 1940s the MOAP placed advertisements in the city's major labor dailies, the Congress of Industrial Organization's (CIO) *Labor Herald* and the AFL's *East Bay Labor Journal*, encouraging workers to see industrialists, rather than unions, as the principal architects of postwar prosperity. "Hundreds of eastern industrialists," one read, were considering locating plants in Alameda County to guarantee prosperity "through new jobs, new payroll, and stabilized employment." The MOAP stood for something quite important in midcentury Oakland: an employer and property-owners' vision of how to develop and sell an entire region to outside owners of capital. This broad class vision came to shape planning, politics, and even constructions of race in the three decades after World War II. In short, it mattered.[18]

The elaborate imagery and idealized civic grandeur of the MOAP revealed a set of assumptions about the interplay between localities like the East Bay and the larger structures and institutions of postwar capitalism. Capital moves according to a known, though unpredictable, logic. Localities can organize and mobilize to attract, capture, and make use of that capital. The MOAP's central message came down to the Chamber's assertion that if capital and labor could be harmonized through systematic industrial and residential expansion, the region's prosperity, and interclass rapprochement, was assured. The message was presented as self-evident. A radiant California climate, an easy urban-suburban interface, high-income markets, garden living, new industry, reliable transportation, and a stable working class with middle-class ambitions, when combined, became the industrial garden. It was a local version of the industrial Keynesian foundation under much of the midcentury American economy and social order: accelerated consumption by a homeowning working class yielding economic growth and social stability. It was the conceptual and ideological basis of growth liberalism.[19]

Organized labor shared much of that vision. Homeownership, especially in the years following the war, remained a goal of virtually every working-class family. Leaving behind the crowded, worn, turn-of-the-century homes and apartments in West Oakland for newer single-family dwellings in North and East Oakland or the developing suburbs to the south was a visible sign of class advancement for Oakland's workers. But organized labor's stance toward the MOAP and its Chamber promoters was more complicated. The MOAP assumed that the Chamber of Commerce, merchant groups, industrialists, developers, and real estate interests would guide postwar development, that the owners and political guardians of property would command the postwar march of progress. Organized labor, however, had spent much of the 1930s and early 1940s building its own institutions, its leaders participating—through collective bargaining, serving on a variety of tripartite boards and committees, and in appearances before the War Labor Board—in the setting of wage levels and standard working conditions. Reluctant to relinquish the power it had gained during the war, labor, while endorsing much of the Chamber's postwar plans, was unwilling to surrender control over the local economy entirely to Oakland's business, industrial, and propertied interests.

The General Strike and Oakland's Working Class

Oakland's AFL and CIO unions never articulated a postwar scenario as coherent as the Chamber of Commerce's. But labor's economic strength nonetheless translated into public defiance of business supremacy. This defiance reached both real and symbolic heights in the late 1940s, as Oakland's trade unions fought to shape local wages and working conditions following the end of wartime wage and price controls. In the process, Oakland's working class, representing the largest share of the city's residents, launched one of the most celebrated and colorful civic mass demonstrations in the postwar nation, the general strike of 1946. A brief affair remembered for its street celebrations and romanticized solidarity, the strike brought Oakland's class fissures into sharp relief. If the MOAP represented the vision of Oakland's business class for a metropolitan industrial garden shaped by businessmen, the general strike reminded Oakland that the city's working-class residents were not uncomplicated ciphers with no economic power of their own.

The general strike showcased labor's power and provided a stage for workers' transgression of the city's class and spatial codes, put forth by Oakland's business and political establishment, in which power and decision making lay in "downtown" institutions while the city's working-class neighborhoods remained passive wards. "The city of Oakland is not going back to the jungle," Oakland's mayor declared after the strike's declaration, dismissing labor's actions as the onset of anarchy. When workers formed picket lines on downtown streets, battled police for control of the sidewalks, and marched downtown during the general strike, they politicized the metropolis, refusing to see it as neutral. They saw the city as divided, both materially and metaphorically, between "downtown" and the neighborhoods. The strike was a symbolic expression of this understanding that prefigured more substantial political confrontations in subsequent years. "This is fascism in America!" Harry Lundberg of the Sailor's Union exclaimed before a crowd of fifteen thousand workers in Oakland. "Those [Nazis] were just average finks, the superfinks are the city administration of Oakland."[20]

Lundberg spoke for Oakland workers, but he would have found a sympathetic audience in union halls and civic auditoriums across the United States in 1945 and 1946, where a powerful tide of militancy had risen among the nation's laboring classes. The unprecedented growth in union membership between 1935 and 1945, the incorporation of both AFL and CIO leaders into wartime planning, and the institutionalization of labor relations within the New Deal state had in the space of a decade transformed organized labor in the United States into an influential axis of political and economic power. What remained was to solidify and extend that power. Toward that end, men and women throughout the United States participated in a record-breaking number of strikes in 1946. Over 4.5 million workers in everything from basic industry to clerical work, retail sales, and transportation walked off the job. Rooted in the economics of postwar conversion, most involved a single issue: wages. After

Congress allowed wartime price controls to expire in June 1946, the cost of living climbed quickly. Between June and December, food prices rose 28 percent and the cost of consumer goods 15 percent, placing workers on a harsh downward spiral, a difficult adjustment even in the warmth of national postwar celebration. Though divided between affiliates of the AFL and CIO (in 1946 an estimated 100,000 workers in Alameda County belonged to AFL unions, 20,000 to CIO unions), trade unionists of any stripe agreed that the labor movement had to act. Trade unions attacked the sudden inflation on two fronts: by reworking existing or expired contracts in union shops and by extending unionization to unorganized workers. Both fronts opened in Oakland in the months following the end of World War II.[21]

It was the second front, extending unionization to unorganized workers, that brought Oakland's labor movement into conflict with the city's powerful and vehemently anti-union Retail Merchants Association (RMA) and precipitated the general strike. Strengthened by wartime organizing drives, federally mandated union shop rules, and maintenance-of-membership clauses in war contracts, Oakland's trade union movement, like that of the nation as a whole, emerged from World War II as a powerful social and political force. Between the 1910s and World War II, the majority of Oakland's transportation and production industries had been unionized. Large numbers of Oakland's workers, however, primarily in clerical and sales occupations—where 57 percent of the workers in the late 1940s were women—remained unorganized. Beginning in 1946, Oakland AFL locals of the Office Employees International Union (Local 29) and the Department and Specialty Store Employees Union (Clerks Union, Local 1265) campaigned to organize them. Union organizers in Oakland imagined the local economy as a series of interconnected workspaces through which goods passed—ships, docks, trains, warehouses, trucks, and finally retail stores or, alternately, factories, warehouses, trucks, trains, retail stores, and sales floors. Women worked in every sector of the local economy but were disproportionately represented at the one end of this chain where labor's power remained the weakest: the stores where goods were sold. Erased as workers in the MOAP, women held the key to the march of postwar union progress.[22]

Kahn's and Hastings were the city's landmark downtown department stores and the largest employers of nonunion workers in the central business district. They stood squarely in the path of East Bay labor's postwar march. Between 1933 and 1939, as head of the Downtown Oakland Property Owners Association, Irving Kahn directed one of the largest urban renewal projects in the United States in which eighty-five Oakland buildings were remodeled and renovated—a first step in rescuing downtown from the crisis of the depression. Kahn and his RMA associates hoped to minimize union interference with the property values and profit-generating capacities of downtown real estate, both of which had declined precipitously during the 1930s. Encouraged by their victory in a spring shoe clerks' strike, however, Local 1265 and its new, mostly female, members at Kahn's and Hastings decided to test retailers' resolve. Determined and dug in for a long fight, the RMA refused to bargain in good faith with the clerks' union. In response, Local 1265's leaders struck both stores in early November. For their part, Oakland's AFL leadership interpreted the RMA's quick dismissal of Local 1265 as the leading wedge in a business offensive against all organized labor. Oakland business, an AFL editorial declared, intended "to repeat the program that followed World War I, the establishing of an open shop plan throughout industry," warning that "the Kahn's and Hastings strike is part of an overall strategy to smash labor."[23]

Figure 1.2. During the 1946 general strike, working men and women gathered in the streets of downtown Oakland to support striking department store employees. Oaklanders were part of a nationwide strike wave in 1946 that represented organized labor's efforts to ensure that postwar demobilization did not erode workers' standard of living. Oakland's strike was also unique because behind it lay a drive to organize new workers: female department store clerks. Courtesy of the Labor Archives and Research Center, San Francisco State University.

A twenty-eight-day strike ensued, during which each side delivered rhetorical diatribes at the other that escalated with each morning edition of the *Tribune*. In an attempt to resolve the strike in late November in favor of the employers, business leaders, including executives from Kahn's and other department stores, the chief counsel for the RMA, the head of the United Employers, the director of the Oakland Central Bank, and the publishers of the *Tribune* and the *Oakland Post-Inquirer* met with city officials, the district attorney, and the police chief. Store representatives announced their intention to break the strike with nonunion deliveries. City officials endorsed the move, and the police chief pledged full protection. Some 250 Oakland police officers were outfitted with tear gas and riot gear and assigned to protect the scabs the following weekend. Outraged at this betrayal and the business-government collusion it symbolized, AFL leaders called for the general strike the following day to protect the integrity of the union movement. The gradual escalation of engagement between the Clerk's Union and the city's AFL leadership on one side and the RMA and city hall on the other had divided the city, lending the general strike the aura of both public theater and dire class conflict.[24]

On 2 December 1946, Oakland union leaders representing some 100,000 AFL workers and 142 union locals in Alameda County called for a "work holiday" to support the retail clerks at Kahn's and Hastings. The next morning Oakland streets sat quiet as city buses and streetcars, operated by the unionized Key System, remained parked in the yards. The city's bustling port, warehouses, and machine shops grew silent as AFL teamsters, sailors, and boilermakers walked off their jobs. Cannery workers from the Fruitvale district and machinists from Elmhurst in East Oakland, railroad porters and day laborers from West Oakland, carpenters and other building tradesmen, and waiters, waitresses, and cooks from downtown hotels and restaurants, AFL unionists all of them, joined in the citywide work stoppage and accompanying mass protests in downtown Oakland. For fifty-four hours, traffic snarled on the Bay Bridge, construction sites remained silent, and the city's commerce ground to a halt. The city literally stopped.[25]

Every major AFL union official in Alameda County endorsed the general strike, and the CIO appeared ready to back the AFL-led effort as workers turned out in the tens of thousands on the night of 3 December to hear Robert Ash, secretary of the AFL Central Labor Council, denounce both merchants and city government—the "downtown" interests. His words resounded in the Oakland Auditorium, encouraged by cheers and massive applause, uniting the city's labor movement behind what the *Contra Costa Labor Journal* called "a fight to the finish in no uncertain terms." Back on the street, tension was palpable. "There were so many people there. They had cops all around the place, both Hastings and Kahn's," a picket captain for the Clerks Union explained of the scene downtown. By six o'clock the next evening, however, the strike was over. Teamsters Local 70, on direct orders from International Teamsters head Daniel Tobin and West Coast Vice President Dave Beck, had called its members back to work. The teamsters forced strike leaders to accept a settlement brokered by new city manager John Hassler. Workers' moods were mixed. The strike had allowed them to breach momentarily the class and spatial boundaries of the city, forcing "downtown" to take the collective will of Oakland's workers and neighborhoods seriously. For this, they celebrated. But the strike ended quickly, resolved little, and left rank-and-file workers and union leaders tempered by stinging defeat, discouraged by the intransigence of city officials, and offended by the ruthlessness of the police.[26]

Neither the Clerks Union nor the AFL Central Labor Council expected the organizing campaign at Kahn's and Hastings to proceed unchallenged, but neither one anticipated the ferocity with which the RMA, Mayor Herbert Beach, and the Knowland-owned *Tribune* would attack and discredit Oakland's moderate labor movement. The presence of the police was but one sign of the hardening anti-union stance of the business community. The strike at Kahn's and Hastings also fell in an important campaign season with implications for the entire state of California. William Knowland, son of Joseph R. Knowland—a former mayor of Oakland and then publisher of the *Tribune*—was running for reelection to the U.S. Senate in the fall of 1946. Backed by his father's *Tribune*, Knowland orchestrated a fiercely anticommunist, antilabor campaign and won handily, heading for Washington, DC, as part of the conservative Congress of 1946. His campaign victory that November encouraged the RMA and other downtown interests to toughen their stance against the Clerks Union and helped to push the two sides toward a more bitter confrontation.[27]

As a public performance, the general strike pitted workers against employers in memorable rhetorical clashes. Ideologically, however, labor offered less an alternative vision of the postwar world than an addendum to the protean concept of the industrial garden: labor wanted a union shop. Oakland's bread-and-butter AFL establishment stood for "efficient city government" and "progressive thinking and planning" more than for class insurgency. Organized AFL labor, while poised to challenge the downtown oligarchy's threat to shopfloor progress, accepted the broad terms of the MOAP and its invocation of Keynesian industrial growth and accelerated consumption. Guaranteed a union shop, to labor in the industrial garden looked pretty good. Oakland's general strike was led by trade unionists who, in the coming national political struggle of 1946–48, would align with Harry Truman and the liberal wing of the Democratic Party, not with Henry Wallace and the Progressive Party. Nonetheless, the general strike demonstrated how far these trade unionists would go to protect the economic interests of their laboring constituency.[28]

Oakland's labor movement was by no means of a single mind in the mid-1940s, however. Most AFL locals were led by business unionists who followed the moderate, pocketbook tendencies of their skilled and semiskilled members in the traditionally powerful unions: building trades, machinists, and teamsters. The East Bay's registered working-class voters were overwhelmingly Democratic, and a cadre of progressive trade union leaders enjoyed substantial influence in the Labor Council, but the local AFL labor movement as a whole, like that in the nation at large, rarely looked beyond the shopfloor. In contrast, led by social democrats, syndicalists, and communists, the East Bay CIO, like its San Francisco counterpart, favored social unionism and progressive political commitment. With small groups of workers in the auto plants, canneries, newspapers, hospitals, utilities, and on the docks, however, the East Bay CIO could never rival the AFL in numbers or influence. Even following the war, the East Bay CIO expanded little beyond its existing core, while the AFL labor movement, centered in the building trades, small-scale manufacturing, ship-building, transportation, and retail and wholesale trade and services, was in a much better position to increase its rolls. Those AFL and CIO leaders who found common cause in their opposition to city hall, and there were many, had therefore to manage a divided constituency and sensitive interfederation politics.[29]

The general strike briefly joined two political arenas that would grow increasingly distinct and differentiated over the course of the postwar period: shopfloor labor relations and urban governance. Oversight of labor relations by the apparatus of the New Deal state, pattern bargaining by the largest nationwide unions, and containment of trade unionism within the industrial and transportation core of the economy quickened after 1945 what had already been a long-term trend within the United States: the divorcing of workplace politics from the constitution of urban political regimes. With the important exception of major cities dominated by building trade unions and Democratic ward-based machines—primarily Philadelphia, Chicago, and New York—trade union politics and municipal governance did not overlap. The workplace politics of low-wage department store clerks escalated into a broader civic conflict because those clerks challenged downtown retail employers, the core group within Oakland's incumbent political regime, and one fighting for economic survival. This made the general strike unique in postwar labor politics, because, unlike in steel, auto and airplane manufacturing, mining, railroad, and textiles, workplace issues were resolved in the context of municipal politics rather than by national bargaining or by federal intervention or mediation. Not until the growth of municipal employee unions in the late

1960s and 1970s—and a handful of celebrated strikes in major cities across the country—would shopfloor labor issues play a comparable role in city politics.[30]

Who were the workers who challenged the downtown establishment in 1946? By the late 1940s, the East Bay's working class was overwhelmingly native born: in 1940 only 14 percent of Oakland's total population of 302,163 had been born outside the United States. Of those, most had immigrated from Germany, England, Italy, and Mexico, though in smaller numbers than to California's largest city, Los Angeles. Since the 1940 count reflects the impact of the first stages of wartime migration, an earlier census provides a clearer picture of Oakland's prewar makeup. In 1930 just under 20 percent of Oakland's total population of 284,063 was foreign born. Italy, Ireland, England, Canada, and Germany accounted for about half of the immigrants, with smaller numbers from Scandinavia (13 percent), Portugal (7 percent), and Eastern Europe (7 percent). Unlike Detroit, Chicago, Pittsburgh, and other major centers of U.S. industrial activity in the 1910s and 1920s, the East Bay economy did not produce entry-level industrial jobs in sufficient numbers to become a principal destination for the huge numbers of Polish, Slavic, and Russian immigrants teeming through America's industrial economy in the early decades of the twentieth century. Similarly, Oakland was not a major destination for southern African Americans before World War II. The prewar black migrations that made Chicago, Detroit, New York, and Pittsburgh centers of the northern black proletariat and middle class had drawn Oakland into the margins, not the center, of the African American diaspora. Prewar Oakland was shaped predominantly by Northern European immigrants, native-born Protestants, and Italians who left San Francisco following the 1906 earthquake and fire.[31]

For Euro-American workers in Oakland, progress meant physical mobility. Nick Petris, a future member of the California Assembly, recalled that West Oakland in the 1930s was "a marvelous mixture of people. We had every nationality that we knew of in that neighborhood. We had Chinese. We had Mexican, Portuguese, Greek, Italian, Yugoslav. Our immediate neighbor was a black family." By the late 1930s, however, the Petris family had moved out of West Oakland across Market Street, the unofficial neighborhood boundary. "And that seemed like moving to an entirely different area," Petris remembered. In the early 1940s, when wartime migration brought a flood of newcomers to West Oakland, the Petris family moved "way out in East Oakland" to a new home in a suburban setting, from where a streetcar ferried his father to work. The Petris family was hardly alone. Manuel Fernandez, a Portuguese immigrant and former West Oakland resident, explained that as people "got jobs and made more money, they bought a better home and a better place." If not to East Oakland, the city's 1920s-era streetcar neighbor-hoods near the General Motors and Durant Motors factories, homebuy-ers moved to North Oakland in the tree-lined shadows of the foothills. Others moved even farther out, to Albany or El Cerrito north of Berke-ley. In far East Oakland, between Fruitvale Avenue and the San Leandro city line, row upon row of stucco California bungalows created an invit-ing garden landscape in stark contrast to much of the residential, com-mercial, and industrial mish-mash of West Oakland.[32]

Class mobility among midcentury Oaklanders should not be exagger-ated, but incremental advancements in status were measured in multiple ways by people throughout their lives. Studies of Oakland during this pe-riod emphasize an overall class stability. People rarely leapt far from the occupational status of their parents. But property ownership in a North or East Oakland neighborhood—and in suburbs like San Leandro and Hay-ward and bedroom communities like Albany and El Cerrito—represented calculable progress. "The better class of people were moving out to San Leandro," Fernandez remembered of the 1940s, an assessment typical of the mobility-as-success paradigm of class. Moves meant more than a larger yard, bigger bedrooms, and a quieter street. They meant gains in a moral economy defined by homeownership. Oakland lacked the row houses, tenements, and dense apartment flats of eastern and midwestern cities, a feature of the landscape that never failed to surprise the eastern journalists, poverty warriors, and federal civil servants who came to Oakland in the late 1960s to study the city's poverty and black power politics. With the exception of Lake Merritt's apartment district and a few scattered apartment buildings in West and North Oakland, the city's housing stock was composed entirely of detached, single-family homes. Moreover, more than half of the homes in Oakland in 1950 were built af-ter 1920, making them relatively new in comparison to most American cities outside the sunbelt. "Everyone has slightly more than his own little flat here," an Oakland resident told an interviewer in the 1960s. "Oak-landers are less likely to actually know their neighbors but more likely to know the kinds of society their neighbors stand for," a 1960s study of Oakland tellingly observed.[33]

The city's white workers sought the status mobility and garden living offered by homeownership in North and East Oakland and in neighbor-ing communities like San Leandro, Albany, Berkeley, and El Cerrito. The postwar housing boom, underwritten by Veterans Administration (VA) and Federal Housing Administration (FHA) loans and mortgage guaran-tees, allowed white Oaklanders to carve new working-class space outside of the older parts of the city. As West Oakland developed into the East Bay's principal African American community in the mid-1940s, whites left in larger and larger numbers. New housing developments in East

Oakland and nearby suburbs provided them with residential mobility. Despite Oakland's horizontal neighborhoods of detached houses, the city's homeownership rate (49 percent in 1950) was still below the state's (54 percent), and increasing numbers of postwar homebuyers looked to nearby cities for their first purchase. The late 1940s was a decade of transition in West Oakland. Residents could still map parts of their community by national group or parish affiliation, but those classifications were losing their resonance. By 1950 the working-class space of the flatlands as divided less by national enclaves than by the racial categories "white" and "black."[34]

Immigrants and their children made West Oakland a lively port of entry in the first half of the twentieth century, but Oakland itself was never primarily an immigrant city. Native-born whites with northern European backgrounds constituted the majority in Oakland's neighborhoods in the 1940s. Oakland boosters had marketed the city to the American heartland in the first half of the century as a land of plentiful jobs, sunny clime, and affordable real estate. Protestant middle Americans flocked to the East Bay in response. They arrived in fewer numbers than went to Southern California, but the city's skilled workforce and the bulk of its middle class was composed largely of such migrants. In addition, during the 1930s the East Bay drew thousands of "Okie" migrants from Texas, Oklahoma, Missouri, and Arkansas, a migration that brought to the city a culture of "plain folk Americanism" with its populist Protestant fundamentalism. Relatively few native-born whites settled in West Oakland, however, preferring Berkeley, North and East Oakland, and the foothill districts that later commentators would call the "Bible belt." The dominant presence of these native-born whites, including large numbers from the Midwest and Upper South, contributed to Oakland's small-town feel in the 1930s and 1940s. Observers noted that despite West Oakland's gritty immigrant cosmopolitanism and blend of Europeans, Mexicans, and African Americans, the city as a whole featured a small-town civic culture. "Oakland will be a third-rank city," one resident told interviewers in the 1960s with tongue in cheek, because the politicians, like their unsophisticated constituency, "sit around a pot-bellied stove and chew tobacco, spit it in spittoons, and have an occasional drink."[35]

While it is possible to speak of a population "gold rush" in the East Bay during the war, and while Oakland was overwhelmed with the numbers of wartime migrants and their strain on city services, the waves of wartime migration distributed people throughout the East Bay corridor in familiar patterns. Oakland itself absorbed 82,000 new residents between 1940 and 1950, the majority during the war. Adjoining East Bay cities also experienced pronounced population growth. Richmond, Alameda, and Berkeley together gained 132,000 new residents between

1940 and 1950, many of them working-class migrants who remained in the East Bay after the war. Much larger African American communities thrived in Oakland and Richmond at the end of the war, and migrant "Okies" established enclaves in parts of Oakland and peripheral cities in Alameda and Contra Costa counties. But with the exception of a much larger African American population, the East Bay's working class remained in the late 1940s quite similar to its prewar form: large numbers of native-born workers of northern European background, and significant, but smaller, numbers of immigrants and the children of immigrants from Ireland, Italy, Germany, Portugal, Mexico, and Eastern Europe.[36]

Skilled and semiskilled workers in small establishments predominated in Oakland's diversified workforce. A statistical portrait of Oakland's male workers in 1940 and 1950 reveals their even distribution over manufacturing, services, and trade, while a smaller percentage could be found in transportation. The war boosted employment between 1940 and 1945, but by 1950 Oakland had registered only moderate overall gains in manufacturing, trade and transportation. Only the service sector, buoyed by large increases in government employment, showed remarkable growth. The Oakland Army Base and the U.S. Naval Supply Depot, federal installations of enormous importance during the war, continued to employ large numbers of workers in the late 1940s and early 1950s as the occupation of Japan, the Cold War, and the Korean War kept the West Coast military establishment busy. Still the center of East Bay retail and finance, Oakland employed a large number of trade and service workers in addition to the substantial number of manufacturing and transportation workers who gave Oakland its reputation as a smokestack city of blue-collar teamsters, craft workers, factory operatives, and dockworkers.[37]

One-third of Oakland's paid workers were women. Though significant numbers worked in manufacturing, working-class women were concentrated in retail and wholesale trade, hotels and restaurants, and as clerical workers in financial, real estate, and other service industries. These women, as employees of banks, department stores, and other trading establishments, figured prominently in the AFL's postwar plans for extending union membership to important unorganized sectors of Oakland's economy. Indeed, the growing numerical strength and militancy of the Clerks Union in the middle 1940s was largely a product of this female labor force. Women also worked in Oakland's sizable canning industry, in health care, and, particularly among the city's African American women, in private household work. As in the rest of the nation, women's notable access to traditionally male-dominated occupations in East Bay manufacturing during World War II gave way after 1945 to older patterns of job distribution and discrimination. Women welders, burners, riveters, and carpenters during the war became clerical workers, maids, retail clerks, and waitresses after 1945. The doubling of women's employment in clerical and sales between 1940 and 1950 signaled early evidence of a long-term postwar trend within the East Bay economy: the feminization of downtown employment and the gradual shift away from manufacturing toward services.[38]

Wartime migration deepened the East Bay's labor pool and brought both skilled and unskilled workers to the region in record numbers. An estimated 500,000 people came to the San Francisco Bay area as a whole between 1940 and 1944. Though San Francisco, Oakland, and the East Bay drew migrants from every part of the country, the "near South" states of Texas, Louisiana, Arkansas, and Oklahoma sent the largest numbers, accounting for 28 percent of the Bay Area's out-of-state migrants, both white and black. Migrants also came from rural parts of California and from smaller cities not affected by wartime employment. Just over 160,000 Bay Area migrants originated within the state. "Boomtown" jobs in the shipyards tended to go to migrants, while people who had lived in the East Bay prior to the war were employed in larger numbers in Oakland's older manufacturing and distribution sectors. The employment picture between 1940 and 1950 suggests that the wartime boost did not reorient Oakland's workforce around new occupations or industries, nor did reconversion, as many feared, result in massive layoffs and a surge in unemployment, with the important exception of the shipyards. In the short term, Oakland continued to produce jobs and expand its occupational base.[39]

More so than in many American cities in the 1940s, unions were important to the lives of Oakland's workers. But unions competed with family, church, civic groups, and neighborhoods as sources of identity and ideology. Most men and women in industrial or low-level white collar jobs— who would have identified as middle class or as "working people"—shared a set of attitudes drawn from a broad set of influences. The moral conservatism of midcentury religion, the egalitarianism fostered by civic associations and popular notions of "the public," the sense of sacrifice and collective endeavor engendered by the war in both battle and on the homefront, and aspirations of homeownership all contributed to a white working-class populism in this era. Though African Americans occasionally shared in that populist public culture, white racism prevented their more thorough inclusion. It would be a mistake to locate the interests and identities of Oakland's workers solely in the institutions of organized labor and to assume that trade unionism reflected working-class aspirations in a transparent way. But it would be an equivalent mistake to overlook a critical process in Oakland in this era: trade unions' entry into the public sphere to make political claims about the city, its workers, and its citizens and to vie for civic power. The general strike's bitter conclusion one day after armed police protected strike-breakers and dispersed a

Figure 1.3. A union representative from Local 6 of the International Long-shoremen's and Warehousemen's Union talks with workers at Oakland's Associated Packing in 1947. As the leading CIO union on the West Coast, the ILWU was committed to organizing the men and women who labored on the Bay Area's waterfronts. An important force for progressive politics in California, the ILWU advocated multiracial class unity and an international solidarity of all workers. Courtesy of the ILWU Library, San Francisco.

peaceful picket left the trade union movement determined to reverse the balance of power in a local political equation that had swiftly turned against them.[40]

African American Workers in Postwar Oakland

A different, though nonetheless urgent, set of circumstances confronted Oakland's African American workers. Trade union roots were strong in Oakland's black community, anchored by the Brotherhood of Sleeping Car Porters, the Dining Car, Cooks, and Waiters Union, and the ILWU. African American workers who participated in the general strike did so because they believed that organized labor, despite its imperfections, promised a better, more secure future for Oakland's working class. But for the majority of black workers, both those who had lived in Oakland prior to 1940 as well as the wartime newcomers, the general strike's symbolic evocation of working-class camaraderie was illusory. Oakland's Jim

Crow social relations, including ubiquitous discrimination against African American workers within the union movement itself, seemed a far more pressing problem than the downtown merchants. In the year prior to Oakland's general strike, 1945, African American leaders took that discrimination head on. The Alameda County NAACP and the Shipyard Workers Committee against Discrimination sued Oakland's private bus and train company, the Key System, before the federal government's Fair Employment Practices Commission (FEPC), charging the company and the operator's union with discrimination in hiring and membership. If a ruling against the Key System could begin to break Oakland's color line, the FEPC suit represented an opportunity to shape postwar industrial relations as important to African American workers as the general strike was to the whole of Oakland's working class.

The struggle to desegregate the Key System embodied African Americans' larger engagement with the industrial garden. Many African American migrants, as well as national black publications like the *Crisis*, celebrated California's openness in the 1940s. The *Crisis*, the monthly journal of the NAACP, extolled the state in which black "children go to the same schools as other children" and black men "can walk down the street without having to move toward the curb when a white man passes." Longtime African American residents of California were far more realistic about the state's racist past and segregated present, however. Black railroad and dock workers, in particular, found the color line in employment and social relations no less stubborn in the golden state than in other parts of the country. Nonetheless, the war years provided a setting for the first large-scale assault on Pacific Coast Jim Crow, because, just like their white midwestern and southern migrant counterparts, African Americans believed that California's promise of garden living and expanding opportunity spoke to them and symbolized their ambitions.[41]

Seizing that opportunity seemed all the more consequential in 1945 because wartime migration had drawn large numbers of African Americans to Oakland. In a 1944 survey, the U.S. Bureau of the Census reported 21,770 African Americans living in Oakland, up from just over 8,000 in 1940. By 1950 Oakland's black population numbered 42,355, a fivefold increase in the space of a decade. Sam Kagel, Northern California War Manpower Commission director, called the movement of tens of thousands of black workers to Oakland, Richmond, and San Francisco during the war part of "the greatest migration of people in history." Labor recruiters combed the southern states in the early years of the war, drawing rural and urban African American workers alike to Bay Area shipyards. As in Los Angeles and other northern and western centers of the defense industry, migrants settled in the region permanently after the war, joining a small, but well-established prewar African American community. Undersized by the standards of northern African American centers like Chicago and Philadelphia, Oakland's black community was no less dynamic and engaged in the process of forging lives in a city where black people faced opportunity in equal measure to reminders of their second-class status.[42]

C. L. Dellums, International Vice President of the Brotherhood of Sleeping Car Porters and member of the Alameda County NAACP and the Alameda County Central Labor Council, led attempts in the late 1930s to open the city's bus and streetcar jobs to black workers. Time after time, he met determined opposition from both the company and the union. The Key System's high-profile jobs and its role as a prominent employer and city contractor placed the railway company in a position to set local standards for occupational access. It was the only mass transit system connecting the East Bay to San Francisco, across the Bay Bridge, and the only system linking the East Bay cities of Oakland, Berkeley, Richmond, San Leandro, Hayward, Albany, Alameda, El Cerrito, and Emeryville. Within Oakland itself Key System lines connected the working-class residential districts of West and East Oakland to downtown, the port, and the city's industrial belt. In the pre-interstate freeway era this transportation network provided Oakland's working families with access to jobs, shopping, and entertainment. By the beginning of wartime mobilization, however, the company had still not hired its first African American operator, turning away dozens of qualified black applicants.[43]

Wartime conditions brought new opportunities to open Key System jobs. The Richmond Shipyard Railway, operating as a division of the Key System, transported workers between Oakland, Berkeley, and the giant Kaiser shipyards in Richmond where tens of thousands of workers were building Liberty Ships. The Key System contracted with the U.S. Maritime Commission to operate the Richmond Railway, placing the company under the authority of President Roosevelt's Executive Order 8802 mandating fair employment in all war industries. In addition, during the first two years of production in the shipyards and other war-related industries, labor shortages encouraged employees to jump from job to job seeking the highest return on their labor. Oakland's Key System fell victim to workers literally "jumping the streetcars" for better prospects in the shipyards, creating chronic labor shortages. In any number of ways, then, when African American labor leaders and the Alameda County NAACP reorganized their campaign to integrate the Key System in the early years of the war, conditions appeared favorable.[44]

The center of midcentury East Bay African American social life and politics was West Oakland. Compact neighborhoods of tree-lined streets, Victorian two-flats, single-occupancy hotels, workers' cottages, and a few scattered bungalows, West Oakland lay nestled in between the downtown business district and the warehouses, rail yards, and factories of Oakland's

Figure 1.4. From left: H. Claude Hudson, C. L. Dellums, Tarea Hall Pittman, and Nathaniel S. Colley of the West Coast Region, NAACP. Dellums, a vice president of the Brotherhood of Sleeping Car Porters, hoped to use the wartime federal Fair Employment Practices Commission to break Jim Crow employment discrimination in the Bay Area. After the war, Dellums would become California's principal advocate for a statewide FEP law. Courtesy of the *Oakland Tribune.*

port and industrial flatlands. Prior to World War II, West Oakland offered inexpensive housing mainly to two groups of workers: working-class Euro-American refugees from San Francisco's 1906 earthquake and fire, and African American workers employed by the Southern Pacific Railroad, the Pullman Company, and Oakland's numerous other freight yards and warehouses. Above all, the Southern Pacific dominated West Oakland's industrial, as well as social, geography with its massive switching and maintenance yards, roundhouses, car assembly and repair shops, creosoting plant, and shipyards (the Southern Pacific built ferries for San Francisco Bay). The Western Pacific operated smaller yards, and the Pullman Palace Car Company maintained its northern California headquarters there as well. In the 1930s, 60 percent of African American income there came from the railroads. And the paychecks mattered. "If you had a job with S.P., you could get credit anyplace," one resident remembered. But paychecks were only part of the story. West Oakland stood at the axis of the West Coast's black railroad working-class culture, nurtured and sustained by employees of the Pullman Company and the Southern Pacific. Black workers nourished a variety of institutions, including the Brotherhood of Sleeping Car Porters, the city's two oldest African American churches, the Alameda County NAACP, fraternal and civic associations, women's clubs and auxiliaries, DeFremery Recreation Center (an important focal point of community organization, youth entertainment, and athletics), and substantial black commercial and professional districts, principally along Seventh Street. The Brotherhood's West Coast headquarters was located in offices in West Oakland, where C. L. Dellums, a close partner of A. Phillip Randolph's, lived and worked.[45]

The Brotherhood fostered a rich organizational and social tradition that extended beyond pure trade unionism and linked West Oakland to other black communities nationwide. Pullman porters returning to Oakland after sometimes weeks of absence brought with them black newspapers from Chicago, Los Angeles, New York, and occasionally even Atlanta, New Orleans, and Birmingham. Paul Cobb, who became one of West Oakland's most important community organizers in the 1960s, remembers porters bringing newspapers into his grandfather's grocery store near the Southern Pacific tracks. As a young man, he marveled at the stories from black communities in Chicago, Memphis, and Philadelphia, narratives of black life and politics—and black-white relations—that became the foundation of his early political education. In places like Cobb's corner store, Brotherhood members joined black ILWU, MCSU, and Dining Car Cooks and Waiters Union members in a cosmopolitan laborite culture that blended politics, trade unionism, and human rights. Defeating economic and social segregation was a central aim of this culture, but otherwise it was far from politically uniform, as black trade unionists ranged from the communist left to the liberal center.[46]

West Oakland was a port of entry for African American migrants as much as for European immigrants. Like their immigrant neighbors, black families measured social progress in terms of economic and spatial mobility. They sought the status that a move to South Berkeley or North Oakland signified. "Berkeley was always the first step up" for East Bay African Americans, Norvel Smith recalled. "You came into West Oakland, then North Oakland, and if you really made it, with a civil service job or something, you moved into South Berkeley." Many could and did ultimately make that move. Many more could not. For the generation of black Oaklanders who came of age before World War II, segregation thoroughly shaped city life. "There's very little difference between the segregation here in California and the blatant things that go on in the South," Arthur Patterson told an interviewer. C. L. Dellums recalled that "[m]ost of the complaint cases we had in those days [1940s] were discrimination in places of public accommodation, police brutality cases, and thirdly, of course, were cases of discrimination in employment." Housing, too, was segregated. Isaac Slaughter, who came to West Oakland in 1944, remembered that there was "such a small part of the city that black folk could live in that they were sleeping on top of each other." In 1950 nearly 90 percent of the city's black population resided in 22 percent of its census tracts concentrated in West and North Oakland."[47]

Black workers in the 1940s found employment as cooks, waiters, Pullman porters, car cleaners, and redcaps, and, though less commonly, in the manufacturing, machine-tool, and repair shops of the Southern Pacific. "At one time around here, it's all they had was cooks and waiters, redcaps and things," Royal Towns, a black Oakland fireman, told an interviewer. Nevertheless, railroad work conferred status. "In those days, people looked up to you if you was a railroad man," Robert Edwards, a dining car waiter working out of West Oakland, recalled. Porters, waiters, and cooks were considered elite workers within the black community, but their daily labor serving a white clientele nonetheless brought them up against the color line. Edwards recalled the work environment in the 1940s and 1950s as "highly Jim Crowed. They just did not believe in promoting blacks to any positions of authority. [And] they had special places for the black passengers to eat. They were always served behind the curtain." Moreover, skilled occupations on the railroad, in the switching yards, and in the machine shops remained the domain of white workers, whose unions, known as the Railroad Brotherhoods, maintained strict color bars. As in housing, black workers confronted the employment color line and fought to erase it, even as they shaped a life within the spaces segregation allowed.[48]

African Americans in West Oakland developed a unique geographic relationship to work. In ways largely untrue of the vast industrial cities of Chicago and Detroit, black workers in Oakland did not have to travel long distances through hostile white neighborhoods to reach jobs crucial to the community. Work, in many ways, came to them. The docks, the railroad tracks, and West Oakland's small factories lay within easy walking distance or a short bus or streetcar ride of the majority of African American homes. The Southern Pacific yards lay so close to West Oakland's black neighborhoods that "you could hear the trains blowing when they would come in," according to Tippy Alexander Jones. "Some people knew the numbers. They would say, 'here comes old number 17.'" Of greater importance, for the laboring elite of West Oakland's African American working class—the sleeping car porters, dining car waiters, and merchant marine cooks—work took them out of West Oakland and even outside California (an opposite trajectory applied to longshoremen, who came into contact in Oakland with ship workers from around the

Figure 1.5. Dining car waiters in Oakland were among the African American working-class elite, but, serving an all-white clientele, they nonetheless confronted the color line in its most stark form. Their union, the Brotherhood of Sleeping Car Porters, combined working-class solidarity with civil rights advocacy and provided an institutional center of gravity for midcentury West Oakland's black communities. Courtesy of the Union Pacific Railroad Archives and the African American Museum and Library at Oakland, Railroad Collection.

world). Despite the vicious racism that confined black workers to the worst and most menial jobs, the experience of labor for this small but important working-class elite was a cosmopolitan one. This dual experience, of immediate spatial confinement in West Oakland and of expansive connections to and exchanges with a much larger world, became the foundation of Oakland's African American working-class culture.[49]

In urban black American communities, from Chicago's Southside to Detroit's Paradise Valley, Harlem and North Philadelphia to West Oakland, a great deal was at stake in the late 1940s. The war had elevated racial liberalism from the margins of political discourse to the center of the nation's wartime antifascism. If African Americans could translate this rhetorical commitment to racial equality into real gains in employment and housing, the long-unfulfilled promises of Reconstruction in the agricultural South might be realized in the postwar industrial North and

West. In the Double-V campaign, black communities across the nation called for victory over racism in Europe and victory over racism at home. The *Chicago Defender* declared that "the Negro is damned tired of spilling his blood for empty promises of better days." America must "bomb the color line," the paper announced during the war. How sincere the nation, its citizens, and institutions were in the newfound racial liberalism remained an open and heated question in African American households throughout the country. But the issue at stake in those households was not simply the defeat of Jim Crow. Midcentury African American communities embraced multiple political currents, from ideologies of racial uplift and integrationism to neo-Garveyite black nationalism and black capitalism to progressive trade unionism (as in the Brotherhood of Sleeping Car Porters) and, especially in the East Bay, radical laborite socialism and communism.[50]

In addition to the Brotherhood, a handful of other East Bay unions exerted positive influences on black employment and culture. Two progressive, CIO-affiliated unions joined the Brotherhood and the Dining Car Cooks and Waiters (both AFL) in the 1940s as crucial strongholds of African American trade union membership in Oakland and San Francisco: the ILWU and the MCSU. Between 1934 and 1937, the era of the brutal Pacific Coast dock wars, these unions forged an intense solidarity, and Harry Bridges and cosmopolitan radicals of both communist and syndicalist persuasion turned this solidarity into a force for racial equality. African American workers made up one-fourth and one-third of the membership of the ILWU and MCSU, respectively, by the early 1950s, and an important black leadership group developed within each union. Neither union earned a perfect record regarding racial matters—job upgrading in the late 1940s and 1950s, in particular, seemed to favor white workers—but the importance of the Bay Area locals of the ILWU and MCSU to shopfloor racial equality and civil rights is definitive. They, along with the Brotherhood, stood at the center of the Bay Area's African American trade union culture and remained an influential force in all of the region's midcentury black communities. The Brotherhood's anticommunism produced some tensions with the ILWU and MCSU, which embraced left radicals, but not enough to prevent their cooperation in coalitions.[51]

World War II transformed few places in the East Bay as dramatically as West Oakland. Tens of thousands of African American migrants from the southern states, recruited to the East Bay by Kaiser, the Moore Dry Dock Company, and the federal government, settled in the flatlands of West Oakland. Housing discrimination in other parts of Oakland and in the nearby cities of Albany, El Cerrito, Alameda, and San Leandro crowded these black migrants into established "Negro" districts. In subdivided homes, apartments, and hotels overbooked and bursting, these newly arrived workers made the best of cramped conditions. As the war progressed and increasing numbers of black migrants arrived, West Oakland's European descendants took advantage of white-only wartime public housing or the restricted private working-class housing projects built in satellite communities like San Lorenzo. Still, West Oakland boomed. By the middle years of the war, African American West Oakland was thriving on the income of its thousands of new African American residents. Seventh Street's commercial district flourished with black-owned businesses and professional offices, Slim Jenkins' jazz club on Seventh and Wood streets headlined a famous (now legendary) nightclub scene; women's clubs, churches, and fraternal lodges thrived; and the district developed a special sense of transplanted community as southern migrants from the same towns and even neighborhoods in "near South" states settled close to one another.[52]

Both sides of the community, new and old, hoped that federal wartime initiatives would help to ease local employment discrimination. The war had delivered jobs, but also the familiar job ceilings and segregation characteristic of "Negro work." When the FEPC hearings opened in March 1945, U.S. Attorney Bruce Hunt charged both the Key System and the union, Division 192 of the Amalgamated Association of Street, Electric Railway, and Motor Coach Employees, with discrimination. Spelling out his claims, Hunt contended that "the Key System for a long period of time has refused to utilize the services of occupationally qualified Negroes," and that the transit union "discriminates against Negroes in that it rejects them for membership because of their race." The case was straightforward. Eight individuals had applied for work with the Key System and been rejected despite their obvious qualifications. Several of the eight plaintiffs had applied with the assistance of either the NAACP or the Shipyard Workers Committee against Discrimination, a wartime organization of African American workers with a strong left affiliation and branches in the East Bay and San Francisco.[53]

The Alameda County NAACP and the Shipyard Workers Committee against Discrimination were part of a much larger network of organizations that challenged racial discrimination throughout the Bay Area during the war. Tactics varied, but most focused on the shipyards, the largest wartime employer of black workers in the region. In Oakland, Richmond, San Francisco, and Sausalito, the principal shipyard union, the AFL-affiliated International Brotherhood of Boilermakers, Iron Shipbuilders, and Helpers of America (Boilermakers), established segregated locals, known as auxiliaries, for African American workers. Overseen by white "parent" locals, these auxiliaries insured that black workers remained powerless and trapped in the tenuous last hired/first fired category. Segregated units were not even parties to the master employment contract. Joseph James in San Francisco and Sausalito and Ray Thompson in Oakland led the Shipyard Workers Committees that fought this Jim Crow system. Thompson was never able to get FEPC hearings in the East Bay shipyards, and all of his discrimination suits either stalled or failed, but he, along with Dellums, did succeed in getting FEPC hearings on the Key System. The committees themselves included a number of activists from the left, including Communist Party members, making them vulnerable to postwar purges and antiradical propaganda.[54]

Thompson and Dellums won an odd, eventually empty, victory. Spokesmen for the Key System denied racial discrimination, arguing that if Division 192 refused to admit African Americans the company had no alternative but to comply under its union shop contract. Passing the buck to the union, a common strategy among employers in the highly unionized Bay Area, proved to be a fortuitous subterfuge for the transportation company: the FEPC hearings came to hinge on the question of union, not company, discrimination. With the focus shifted to the union, Hunt and his witnesses regrouped and presented overwhelming evidence that Division 192 refused to admit black workers, preventing their employment as operators in the entire East Bay. In a survey of Division 192 members ordered by the FEPC, 93 percent of white workers indicated that they would object to working alongside African Americans. Confronted with this overpowering evidence and the company's dodging of responsibility, union representatives Alfred Brown and Cyril Marelia walked out of the hearings. "We believe the method of handling these proceedings is un-American, un-democratic," Marelia told FEPC representatives. The FEPC ruled against the union and sanctioned the company for conspiring in job discrimination. In the face of the ruling, the Key System, without directly admitting guilt, capitulated and agreed to abide by fair employment practices. Despite the Key System's capitulation, black activists immediately recognized the pyrrhic nature of the victory. In a frank personal letter to Hunt the same month as the ruling, Dellums wrote that "too many people feel that the hearings might have been window dressing or white washing."[55]

Dellums was right. The FEPC hearings failed to dismantle the color line in either Key System or broader local employment. "They will try anything that might delay the issuance of the directives," Dellums wrote to Hunt, predicting that the Key System would attempt to wait out the FEPC and stall on hiring black operators. Congress subsequently eliminated the FEPC in 1946, stripping from the movement a key enforcement mechanism. The Key System did not hire its first African American operator until 1951, six years after the FEPC hearings. Their closed door policy reflected conditions throughout most of the Bay Area and nationally, in which blue-collar jobs of high public visibility were reserved for white workers. In hospitals, hotels, restaurants, department stores, transportation, and other services, a "front-of-the-house/back-of-the-house" racial line restricted black workers to jobs invisible to the public. This arrangement, and set of attitudes, persisted well into the 1960s and 1970s in both Oakland and San Francisco despite Northern California's reputation for racial liberalism. Most unions erected impenetrable boundaries around membership rolls, and local employers rarely challenged this racial favoritism, often maintaining their own informal Jim Crow hiring methods. Moreover, the Key System's tactical response to the FEPC ruling embodied an approach to fair employment that employers would use with increasing frequency in subsequent decades: capitulate to public pressure, while stalling on hiring black workers behind the scenes.[56]

Because of the region's high rate of unionization, patterns of racial discrimination in the labor movement set local employment standards. In a major study undertaken at the University of California in 1947, one-third of more than one hundred unions surveyed reported no black members. One-half of all black union members were general laborers, back-of-the-house food service workers, or janitors. On average, CIO unions showed larger numbers of African Americans than AFL locals, but the CIO was a small presence in Bay Area industry. In the crucial fields of transportation and construction, dominated by the Teamsters and Building Trades, respectively, a nearly solid color line prevailed. Many unions in the Bay Area used the power of white worker solidarity and the union contract to deny black workers membership or to subordinate them in second-class status within the union. The California Supreme Court, in *James v. Marinship*, brought the segregated auxiliary system within the shipyard unions to an end toward the close of the war, but postwar layoffs and reconversion all but eliminated the shipyards as major employers of black workers. African American workers, who in the mid-1940s gained access to union-controlled jobs and the higher wages that accompanied them, did so in spite of this widespread discrimination. And even then they often confronted steep racial barriers to advancement within the workplaces controlled by those unions.[57]

Few African American women encountered unions in their places of employment, but women shaped Oakland's postwar African American working-class community in other critical ways. Migrant women transplanted southern folk traditions to their Oakland neighborhoods. They constructed informal bonds across the community, reciprocal relationships of exchange and mutual dependence that provided newly arrived families with essential goods and services: from childcare and weddings to health care, jobs, food, and shelter. This kind of face-to-face social networking, an essential feature of rural southern African American tradition, gave West Oakland's bustling streets and neighborhoods a sense of safety and familiarity while quietly holding families and homes together. Moreover, women's social networking translated into politics. In churches, the NAACP, the East Bay Parent-Teacher Associations, the East Bay Democratic Club, and numerous other community, civil rights, and political organizations and institutions, migrant women, as well as their more established counterparts, brought an aggressive advocacy to East Bay political culture. Black women's labor, too, sustained the community. In an era when few black men outside of the laboring elite were permitted to hold positions that paid a family wage, women performed an untold range of jobs: in the service sector, as domestics, in factory work, and in informal labor, such as laundering, babysitting, taking in and cooking for boarders, in addition to raising children and providing for a home. African American women added important elements of both formal and informal work and politics to the more male-centered trade union culture in Oakland's growing black community.[58]

California's version of segregation meant that African American workers in every sector of the local economy faced job ceilings. Census figures suggest that World War II offered African American migrants only a tenuous foothold in the local job market, with most finding postwar work in familiar semiskilled and unskilled jobs and in the service sector. The thousands of African American men and women recruited to work in the wartime shipyards found the conversion to civilian production especially difficult. Sixty percent of African American men in 1950 found work as blue-collar laborers, as machine operatives, or in back-of-the-house service work. African American women found that their wartime employment in the Moore and Kaiser shipyards did not easily translate into postwar opportunities beyond the usual household service. Half of all black women workers labored in 1950 as private domestics or in other kinds of service work. Groups like the NAACP and the Urban League continued to fight discrimination in employment in the late 1940s and early 1950s, but progress was often slow and incremental. African American workers, especially men, did make substantial inroads in one area of employment, federal government jobs, that would remain a foundation of black opportunity in the postwar decades. The Oakland Army Base, the U.S. Naval Supply Station, and the Naval Air Station at Alameda took on large numbers of black workers during the war and kept them. While not free of discrimination in job assignments and pay, these military installations, all three located in or near West Oakland, acted as something of a community bulwark against the more pervasive bias in the private sector and the large-scale postwar layoffs in shipbuilding.[59]

Workplace segregation provided the most obvious example of regional Jim Crow practices, but a more general, widely observed, social separation of the races defined a variety of settings. Through the mid-1940s, signs announcing "We Refuse Service to Negroes" sat in the windows of many hotels, bars, and restaurants, particularly in the areas of downtown closest to West Oakland and in cities like Albany and San Leandro that remained closed to African Americans. The signs disappeared fast on the heels of the war, but in practice segregation in many types of public spaces persisted through the 1950s. Oakland's educational system, relatively integrated prior to the war, emerged in the late 1940s on a steep path toward almost complete segregation. Parts of the East Bay escaped these hardening racial lines, especially areas in Berkeley and North Oakland where churches, schools, and civic organizations continued to bring some black and white residents together, but this was confined largely to the established middle and professional classes. Recent working-class migrants, black and white, tended to live in monoracial worlds. Despite the reality of racial separation, many in Oakland's white community perceived black migrants as intruding on what one local observer called "the old and peaceful understanding between the Negro and the white in Oakland."[60]

World War II marked a watershed for Oakland's African American community, a moment that embodied the possibility of further victories against Jim Crow or the prospect of a retrenchment and return to prewar forms of segregation and oppression. Extending wartime racial liberalism remained the foremost priority for black activists across the political spectrum, because signs of an emerging backlash were eminent. The Key System, one example among many, symbolized the containment of racial liberalism within the rhetorical and institutional environment created by the war. What was won could quickly and easily be lost. But African Americans, from activist leaders to ordinary men and women, were determined to shape a political culture in Oakland and the East Bay that included them and their ambitions. Their first act of resistance was simply to stay, to make the new life California and its industrial garden had offered during the war permanent—in the face of white assumptions that their "stay" was temporary, a product of wartime emergency. But further progress was contingent, not guaranteed; subsequent victories would be won through struggle, not patience. The year 1945 marked this divide in palpable and indisputable terms.

In 1940s Oakland a disparate range of interests embraced the optimism and promise of the industrial garden. Its protean qualities allowed workers and business leaders, African Americans and white Euro-Americans, to see in California living expressions of their own values and ambitions. Space as an analytical category is amorphous; the industrial garden in Oakland and the East Bay in the postwar decades was anything but. It cut in many directions, but cut it did. How residential and employment opportunities would be distributed, how homes would be financed and property taxed, how communities would be formed and defined, how and where investment capital moved, relocated, and fostered new economic relationships—such questions turned on the concrete production of social relationships in and through the postwar metropolis. Power in the booster MOAP's industrial garden remained latent, beneath the surface, diffuse. But power in the industrial garden as its adherents struggled to build and modify it was none of these things. Power had real locations, granted privileges, and imposed limits—according to class, property ownership, race, gender, political district, and city. The necessary precursor to the industrial garden's realization, power was everywhere divided, coded, and fragmented, making the garden and its ideological foundations in growth liberalism an extraordinarily broad arena in which postwar social conflict and negotiation would unfold. The dream of the industrial garden was finally about producing both space and power.

The history of Oakland's shifting political terrain in the years after World War II was linked to the city's distinct urban spaces. Oakland's residential, commercial, and industrial districts were not passive backdrops to some more fundamental action. They were in constant motion as people and capital moved to and through them and as groups and organizations sought to shape them, producing and reproducing local physical, social, and political relationships. West Oakland, with its working-class ethnic and national neighborhoods, its factories, rail yards, and port, its concentration of African American railroad workers, and the strong trade union presence among both white and black workers, made that neighborhood an enormously important and dynamic center of political culture in the 1940s. East Oakland, with its factories and working-class bungalows, its suburban distance from downtown, and its greater proportion of homeowners, looked and felt like the middle landscape imagined in the MOAP. The city's downtown commercial districts, dominated physically by the *Oakland Tribune*'s tower just off of Broadway and united politically the interlocking interests of retailers, property owners, and boosters, had become by late 1946 symbolic of Oakland's propertied class, the power of which lay in its ownership of the city's best real estate and its influence over the city council. These places carried more than discursive significance. They were physical and cultural spaces of work, residence, and property where people came to understand and articulate their interests.

Oakland's business class and white and African American working-class residents defined postwar progress in different, conflicting ways. Resolving those differences was an issue of politics—the everyday politics of social struggle and the formal politics of elections. Downtown property owners could imagine themselves guardians of the city's economic future, but class power is produced through political contest, not the suggestive symbolism of planning documents. Business dominance in the city would have to be won; it could not simply be asserted in the rhetoric of promotional literature. Neither could liberal rhetoric alone reconcile divergent class and racial interests in the neighborhoods and shopfloors of the city. Working-class black and white Oaklanders shared the flatlands, but spatial proximity did not translate into a political alliance. The class struggle in mid 1940s Oakland, as nationwide, intensified racial divisions as it forged unity among white workers. While black workers participated in the general strike, they understood that trade union solidarity could just as easily mean white racial privilege as interracial unity. The Key System hearings and experience in the wartime shipyards revealed that truth in no uncertain terms. In the years immediately following World War II, Oakland faced crucial decisions about its long-term postwar fate. The city itself could be remade and improved, but who would remake it? If the MOAP's industrial garden was the city's model for postwar development, how would the real class and racial politics in Oakland's streets be resolved? As business, labor, and African Americans looked to open new possibilities for Oakland in the late 1940s, the answers remained uncertain and contentious, the questions looming over the East Bay even as the clouds of global war retreated and dispersed.

2

Working Class

THE RAUCOUS CELEBRATION and heated social tensions on display in Oakland's general strike spilled over into electoral politics. Drawing on the civic divisions exposed by the strike, labor leaders between 1945 and 1950 attempted to forge a progressive coalition, rhetorically united as "the public," to defeat the conservative political forces that governed the city. Their attempt raised fundamental questions confronting postwar America. How would the class struggle that had divided the nation in the 1930s be resolved, and would trade unionism, empowered by the New Deal state, remain an instrument of working-class mobility? How would the nation's working class preserve the New Deal's promise of greater economic security and extend the reach of the welfare state into urban neighborhoods? For African Americans, there was an additional set of questions. Could New Deal liberalism be expanded to encompass racial equality, including in the economic realm? What were the appropriate vehicles for challenging racial oppression in the midcentury United States? These questions were contested after the war in the local politics of cities like New York, Philadelphia, Baltimore, Detroit, Los Angeles, and Oakland. Their resolution would shape the future of the nation. In Oakland, their resolution raised the unprecedented possibility of a new working-class politics with racial inclusion.[1]

That possibility was foreclosed as swiftly as it was opened. The drama of assembling Oakland's progressive coalition of labor, professionals, merchants, and homeowners, white and black, was matched by its disintegration within five years. The narrative of that failure is the story of American liberalism at midcentury with all of its promise, contradictions, and dedicated enemies. The progressive coalition collapsed in Oakland for three critical reasons. First, the political power of property holders made defining and mobilizing a broad and consistently progressive "public" difficult if not impossible. A variety of property owners broke away from the liberal coalition when their economic interests came under threat. Second, white liberals' accommodation to racism and segregation fractured solidarity across racial lines and marginalized African American political objectives. Drawn into progressive politics by promises of inclusion and access, black Oaklanders were disillusioned with the token attention that white liberals devoted to their agenda. Finally, the downtown business class proved determined and resourceful, wielding a potent anticommunism against the coalition. Their manipulation of the postwar red scare constituted a cynical and self-interested, but nonetheless effective, strategy to defeat calls for urban reform. The liberal defeat marginalized trade unions in local politics and, as nationwide, helped discourage the mobilization of explicitly working-class-oriented political movements after the early 1950s. Most important for the East Bay, the liberal defeat left the owners and guardians of downtown property in control of Oakland's political machinery.[2]

Developments in Oakland reveal a great deal about postwar California and the nation. Defeated and bruised in Oakland, liberal Democrats nonetheless controlled the legislature in Sacramento by the end of the 1950s. This statewide alliance between African American voters of all classes and trade unionists based in northern California with important pockets of support in Southern California dramatically expanded California's welfare state in the 1960s and passed fair employment and housing laws. Broadly, then, this chapter follows two overlapping processes in the first decade and a half after World War II: liberalism's search for a location of political purchase and leverage, and African Americans' pushing of liberalism to advance their interests. Each process involved contests between different views of rights as well as constant negotiation between social reform and particularist, place-based interests. How these political movements imagined social reform and where their successes and defeats came would have far-reaching material consequences. The political contests in Oakland between 1945 and 1950, and their subsequent expression statewide, were fought over how the anticipated benefits of postwar economic growth would be distributed. They were part of a much larger national struggle in the years immediately after World War II over the extent and reach of the American welfare state. The crushing defeat of labor's national postwar agenda—including full employment, national health insurance, and a higher minimum wage—by the 1946 Congress made local and state progressive movements the vanguard in defining a postwar pluralist, labor-based, working-class politics. To follow those politics, we must move from group to group and neighborhood to neighborhood across Oakland and, eventually, to the state capital.[3]

Defining "the Public" in Postwar Politics

Peacetime reconversion raised questions about Oakland's economic future and questions about the nature of postwar urbanization. What kinds of civic improvements would the city undertake? How would health care be organized? Would property taxes fund new projects or would citizens pay through a city sales tax? Would the city support public housing to help ease crowded conditions in West and North Oakland? Would there be rent control? Would economic development come with a union shop and protections for social welfare? Would jobs be open for African Americans? In short, who would benefit from postwar economic development and how would its costs be distributed? These would not be the arcane decisions of city planners and municipal bureaucrats. They were ideological, contested, and lay at the heart of what the spatial and political narrative of postwar Oakland would become. As the war came to a close, as thousands of decommissioned soldiers streamed into the East Bay, as war workers endured layoffs, as the events of the general strike unfolded, and as African Americans faced a housing and employment crisis, the resolution of these basic propositions looked to have momentous consequences. Could a liberal vision of Oakland, driven by neighborhood issues and the organizing power of the labor movement, survive both opposition from conservative downtown property interests and the tensions and elisions within liberalism itself? At the core was the question of who got to define the public interest, even "the public" itself.[4]

Labor leaders believed that they were best prepared to offer such a definition. Oakland's emerging liberal coalition in the 1940s included a broad interracial alliance of CIO social democrats and AFL craft unionists, civil rights activists, Communist Party radicals, merchants, and liberal professionals, all uneasily held within the Democratic Party. Robert Ash, a former teamster and secretary of the Alameda County Central Labor Council (AFL), Jack Reynolds from the Building Trades Council, and representatives of the CIO Political Action Committee worked to unite the group. Sharing the MOAP's vision of economic growth, the coalition sought a moderately social-democratic version of urban reform. A union shop, modernization of the schools, reform of city elections, and moderate income redistribution through more equitable property taxes had long topped reformers' wish list. Disillusioned with their relative powerlessness in a political culture dominated by antilabor Republicans and downtown business interests, Ash, Reynolds, and CIO labor leaders sought a more consistent, long-term voice in the design and implementation of postwar plans. Above all, Ash hoped to convince the city's voters that labor represented the public good, that, in his words, "the plans and actions which benefit labor as a whole also bring progress to the community as a whole." Labor leaders placed themselves at the head of a reform movement to advance the interests of the city's workers. Downtown business, Joseph R. Knowland, and the *Oakland Tribune* stood in their way. The basic proposition thus turned on a simple axis: would Oakland's conservative Republican establishment or trade unionists and their liberal allies control the postwar city and determine its course?[5]

Oakland politics took shape in the *Tribune*'s offices and on its editorial pages. In the 1930s Knowland, the *Tribune*, and downtown merchants had consolidated control over the Republican Party, from candidate selection to platforms and public appointments. The *Tribune*'s endorsements, in turn, helped to maintain conservative Republican dominance of the city council, county board of supervisors, and district attorney. Such dominance was remarkable because Alameda County consistently boasted a Democratic electoral majority; after 1936 Democrats never accounted for less than 56 percent of registered voters. While not a "machine" in the traditional parlance of big-city American politics, beginning in the late 1930s the *Tribune*'s system was something akin to an anointing process. Because of its at-large electoral system, Oakland politics were newspaper-advertising-dependent and expensive; anyone who wished to be considered a serious candidate for the council had to have citywide recognition, which the *Tribune* and Knowland could provide. In addition to the newspaper's local influence, at the end of World War II, J. R. Knowland's son, William, had become a U.S. senator. Both father and son were among California's most vocal critics of the labor movement and radicalism of all varieties. Both used the *Tribune* to castigate the political projects and social programs sponsored by the left-liberal wing of the labor movement and Democratic Party in the mid-1940s.[6]

Labor leaders in the main did not envision a limit to growth or brakes on the MOAP. Few with an interest in the city's future doubted that a full program of economic growth and the spatial modernization of the metropolitan East Bay "with Oakland at its center" represented the best hope for sustained prosperity in the postwar decades. Instead the liberal insurgents charged that city officials in 1945 were proceeding too slowly with important civic improvements, threatening to choke industrial expansion. The *East Bay Labor Journal* warned of "the economic strangulation of Oakland and its growth by the political machine dominated by J. R. Knowland of the *Tribune*." AFL leaders called for "orderly growth" and "efficient city government," rather than the "selfish interests and machine politics" they saw in downtown's political clique. They embraced a range of reforms and initiatives and wanted immediate action on them: modernization of the transportation system, support for postwar industrial expansion (a link to full employment), a forty-hour work week for city employees, public housing developments and slum clearance, and improvement of schools and recreation facilities, as well as democratization of city government and the election process through the creation of a district election system. The latter would create a more democratic system of municipal representation. Efficiency, openness, and economic growth were the cornerstones of the liberal campaign, part of a joint AFL and CIO nationwide urban reform agenda in 1945, the twin aims of which were maintaining full employment and improving urban quality of life.[7]

Trade union liberals and progressives emerged as the principal spokespeople for postwar urban reform in Oakland. This did not mean that there was unanimity among labor's advocates. The communist left, in particular, took more radical stands on public ownership of transportation and other municipal services than did liberals. The left was far more engaged in struggles for racial equality, both during and after the war, than virtually all white AFL trade union leaders, middle-class liberals, and many among the noncommunist CIO as well. And leftists in general pushed more aggressively for expansions of the welfare state and for extending unionization to new groups of workers. Nevertheless, between 1945 and 1950, the East Bay left worked within the liberal reform coalitions headed by AFL and CIO trade unionists and their middle-class allies, believing that such participation would allow them to advocate from the inside.[8]

Knowland was not the venal civic oligarch portrayed by the *East Bay Labor Journal*, but Oakland's political insularity was nonetheless real. "The business of districts does not have much meaning in municipal elections," the *People's World*, the Communist Party's West Coast daily, complained in 1945. The city's at-large system "provides no representation from the district as such." Like the *World*, most observers noted that the city's at-large system tended to produce a withering apathy among the majority of eligible voters. Turnout rarely exceeded one-third and commonly sank to less than one-quarter of the electorate. District- or ward-based political systems, with their more proportional distribution of political rewards, tend to encourage greater voter participation and offer better opportunities for grassroots mobilizing. At-large systems, for instance, have long been associated with disfranchising the black vote. Voter apathy in Oakland handed the downtown interests even more leverage. Mobilizing heavily working-class neighborhoods remained the stumbling block for the liberal coalition in its quest to secure a place in postwar planning. The consequences of failing, the *People's World* feared, would be further civic decline. "Under this system," the *World* explained, "the Negro people have no assurance of real representation in order to bring forth West Oakland's many unsolved problems of housing, transportation, health, and recreation." Black Oaklanders were especially marginalized within this system, but workers as a whole, black and white, faced steep disadvantages in the city's political structure. Ash and his CIO compatriots had long hoped that labor's fabulous membership gains since passage of the Wagner Act in 1935 could be translated into electoral power. In Oakland, this meant reversing Progressive-era reforms, which had eliminated ward-based voting, and reviving neighborhood-level politics. It meant changing the scale of politics.[9]

The first real test between liberals and the incumbent political administration came in the 1945 municipal elections. Early in that year, representatives of the CIO-PAC and the AFL Central Labor Council formed the United for Oakland Committee (UOC), a nonpartisan political coalition established to support reform candidates for the Oakland City Council. The CIO-PAC and the Labor Council provided the ideological and organizational framework for the UOC, but business leaders and professionals gave the coalition a strong cross-class character. The UOC's considerable business support came from both merchants and industrialists who believed that the cronyism and inefficiency of the downtown elite threatened economic growth. Patrick McDonough, chairman of the Democratic County Central Committee and owner of McDonough Steel Company, and Earl Hall, former chairman of the Uptown Property Owners Association—rival to the Knowland-backed Downtown Property Owners Association—served as co-chairs of the UOC, while the UOC's candidates came from labor's ranks. It is testimony to the degree of labor-capital rapprochement achieved during World War II and the ideological consensus behind postwar growth, as well as the organizational strength of AFL Labor Councils and the CIO-PAC in the Bay Area, that trade unionists, not middle-class reformers, led the UOC.[10]

Despite the appeals of black leaders and white leftists, the UOC's stance on race fell far short of African Americans' goals and expectations. The coalition appealed to African Americans on bread-and-butter union issues but failed to break new ground on discrimination in housing and employment. UOC leaders, particularly members of the CIO Minorities Committee, reached out to African American voters in West Oakland, and C. L. Dellums provided the crucial link between AFL labor and Oakland's black electorate. But this was a limited alliance. White UOC representatives wanted West Oakland's votes, and hoped that Dellums and black ILWU activists could deliver them, but the coalition made few concessions to African American workers. The UOC downplayed fair employment— even as the NAACP and Shipyard Workers fought to end discrimination in the shipyards and on the Key System—and fair housing, issues central to West Oakland's future. Such reluctance to make antidiscrimination a more fundamental part of its program in 1945 set the stage for half-hearted courting of the black vote between 1947 and 1950. And it set Oakland apart from a city like New York, where progressive, labor-led postwar political movements made fair employment a central component of their political objectives.[11]

Trade unionists had high expectations, but the UOC campaign fizzled at the polls. Voter turnout was typically miserable, less than 30 percent of registered voters. Every incumbent was returned to the city council. Ash, who ran for a council seat, and the other UOC candidates had failed to translate their criticisms of the city and their fears about postwar stagnation and unemployment into an effective grassroots message. They offered instead a thin version of laborite liberalism that differed marginally from the paeans to economic growth issued by the conservative council incumbents and the *Tribune*. Lacking a real mechanism for neighborhood mobilization like a ward system, labor leaders fell back on a rhetoric of growth that stirred few passions in the voters. Within the UOC, disillusionment with Knowland and the city council ran deep. But UOC representatives mistakenly believed that their own passionate antidowntown convictions were sufficient to mobilize the city's working-class voters. When Ash told workers on the eve of 1945 balloting that "labor must constantly be on the alert to protect its interests," voters were unmoved. In 1947, following the general strike, it would be a different story. In the aftermath of the strike, union leadership made a compelling case to its members and to Oakland at large that the interests of "labor" and "the public" were synonymous and threatened. The general strike changed the political calculus.[12]

Labor and liberals had a second issue, however, one that would have a more lasting effect than the temporary outrage and euphoria produced by the general strike. That issue was taxes. In 1946 the CIO *Labor Herald* splashed "Oakland Tax Rate Burdens Little Guy" across its front page and in a series of stories detailed a property assessment scheme that had saved downtown landholders millions of dollars in taxes during the previous decade. Assessments on small businesses and homes had increased since the 1930s, while assessments on key downtown properties, including those owned by the *Tribune* and the city's major retail stores, had decreased. The *Labor Herald* charged the "local Republican machine" with cheating the "neighborhood merchant and the small homeowner." Across the nation in the 1940s, taxation was a working-class issue with a progressive cast. Laborite activists paid attention to taxes not because they were antistatist but because they wanted to hold employers and other capitalists and property holders responsible for their share of the fiscal burden of social services and other city programs. In 1947, against the background of the general strike and the tax controversy, liberals in Oakland established the Oakland Voters League (OVL) and prepared to launch another challenge to council incumbents.[13]

Like the UOC, the OVL joined labor and middle-class reformers in a coalition dedicated to economic growth accompanied by social welfare. The OVL in 1947, however, was more specific and aggressively socialdemocratic in its ambitions for the city's future than its UOC predecessor. OVL leaders called for substantial investment in public housing, rebuilding the city's schools and recreation facilities, local rent control ordinances, an overhaul of the city's public health system, and a public-owned transportation system. "We need councilmen who support all the people, not just those who run newspapers, department stores, and banks!" AFL attorney J. F. Galliano shouted at an Oakland labor rally in the spring of 1947. In response to the city's handling of the general strike, the OVL demanded city council neutrality in all labor disputes and repeal of anti-picketing and antihandbill ordinances. The official OVL platform also called for repeal of the sales tax and for increased assessments on downtown property. Finally, the OVL called for the creation of a civic unity commission to study discrimination in city employment, a positive step forward, if not a leap, on civil rights. Rather than running candidates from the ranks of organized labor, OVL representatives interviewed candidates already in the running and issued endorsements prior to the election, an aim for broader appeal. The OVL's endorsed candidates included Vernon Lantz, a chemist; Raymond Pease, a railroad engineer; Joseph Smith, an attorney; Scott Weakley, a radio producer; and Ben Goldfarb, an insurance salesman. OVL leaders hoped that with a strong platform and an antilabor city administration against which to run, the liberal coalition would turn out the votes.[14]

Of the multiple problems confronting working people in Oakland, the severe housing shortage was among the worst. Federal war housing projects remained full, and the city had not added enough new housing during the war to accommodate both wartime migrants and returning veterans. Between 1940 and 1947, the city's population increased by 100,000 people, but available housing increased by just under 14,000 new units. The crunch forced rents up. Oakland Housing Authority surveys found almost no housing units in the late 1940s and early 1950s "offered at rentals within the reach of lower-income families." Dorothy Boyich of West Oakland's Peralta Villa Tenants Association told Congress in 1947 that the housing crisis had to be understood "in human terms." People "fear eviction because they wonder every time they go to the grocery store just how much longer they can continue eating and also have enough left to pay the rent." In African American neighborhoods in West Oakland, overcrowding had reached near crisis proportions by the early 1950s. Between 1949 and 1951, less than one-half of 1 percent of the building permits issued in the Bay Area were for private dwellings open to African Americans (600 out of 75,000). The OVL hoped that additional units of public housing and strengthened rent control ordinances would ease the citywide housing strain while the construction industry caught up to demand. Decent housing was one of the core promises of Rooseveltian liberalism and California iconography and a fundamental ambition of most working families. Housing problems struck people on a visceral level and, along with the general strike and taxes, gave working-class voters ample reason to send city officials a loud and defiant message at the polls.[15]

Much of Oakland's middle class had grown disenchanted with the city's existing leadership as well. Downtown's preferential tax assessments, coupled with the council's inattention to repeated calls for neighborhood improvements, led *The Montclarion*, voice of the hillside district's liberal professionals, to declare on the eve of the election that "stupidity is intolerable in the leadership of the East Bay's greatest city, a metropolis that will one day be the industrial center of northern California." According to *The Montclarion*, the war had transformed Oakland, but the city's leaders, dominated by Knowland and his "political machine and its henchmen," had failed to respond to the multiple challenges associated with rapid growth. High taxes and poor city services headed their complaints, but hillside residents found most distasteful the arrogant cronyism and inefficiency of the *Tribune*'s control of the city council. *The Montclarion* joined with hillside members of the Committee for Responsible Government and the OVL in calling for a new city charter, one that would provide for the election of council members by district and for an elected, full-time mayor.[16]

Activists from the left participated fully in both the OVL and UOC campaigns, though in neither did they win nor were they allowed a dominant voice. The Alameda County Communist Party (CP) was one of many radical groups active in the OVL campaign, and numerous CIO leaders moved back and forth between unions (especially the ILWU), the CIO-PAC, and the CP during the 1930s and early 1940s, building the bridges of the Popular Front. The UOC and the OVL emerged within the kinds of political frameworks the Popular Front had been designed to nurture: alliances between the left and liberal reformers in coalitions that sought broad political power for the nation's working class. Across the bay, San Francisco's sizable CP organization, including its organ the *People's World*, watched developments in Oakland with a rising sense of pride and accomplishment. The OVL proved, one *World* editorial concluded, that "united labor can attract the support of small business and other elements of the middle class" and that "united labor action *pays off.*" The weakness of the CP and other left activists within the OVL, however, meant that the issues they pushed harder than any other white-dominated group—black equality and black rights—won little hearing. During the 1947 campaign, for instance, Paul Heide of ILWU, Local 6, delivered a stinging indictment of police brutality against African Americans before the Oakland City Council, yet the OVL ignored this and virtually the entire political agenda of black West Oakland. These glaring omissions aside, the OVL functioned as the sort of open-ended, relatively fluid forum for political cooperation that left activists supported across the country in the middle 1940s.[17]

To the city's conservative leadership, the OVL program smacked of left-wing extremism. Knowland's *Tribune* red-baited the progressive coalition with ham-handed editorials characterizing their program as dangerously statist. Knowland referred to the council candidates as "left-wing" crusaders controlled by the "communistic" arm of the city's labor movement and claimed that the OVL's plan for shifting city taxes onto business and industry promised "staggering tax burdens" that would cripple free enterprise in Oakland. But the OVL platform and its principal issues—the general strike, housing, and taxes—fell within the liberal Democratic mainstream in 1940s' America and appealed to a broad range of workers, homeowners, and small merchants, most of whom would have refused radical affiliations. Dellums authored a scathing letter to the city council in which he called the *Tribune*'s downtown interests "sanctimonious scarecrows" who delivered "prophecies of doom, disaster and socialism every time we debate some measure to benefit men and women of our nation with low incomes." The *Tribune*'s red-baiting failed. With unions orchestrating a massive get-out-the-vote drive, turnout in 1947 reached 65 percent of those registered, twice the usual average. Four of the five OVL candidates won seats on the city council; the fifth, Ben Goldfarb, lost by less than one thousand votes. In the words of the local CIO newspaper, labor unity had "rocked the municipal stooges of the Knowland machine on their heels."[18]

On Labor Day of 1947, tens of thousands of AFL and CIO unionists massed in downtown Oakland for a march celebrating the OVL's success, especially the symbolic defeat of Knowland and the *Tribune*. Floats depicting labor's aspirations—full employment, public housing, a more open city government—joined bands, flag teams, and sign-carrying marchers who proclaimed that in Alameda County labor represented "the public." Despite their behind-the-scenes marginalization, the United Negro Labor Committee produced a magnificent interracial float that embodied their hoped-for black-white unity, and representatives of the Civil Rights Congress, a communist-led interracial organization, also joined the parade. Labor Day in 1947 marked a special victory and labor's hope that the hermetic world of downtown interests had been broken. Now, it was felt, trade unions and their allies would have a hand in shaping postwar development in Oakland.[19]

The unity and electoral power orchestrated by the liberal alliance in 1947 was unprecedented in Oakland. It did not last long. The strength of the OVL coalition lay in its ability to translate an array of urban reforms into a single platform and slate of candidates that could ride the general strike's momentum. Those reforms spoke to a broad group of Oakland workers, middle-class liberals, and merchants who approved of economic growth but did not want to see the city sacrifice social welfare, homeowners, and small businesses in the process. But OVL unity hid deeper problems. The league, for instance, had no control over its candidates once they took office. They proved to be frustratingly independent, and they

Figure 2.1. In 1947 the Oakland Voters League hoped to "take the power out of the tower" by winning a majority of seats on the Oakland City Council for progressive candidates. The "tower" was the Tribune Building, pictured at left, representative of the Knowland family and the Republican "machine" that dominated municipal politics. The OVL had broad, cross-class support, but its electoral base was Oakland's workers, who temporarily united in a major push to reform city government. Courtesy of the ILWU Library, San Francisco.

constituted only four seats of a nine-member council. Moreover, the labor movement remained divided, not just between the AFL and CIO, but between small groups of radicals, the liberal leadership corps, and the more conservative rank-and-file. In the immediate aftermath of the general strike, those differences mattered little since city hall had antagonized workers and organized labor writ large. Once the sting of the city's reaction to the strike and the glow of OVL electoral triumph had worn off, however, labor unity proved more difficult to maintain. An even more troubling problem came in on the first winds of the Cold War. As local and national politics shifted toward strident anticommunism, the *Tribune*'s antiradical attacks began to work, consuming the OVL program and the four city council members in endless defense of their Americanism. The redbaiting that had failed in 1947 worked increasingly well for conservative

Republican interests after 1948. Finally, the core of the OVL's nonlabor leadership came from merchants, insurance brokers, and real estate interests in East Oakland and certain hillside districts like Montclair. These groups bitterly opposed Knowland but did not share the broad reform vision embodied in the OVL platform. East Oakland, especially, was far from the hotbed of laborite social-democracy that Ash, Reynolds, and the CIO-PAC hoped it would become.

East Oakland in 1947 was a simmering mix of homeowner, antidowntown, tax reform, and municipal reform politics. Potent and unpredictable, that mix would bring to an end the brief flowering of the liberal coalition. Civic and business leaders in East Oakland complained of poor transportation, high taxes, and lack of capital improvement projects in their neighborhoods. But a more general resentment of Knowland, the Oakland Chamber of Commerce, and the Downtown Property Owners Association motivated them. The primary spokesman for antidowntown sentiment in these, the city's most far-flung, neighborhoods was Gil Westoby, editor of the *East Oakland Times*, a newspaper established in 1947 to compete with Knowland's *Tribune*. Westoby's *Times* reveled in exposing the insularity of the city's public officials. Westoby himself represented a group of merchants and real estate interests who had helped to establish the commercial and residential districts of East Oakland in the 1920s and 1930s. Entrepreneurs and self-styled small-r republicans with a financial stake in the neighborhoods, this group joined the liberal coalition out of long-standing opposition to Knowland and other downtown property holders. Encouraged at first by the OVL victory, Westoby and other moderates in East Oakland quickly lost faith in the new council members because the OVL did little to ease the tax burden, Westoby's principal concern. Before the four OVL council members had been in office much more than a year, East Oakland civic groups launched a major recall (evicting an officeholder before his or her term expires) and charter-reform campaign, based on the tax issue, that split apart the OVL coalition and revealed deep rifts within the city's liberal reform movement.[20]

William Clausen, president of the Elmhurst Merchants, spearheaded East Oakland's tax revolt, with Westoby giving him vocal support in the editorial pages of the *East Oakland Times*. Clausen embodied the complicated political currents hidden beneath the OVL's electoral unity in 1947. He was a Roosevelt Democrat, owned a hardware store on the main commercial thoroughfare in East Oakland, and hated taxes. Furious that the city council had done nothing to reduce property taxes in the outlying parts of the city, in December 1948 Clausen demanded the recall of *all nine* city council members and the drafting of a new city charter framed by "fifteen free holders." Clausen's group, the East Oakland Tax Protest Association, had surveyed Oakland's homeowners and businesses.

They discovered, as the CIO had before them, that increases in the tax burden on downtown property owners over the previous two years were proportionately much smaller than "that in the outlying business districts and the enormous increase to the small homeowner." The OVL candidates had promised tax reform, Clausen argued, but failed to deliver. Clausen created a second organization, the League for Better Government, meant to unite civic, business, and labor groups and to extend his appeal beyond East Oakland. The petition circulated by the league called for elimination of the council–city manager system and its replacement by an elected mayor and other "modern methods" of government; the latter included provisions for making the recall of city officials easier. Determined to operate outside the OVL coalition, Clausen hoped to embarrass the city council and pressure it, with Westoby's editorials raging every week, into calling a "free holder" meeting.[21]

The insurgent Clausen placed the labor side of the OVL coalition in an awkward position. Because Pease was the only OVL council member to support the league's call for a new city charter, Clausen denounced and abandoned the other three. Both the AFL and CIO councils initially supported Clausen's efforts and endorsed the League, but backing him ultimately meant forsaking Lantz, Smith, and Weakley, whom they had worked so hard to elect. None of the OVL council members were up for reelection in 1949, but Clausen's public crusade forced OVL coalition members to take sides. Robert Ash, never satisfied with the OVL four, went with Clausen, as did Reynolds and the Building Trades Council, but the CIO split along self-described lines of "left" and "right." The left stayed with the OVL four; the right backed Clausen. Clausen made one last appeal, with petition signatures in hand, to the city council either to enact charter reform or to place the issue before the public for a vote. When that effort failed, nothing remained to reunite the various factions within the labor movement or to repair the relationship between OVL leaders and the council members. Several liberal candidates ran for city council in 1949, but without a unified coalition behind them none came close to winning.[22]

Tax reform was the first major issue to damage Oakland's liberal coalition. Public housing was the second. Together they proved fatal. The housing backlash had been building since the 1947 election but did not explode until 1950. In response to the OVL's call for the construction of public housing during the 1947 campaign, the Oakland Real Estate Board, the Apartment House Owners Association, and other development interests formed the Committee for Home Protection (CHP). As chief guardian of the city's private real estate market, the CHP opposed state interventions in the buying, selling, and renting of residential space that lowered, rather than raised, property values and rents. In 1948 the CHP sponsored a citywide referendum banning public housing in Oakland. The referendum passed, an early indication that the OVL agenda would face mounting hurdles. However, in 1949 the city council, behind a united OVL bloc and one dissenting incumbent vote, ignored the public mandate and voted five to four in favor of building three thousand new units of public housing. Outraged, the CHP filed petitions to recall three of the prohousing council members. A special recall election was scheduled for the spring of 1950.[23]

The subsequent campaign rent the remaining OVL forces. With financial and political support from the California Real Estate Association, one of the most powerful political organizations in the state and a dedicated opponent of public housing, the CHP launched an all-out red-baiting attack on the OVL council members, characterizing the three as proponents of "socialized housing" and "CIO communism." Knowland's *Tribune* joined in, again accusing the OVL of radical extremism and attacking public housing as a threat to the city's private developers. With Oakland's political climate under the heavy hand of anticommunism, manipulated by Knowland's *Tribune*, Clausen then emerged to play a critical, if ironic, role in the recall election. City election rules allowed candidates to file against the sitting council members who were up for recall. Fresh from his tax revolt and charter-reform crusade, Clausen ran for a seat and won, largely on the strength of an endorsement from the CHP, which found him "unalterably opposed to socialized housing." To their credit, Reynolds and Ash then withdrew their support from Clausen and backed Weakley, refusing to bow to the *Tribune*'s anticommunist crusade. In the tense antiradical environment of early 1950s Oakland, Clausen in a single stroke abandoned the OVL coalition to vicious red-baiting and drew both tax reform and anti–public housing voters into his camp. The other two OVL council members survived the recall bid but lost in the general election in 1951 to CHP-backed, anticommunist candidates. Public housing, a critical concern in a city strained by wartime migration and massive overcrowding in African American neighborhoods, was dead. So was the OVL.[24]

The general strike had forged a sense of common working-class interests in Oakland, and the push for tax reform had made possible cross-class alliances among labor, middle-class homeowners, and antidowntown merchants. The UOC and the OVL stayed within the boundaries of the paradigm of growth liberalism—economic expansion, modest social welfare, and increased wages in an economy directed by employers—a paradigm in which a majority of both AFL and CIO unionists had invested deeply. Furthermore, American populist rhetoric had bequeathed to midcentury liberalism a language in which "labor" and the "small taxpayer" could be fused into the more protean "public," temporarily uniting black and white, labor and middle class, skilled and unskilled. All of this seemed

AMERICAN CAN CO.
FACTORY 99A
Oakland.Calif. 1948

Figure 2.2. Progressive labor leaders in the late 1940s believed that Oakland's workers, like these at American Can, could become a broad social force pushing for extensions of the welfare state, both locally and nationally. Many African American labor leaders hoped, against ample evidence to the contrary, that trade unions would become allies in their struggle to advance racial equality in the economic realm, both locally and nationally. Courtesy of the Oakland Library.

to predict success. But the unraveling of the OVL revealed that on both issue and structure the nature of Oakland politics favored property-holding interests. The desire for high property values and rising rents led property holders, big and small, to oppose labor's interest in public housing. Single-issue, antitax merchants abandoned the coalition as soon as their economic agenda was not met. And downtown interests simply could not imagine an Oakland not run by their patrons. Moreover, Oakland's political structures, including at-large voting and recall, gave numerous advantages to the entrenched elite who were also more than willing to draw on the inflammatory and polarizing rhetoric of anticommunism to marginalize progressive concerns and characterize them as subversive of American life.

The popular mobilizations stemming from the general strike temporarily masked this control that property holders exerted over Oakland politics. Blocked at the national level by a resurgent congressional right, lobbied strongly by the National Association of Manufacturers (NAM) and other industry groups, progressives were stymied at the local level in the late 1940s primarily by the political power of property—especially those who controlled and managed downtown property, the principal engine of capital accumulation among local interests. However, fissures within the liberal coalition and their interaction with political structure also played a role in the outcome. On labor issues, white workers could be progressive. In contrast, on neighborhood issues, those same workers were more inclined to be conservative and more vulnerable to racist and Americanist appeals. Because city politics is about the latter in much greater degree than the former, local urban progressive coalitions faced unique challenges in this late 1940s political push. The workplace issues raised by the general strike were irresolvable in the municipal political sphere, and neighborhood politics destroyed the coalition by halving off constituencies issue by issue, piece by piece. The political forces that destroyed the OVL were propelled by questions of property taxes, urban resources, and home values rather than by work or labor relations and prefigured a more profound reorganization of politics, and their language of race and class, in Oakland and the nation in the quarter century after the OVL's defeat.[25]

Black Politics: Coalition Building in the Flatlands

African Americans in Oakland participated in the UOC and OVL campaigns, but they remained junior partners with minor influence. Black voters were recruited into the coalition through CIO and Popular Front institutions—the Political Action Committee, the Negro Labor Council, and the Civil Rights Congress—and through the United Negro Labor Committee, a group comprised of black CIO and AFL unionists who forged connections to African American Democratic political clubs in West Oakland. But these institutions, successful on a small scale, never realized an interracial political alliance of great depth. In 1947, for example, the United Negro Labor Committee asked the OVL to develop a platform that addressed police brutality, job discrimination, and housing segregation, black Oakland's top three concerns. The OVL refused. The white laborite political culture that produced the OVL muted explicit race talk in the interest of white working-class unity and alliances with white homeowners, merchants, and professionals, forcing African American political objectives to the margins.[26]

African Americans in Oakland thus confronted a challenge common to 1940s black communities throughout the urban North and Pacific Coast and in major southern cities like Memphis and Birmingham. The question had preoccupied black America since Emancipation, but labor activism between 1935 and 1945 and the massive proletarianization and movement north and west of African Americans since 1917 placed renewed emphasis on resolving it. Should African American workers stress their common fate with white workers and develop interracial, class-based strategies for advancement, or did such an approach represent a Faustian bargain with an irredeemably racist institution, organized labor, that would compromise and betray black interests? The midcentury American labor movement embraced a wide range of political ideologies, from radical to reactionary, but the great bulk of working-class economic and electoral power remained invested in the reformist New Deal welfare state, its Kenysian growth liberalism, and its promise of security to workers in the core of the economy. It remained to be seen how and if this political structure could be leveraged into a force for racial equality and whether or not it was even in the best interests of African Americans to make the effort.[27]

In the 1940s African American Oakland's three leadership poles—trade unionists, ministers, and professionals—pursued various kinds of reform in creative, and sometimes anxious, tension. C. L. Dellums was the city's most prominent black leader and one of the most important civil rights figures in California. A dapper sophisticate who never backed off the struggle for black equality, he led the West Coast Brotherhood of Sleeping Car Porters for thirty years and, like his friend and mentor A. Philip Randolph, transcended the confines of trade unionism. In addition to Dellums, other officials of the Brotherhood and the Dining Car Cooks and Waiters Union—crucial figures in the black working-class railroad culture—gave Oakland's labor–civil rights coalitions strong support. In the CIO, the heavily African American and racially progressive ILWU and MCSU took solid civil rights stands. Outside of organized labor, Oakland's civil rights leadership included a number of professionals, attorneys, religious leaders from the African Methodist Episcopal (AME), Christian Methodist Episcopal (CME), and Baptist churches, and newspaper people like E. A. Daly. Daly, publisher of the East Bay's largest African American weekly, the *California Voice*, headed West Oakland's small circle of Republicans, mostly business and professional families. Wartime population growth in West Oakland, the rapidly declining living conditions there, and the rising tide of black unemployment after demobilization gave African American leaders, especially laborites like Dellums, new incentive to press the city for expanded opportunities in housing and employment.[28]

It was an incentive in search of a vehicle. One promising, but precarious, possibility was pursued by black and white activists in the Communist Party and other organizations on the left. Their most propitious alliance of the postwar era was Oakland's branch of the Civil Rights Congress (CRC), a Popular Front holdover that focused on police brutality against black residents of West Oakland. Backed by the ILWU, white radicals, and progressive African American ministers, the CRC focused on fighting the provocations of the Oakland Police Department, the target of numerous allegations of racism and police brutality in the 1940s and 1950s. After a series of mass arrests and beatings in the late 1940s, the CRC filed civil suits against the City of Oakland on behalf of dozens of West Oakland residents. "Legal lynchings in the form of frame-ups are multiplying," the CIO-sponsored Bay Area Conference on Negro Rights asserted. "Abuses of the civil rights of Negroes have reached a new level." In early 1950 these cases prompted the California Assembly to hold hearings on police brutality in Oakland, among the first such hearings in the nation. Over fifty witnesses testified before legislators and an audience of hundreds of West Oakland residents on a range of "brutalities contradicted only by the police themselves." The committee's final report, while lenient on the police, confirmed that racial bias played a role in the events. The CRC's exposure of police racism, however, produced only token changes, and on the heels of the 1950 hearings the CRC fell victim to red-baiting and FBI investigations and repression. Frank race talk remained a productive contribution of black and white radicals to progressive politics in Oakland in the late 1940s and early 1950s, but anticommunism, the collapse of the OVL coalition, and splits between left and right within the CIO narrowed the possibilities for deeper changes.[29]

Despite the CRC's initial success, communist-led and communist-linked efforts at racial unity in the East Bay divided Oakland's African American community. Franklin Williams and Tarea Hall Pittman of the East Bay NAACP followed national NAACP policy by purging CP members after 1948 and distancing themselves from the party, which they accused of "attempting to mislead the Negro community." E. A. Daly and the *California Voice* editorial staff detested left-wing radicals, especially white communists. Other African American groups in Oakland, including the Men of Tomorrow (a prominent service organization), the East Bay Democratic Club, and West Oakland's District Community Council, rejected any direct affiliation with white radicals and kept black radicals at arm's length. In part, this was pure political expediency. Already underrepresented in Oakland's postwar political culture, most middle-class African Americans believed that they could ill afford association with such thoroughly marginalized groups. Moreover, since the AFL and CIO left wing and the Communist Party were the only white voices in the East Bay addressing issues in the African American community, interracial unity and equality within the OVL coalition depended on a fraction of a fraction—not a promising political calculus. Nonetheless, the NAACP's bowing to anticommunism in Oakland, as nationwide, further crippled the possibility of a true interracial progressive politics in the late 1940s.

The rapid marginalization of black radicals after 1948 silenced a major voice and organizing model in the larger struggle over race and class in the East Bay and nation. As a consequence of these tensions, purges, and practical political calculations, by the late 1940s the push for racial equality would be carried forward largely by liberal civil rights leaders, black and white, not radicals.[30]

The most successful dimension of this push in the immediate postwar years had its roots in the black railroad culture and African American professional and middle-class circles. The East Bay Democratic Club, the Bay Area's most important African American political organization, based in Oakland and Berkeley, joined with liberals within the Berkeley Democratic Party to run a candidate for the California Assembly. Both groups wanted an African American in the state legislature who would represent the working-class, and increasingly black, flatlands. In 1948 Byron Rumford, an African American pharmacist who lived in south Berkeley near the Oakland border, won election to the California Assembly from the seventeenth district, a compact area that included West and North Oakland and one-third of Berkeley. Rumford's electoral coalition united blacks in Oakland with CIO labor, a handful of AFL progressives, and Berkeley's labor and middle-class liberals in a set of political relationships that would endure for more than thirty years. Rumford lacked any previous political experience, but in short order emerged as a crucial figure in Sacramento, sponsoring the state's first fair employment and housing legislation and remaining a close ally of organized labor throughout his eighteen-year political career.[31]

Behind Rumford lay the architect of postwar black political strategy in the East Bay, D. G. Gibson. Born in Texas, Gibson, a World War I veteran, settled in Oakland in the early 1920s as a railway dining car waiter. He parlayed his earnings into real estate and then ownership of a local newspaper and magazine distributorship catering to the African American community. He founded the Appomattox Club and campaigned for Roosevelt in the 1930s, established the East Bay Democratic Club with Rumford and others in the 1940s, and served as cochair of the Democratic Seventh U.S. Congressional District (Berkeley and West and North Oakland) from 1954 until his death in 1973. During that period, Gibson helped advance the careers of most African American political leaders in the East Bay. "D. G. Gibson may very well be the father of all of us who are now active in the black political arena," former California Assembly leader and San Francisco Mayor Willie Brown observed in the 1970s.[32]

Throughout his life, Gibson combined business, politics, and civic activism. He linked the black communities of Oakland and Berkeley with progressive whites through the YMCA, the East Bay Business and Professional Men's League, and the Port of Oakland Club, in addition to his

Figure 2.3. Some of the leaders of the East Bay Democratic Club, c. 1955. Back row, from left, Albert McKee, Allen Broussard, Hiawatha Roberts, Zeke Griffin, and unknown. Front row, left to right, Byron Rumford, Lionel Wilson, D. G. Gibson, and Charles Wilson. The picture does not include Norvel Smith, Evelio Grillo, and Leonard Jones, three other important East Bay Democratic Club strategists. Courtesy of the Bancroft Library, University of California, Berkeley.

connections in the Democratic Party. A tireless networker and political entrepreneur, he and his principal collaborator, Evelio Grillo, a Cuban immigrant and consummate strategist, made coalition politics work for Oakland's African American community. Rejecting an older tradition of African American political strategy in which anointed spokesmen or brokers negotiated political favors and compromises with local white institutions, Gibson dedicated his life to building coalitions based on black electoral power. His approach influenced black politics in West Oakland from Rumford's campaign in 1948 to the Black Panther Party's electoral mobilizations in the 1970s. The seventeenth state assembly district in the Oakland-Berkeley flatlands, under the leadership of the East Bay Democratic Club, became an enduring lever of East Bay African American power.[33]

Because the boundaries of African American residence took in more of the assembly and congressional districts than they did of Oakland, Gibson's

East Bay Democratic Club would have far more success in the 1950s and 1960s running candidates for state and federal offices than electing city council members in Oakland. The politics that Gibson and Rumford nurtured thus occupied a very particular space in the geography of power in Oakland, the East Bay, and California. By the late 1940s East Bay African American communities extended from West Oakland through North Oakland and into South Berkeley, along residential lines in the flatlands that corresponded closely to California's seventeenth assembly district and the seventh U.S. congressional district. Citywide balloting for all city council positions continued to prevent any single community from controlling an elected seat in municipal politics. This dimension of Oakland's political geography shaped West Oakland's future in dramatic ways. Until the 1970s West Oakland's African American community had more political influence in state and national institutions than in municipal ones. With more power in Sacramento than Oakland, East Bay African Americans could expect a certain quid pro quo at the state level that was unimaginable in their own city. The consequences of this governing structure were evident in the late 1950s and early 1960s when no substantial political opposition stood in the way of the City of Oakland's massive physical destruction of large parts of West Oakland for public housing and freeway and rapid transit construction. Such redevelopment decisions were made at the local level, despite the federal and state subsidies that lay behind them. The concentration of black residence in West Oakland, the oldest part of the city, combined with virtual local political disfranchisement, left the community without even token leverage to gain a share of economic growth, to channel civic resources into their communities, or generally to participate in shaping the postwar city. This powerlessness left black Oaklanders vulnerable in the long term to high rents, declining property values, deteriorating housing stock, overcrowding, and redevelopment.[34]

At the same time, West Oakland's African American political leaders deliberately shifted their political engagement toward Sacramento. By 1948 black political and labor leaders, like Gibson and Dellums, understood the weaknesses of municipal elections and alliances like the OVL as vehicles for challenging racial oppression and advancing their interests. Election rules diluted neighborhood electoral power, white-dominated unions, business groups, and the *Tribune* controlled local political channels, and city government was limited in its ability to legislate changes in housing and job discrimination. For these reasons, West Oakland's commitment to city politics remained tenuous and uneven throughout the 1950s and early 1960s as black leaders looked to state and national legislatures as vehicles to destroy Jim Crow. Local municipal politics can be an effective arena for advancing progressive agendas, but their success depends on political structure. Because of the deficiencies in the East Bay, black Oakland,

no less than African American communities in the South, required intervention by a higher level of political authority to overcome entrenched
local barriers to equality. Rumford's election and Gibson's rise represented
important new possibilities for the legislation of racial equality at the
state level and, eventually, the federal.[35]

Black Workers and Fair Employment at Midcentury

No one was more influential in translating African Americans' voting
power in the East Bay into concrete reform than C. L. Dellums. From his
base in Oakland, Dellums shaped a labor–civil rights coalition in the
1950s to push for a fair employment law in the state legislature and, he
hoped, to transform the place of black Americans in California. His long
association with A. Philip Randolph had convinced Dellums that a commitment to both civil rights and trade unionism was essential to the social
and economic progress of African American workers. Indeed, Dellums
understood African American liberation as fundamentally grounded in
economic rights. But for those who, like Dellums, had worked on fair
employment during the war, the late 1940s presented new challenges. No
longer could African American labor and community leaders appeal to
employers' patriotism and the urgency of the war effort to break down
barriers for black workers. Even the federal FEPC—though in the final
analysis a weak instrument—was now gone, leaving fair employment
advocates with no legal leverage. "Without FEPC," *The Black Worker*,
the Brotherhood's newspaper, insisted, "Negroes and all other minorities
will face terrible days in the postwar period." As the postwar picture
developed, the Alameda County NAACP insisted upon "the *fair* distribution of jobs," a claim that drew on, and underscored the influence of,
a midcentury language of "fairness" common to broad sectors of the
American public, black and white. Dellums hoped to extend wartime liberalism into the postwar world by making the FEPC a permanent feature
of the economy.[36]

Unemployment and occupational downgrading hit postwar African
American communities in Oakland and San Francisco harder than those
elsewhere in the United States. After finding wartime employment in
manufacturing at a higher rate than African Americans in the country as
a whole, Bay Area black workers became casualties of the massive postwar layoffs in the shipyards in equal proportion. By 1950 unemployment
among Oakland's African American workers was 20 percent for both men
and women, twice the rate for white workers. Statewide comparisons
provide even more telling evidence of difficult postwar adjustment. Unemployment among Bay Area black men was more than twice the overall

California unemployment figure and six times as great among African American women. Additionally, younger men and women, less established in the labor market and lacking higher skills, fared worse in the postwar job search than older workers. In 1950, 29 percent of black men between the ages of twenty and twenty-four were jobless, twice the rate for men between forty and forty-nine.[37]

Generational differences in unemployment pointed to a growing internal differentiation within the city's African American working class. Older workers proved far more able to consolidate the gains they had made during World War II than younger workers. Large numbers of black workers, both migrants and prewar residents, acquired skills, seniority, and familiarity with local labor markets and employment opportunities during the war. Wartime job experience, the presence of a handful of African American and multiracial labor unions, and expansion of the black middle class all helped substantial parts of Oakland's growing black community to locate well-paying jobs in the postwar years. There was a flip side, however. Segregation persisted in large sectors of the economy, and jobs available to younger black workers were limited. As the NAACP observed in 1948, Oakland and the East Bay's automobile industry remained white-dominated and segregated; downtown employers in retail stores, restaurants, and offices continued to resist fair hiring; and city services, including transportation, the police force, and the fire department, hired few African American workers and segregated those they did. At the close of the 1940s, despite substantial progress during the war, Oakland's employment patterns continued to reflect a Jim Crow occupational hierarchy.[38]

Dellums and other black leaders were also distressed by racial discrimination in the labor movement. Unions in Oakland exerted enormous control over access to jobs, in many cases more than employers did. By one count in the late 1940s, 75 percent of all employees in Oakland worked in union-controlled shops. In Oakland alone, unions operated eighty-one different hiring halls. When Dellums raised the issue of fair employment with individual union leaders or with the Labor Council as a whole, he heard dodges reminiscent of the Key System's FEPC hearings. Unions blamed employers for discrimination. Employers blamed the unions. In 1948 the NAACP singled out General Motors, Chrysler, the Key System, and the Bethlehem Pacific Coast Steel Corporation as "sponsors of unfair racial labor policies," but all of those companies excused at least part of the problem by pointing to the unions, including the United Auto Workers and United Steel Workers, that exerted some influence over the applicant pool and enjoyed substantial shop floor power. This "vicious cycle" infuriated Dellums, who saw it as a major obstacle to black economic advancement.[39]

Not all unions were obstacles to fair employment. The AFL as a whole had a poor record on racial equality, both nationally and in the Bay Area. But a number of AFL unions, particularly the Building Service Employees, certain locals of the Carpenters Union, and the Laborer's Union, while not models of racial egalitarianism, nonetheless developed a large membership among both white and black workers in the middle and late 1950s. Public-sector AFL unions, still in their infancy in the 1950s, advanced fair employment. The CIO demonstrated an even stronger commitment to fair employment. Efforts by CIO council leaders and African American workers in Oakland and Alameda County, along with the NAACP, helped to increase black access to the East Bay's automobile and steel industries in the early 1950s. The ILWU's two locals—Local 6 in the warehouses and Local 10 on the docks—in both Oakland and San Francisco embraced civil rights positions and earned good records in admitting black members. Similarly, CIO machinist, electrical, and office workers unions in Oakland promoted some equality in their locals that were far ahead of most AFL unions in the region.[40]

Together, unions and employers in Oakland practiced forms of racial discrimination that were difficult to disentangle, with both labor and management often working in tandem against black hiring. A "silent conspiracy," Horace Hazzard, chairman of the CIO minorities committee, announced at a CIO-sponsored conference on employment problems in 1948, "is barring the minority groups from jobs in industry after industry, purely on a basis of discrimination." Organized labor had more control over hiring in the Bay Area than anywhere else on the West Coast, complicating the battle for desegregation. Still, this did not make labor the sole defender of Jim Crow. Employers protected the color line as vehemently as many unions. Further, the question of union discrimination was far more complex than whether or not labor had large numbers of African American members. A handful of unions boasted sizable numbers of black workers but either segregated those workers in Jim Crow locals or, more typically, discriminated in other ways—on job assignments, seniority, promotion, apprenticeship training, and so forth. In the 1960s state and federal courts, the California FEPC, and the U.S. Equal Opportunity Employment Commission would find that both unions and employers were responsible for the postwar legacy of employment discrimination. But for the present, holding either party responsible and accountable to more than abstract notions of equality remained a difficult, slippery task.[41]

The efforts of the NAACP to promote job equality yielded mixed results. In 1954 the Northern California NAACP held a "Fight For Freedom Day" to highlight the region's continuing employment problems. "The employment situation for Negroes here on the West Coast is even more critical than in the East and Midwest," the NAACP's regional secretary,

Franklin Williams, explained on the eve of that organization's first large-scale assault on racial bias throughout the Bay Area. The Oakland NAACP branch had waged a successful campaign to integrate the Oakland Fire Department in 1952 and had worked with General Motors and the UAW to open more jobs to black workers at the Chevrolet plant in East Oakland, but Williams's comment signaled the NAACP's commitment to a broader program of job equality. In 1955 the NAACP, along with black ministers and fraternal lodges, founded the East Bay Organizations Employment Committee and sponsored a two-year "Spend Your Money Where You Can Work" campaign. Employing boycotts, informational leafleting, and occasional demonstrations, the campaign focused on hiring discrimination in the city's large downtown service sector, especially the department stores. The Retail Merchants Association, labor's nemesis during the 1946 strike, endured the boycotts and stonewalled the Employment Committee, while derisive editorials in the *Tribune* sought to squash public sympathy. They finally made only token changes in hiring policies, preserving the front-of-the-house/back-of-the-house racial line in downtown employment. As late as 1960, tens of thousands of African Americans lived in West and North Oakland, but only blocks away in the downtown retail center one could not see a black waiter, waitress, clerk, receptionist, salesperson, or bellman in the restaurants, department stores, and hotels. Oakland's NAACP did not abandon local work on fair employment after the disappointing "Spend Your Money Where You Can Work" campaign but for the remaining years of the decade devoted the bulk of its resources to lobbying in Sacramento for a state equal employment law.[42]

Dellums and other East Bay NAACP leaders believed that a state law would give the struggle against employment discrimination critical leverage. Throughout the 1950s, Dellums and Tarea Hall Pittman, from Berkeley, worked in Sacramento for a Fair Employment Practices (FEP) bill, first through the NAACP and then, after 1952, through the Fair Employment Practices Committee, a statewide lobbying group. Byron Rumford joined Gus Hawkins from Los Angeles as the principal architects of FEP legislation within the California legislature, proposing an FEP bill at the beginning of each session from 1950 through 1959, when it finally passed. The road was long and arduous. When Dellums and Pittman held their initial press conference at a church in Sacramento in 1951, having invited all eighty members of the assembly and forty members of the California Senate, only three turned out: Rumford, Hawkins, and Vernon Kilpatrick, a white liberal from Los Angeles. Undaunted, Dellums met the following year with C. J. Haggerty of the California State Federation of Labor (AFL), John Despol of the CIO, Ed Roybal, a Los Angeles city councilman, and a handful of other civil rights, Jewish Labor Committee, and NAACP representatives. This group became the nucleus for the California Fair Employment Practices Committee, which Dellums chaired until 1959. It represented the seeds of the state-level alliance of liberal, labor, and black civil rights forces that Dellums had long sought, an alliance that grew stronger over the course of the 1950s even as local labor-civil rights initiatives weakened and failed in Oakland.[43]

Dellums, Rumford, and Pittman nurtured this labor-civil rights coalition primarily at the level of state politics. It was smaller and weaker in the mid-1950s than in states like Michigan and New York, where Democratic machines had incorporated much larger black electorates along with labor in the 1930s and 1940s, but it would nonetheless become a central feature of California liberalism. Dellums and Pittman, the NAACP's full-time lobbyist for the FEP, worked with labor leaders and other California Federation of Labor and CIO officials, and by the mid-1950s the majority of the FEP Committee's funding came from two sources: the NAACP and trade unions. When FEP legislation finally did pass in 1959, the bill was helped through the assembly by new Democratic Governor Pat Brown and a Democratic legislative majority that had been swept into office in 1958 on the strength of African American and labor votes. Both groups had mobilized huge turnouts in Northern and Southern California to defeat Oakland's home-grown antilabor gubernatorial candidate, Bill Knowland. California's 1959 FEP bill was a seminal achievement, civil rights advocates believed, because the power of the state was now behind employment desegregation efforts, a goal of African American politics since the 1930s.[44]

The East Bay Democratic Club, and the Dellums-Gibson-Rumford-Pittman quartet, derived their political power in the FEP battle from a decade of organizing and building institutions in black communities. Rumford, the legislator, and Pittman, the activist, advocated a racial liberalism that emphasized a strong governmental role in making modern society free of racial discrimination. Dellums, the laborite, and Gibson, the working-class party leader, shared this agenda, but they came out of and drew their authority from the labor movement and all-black organizations. The Brotherhood and other African American railroad unions—built "with Negro leadership and Negro money," in Dellums's words—were places where creative leaders and shopfloor solidarity transformed segregation into economic and political leverage. "Negroes will have to pay for their own organization," Dellums declared, "their own fights, by their own funds as well as their own energy." The capacity, then, of Gibson, Dellums, the East Bay Democratic Club, and the NAACP, to broker with liberal white leaders was based on this grassroots strength. "D.G. organized the black vote for the first time so that the black vote meant something," former Oakland NAACP chairman William Patterson remembers. "They got people to buy in and subscribe to it. If we give you our vote on this, then you got to help us do that." Oakland's story underscores that coalition-building with whites in the postwar North and West toward civil rights legislation was possible because of black political mobilization, not a supposed sea change in white attitudes.[45]

Keep Mississippi Out of California

California's labor–civil rights alliance faced its first major test in the 1958 election. That year, voters defeated Bill Knowland's bid for governor, turned back an anti-union ballot initiative, and elected a Democratic majority to both houses of the state assembly where the FEP law passed in the first months of 1959. This tide of California politics swept Democrats into state and national offices in record numbers, but Oakland did not merely ride the swells. The contests of 1958 extended to the state level the objectives that had preoccupied Oakland liberals since the OVL campaign in 1947: labor defeated Knowland, and Dellums won a fair employment law. Oakland's liberal forces celebrated the defeat of Knowland and a right-to-work initiative, Proposition 18, claiming that they had taken the first important steps toward creating a statewide political coalition that would both promote working-class mobility and guarantee racial equality.[46]

In the middle of the 1958 campaign, the San Francisco and Los Angeles offices of the NAACP issued a pamphlet entitled "Keep Mississippi Out of California." On the cover, an employer in white shirt and black tie whips a kneeling "California Worker" with a "Right-to-Work" lash. A Nazi insignia and the states "Tennessee," "Arkansas," "Texas," "Alabama," "Georgia," and others from the South leap from the whip. Encouraging their members to "fight sharecropper wages!" and "expose the fake 'right-to-work' plot of the enemies of FEPC," the NAACP pamphlet called on the state's African American voters to reject Proposition 18. Franklin Williams, regional secretary of the NAACP, warned voters that "California minorities will suffer a severe blow if a destructive 'right-to-work' law were enacted to handcuff and straightjacket organized labor." If passed, Proposition 18 would outlaw the union shop in California, a state where union membership stood just below 50 percent in the late 1950s. In states where right-to-work laws had been implemented in the wake of the Taft-Hartley Act of 1947, principally in the South and Southwest, union membership had declined and organized labor remained ineffective. They were a particularly important weapon in southern employers' and politicians' defeat of the CIO's Operation Dixie in 1948. The stunning imagery of the NAACP's campaign against Proposition 18

Figure 2.4. In the 1958 California election, the NAACP encouraged African American voters to "keep Mississippi out of California" by defeating the right-to-work Proposition 18. With major Democratic victories across the state that year, a labor–civil rights coalition took shape in Sacramento. Courtesy of the Bancroft Library, University of California, Berkeley.

suggested to voters that the white supremacy of the Old South survived in the anti-union crusade of right-to-work advocates in California. In the name of fair employment and the rights of organized labor, the NAACP made defeating Proposition 18 a top priority in the 1958 election. In the process, African American Californians forged important ties with trade union leaders to ensure that labor would remain an ally in the fight for a state FEP law.[47]

For labor's part, defeating Proposition 18 meant establishing in the public mind the fundamental connection between trade unionism and economic progress. Labor officials spoke for a broad notion of community in which unions defended high wages and middle-class California living standards. Rarely in late twentieth-century California did unions so deliberately address their role in public life. Through the labor-sponsored Citizens Committee Against Proposition 18, unions reached local civic groups, business associations, Chambers of Commerce, political clubs, PTAs, churches, and a host of other grassroots forums and institutions. Trade unions guarded the health of the state's economy, labor leaders declared in campaign speeches and advertisements. Collective bargaining guaranteed workplace democracy. Union wage rates protected the incomes of all Californians. Most important, union wages made homeownership possible. The campaign against Proposition 18 revisited the UOC and OVL platforms, stripped them of their more social-democratic elements, and emphasized the centrality of the union shop to industrial-garden progress, economic development, and consumer democracy. It was a combination at the core of the growth liberalism for which California became famous under Knowland's eventual vanquisher, Pat Brown, who served as the state's governor from 1958 until 1966.[48]

Proposition 18's most vocal advocate was U.S. Senator Bill Knowland, Republican gubernatorial candidate and Oakland native. Renowned statewide as "the big switch," the 1958 campaign is remembered in Republican circles for Senator Knowland's pursuit of the governorship at the expense of Republican incumbent Goodwin "Goodie" Knight, who in turn ran for Knowland's U.S. Senate seat. Both lost. Knowland's maneuvering for the presidency (he wanted to launch a campaign for the 1960 Republican presidential nomination from the California governor's chair, not his Senate seat) and his controversial endorsement of Proposition 18 were widely credited with crippling the Republican Party in California until Ronald Reagan revived it a little less than a decade later. Ignoring the warnings of Republican strategists, Knowland sought to mobilize the conservative wing of the party using his father's old strategy of baiting and vilifying labor, a formula that proved disastrous in the late 1950s.[49]

Everything in the 1958 election hinged on Proposition 18. Knowland did not simply endorse the measure. He based his entire campaign on it.

90   CHAPTER TWO

Democratic challenger Brown charged that Knowland's single-issue campaign was fed by "belligerent extremism and shabby political irresponsibility." There was more behind Knowland's campaign, however, than
pure belligerence. The McClellan Committee's congressional hearings on
labor racketeering, held in 1958, had brought union corruption to national
public attention. The criminal and financial wrongdoing of the Teamsters
and International Longshoremen's Association made front-page headlines in California even though no California unions were under investi-
gation. Knowland hoped that the extensive media coverage of corrupt
unions would translate into broad public support for laws aimed at
reducing organized labor's strength. Moreover, Knowland and his family
remained close to the owners of the *Los Angeles Times*, the leading anti-
union newspaper in Southern California. Knowland's strategy depended
on the ability of the *Times* and his father's *Tribune* to revive anti-unionism
as a core conservative issue in order to animate California's political
right. He ran as the friend of ordinary workers, proposing an alternative
"Worker's Bill of Rights" that guaranteed union members freedom from
indomitable "union bosses." In a particularly bizarre campaign move,
Knowland's wife Helen wrote a seven-page letter to two hundred California Republican leaders warning that "California may be the last hope
of saving our country from the piggy-back-labor-socialist monster which
has latched on to the Democratic Party and to some Republicans as
well."[50]

Knowland badly miscalculated the public's interest in the corruption of
East Coast trade unions and underestimated the extent to which a large
portion of the state's suburban voters had purchased their homes and elevated themselves into the middle class with union wages. Within the San
Francisco–Oakland standard metropolitan statistical area, over 95 percent
of manufacturing and transportation workers were covered by labor-
management agreements. In the East Bay, working-class suburbs like San
Leandro, Hayward, and San Lorenzo, and in Southern California places
like South Gate and Torrance and large sections of the San Fernando Valley, were dominated by union households. Organized labor's claim that
unions sustained California's barreling high-wage economy, brought new
homes and consumer goods within reach of the working class, and kept
workplaces safe resonated with voters powerfully in 1958. The newly
united AFL and CIO launched a grassroots campaign in which they
linked the health of the California economy, the housing boom, and suburbanization to the high wages that unions made possible. Campaign
advertisements featured deteriorated schools and overworked drones
returning to homes empty of consumer products, victims of the new low-
wage economy under a "right-to-work" law. A victory for Proposition 18,
in labor's view, meant eviction from the industrial garden.[51]

Racial discrimination was an important subtext of the 1958 campaign because African American activists knew that if Knowland and Proposition 18 were to win in November, a fair employment law would recede even further from reach. Local representatives of the Citizens Committee Against Proposition 18 worked closely with NAACP branches, African American ministers, and black trade unionists to reach black voters with the "no on 18" message. The partnership initially ran smoothly, but in late summer a troubling development forced the opponents of Proposition 18 to redouble their efforts in African American communities statewide. Lester Bailey, field director for the Committee Against Proposition 18, learned that "the proponents of Proposition 18 are flooding Negro communities throughout California with the rumor that the so-called right-to-work issue, if passed, will guarantee Negroes and other minorities Fair Employment Practices." Proposition 18 supporters hoped to benefit from the fact that union racism had made some African Americans distrust the whole union movement. By limiting the power of unions, the argument went, black workers could more easily find employment, ideally in union-free workplaces. Dellums, in particular, resented the duplicity of claims that a right-to-work law could be construed as civil rights legislation. He feared that if African American voters did not stand with labor on Proposition 18, the FEP fight would founder in the legislature permanently.[52]

The "civil rights" argument for Proposition 18 convinced few voters, but the fair employment issue had the potential to work against labor's campaign. By 1958 FEP legislation had been introduced in the state assembly by Rumford and Hawkins and rejected or kept from the floor half a dozen times. Moreover, despite the labor-civil rights coalition in place at the state level pushing for the FEP law, in local communities, factories, and other work places many unions still discriminated blatantly against African Americans or refused to challenge white privilege among rank-and-file workers. Unions, many African American leaders claimed, stood in the way of fair employment, and organized labor's duplicity ran deep. But the labor-civil rights coalition held—and turned out voters in record numbers—because Dellums, Franklin Williams, and Tarea Hall Pittman joined African American leaders and community activists from Southern California in articulating a basic tenet of post–New Deal civil rights philosophy: trade union protections and civil rights laws go hand in hand. Discriminatory unions, Dellums said again and again, could be dealt with through FEP laws, not by destroying the very foundations of trade unionism. The message worked. Postelection samples revealed that African American voters rejected the right-to-work initiative six to one.[53]

The commitment of organized labor and African American leaders to defeating both Proposition 18 and Bill Knowland produced one of the most lopsided elections in California history. The Democratic Party

Figure 2.5. Democratic California Governor Edmund "Pat" Brown signs the state Fair Employment Practices Law in 1959. Immediately behind Brown's right shoulder is Byron Rumford. Behind Rumford on the left is Nathaniel S. Colley, general counsel of the NAACP, and on the right is C. L. Dellums. African Americans from the East Bay played an enormously important role in the state labor–civil rights coalition that passed fair employment and housing legislation in the late 1950s and early 1960s. Indeed, East Bay African American leaders enjoyed more influence in Sacramento than they did in Oakland or Berkeley in this period. Courtesy of the Bancroft Library, University of California, Berkeley.

reaped the rewards. Brown won by over one million votes, Knight was soundly defeated, and 60 percent of the state's elected offices went to Democrats. Democrats fared so well in 1958 mostly because of Knowland's Proposition 18 blunder, but the party's revival also reflected internal growth. Throughout the 1950s local political "amateurs"—middle-class liberals and trade unionists, African American and white—rebuilt the state Democratic Party from the ground up by creating a series of political clubs, of which the East Bay Democratic Club was one of the most important, in the state's largest cities. The liberal-labor-civil rights coalition that elected Brown in 1958, based in these local clubs, became the core constituency for the unprecedented expansion of the welfare state that accompanied California's phenomenal economic growth in the 1960s. Brown and the Democratic-led state assembly poured massive state subsidies into the college and university system, extended broader unemployment insurance, health, and welfare protections to the working class, passed fair employment and housing laws, and embarked on large-scale dam-building and water works in the Central Valley. It was one of the nation's most comprehensive and visible liberal undertakings.[54]

The Democratic majority produced by the 1958 landslide gave Dellums and Rumford the votes and gubernatorial support they needed to pass the FEP bill in early 1959. A fair housing law came in 1963. A turning point in California political history, 1958 marked the beginning of an eight-year period during which the Democratic Party, organized labor, and the NAACP solidified an electoral bloc that placed California ahead of the national curve in its embrace of a postwar liberalism that prefigured the Great Society. From 1958 to 1966 Oakland-based and East Bay leaders and voters played important roles in this coalition. African Americans benefited unevenly from labor's fickle attention to civil rights in local politics and on the shop floor. But the combination of African American migrants, who poured into the state in the tens of thousands between 1942 and the 1960s, and organized labor was nonetheless a potent force in extending the social wage in California. C. L. Dellums and Byron Rumford believed that with the legislative victories of 1959 and 1963—representing three decades of activism and political organizing—they *had* kept Mississippi out of California.[55]

They had, for the moment, but California liberalism in the late 1950s had made both enemies and accommodations that would weaken its political coherence and effectiveness over time. Even the relatively modest fair employment and housing laws won in 1959 and 1963 drew enormous opposition and resistance from the state's Republican Party, lobbyists for employer groups, and, especially, the real estate industry. In the employers' case, this resistance would continue throughout the next decade as Dellums and others attempted to *enforce* fair employment. In the case of the real estate industry, political resistance emerged immediately: the California Real Estate Association placed a ballot measure repealing fair housing before the state's voters in 1964—about which chapters 4 and 7 have much more to say. This opposition was fierce and mobilized. At the same time, however, the liberals who swept into office in 1958 had their own blinders that gave the coalition stark limitations. It did not, for instance, extend into the state's fast-growing ethnic Mexican population. Among Mexican American civil rights leaders, securing old-age pensions for long-term Mexican residents, ending the bracero program, and unionizing farm workers were the overriding concerns. White and black liberals who reasoned by analogy from African Americans' experience too often missed or dismissed the nature of injustice and discrimination confronting other groups in the state. The statewide liberal coalition that enjoyed such

success in 1958 was composed of leaders who understood the state's
racial terrain largely in terms of black and white; advocates for ethnic
Mexicans and other groups of Californians, including Chinese and
Filipinos, would have to engage in their own push to broaden liberals'
perspective.[56]

By the end of the 1950s, East Bay liberalism had endured a bumpy
ride. It could claim gains to counter the losses. One of its most telling
characteristics was its diverse locations in political space. The municipal
political power mobilized by the progressive wing of the labor movement
in the 1940s proved weak in the face of the power of property as an issue
and property holders as a class. Place and property shaped local interests
in ways that mitigated against a unifying political identity invoked by
"labor" or the "public." Even the city's famous general strike provided
only a temporary stabilization of labor's hoped-for coalition. This shifting political landscape was part of a national narrative in the 1940s. Urban
reformers within the CIO Political Action Committee and the progressive
wing of the AFL found the going rough in cities throughout the country
after World War II, falling short of their objectives or failing outright.
Blatant racism and whites' accommodation to segregation, the rhetorical
and political buildup of Cold War anticommunism, and a business backlash
against the New Deal together stymied progressive reform. In Oakland,
postwar liberals were unable—because of both liberalism's own limitations
and its extraordinary opposition—to define a universalist vision of the
city's future and to win political power. Liberalism was in full retreat in
Oakland politics, where Knowland returned in 1958 to run the *Tribune*,
the at-large election system discouraged political reform, and a small circle of downtown property holders, attorneys, and business people shaped
the political climate.[57]

From another vantage, however, liberalism looked ascendant in the
East Bay. African American and white workers joined together in the late
1950s to vote overwhelmingly Democratic in state and national elections. Blacks and whites lived in relative proximity in the East Bay flatlands, from Richmond in the north through Berkeley and out to East
Oakland. Moreover, in both Berkeley and Oakland a liberal middle class
of professionals and civil servants was becoming outspoken and active.
During and after the war, African American organizing and struggle had
pushed racial equality onto progressives' agenda. Across the bay in San
Francisco, too, there was an emerging liberal establishment of institutions and organizations—as in the East Bay, based in CIO labor, progressive AFL leadership circles, veterans of the Popular Front, black churches
and the NAACP, and middle-class professionals. All of this carried over
to Sacramento in 1958 with the enormous Democratic electoral victories
and in subsequent years with the passage of fair employment and housing

legislation. While politics cannot be reduced to a spatial typology, the political boundaries drawn across and through the East Bay, and the political structures in place locally, meant that liberalism was fractured and located in quite distinct places by the 1960s. As a result, liberals and civil rights advocates could register certain victories while still facing huge obstacles in other political contexts.[58]

For East Bay African Americans, the struggle for equality and desegregation in the decade after World War II had produced mixed results. Black and white workers may have lived in relative proximity, but that was all. Few whites wanted African American neighbors or cared much about changing patterns of job discrimination that benefited them and disadvantaged blacks. White and black Oaklanders understood liberalism quite differently: whites as part of a larger set of guarantees of their own economic security, African Americans as the most likely vehicle for destroying Jim Crow and opening housing and labor markets. Moreover, the political marginalization of African American communities in Oakland meant that black leaders lacked the leverage to secure municipal resources—city jobs, community economic development, or fair allocating of city contracts, for instance—or to shape city policy. But the struggle to find a reliable vehicle for desegregation and African American rights was far from over. Black political power in the East Bay's seventeenth state assembly district would endure as leverage in Sacramento. And African American political leaders and grassroots activists alike in Oakland, realistic in the face of their local powerlessness, would continue to search for appropriate vehicles to advance their and their communities' interests.

Finally, in both East Bay and statewide political contests between the late 1940s and the late 1950s were glimpses of an emerging conservative movement. Knowland's effort to mobilize conservatives in 1958 failed as an electoral strategy, but it succeeded in pushing the Republican Party further to the right—further away from the moderate pragmatism of party stalwarts like Hiram Johnson and Earl Warren. The advance of California conservatism in the next decade would take place primarily in Southern California, and primarily under the leadership of right-wing Republican Party activists from Los Angeles and Orange counties. The Bay Area remained a Democratic and liberal stronghold. However, the right's assertion that liberalism fostered a coercive state that constrained personal liberty and violated "property rights" would ultimately appeal ideologically across party lines, even in Oakland and the East Bay. As was evident in Oakland politics in the late 1940s, liberalism was constrained by tax reform advocates, by appeals to property rights, and by a relatively weak commitment to racial equality within its own ranks. After 1958 the conservative movement in California would take advantage of these fissures far more successfully than Knowland had.[59]

3

Tax Dollar

Driving south from Oakland into the adjacent suburban community of San Leandro, an observer in 1948 would have found it impossible to know when he or she had crossed from one city into the other. The tree-lined streets and 1920s-era bungalows common to both would have offered no clue. Even the industrial landscape would have struck the casual observer rolling past small machine shops and warehouses as a single piece. Not far from the fading brown brick of the General Motors Durant plant on East Fourteenth Street in Oakland was the red brick Caterpillar Tractor plant in San Leandro. Both would have hummed with activity and spilled workers onto the streets at shift change in the late 1940s. San Leandro looked like a good deal of East Oakland in 1948, but their post-war histories would be very different. To understand why, we must cross Oakland's boundary and move into the expanding neighboring suburbs. Between the end of World War II and the middle of the 1960s, East Bay residents created new suburban cities and expanded older ones at an astonishing rate. But first-generation postwar suburbanites did not so much "flee" the city as create industrial and residential property markets out of undeveloped agricultural flatlands. Their actions were as much a part of Oakland's history as the general strike, because from the beginning, suburban city building was predicated on maximizing property value and keeping taxes low, development strategies that would shape the entire region.

Between 1945 and the early 1960s, cities south of Oakland, between East Oakland and San Jose, emerged as the industrial garden imagined in the Metropolitan Oakland Area Program. By the 1970s one could trace a straight line on a map following this landscape from Oakland's southern edge through San Leandro, Hayward, Union City, Newark, Fremont, and Milpitas to San Jose's northern boundary forty miles away in the South Bay. San Leandro and Hayward alone existed as corporate cities prior to the mid-1950s. The others incorporated during that decade, as civic entrepreneurs from the scattered towns, farms, and orchards of the East Bay flatlands forged new municipalities. Conceived as locations of both employment and residence, of factories and homes, the suburbs they created were designed locally but depended on national developments: the unprecedented postwar federal mortgage guarantee program, new federal interstate highways, and capital mobility. This pattern of growth elaborated the MOAP's suburban vision, but it also undermined Oakland, creating cities and economic networks that would compete with, as much as complement, the presumed "center" of the new industrial West.[1]

Postwar suburbanization in the United States was driven by the politics of making markets in property and in maintaining exclusionary access to those markets. Cities are fundamentally based on leveraging property into one version of community or another—they are the result of the social production of markets, the social production of space. "During the last half of the twentieth century carefully selected property will increase to prices that would now seem fabulous," Fred Cox, president of the Southern Alameda County Real Estate Board told an audience in 1950. Such prices would be produced by "a great increase in population, tremendous industrial development and amazing commercial growth." In the postwar decades, three primary sets of interests came together to shape suburbanization and the kinds of suburban markets celebrated by Cox: the federal state, local city-builders, and white homeowners. Each brought an ideological and material investment in the process of market creation. The resulting "compact" between these different agents, worked out over more than a decade, made the postwar suburb possible. Suburban forms varied across the United States, but as a whole they represent one of the nation's most far-reaching and influential sociospatial constructions of the second half of the twentieth century. In the East Bay, we will look closely at several highly influential examples. Before doing so it is necessary to review the role each of the three architects of suburbia played in the process of city building.[2]

First, postwar homeownership developed with the assistance of massive state subsidies. The federal government dramatically democratized the housing market for whites while simultaneously enforcing a racial segregation that resembled apartheid. State intervention in the housing market made financing single-family homes more profitable to lenders, more accessible to white buyers, and virtually unobtainable for African Americans. Beginning in the 1930s, New Deal federal housing policies defined black and mixed-race communities as high risk, and the government refused to extend its generous mortgage guarantee programs into such neighborhoods well into the 1960s. Thus, for more than thirty years, the Federal Housing Administration and the Veterans Administration, the principal agencies in charge of implementing the federal state's housing policy, underwrote segregation. Because of the enormous sums of capital involved—billions of dollars annually—their actions gave contour to the entire national housing market; the market was shaped in the image of these agencies. The federal government, according to the 1961 report by the U.S. Commission on Civil Rights, "created the machinery through which housing discrimination operates." America's postwar housing boom—a

twenty-five-year building bonanza with long-term social consequences—
was possible because of federal underwriting of home finance, a policy
that pressed African Americans to the extreme margins of the nation's
aging residential communities.[3]

The second architect of suburbanization, local city-builders, came in the
East Bay from a broad, diffuse entrepreneurial political class that managed
municipal incorporation campaigns between Oakland and San Jose.
Unlike California's celebrated "community builders," who constructed
entire cities from a single massive property—and made famous such places
as Irvine, Rancho California, Huntington Beach, and Foster City—the
East Bay's suburban civic founders were neither large landholders nor,
with a few exceptions, major developers. They were almost universally
middle-class professionals, industrialists, modest landholders, and merchants, men and women who had smaller, though no less real, financial
stakes in incorporation. This group included representatives of the real
estate industry, with their investment in segregation, but that industry
itself did not control incorporation in every instance: more fluid alliances
and political combinations were possible. Nonetheless, city-builders set
out to create and maximize two kinds of property markets, one in industrial land the other in residential. They did so in order to finance public
services, maintain home equity, and, in the optimistic and market-driven
logic of American development, to ensure future economic growth. This
city building was political because interests differed over how those markets would be created and racialized, and territorial because the way municipal boundaries were drawn, how the tax burden was distributed, and
where people lived in relation to where they worked depended on both an
imagined and real geography.[4]

The third agent of suburban city building, white homeowners, was also
the most diverse group. Homeowners were first-time buyers from West
Oakland, families of World War II veterans purchasing property with the
assistance of the VA. Homeowners were migrants from Iowa or Oklahoma, coming to California for new jobs. Homeowners were longtime suburban residents, people who had lived in southern Alameda County for a
decade or more, perhaps purchasing new homes in a Fremont subdivision.
Homeowners were an occupationally varied lot: factory workers, public
employees, carpenters, nurses, office workers, attorneys, merchants,
home workers, and engineers. They were diverse in class background and
place of origin, but the structure of the housing markets into which they
entered in the postwar decades would begin to give them a common identity, to shape for them a set of concerns and interests that would unite
more than divide them. These issues started with the concrete economics
of taxes and home values. No investment an average family in midcentury
America would make in their lifetime was larger than that in their home,

and in California, perhaps more than anywhere else in the nation, the detached, single-family home had been elevated in popular culture as the
preeminent symbol of both independence and assimilation. Together, markets and culture—and later, electoral politics—encouraged homeowners
in suburban California to identify property ownership first and foremost
in terms of their own individual financial interests.[5]

Over time, the product of the suburban compact between the federal
state, city-builders, and homeowners in the East Bay was a set of expectations and ideologies that could be mobilized politically. Three key elements lay at the core of those expectations. First, homeowners came to
expect, and later demand, low property taxes. Second, they came to expect and rationalize racial segregation. Finally, they came to accept as
natural the conflation of whiteness and property ownership with upward
social mobility. None of these expectations emerged in a linear fashion
from a single source, nor were they unchallenged. Their origins predate
the postwar suburb. But their particular conjuncture at this moment in
concrete sociospatial formations like those in the East Bay stands out historically. In these suburbs, homeownership stood at the core of political
identification, and small property holders emerged as the most important
social class and political constituency. Capital mobility, national economic
restructuring, and the extraordinary growth of California's population
during and after the war propelled the process of suburban formation in
the East Bay, but homeowner expectations were the glue that held the
new cities together. Far from the cradle of republican independence and
American voluntarism its proponents proclaimed, homeownership among
white families was one of the most state-subsidized features of the postwar
national economy. "[I]t has been said of housing," the U.S. Civil Rights
Commission wrote in 1961, "there is no nondefense segment of American
economic life so dependent on the federal government."[6]

Property is fixed space that over time produces capital, which in turn
consists of assets that can generate, through investment, other financial
enterprises. Postwar American suburbanization is thus best understood
in terms of the processes by which property was converted into capital
and its corollaries: value for homeowners, profit for boosters, and taxes
for public officials. Home equity was a precious form of personal or familial wealth embedded in present and future property values. But it was
also "value" of a different sort in a moral economy, irreducible to mere
capital. For city-builders and boosters, property was an elemental engine
in the production of profit: the sale of land to developers and industry
and the conversion of residential and industrial land into home sales
and jobs, all of the economic activity described simply as "growth." Public officials shared both sets of concerns. But their interest in property
was finally about how best to tax it in order to finance the administrative

infrastructure of the city itself: schools, fire protection, police, water and sewer lines, and all of the services and amenities required for a city to survive. To public officials property was *taxes*. In the context of broad movements of capital across the region and the nation in the 1940s and 1950s, East Bay suburban growth nonetheless hinged on these intensely local concerns.[7]

What follows is a look at the creation of three suburban cities in the East Bay that, while vastly different in many respects, embody the features of the postwar suburb outlined above. These local case studies of suburban development underscore the "pull" factors that encouraged white people to buy homes and make a cultural and financial investment in suburban communities, rather than the "push" factors that propelled them to leave larger cities. Such an effort demonstrates that white suburbanization in this period represented the complicated intersection of public policy and subsidy, economic individualism and self-interest, and regional development and underdevelopment, rather than the vague and impressionistic "white flight."

San Leandro: The Industrial Garden Realized

San Leandro entered the national iconography of suburban industrial growth in 1966 when it was named a "model municipality" by the *Wall Street Journal*. In the 1920s San Leandro had served as a bedroom community for both San Francisco and Oakland commuters and as a truck farming center that provided vegetables, fruit, and cut flowers to nearby cities—the "land of sunshine and flowers," boosters bragged. Its streets and neighborhoods were indistinguishable from those of East Oakland, where the modest homes of skilled workers, merchants, and semiprofessionals blended into San Leandro's northern edge in a suburban ménage typical of the East Bay's flatland geography. Despite its size (22,903 in 1940) and semirural orientation, however, San Leandro had attracted a few notable industries—a Caterpillar Tractor assembly plant and Frieden Calculators, in particular—before the war. After 1945 the city's civic leaders, developers, and wartime newcomers added to that industrial base by converting nearby agricultural land into cheap factory and housing sites in pursuit of what they termed "balanced development." San Leandro's choices underline how "model municipality" was understood, not just by the *Journal* but by those who built the city. Civic leaders and homeowners chose industrial growth led by low taxes as one foundation and racial segregation as another. From the beginning, the industrial garden was a contested idea. Power would determine *whose* vision was ultimately expressed on the ground. Through their choices and politics,

San Leandro residents realized one version of suburbanization: dynamic industrial job growth and pastoral neighborhoods enclosed behind the exclusionary walls of apartheid. It was a civic space that would profoundly influence the future of both Oakland and suburban Alameda County.[8]

Between 1946 and 1948 the San Leandro City Council hotly debated the direction and pace of industrial development, offering, in the words of the city's principal newspaper editor, George Thompson, "two approaches [that] should be thrashed out without animosity." On the one hand, the city could encourage industrial investment by allowing companies to build new factories on unincorporated land outside of the municipal tax district. On the other, the city could require industry to locate within San Leandro while expanding its municipal boundaries to incorporate existing and future factories. In the latter instance, according to Thompson, "with industry paying its full pro-rata share of city government costs, and thereby in the long run reducing all city taxes," the results would "make this community a better place in which to live and work." In 1947, however, the council struck a deal with Chrysler Motor Parts in which the latter received a full slate of municipal services—including water, sewer, fire, and police—while remaining outside San Leandro's city limits, its properties off the tax rolls. Thompson and others fumed at the council's apparent pandering. "The average homeowner should not be expected to underwrite the costs of industry," Thompson editorialized. "Those same industries, sharing in the benefits which the community has to offer them . . . must be made to realize their community responsibility."[9]

Thompson's language was bursting with a largely inchoate, but nonetheless powerfully persuasive, discourse that championed homeowners by echoing American traditions of populism. Dating to the late nineteenth century, the latter emphasize the interests of a broad, diffuse, quasi-egalitarian "public" or "people" against various elites and entrenched economic and political institutions. Wedded to capitalism, populists in U.S. history have rarely endorsed radical prescriptions for social change, preferring reforms that restore power to local interests. But their most distinct element is the desire to hold large business and state institutions responsible to the lives and interests of average people. In places like the East Bay suburbs, populism was refashioned in the postwar decades in the form of a homeowner-centered faith in the righteousness of the "small taxpayer." Homeowner populism brought property taxes to the fore of local politics and tied the fulfillments of suburban living to the tax revenues generated by corporate industrial property owners—whose fiscal responsibility homeowners had constantly to monitor. In this period, under the conditions of city building, a low tax burden was understood by people like Thompson as part of a common-sense "fair" distribution of local economic burdens.[10]

Civic leaders, neighborhood associations, industrialists, and politicians all understood the enormous relevance and long-term consequences of mundane decisions about sewer bond measures, municipal boundaries, and the siting of industrial property. The East Shore Park Civic League, a neighborhood association representing new wartime residential development, emerged as the city's most vocal advocate of using industrial property taxes to improve municipal services and the physical infrastructure of the city—especially sidewalks, sewer lines, street lights, and other amenities in East Shore Park itself. Between 1946 and 1948 the League grew disenchanted with the existing city council, which was composed of an established generation of San Leandro businessmen who had governed the city since the 1930s, lived in the older downtown, and who, so it appeared to the organized newcomers, overburdened new homeowners to accommodate corporations like Chrysler. Barbara Burbank, a self-declared "scribe" for the East Shore Park Civic League, asked her readers if they "know how much of the city taxes come from your neighborhood?" and "how much of that is *spent* in your neighborhood?" The league was not antitax in an absolute sense, but like their tax-conscious compatriots in East Oakland, East Shore homeowners believed that neighborhoods should be shielded from high taxes by shifting the city's fiscal burden onto those businesses and industries that could, in Thompson's words, "well afford to pay."[11]

In 1948 the East Shore Park Civic League translated these concerns into electoral politics, when they swept the incumbent city councilmembers from office with a reform slate pledged to "let the people decide and know where their tax dollar is spent." Joseph Bellini, an East Shore Park pharmacist, headed the slate, and the league orchestrated a grassroots campaign for the Committee for Better San Leandro Government, a citywide coalition that sponsored the reformers. According to the *News-Observer*, the city's governing clique "forgot to remember that there are thousands of little property owners who were not impressed with the desirability of underwriting the manufacturing costs of such enterprises as the Chrysler corporation." The *News-Observer* underscored that in San Leandro both working- and middle-class homeowners had common interests in holding corporations responsible for their "fair share" of the local tax burden. Both groups could identify corporations like Chrysler as either adversaries, if the companies received a taxpayer-sponsored free ride, or allies, if the companies could be harnessed, through property taxes, to the improvement of civic life and the reduction of *homeowner* taxes.[12]

The electoral victory of 1948 set the stage for a political and administrative consensus in San Leandro that carried the city through a remarkable period of industrial and residential growth. With plenty of neighboring "vacant" agricultural land for new and expanding factories, San Leandro enjoyed what its boosters liked to call "natural advantages." The new city council, the city manager appointed by the 1948 reform slate, and the Chamber of Commerce developed an industrial strategy designed to transform San Leandro from the "city of sunshine and flowers" into the "city of industry." As long as new businesses located within the municipal boundaries, taxes on industrial property would fund city services. Yet the property tax rate would be deliberately low, both to accommodate the "thousands of little property owners" who voted and to attract new industrial capital seeking entry into the Bay Area's rapidly expanding postwar markets. There could hardly have been a more ironic reformulation of the Metropolitan Oakland Area Program than this low-tax industrial strategy. Regional East Bay growth "with Oakland at the center" worked rhetorically but yielded in reality to intercity competition. Between 1948 and the late 1960s, San Leandro competed for new investment with nearby Oakland, Hayward, and Fremont, as well as with the South Bay and San Francisco Peninsula, by driving its property tax rate to the lowest level in California.[13] (See appendix tables 4–6.)

While San Leandro's city manager coordinated with business and political leaders on an industrial strategy, homeowners and real estate developers articulated a related, but still distinct, exclusionary racial strategy. Prior to World War II in San Leandro, as in the southern East Bay generally, a hierarchy of social status delineated people according to race, nation of origin, and religion. The city's large Catholic Portuguese population, for instance, included a sizable middle class of merchants and professionals who had achieved some social standing in the eyes of the city's residents of northern European, Protestant background. Nonetheless, working-class Portuguese often found themselves denigrated by Anglos, because of the latter's distaste for the "Spanish" or "Mexican" workers who provided much of the region's agricultural labor. Ethnic Mexican laborers and Japanese truck farmers experienced housing discrimination and other abuses, as did the fewer Chinese American residents. Middle-class Mexican, Japanese, and Chinese American merchants and professionals, however, could occasionally break into civic leadership circles—the longtime mayor of Union City in the 1960s, for instance, was Japanese American. This hierarchy of race and nation did not disappear, but after the war San Leandrans specifically targeted newly arrived African Americans in Oakland for legal exclusion. "Faced with the great influx of colored population into the East Bay during the war years," the News-Observer explained in a frank page-one story, San Leandro residents erected legal barriers of segregation. Thompson's "thousands of little property owners" were "all white Caucasians" according to the newspaper.[14]

Homeowners in San Leandro defended their rights against corporate property owners while trampling on the rights of African Americans at the same time. They crafted a populism, which, like its nineteenth-century counterpart, embraced both the possibility of an inclusive progressive politics of the "little guy" and an exclusionary racism mobilized against blacks. For San Leandro's real estate brokers and homeowners, racial restriction was rationalized as a way to maintain low property taxes and high property values. Segregation was reinforced by the fact that the federal government had promoted white-only suburbanization since the 1930s, first through the Home Owners Loan Corporation, then through the Federal Housing Administration (FHA), whose *Underwriting Manual* in 1938 maintained that "it is necessary that properties shall continue to be occupied by the same social and racial groups." That same manual recommended restrictive covenants, like those ultimately developed in San Leandro, to insure against "inharmonious racial groups." Between the end of World War II and the 1960s, the FHA and VA guaranteed more than $3.3 million in home loans in San Leandro, an enormous subsidy for white homeownership denied to African Americans. The view that African Americans lowered the value of property became widely accepted by whites and encouraged both homeowners and real estate agents to utilize an array of devices to maintain racial exclusivity even as federal policy slowly changed in the postwar era.[15]

Immediately after the war, San Leandro residents erected a figurative white wall along the city's border with Oakland. M. C. Friel and Associates, a Hayward real estate firm with expertise in racial covenants, became the East Bay's leading consultant on shoring up segregation. In 1947 Friel developed a plan to place as much of San Leandro's residential property under restrictive covenants as possible, limiting future property sales to "members of the Caucasian race." Such restrictions had been used in San Francisco and parts of the East Bay for decades to contain the mobility of Chinese and Japanese residents, and while Friel's postwar covenants perpetuated such exclusions, his 1947 tactics were aimed at newly arrived African Americans. The *San Leandro News-Observer* reported in the autumn of 1947 that Friel outlined his "plan for protecting property values" in an address "before the board of directors of the Chamber of Commerce," which concluded with "the board giving its approval of the program and authorizing that a letter of approval of his program be furnished Friel." In undisguised language the *News-Observer* announced that the "sudden increase in the East Bay Negro population" meant that "local neighborhoods are spontaneously moving to protect their property values and calling upon Friel's company to assist them."[16]

San Leandro's campaign of racial exclusion earned the city a regional reputation. The *San Francisco Chronicle*, reporting on Friel's efforts in early 1948, lamented that the "closed door" policy of cities like San Leandro had exacerbated the postwar housing crisis in the "Bay Area's non-white districts." Such liberal lamentations, however, did little to disrupt patterns of racial segregation. Even the U.S. Supreme Court's ruling against covenant enforcement in 1948 (*Shelley v. Kraemer*) slowed but did not halt the process. Already known in the East Bay for designing racial covenants that could survive close legal scrutiny, Friel responded to the Court's landmark decision by reconfiguring San Leandro's covenant agreements into "neighborhood protective associations," pseudo-corporations of homeowners that could legally select acceptable homebuyers through "corporation contract agreements" as long as "race and creed" were not taken into account. This new approach attracted the attention of C. L. Dellums in Oakland, who warned NAACP members when Friel ran for U.S. Congress from a South County district in 1950 that he was "viciously anti-Negro." As they erected impenetrable racial barriers that would stand for a generation, white real estate interests and homeowners justified this racist practice as a protection of their investment.[17]

San Leandro's zealous pursuit of racial homogeneity and rising property values in the late 1940s and into the 1950s, as well as its policy of racial restriction, occurred under no pressure from actual African American mobility. African Americans could not purchase homes anywhere in East Oakland until 1950 because of policies enforced by the real estate industry in Oakland. During 1947 and 1948, Friel's most active period in San Leandro, no black homebuyers could purchase property within miles of the city. Yet its residents pursued restrictions with fervent determination. As parts of East Oakland opened to black families in the 1950s and 1960s, San Leandro remained firmly closed, halting African Americans' pursuit of homeownership at Oakland's southern boundary and sealing off large portions of southern Alameda County. During those same decades, San Leandro's industrial growth and its obvious prosperity contrasted sharply with East Oakland's deindustrialization (including the closing of two automobile factories) and the emergence there of the city's poorest African American neighborhoods. Such consequences were not the product of white "backlash." They were the product of an assertive, aggressive segregation policy pursued by the federal state and supported by local white consensus before African Americans had even arrived in nearby neighborhoods.[18]

San Leandro's postwar strategy of growth remained remarkably stable over the three decades between the end of the war and the middle 1970s. Like Oakland, San Leandro had both a white-collar, foreman/managerial, and small business middle class ensconced in prewar homes near its small downtown and pressed against the hills in postwar cul-de-sac developments, as well as a working class of skilled tradespeople, clerical workers, and factory employees and their families living in a range of bungalows and ranch houses in broad flatland neighborhoods like East Shore Park. Unlike Oakland, however, no Republican establishment, hostile to organized labor, dominated the city politically. Unions remained widely popular. An admixture of long-time residents of Portuguese descent (throughout the 1940s and 1950s Portuguese holidays and parades gave the city its most prominent public rituals) second- and third-generation Italian and Irish families, and Protestant middle Americans, San Leandro was a decidedly working-class city in which nearly three-quarters of residents were clerical, factory, transportation, or construction workers. The white working-class identity that arose in places like San Leandro in the postwar decades did not reflect a transparent process of assimilation, however, but was a complicated product of white privilege, increasing affluence subsidized by state housing policy, rising wages that unions made possible, and spatial remove afforded by suburbanization. San Leandro residents shared a sense of participating in the creation of a civic space that excluded African Americans, which gave at least one concrete meaning to the otherwise impressionistic terms "Caucasian" and "white."[19]

San Leandro's postwar development illustrates the social production of space in postwar metropolitan America. Homeowners used a public discourse of fairness to make claims on the property of industry. These were not radical redistributive claims, but rather an insistence that homeowners and industry should share the city's tax burden, claims that embodied a set of spatial structures linking various kinds of property in the city to one another and to the larger city-building project. In this structure, political boundaries became economic boundaries. Because San Leandro was a municipality—and not, for instance, a neighborhood within a larger city like Oakland—it could deploy the *powers* of a municipality to set tax policy, annex outlying industry, and establish zoning patterns to create potential markets for investment and to leverage property taxes into public services and infrastructure. These public powers, unavailable to big-city neighborhoods, were crucial components and tools of postwar suburbanization, because they reified physical boundaries and made them markers of profit potential and indicators of safe investment. At the same time, real estate brokers and homeowners mobilized private contracts and agreements among property holders into an apartheid-like set of racial restrictions on mobility. These restrictions enjoyed official local support through the San Leandro Chamber of Commerce and city council and federal support through FHA and VA redlining, but their most fundamental characteristic was an agreement among local property holders on how to construct and organize the city as racial space.[20]

Between the late 1940s and the late 1960s, two great rivers of public and private capital surged through the nation, enriching and developing certain kinds of places, primarily suburban, and contributing to the underdevelopment of others, primarily urban. San Leandro had positioned itself well in relation to these currents and stood to benefit enormously from them. The first was the unprecedented federal underwriting of private home construction through the mortgage guarantee programs of the VA and the FHA. During the 1950s VA and FHA financing accounted for as much as one-third of the total housing starts nationwide. Mortgage guarantees represented billions of dollars annually, sums that went to suburban locations at a rate three times that to central cities. The second river had two forks. One was federal military contracts that fed private companies like Lockheed, Boeing, Douglas Aircraft, Convair, and dozens of others. California received more than an ample share of these contracts—upon which entire communities were built in places like Sunnyvale, Pasadena, and Long Beach—but San Leandro and the East Bay were minor recipients of this kind of largess. A second fork, however, did flow through San Leandro: manufacturing capital decentralizing from the nation's older industrial heartland in the East and Midwest and seeking new, moderate-sized facilities to produce consumer products for southern and West Coast markets. Largely a postwar extension of the branch plant pattern of industrialization that had contributed to Oakland and the East Bay's prewar growth, industries based in the East or Midwest opened branch plants in California employing between 150 and 500 workers throughout the 1940s and 1950s. Other local businesses followed, some looking to leave older facilities and high taxes in cities like Oakland, others looking for land on which to build a first plant or warehouse.[21]

Having positioned itself to capture these postwar capital flows, San Leandro enjoyed a two-decade boom envied by its East Bay civic rivals. Between 1948 and 1957 the city added 15,000 industrial jobs and over $130 million in capital investment in property and facilities. Caterpillar Tractor, Chrysler and Dodge parts and assembly divisions, Frieden Calculators, General Foods, Pacific Can Co., Peterson Tractor and Equipment Co., California Packing Corporation, Kaiser-Frazer Aircraft, and Crown-Zellerbach all had new or expanded factories or processing plants in San Leandro by the end of the 1950s. In just five years, between 1951 and 1956, the city's assessed property valuation nearly tripled, from just over $31 million to just over $85 million; by the early 1960s industry in San Leandro paid more than one-third of the cost of city government. When the *Wall Street Journal* hailed San Leandro as a national model of small-scale industrial success in 1966, the paper crowed that the city had "managed to get all the benefits of lavish public spending while putting a surprisingly small bite on the local taxpayers." San Leandrans had created a working-class city with middle-class amenities: the industrial garden.[22]

As the 1948 election had demonstrated, however, San Leandro's business community was constrained by an active, tax-conscious group of homeowners and neighborhood associations. Beginning in 1949, the Chamber grafted onto its already elaborate, MOAP-like campaign to attract industry a parallel program designed to convince homeowners of "their stake in terms of personal benefits and in the continued growth and expansion of industrial and business firms in San Leandro." With declarations like "San Leandro industry helps pay your taxes!" and "San Leandro industry puts money in everyone's pocket!" a series of Chamber pamphlets and advertisements blanketed the city in the late forties and early fifties. Addressed to homeowners, this super-charged booster literature translated the city's industrial strategy into easy bites of colloquial economic wisdom. San Leandro's homeowners did not subscribe to anti-industry, redistributive politics of a radical stripe, but the Chamber nevertheless understood that the sorts of nitty-gritty concerns residents did have about taxes, city services, and quality of life amenities could lead them to oppose certain kinds of industrial development in the future, especially so-called "smokestack" growth. Here was the antidote: constant messages that industry was on the homeowners' side, keeping taxes low, schools good, and jobs local.[23]

San Leandro's public officials navigated the city according to the logic encouraged by postwar American growth economics: expand the pie and everyone's piece is bigger. The city avoided the potential pitfalls of its low-tax development strategy—underfunded schools and poor city services—with two conservative fiscal tactics based on an inflationary property market. First, with the exception of the 1947 bonds for sewer facilities, between the early fifties and mid seventies the city never went into bonded debt, adopting instead a "pay-as-you-go" philosophy. With no debt payments, the city could dedicate tax revenues solely to schools, fire and police, and other basic municipal responsibilities. Second, as the value of existing property in the city increased, and as new property was added through annexation and capital investment in plants and factories, the city could lower its tax rate annually without decreasing its overall revenue. These tactics worked well for thirty years because of the spatial context in which they were deployed. The total amount of property tax paid by both individual homeowners and industries remained stable or increased slightly, but because the city in turn reduced the property tax *rate* every year—and did so with a consistency unmatched by any other comparable city in the region or state—San Leandro property holders and industry enjoyed a comparative advantage over those in nearby cities. Cutting the tax rate was both an economic incentive to attract industry and a socio-political tactic designed to incorporate local homeowners into an ideological and political consensus about the benefits of growth.[24]

Figure 3.1. In the 1940s the San Leandro Chamber of Commerce hoped to convince homeowners of the benefits of industrial growth. Industry would bear a large part of the tax burden, the chamber stressed, making homeownership in San Leandro profitable by reducing the strain on the "family budget."

Figure 3.2. San Leandro expanded enormously in the postwar decades, enlarging both its physical boundaries and its industrial districts. In twenty years, San Leandro homeowners and public officials transformed the "city of sunshine and flowers" into the "city of industry." This advertisement, sponsored by the San Leandro Manufacturers' Association, emphasized how homeowners benefited from the city's rapid industrialization.

That ideological consensus, and the material benefits that underlay it, provided a powerful incentive for prospective San Leandro residents. Through much of the 1950s, the city grew by expanding its geographic boundaries to incorporate nearby residential and industrial developments. In the intricate local homeowner politics characteristic of suburban city building in this era, San Leandro officials pitched their city to homeowners associations representing outlying tract developments with names like Mulford Gardens, Fairmont Terrace, Hesperian Gardens, and Hillcrest Knoll. George Thompson explained during the 1949 campaign to convince Foothill Manor residents to annex themselves to San Leandro that they could "enjoy local city government, by becoming a part of San Leandro, without an additional cash cost to the family budget." City Manager Wes McClure made elaborate presentations to group after group of homeowners, highlighting the city's low tax rate, good schools, and reliable services. Through annexation, San Leandro doubled in size during the 1950s, extending the philosophy and benefits of homeowner populism deeper and deeper into southern Alameda County. By the end of the 1960s the city's population stood at just over 68,000—more than half a dozen outlying communities had annexed to San Leandro during the previous decade and a half.[25]

San Leandro was touted in both local and national planning and development circles in the 1960s as a "model municipality." It modeled to the nation a combination of fiscal conservatism and racial exclusivity that made the city's property markets and industry the envy of Bay Area cities. "Since 1947 some 600 companies have moved to town," gushed the *Wall Street Journal* in its effusive 1966 article celebrating San Leandro, "adding some $200 million in property to the tax roles." Articulating a cornerstone of postwar U.S. ideology, the *Journal* even argued that the city was successful because "it hasn't been forced to absorb a heavy influx of minority groups and unskilled workers." In a cultural construction of far-reaching implications, the *Journal* presented racial diversity as self-evidently bad for business. In San Leandro, industry paid the taxes, the federal government guaranteed mortgages, and racial exclusivity confined this industrial garden to whites only. With homeowner populism elevated to a civic creed, San Leandrans had made the California industrial garden a national model.[26]

Milpitas: "The Neighborhood Where Democracy Lives"

Public officials and homeowners in other East Bay cities hoped to duplicate San Leandro's achievements. In Milpitas, a brand-new suburb in 1955 of several thousand residents on the northern edge of Santa Clara

County near San Jose, local civic founders held up San Leandro as a model of industrial and residential growth. But Milpitas homeowners and city-builders produced a set of social and political relationships distinct from those in San Leandro. Milpitas shared with San Leandro a local political culture shaped by issues of property. Segregation, however, was contested from the beginning. The emerging racial geographies of postwar Oakland and San Jose intersected in Milpitas. A crossroads suburban community where African American, white/Anglo, and ethnic Mexican communities lived and worked in close proximity, Milpitas never practiced racial segregation in the manner of San Leandro. Instead, local residents, especially United Automobile Workers (UAW) activists, pushed for racial democracy and integration, linked to a liberalism centered on consumption and homeownership. While not totally defeated, their efforts were ultimately contained, a process that sheds light on the extent of the suburban East Bay's investment in segregation and the enormous efforts required to fight it.[27]

The story began in 1954, when city-builders incorporated Milpitas at the urging of the Ford Motor Company. Ford executives wanted industrial property owned by the Western Pacific Railroad along the Oakland Highway as a site to build their newest West Coast manufacturing plant to replace their aging one in Richmond. Eager to do business with a small, undeveloped community rather than nearby San Jose, Ford encouraged local leaders to incorporate as a chartered city before the larger, expansion-minded neighbor to the south could annex the Western Pacific property. By enlarging West Coast production with automated, state-of-the-art factories that offered direct access to California's booming automobile market, Ford and the other major automakers hoped to reduce costs and tap the state's extraordinary postwar growth and consumer might. Eager to acquire the Ford plant and the generous tax base that it promised, five civic activists—a real estate developer, a rancher, a restaurateur, the owner of a mobile home park, and a newspaper publisher—pushed for the incorporation election that created Milpitas. This marriage of Milpitas and Ford produced what one city planning report called "an arrested community meets the twentieth century," an instant industrial city set against an agricultural past. It was also, as its founders well knew, an inflationary market in local industrial and residential property with a guaranteed tax base and four thousand new jobs.[28]

A local observer of the Milpitas transition warned, however, "that there would be a problem in absorbing Negroes." Ford's cramped and outdated Richmond factory north of Oakland employed two thousand workers, 25 percent of whom were African American. These workers lived in the black communities along the bayshore flatlands of Richmond, South Berkeley, and West Oakland. Housing open to black occupancy in suburban communities south of San Leandro in this era was scarce. There were some African American homeowners in the older Fairview section of Hayward and in the unincorporated, industrial community of Russell City, enclaves designated by local real estate brokers for black residency. Housing in the latter dated to well before the war, had poor running water, and remained in a constant state of disrepair. Ethnic Mexicans, too, found their residential options limited to marginal land and older housing stock. The existence of *colonias*, prewar residential communities of Mexican immigrants and Mexican Americans scattered throughout the East Bay corridor, meant that a greater variety of housing options was available to the large Mexican-origin communities in Alameda and Santa Clara counties. But *colonias*, especially in unincorporated districts, experienced problems endemic to aging working-class neighborhoods across the nation: absentee landlords, few, if any, services or amenities (including sidewalks and paved streets), overcrowding, and constant threats of removal and redevelopment.[29]

This deplorable housing situation in the early 1950s prompted action from the union at Ford. The UAW's Richmond Local 560 was small by UAW standards but boasted a strong African American leadership corps and a left-liberal orientation. Ben Gross, chairman of Local 560's Housing Committee and a leader of the black caucus within the union, anticipated the housing shortage in Milpitas, a shortage he perceived as temporary for white workers but more permanent for black employees. Determined not to reproduce "ghetto" life in the suburbs, Gross and William Oliver, national director of the Fair Practices and Anti-Discrimination Department of the UAW, conceived a plan for a private, interracial, cooperative housing development, named Sunnyhills, to be located three miles from the new Ford plant. Absent such a development, "those brothers and sisters who work side by side with us in our plants," Gross wrote in the union newsletter, would "be forced to live in the least desirable areas, in the slums and ghettos."[30]

The forces driving suburban development in the East Bay, especially the real estate industry, would make every effort to crush this incipient integration. Before a single new home could be built on Sunnyhills property, the UAW was challenged by local developers who hoped to define the area's racial geography. Gross, Oliver, and, from afar, Walter Reuther engaged in what Oliver called "a great struggle" with the San Lorenzo Homes Company, developer of an all-white adjacent housing tract. San Lorenzo Homes had become one of the dominant housing developers in the East Bay by building racially restricted developments during and immediately after the war. Its flagship community was San Lorenzo, a racially restricted postwar suburb of five thousand homes and seventeen thousand residents sitting on unincorporated land just south of San

Leandro. With an immense investment in the whiteness of East Bay housing markets, San Lorenzo Homes worked tenaciously to prevent the construction of Sunnyhills. Using its contacts and influence with government agencies, San Lorenzo tried to block county permits for the UAW's interracial project. They intervened at Wells Fargo Bank to prevent a loan allowing the union's developer to purchase the land. And they denied Sunnyhills access to drainage facilities that the company controlled at a nearby site. The developer was also able to compel from the county a sanitation ordinance that forced housing prices at Sunnyhills up by 25 percent. Having stalled the UAW's efforts with these backroom pressures, San Lorenzo Homes came forward with a public offer to finance a "Negroes-only" housing tract behind the Ford plant—literally on the other side of the railroad tracks. San Lorenzo was determined to force segregation onto the landscape in the form of what Gross called a "high wall of prejudice, bigotry, and intolerance."[31]

Local 560 responded with a boycott of San Lorenzo Homes and intense public efforts, assisted by the American Friends Service Committee (AFSC), to win the support of the County Board of Supervisors. In this campaign, Gross and Oliver drew on the emerging statewide coalition of racial liberals that C. L. Dellums and Tarea Hall Pittman were working to cement. Oliver convinced the then-state attorney general, and later governor, Pat Brown, to intervene on behalf of the union. This won the union a hearing with the county. In that 1955 appearance, union representatives were joined by spokespeople from the AFSC, the San Jose Council for Civic Unity, the San Jose Council of Churches, and the local Democratic Party. Persuaded by the arguments of those groups, and by a letter-writing campaign among AFL and CIO locals organized by Oliver, the board approved the project. Meanwhile, enough white members resolutely observed the union's grassroots boycott of San Lorenzo Homes that sales of those lots dropped to almost nil. In a stunning turn of events, a frustrated San Lorenzo Homes offered the union sixty-three completed but unsold homes and seventy-three vacant engineered lots. The union accepted, and in late 1955, almost a year after the Ford plant had begun turning out automobiles, Sunnyhills opened as an interracial cooperative, its homes priced at a modest $10,500 (nothing down for veterans, $50 per month; $850 down for nonveterans, $53 per month).[32]

San Lorenzo's efforts to defeat Sunnyhills underscores the deep investment of the real estate industry in segregation. In the 1950s, before changes in federal housing policy and the Civil Rights Act of 1968, desegregation threatened the financial foundation of home building, because FHA and VA programs had virtually eliminated lending for mixed-race developments. Further, the universally accepted rationalization for segregation—that mixed-race communities depressed property values—circulated within the industry as an unchallenged truism. "That the entry of Non-Caucasian into districts where distinctly Caucasian residents live tends to depress real estate values," a prominent real estate textbook writer and member of the National Association of Real Estate Boards (NAREB) wrote in *Real Estate Subdivisions*, "is agreed to by practically all real estate subdividers and students of city life and growth." That this statement was false in all of its particulars did not inhibit the NAREB from asserting the claim as proven fact. In addition to its investment in segregation, behind San Lorenzo's opposition to Sunnyhills lay the real estate industry's constant quest for market control. The rhetoric of "free" markets espoused by groups like the NAREB belied their real objective: *industry* control over where particular groups of people lived, a key element in the manipulation of markets to maximize profits. Sunnyhills threatened the industry's use of segregation to generate the highest possible returns on land and its control over local housing markets, drawing San Lorenzo's vehement objection.[33]

Its victory over San Lorenzo Homes complete, the UAW promoted Sunnyhills as the Bay Area's "neighborhood where democracy lives," welcoming buyers of all backgrounds into "a truly enlightened development with equal opportunity for all." The visual rhetoric of Sunnyhills featured multiracial groups of children and mixed-race public spaces, in striking contrast to the racially homogenous white images that were ubiquitous in 1950s' real estate advertisements and promotion. In this context, something as simple as a black man and a white man in friendly conversation over a lawnmower represented a subversive rendering of suburban ritual. This kind of iconography, in which the consumption values of the American Dream were linked to "community democracy" and racial harmony, provided an alternative to the dominant segregationist vision promoted by suburban developers like San Lorenzo Homes, in which "democracy" and consumption stood for the right of property owners to limit residency to whites. Local 560 and the UAW International had captured in the mid-1950s the kind of faith in racially mixed spaces and democratic patterns of consumption that progressives in California had begun to push. As Oliver explained to reporters in 1956, "[w]e feel this development will give our union and other people across the nation a chance to uphold our philosophy that people who work together can live together and play together."[34]

Sunnyhills challenged questions of race and property at the core of U.S. social policy in the 1950s and resolved them in a laborite homeowner populism that would have profound implications for the city's future. The Ford workers—African American, white, and a few ethnic Mexican—who filled up the modest "garden-set" ranch-style homes of Sunnyhills in the late 1950s were determined to prove that multiracial residential developments did not adversely affect property values or produce "social tension" but actually nurtured a sense of community mission. The core group of Local 560 activists integrated the local Methodist Church and helped to build Weller Grammar School into a model of multiracial education and parent involvement. But racial democracy was only one element of Local 560's vision. The union built its new hall in the middle of the Sunnyhills development and opened it regularly for community gatherings, fund-raisers, town meetings, political speeches, traveling civil rights figures, and the Sunnyhills Community Breakfast on the first Sunday of every month. Gross and a handful of other Ford workers founded the local Democratic Club, the city's most influential political group for forty years, and threw themselves into civic affairs and a wide range of activities, including political office. To all of these endeavors, Local 560's core group, and Gross in particular, brought a political orientation that emphasized the responsibilities of workers and homeowners to their community and the small-d, average-person democracy possible in a community the size of Milpitas (27,000 in 1970). An extraordinarily optimistic vision, the UAW's housing development and commitment to Milpitas represented the apotheosis of the California CIO generation's belief in and efforts to desegregate both work and neighborhood.[35]

For all of its promise of suburban racial democracy, however, Sunnyhills did not become the wedge for open housing in the East Bay that union activists hoped. By 1962 Sunnyhills had a 15 percent African American occupancy rate, but it never climbed much higher, even as Ford's workforce grew. Further, adjoining real estate developers remained unswayed. A few tracts in Milpitas practiced open selling, but through the 1960s almost no black workers found housing outside of the union-sponsored development. East Palo Alto, an unincorporated area on the edge of upper-middle-class Palo Alto across the bay, became one of the only places where working-class African Americans could find housing. Only about half of Ford's African American employees in 1955 were skilled workers who earned wages near the top of the UAW scale. Among these were the core group of union activists led by Gross, many of whom lived in Sunnyhills. An equal number of Ford's black workers, however, labored in less-favored low-wage jobs, enjoyed much lower seniority, and could not afford even the modestly priced homes in Local 560's development. Confined to the region's most marginal and restricted housing, these workers lived in East Palo Alto, West Oakland, and Russell City, or continued to commute by car pool from Richmond. In a nation in which less than 1 percent of new housing built between 1935 and 1952 went to nonwhite families, Sunnyhills was, as the union boasted, a unique, much-needed beacon of hope and a compelling liberal vision of the transformative possibilities of open housing. But it could not by itself remap the racial segregation produced in the East Bay in the 1950s.[36]

Throughout the nation, real estate interests, public officials, and home-owners developed in the postwar decades a set of legal practices that enforced racial segregation and a set of discursive strategies that encouraged public discussion to proceed as if this was not the case. Because FHA and VA mortgage programs *defined* black and mixed-race communities as unable to participate until the early 1960s—the UAW formed a cooperative and avoided most, though not all, complications with FHA financing—suburban homebuyers came to believe that their communities should be entirely white. The East Bay city-building process demonstrates how deliberate and intentional this segregation was. Once embedded in local housing markets, however, the structure of segregation was enclosed within a language of private rights and free markets deployed throughout the real estate industry to cover patterns of racial exclusion in buying and selling. Market discourses thus functioned to encourage suburbanites to think of their housing decisions as racially innocent, involving only issues of property value and property rights. In this way, over time both the structure of housing markets and the public discourse about them worked to divorce individual white decisions from their actual consequences in the perpetuation of social inequality and white privilege.[37]

Whereas San Leandro's civic boosters had constructed the "balanced industrial landscape" envisioned in the Metropolitan Oakland Area Program, Milpitas remained for decades dependent entirely on Ford. With only a single major employer, the Milpitas City Council and city manager enjoyed little flexibility in setting the property tax rate. Lacking other sizable industrial employers, and encumbered with residential developments targeted at moderate-income Ford workers, property valuation did not increase in Milpitas at the same extraordinary rate as in San Leandro, making it doubly difficult for the city to reduce taxes and compete with its East Bay neighbors for new investment. Compounding these factors, Western Pacific Railroad owned most of the industrial land in Milpitas but after winning the Ford plant in the early 1950s proved unable to attract another major employer. Public officials in Milpitas complained in the late 1950s and early 1960s that Western Pacific had done little to boost the city's employment and tax base and that the city's reliance on Ford was dangerous and untenable in the long run. Dependent on two powerful corporate entities, Ford and Western Pacific, with their own economic agendas and facing their own economic pressures, Milpitas homeowner populists enjoyed less leverage than their counterparts in San Leandro.[38]

Nevertheless, like their compatriots in San Leandro, Milpitas residents forged their politics in the cauldron of property tax disputes. An attempted annexation by San Jose was the defining event in solidifying the city's homeowner populism. In 1960 a group of homeowners calling themselves "Citizens for Milpitas" fought San Jose's efforts to absorb the smaller city and acquire the highly valuated Ford plant for its tax base. San Jose had since the early 1950s been annexing outlying industrial and residential properties, much as the smaller San Leandro had done. Citizens for Milpitas opposed annexation to San Jose on two grounds: that it would increase property taxes on homeowners and that it would threaten local control by placing municipal government in the hands of people who had never lived in Milpitas. Calling annexation "taxation without representation," opponents painted San Jose, in great California tradition, as a greedy "octopus" whose outreaching tentacles engorged the central head. At packed meetings in schools, local housing developments, and the UAW hall, representatives of Citizens for Milpitas laid out in detail the per capita tax base of each city, arguing that with a small population and the Ford factory, Milpitas homeowners enjoyed a tax burden considerably smaller than that in San Jose, a larger, older city with declining infrastructure, lower industrial valuation per capita, and larger numbers of low-income residents. This combination of direct economic appeals and populist iconography—the octopus was how nineteenth-century California progressives had famously represented railroad monopolies—reinforced the small property holder's faith on which Milpitas developments like Sunnyhills had been founded. When they turned annexation back by a margin of more than three to one, Milpitas residents celebrated. Their sense of themselves as homeowners, and of Milpitas as *their* little piece of controlled civic space, had been confirmed.[39]

Ben Gross and a number of other UAW activists emerged from the 1960 annexation fight as the city's most outspoken advocates of low taxes and the rights of homeowners. As pioneers of Milpitas's residential housing tracts, Gross and his colleagues had long fashioned their democratic rhetoric in terms of property, taxes, and homeowner amenities. Indeed, the translation of the UAW's labor liberalism into homeowner populism may have been a more lasting contribution to Milpitas's political culture than Local 560's racial liberalism. During the 1960 annexation battle, Local 560's newspaper, *Plant Slants*, was filled with weekly appeals to defeat the "octopus" San Jose in order to keep property taxes low and avoid consolidation with "a large modern community with tax and financial pains." Local 560's Democratic Club went door-to-door that year registering new voters with the double intent of electing John F. Kennedy president and defeating annexation. Local 560 consistently supported liberal social programs at the federal level, and health, welfare, and unemployment insurance at the state level (major spending programs all), but in local politics the union, encouraged by the structure of property taxes, placed community-centered financial interests in the foreground.

In this emerging political geography, Local 560 and the Milpitas Democratic Club saw San Jose, with its host of "financial pains," as an enemy of their working-class city. As the local newspaper put it in 1964, "it *pays* to live in Milpitas."[40]

Two years after turning back San Jose's annexation bid, Gross ran for city council with a slate of neighborhood activists, veterans of Citizens for Milpitas, who called for lower taxes, more industry, the elimination of blight, and collective bargaining rights for city employees. Gross won a seat and four years later, in 1966, was elected mayor, a position he held through the early part of the succeeding decade. Local news stories celebrated his role in solidifying the homeowner populism called forth in the 1960 annexation battle. Gross was seen as a dedicated homeowner and community activist who had been crucial in standing up to San Jose to maintain the independence of Milpitas property owners. Integrationists in the tradition of the progressive wing of the UAW, Gross and other Sunnyhills activists embodied the promise of postwar racial liberalism. They had helped to make their neighborhood a standard of open housing, and Gross himself had carved a place in local politics. But the resistance to the kind of world Gross and his UAW colleagues imagined was deep in the suburban East Bay. For all of Gross's activism, the industrial garden in which Sunnyhills had been forged remained an exception to broader regional patterns of racial inequality. As Ford and Milpitas both grew during the 1960s, new subdivisions encircled Sunnyhills and filled former farms and orchards with all-white neighborhoods. Isolated and contained, the Sunnyhills liberal experiment looked by the end of that decade more and more like an island in a much larger sea.[41]

Fremont and the Dilemmas of Growth

City building in San Leandro and Milpitas yielded two versions of the suburban industrial garden. A third, competing version emerged in Fremont, southern Alameda County's largest suburban community and eventual home of northern California's biggest automobile plant, a six-thousand-employee General Motors factory that opened in 1965. Incorporated a decade earlier, in 1956, Fremont became the county's most elaborately planned city. Its founders, an eclectic group of political entrepreneurs and landholders, envisioned a coordinated series of neighborhoods linked by broad boulevards and ample green space. Industry would, as in San Leandro and Milpitas, provide the tax base and support city services. But Fremont's homeowners and city-builders expressed neither the progrowth, industry-friendly, tax-savvy élan of San Leandro, nor the working-class, homeowning everyman ideology of Milpitas autoworkers.

Fremont's founders decried "runaway growth," kept local developers in close check, and designed a community that for many years was affordable only for the region's managerial and professional classes. The results stirred controversy. Imagined as a planned community of controlled growth, Fremont's very success became in the 1960s a source of political discord, as the city's middle-class homeowners faced challenges from both developers and working-class activists. "We're going to wind up with the most beautiful ghost town in the west," a frustrated developer told the local newspaper.[42]

In between San Leandro and Milpitas lay all of the remaining unincorporated, undeveloped land in Alameda County west of the hills, what was known as "South County" (map 3.1). Impelled by the zero-sum logic of intercity competition, city builders there scrambled to divide up hundreds of square miles of farmland and rolling hills, a bonanza of potential factory and home sites, in a series of annexation and incorporation contests in the 1950s. In the suburban city-building environment of that decade, popular doctrine held that all available, potentially profitable land would eventually be incorporated. Property left unclaimed by one city would be annexed by a competing neighbor. The resulting land rush, one of the most ferocious anywhere in postwar California, produced in a few short years three altogether new cities—Newark, Union City, and the sprawling Fremont—and an enlarged, reinvigorated older city, Hayward. In all, between 1951 and 1957, competitive incorporation and annexation converted Alameda County's prewar agricultural hinterland into a collection of cities bigger than Los Angeles (map 3.2). As in San Leandro and Milpitas, these contests turned on fundamental questions of class, racial geography, and competing visions of the rights and responsibilities of property owners.[43]

Fremont's development offers a window on this process of land competition in South County and a view of the class contradictions latent within suburban city building. Two factors in the early 1950s gave rise to the incorporation movement in what became Fremont: disaffection with the County Planning Commission and Hayward's aggressive annexation. Homeowners, small businesses, and a handful of civic activists from five rural communities had grown impatient with the County Planning Commission's lack of a concrete vision for the unincorporated land between Hayward and the Santa Clara County line—tens of thousands of acres. Local gripes and individual complaints found a formal champion in the *Township Register*, the editor of which explained in 1952 that "this township wants its master plan and wants it in a hurry—before shacks overrun our industrial land, before factories are jammed against our homes." At the same time, Hayward's southward extension worried landowners in Washington Township, the county unit containing all five communities,

who saw in that city's expansion a threat to local autonomy and a siphoning of tax revenue to serve population centers in the northern part of
the county. Between 1951 and 1956 Hayward had doubled its land area,
from five to ten square miles, and seemed poised to reach even farther
into South County. Wary of Hayward and frustrated with the planning
commission, the Chambers of Commerce of the five communities organized
local homeowners, landowners, and businesses into an incorporation
movement. By 1955 the Fremont Citizens' Committee had neatly encap-
sulated their philosophy in a question printed on their campaign flyers:
"Home rule? Or high taxes dictated by non-residents?" Proponents of
incorporation cast themselves as modern day American revolutionaries
who sought to protect their communities from unjust taxation by establishing "home rule." It was to be, literally, the rule of the *home*.[44]

Homeowner politics in Fremont combined an emphasis on low taxes
with disdain for "runaway growth," a potent political mix. A small group
of petty bourgeois entrepreneurs and professionals managed Fremont's
incorporation campaign. Local ranchers were prominent in the effort, as
were small businessmen (the chairman of the Committee for the Incorporation of Fremont, Wally Pond, was a local druggist), but the various
incorporation committees included judges, insurance agents, orchardists,
newspaper editors, and engineers. Some among the founders had clear
speculative economic interests in incorporation—a few ranchers and
orchardists, for instance, could expect to receive high prices for land once
the city was established—but the majority identified themselves as
"homeowners" or "taxpayers" and articulated vague and idealistic notions
of what was "best for the community." Still, incorporation finally came
down to a more specific issue—taxes. "We want to see you aren't taxed
one cent more than you need to be," a representative of the Alameda
County Taxpayers Association told Wally Pond and the Committee for
the Incorporation of Fremont.[45]

"Home rule" meant more than lower taxes to Fremont's populist insurgents. It also meant control of development and a "balanced" suburban
landscape. When the County Planning Commission offered to rezone
"1,500 acres of swamp and sugar beets" to accommodate an industrial
park, the *Register* editorialized that such obeisance to industry "destroys
the balance of the area" by setting up "industrial islands . . . whether the
neighbors like it or not." Only incorporation, and home rule, could keep
the County Planning Commission's mistakes from ruining South County,
the editors warned. Fremont's incorporation would return the "balanced
concept of a city, one where homes, factories and stores, parks (and farms,
for a time at least) all have equal place." The MOAP architects could not
have said it better. This combination of a desire for low taxes and a conser-
vationist view of local development, forged into the small-property-holder

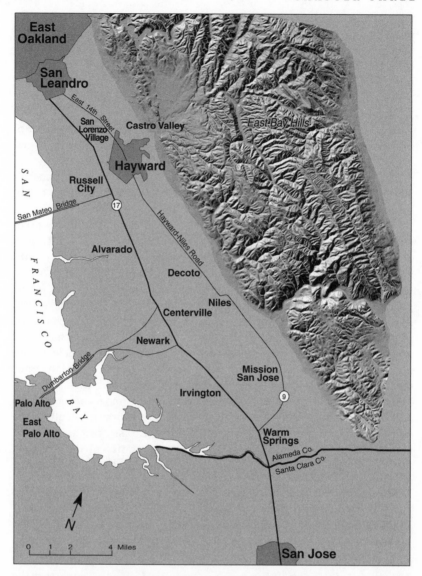

Map 3.1. Alameda County in the late 1940s. Between Oakland and San Jose, only San Leandro and Hayward existed as corporate cities. This vast landscape of unincorporated farmland, orchards, and cattle ranches would in two decades become suburbanized "South County." The place names indicate existing towns, which themselves were part of townships, the county's primary unit of administration. Cartography Lab, University of Wisconsin.

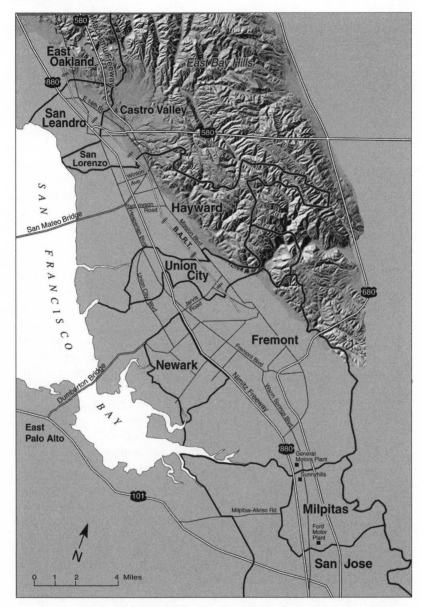

Map 3.2. Suburban Alameda County in the 1960s. The dark lines indicate new municipal boundaries. Between 1945 and 1958 all of the available unincorporated land between Oakland and San Jose, west of the hills, was incorporated into existing or altogether new cities. Only San Lorenzo and Castro Valley, bedroom communities with no industry, resisted this process. Altogether, it was an extraordinary land rush with few equals in California. Cartography Lab, University of Wisconsin.

faith of homeowner populism, became the founding philosophy of Fremont. The township's residents voted overwhelmingly in favor of incorporation in January 1956.[46]

Fremont's political founders were determined that the city would grow slowly without the usual deference to developers. With ample green space, solid housing, and just enough industry, properly separated from residential districts, to supply the tax base, Fremont would become a model garden city. Its planning commission, composed of avowed slow-growth champions from among the proponents of incorporation, envisioned a community of "planned unit developments," coherent neighborhoods with homes built around parks, schools, and community centers. Planned unit developments had emerged in the 1950s as the national planning profession's answer to suburban sprawl, promising greenbelts and pedestrian-friendly geography. To secure their vision, Fremont's founders produced a much-celebrated and relatively novel "general plan" for the city. Urban planning experimentation found an ideal home in Fremont, which after incorporation embraced an enormous ninety-six square miles (almost twice the size of San Francisco), making it California's third largest city behind Los Angeles and San Diego. Nearly 40 percent of that was bay, marshland, and salt ponds, but the remaining 60 percent included vast stretches of farmland, orchards, ranches, vacant fields, and rolling hills. In 1955 only twenty thousand people lived in this expansive area. Fremont had sequestered one hundred square miles of property within a jurisdiction controlled by low-tax, slow-growth advocates determined to place firm reins on development. It was a planner's paradise.[47]

But rather than uniting the new community, Fremont's "general plan" sparked political fires and set the founding group of civic activists against local developers. Based on the prescriptions of the plan, Fremont's planning commission denied dozens of building permit requests by developers and turned down four large housing subdivisions. The commission's strict adherence to what many assumed was a theoretical document incensed the development community, but the general plan was but one thorn in the side of the city's builders. The commission enforced three other controversial policies that raised the costs of building in Fremont. First, they increased the city's minimum housing lot size from five thousand to six thousand square feet. Second, they required developers to cede to the city a percentage of every developed property to ensure sufficiently wide streets—like many Sunbelt cities, Fremont planned for extra-wide boulevards to ease traffic congestion. Third, when a speculative developer charged the local school district twelve thousand dollars per acre for a school site after paying only four thousand, the commission adopted even stricter guidelines on building permits and required "fair prices" on all public property transactions. Accustomed to civic cooperation, if not kowtowing, zoning loopholes, and generous profit margins, local developers grew perplexed by and hostile to the general plan and the planning commission. The conversion of property into profit, of land into capital, would proceed in Fremont under the strictest rules that homeowner populists and city-builders had achieved in the San Francisco Bay area.[48]

These strategies kept developers at one arm's length and working-class residents at another. Over the course of the 1960s the general plan alienated both groups. Initial opposition came from developers. "Proplan" and "antiplan" coalitions formed for each local election between 1958 and 1962. Proplan forces won decisively in 1960 and 1962, after which they controlled the city council for more than a decade. The leading opponent of the plan was Jack Brooks, a local builder whose company was responsible for housing one-fifth of the city's residents. Rumblings of discontent could also be heard, however, in older working-class districts along the new city's fringes. In Niles, a community of working families on the far northern edge of Fremont a few blocks from the Pacific States Steel plant in Union City, Mexican American residents and the United Steelworkers local opposed the plan, believing that it and the commission's decisions in the late 1950s had ignored improvements in these existing neighborhoods in favor of directing resources and civic amenities to the newer, more central commercial and middle-class residential subdivisions. Support for the plan, and the conservative approach of the planning commission, was strongest among homeowners in two new housing tracts near the center of Fremont, Mission Ranch and Glenmoore Gardens. Here residents often spoke of the commission and the city council as defenders of "the people" against cynical developers and other landholders who sought to manipulate property "for their own special welfare." These spatial and class fissures—which seemed to bring developers into an odd alliance with blue-collar families living in older housing stock—went unresolved for more than a decade.[49]

Undeterred by criticism, plan advocates claimed that the city's stringent zoning and careful planning had made possible Fremont's selection in late 1960 as the site of a new General Motors production plant. In December of that year, GM promised the massive facility to Fremont, jilting its cross-bay rival, Sunnyvale. Local planners had long known that the city would require an industrial tax base. The original 1956 general plan estimated that an industrial payroll of sixteen thousand workers was necessary for a city the size of Fremont, with a projected population of one hundred thousand. A year later, the News Register warned that only "intelligent planning" and "the importation of industry, to provide jobs and balance the assessment roll with factories" would safeguard the city's future. When GM announced its decision to build a state-of-the-art production plant employing more than four thousand workers in the southern

Figure 3.3. The largest automobile plant in Northern California, operated by General Motors, opened in 1964 thirty miles south of Oakland in Fremont. The vast stretches of open farmland and orchards would within a decade be covered with new housing subdivisions, part of the spectacular growth of suburban California in the 1960s. Courtesy of the *Oakland Tribune.*

industrial zone of the city, plan loyalists could rightly point to their rational approach to growth as reason for the coup. The Southern Pacific Railroad Company, which owned the land and sold it to GM, benefited enormously when Fremont incorporated and the planning commission zoned hundreds of acres of property along SP tracks, former farmland, for heavy industry.[50]

Civic leaders had made Fremont an attractive investment for GM's strategy of national decentralization. The auto company had operated a small factory in East Oakland on MacArthur Boulevard since the 1930s. Without space for expansion, and burdened with an aging and outdated production regime, GM Oakland closed in favor of the new Fremont facility, sending jobs and tax revenue south to the suburbs. When the plant was dedicated in early 1964, its payroll exceeded twenty-four million dollars. Governor Pat Brown, the president of General Motors, Fremont's mayor, and a throng of local political figures, boosters, and businesspeople celebrated the opening of the plant with the kind of civic fanfare, speeches, luncheons, and photo opportunities reserved in this era for rocket launches. The gist of the festivities: General Motors guaranteed Fremont's future. A short two years later, the plant employed 5,400 workers with a payroll of forty-two million dollars and a line of cars that included Buicks, Oldsmobiles, Pontiacs, Chevelles, and GMC trucks. The city's mayor buoyantly declared: "There's no question about it. Fremont has arrived."[51]

Fremont's "arrival," however, produced a spatial landscape in which the idealized proximities and class harmony of the industrial garden went unrealized. Rapid property speculation within the vast new city drove land and housing prices up, as did strict enforcement of the general plan. Developers built enormous subdivisions and sold thousands of homes to a narrow range of middle-class families. Residents of these tracts, especially Glenmore Gardens and Mission Ranch, where homes sold for between $19,000 and $29,000, formed the backbone of the "proplan" coalition. In the general plan's prescriptions for ample green space, parks, and controls on growth and development, these homeowners found their values reflected and protected. But as the city's population increased through the 1960s (from 43,000 to just over 100,000 in 1970) and the General Motors workforce grew apace (from about 4,000 in 1964 to 6,100 in 1969), observers and critics noted that surprisingly few workers seemed to live in the city. Commuting from East Oakland, San Jose, Milpitas, East Palo Alto, Santa Clara, Redwood City, Hayward, and other communities within the Bay Area, GM workers streamed in and out of the plant's massive parking lot at each shift change. "We're creating a beautiful city where most of our workers cannot afford to live," Jack Brooks told the *Fremont News Register* in 1967. By 1970, out of a total population of just over one hundred thousand, not even four hundred African Americans lived in the city; the median income ($11,933) was higher than in any other city in Alameda County and almost twice that in Oakland; and the median housing price was the highest in the county.[52]

The shortage of working-class housing had long been an issue in Fremont. In 1957 Kroehler Furniture, a firm moving to Fremont from Pittsburgh, Pennsylvania, wrote to the Chamber of Commerce complaining about the lack of affordable housing. Kroehler employees could not afford homes retailing for more than eleven thousand dollars, an extremely low ceiling in Fremont. A survey conducted by the Associated Homebuilders of the East Bay in 1964 criticized the general plan for forcing up the costs of building and thus the price of homes. One quarter of the developers surveyed indicated that the lack of affordable housing for workers was the city's principal problem. A report to the city manager in 1967 by the president of the Fremont City Employees Association claimed that 62 percent of Fremont city employees could not afford to purchase a home in the city. A subsequent study by the *Fremont News Register* confirmed that the least expensive houses in Fremont in 1967 were priced at twenty thousand dollars, with mortgage payments out of the reach of workers making less than ten thousand dollars a year. "The fact is," Jack Brooks explained, "this city has no real correlation between housing and industrial development."[53]

The unlikely alliance between working-class activists and property developers in Fremont took its most public form in 1966. That year, a "Committee for Change" ran candidates against two incumbent "proplan" councilmembers. Billed as an "economy slate," the challengers argued that Fremont "must aggressively seek industrial development" and "cut the tax rate for the homeowner." The insurgents claimed that under the "proplan" administration, the costs of city services had increased, but the slow growth philosophy of the council had chased industry away and kept developers handcuffed. Teamster Dave Latham, running as a "working man," joined the chorus of criticism, telling the incumbent mayor that "industry has constantly turned its back on Fremont." Veteran "proplan" spokespersons, and Fremont founders, countered that the "builder-subdivider political slate," if elected, would bring uncontrolled industrial and residential development to the city, exactly what the general plan had been designed to prevent. In the end, one incumbent won and the other was defeated. The proplan council majority held, setting the stage for additional rounds of attacks by both developers and homeowners in subsequent years. But the election had showcased the narrow range of civic debate—and the centrality of taxes and development to local political discourse—while demonstrating how fierce the conflicts could be within that consensus.[54]

The complaints of workers like Dave Latham and developers like Jack Brooks exaggerated the city's stagnation, but Fremont's critics did not lack evidence that the bloom on the industrial garden had begun to wilt. Fremont more than doubled both its population and its production workforce between 1960 and 1970. During that decade the city remained decidedly working class, with over half of its residents employed in trades, clerical work, and as operatives or laborers. Nevertheless, in relation to other East Bay cities, especially San Leandro, Fremont was a more expensive place to live and had fewer industrial jobs and industrial establishments. With a median income somewhere in the middle among Alameda County suburbs in 1960, by 1970 the median and average incomes in Fremont were higher than in any other East Bay city save the professional suburban enclave of Castro Valley. Housing prices, too, were higher. By 1970 families paid more for homes in Fremont than in any other East Bay city. Moreover, while the city had grown, it lagged behind the region's model industrial community, San Leandro, by a considerable margin. Despite its notable success in acquiring the General Motors facility, Fremont in 1972 still had one-third the total number of production plants of San Leandro and about half the number of production jobs. All of this in a city with a population one and a half times that of San Leandro. Finally, Fremont's relative lack of industrial property translated into higher property taxes for homeowners. By the early 1970s Fremont homeowners were paying local property taxes at a rate 40 percent higher than in San Leandro. Indeed, in 1970 Fremont's total combined tax burden was higher than Oakland's, a negative advertisement for the industrial garden suburb if there ever was one.[55]

Emerging New Region

By the middle of the 1960s, the suburban East Bay corridor from Oakland to San Jose looked like what the Metropolitan Oakland Area Program had envisioned. Homes, factories, and other workplaces had proliferated. Working-class families, managers, and professionals enjoyed the advantages of homeownership and the amenities of suburban living—if not always in the same neighborhoods, at least in close proximity. Property values had increased with the new investment and population. Much of the MOAP's vision for the East Bay had been realized. The 1964 christening of the General Motors plant in Fremont confirmed the strength of the East Bay's industrial capacity and the longevity of the MOAP model two decades after the end of the war. But as coherent as the various spaces of the East Bay landscape could appear, the emerging new region was in reality a set of distinct property and employment markets, tax bases, and zones of affluence, segregated by race and divided by municipal political boundaries. Less visible to the casual observer, especially whites, these geographies produced steep differences in the distribution of economic development's local benefits. They produced development and underdevelopment.

In the rise of the East Bay's industrial suburban corridor in the 1950s and 1960s was a trajectory of metropolitan development that the MOAP had foreseen but hoped to counter—decentralization. The city-level industrial and fiscal policies of San Leandro, Milpitas, Fremont, and Hayward, among others, realized the MOAP's vision of suburban industrialization but set in motion processes that would in time undermine Oakland's own growth and financial viability. The spatial and political integrity of cities proved crucial here. Municipal boundaries were not merely arbitrary markers in a hazy metropolitan "sprawl." They represented important forms of publicly controlled space. Neighborhood associations and Chambers of Commerce could mobilize city governments to lower property taxes, to compete with nearby cities for industrial investment, to erect racial residential barriers, and to plan industrial parks and neatly groomed boulevards—in short, to pursue policies that compromised Oakland's economic stability. In the 1950s and 1960s, Oakland's suburbs did all of these things and would over time shift a disproportionate share of the costs of postwar capitalism to Oakland. The competitive reality of the urban system in the United States, in which cities are locked within the capitalist marketplace, placed limits on the degree of metropolitan coordination. Oakland remained the administrative center of the East Bay, but whatever benefits in job growth accrued to the city as a result could not keep pace with the extraordinary growth in jobs and, especially, taxable property value in its southern suburban periphery.

The emergent classes at the center of this story, city-builders and suburban homeowners of moderate income, invested not simply in new towns and homes but in a cultural-economic compact of national historical significance. The terms of suburban development in the East Bay asked residents to equate economic growth, high property values, low property taxes, and racial segregation with upward mobility. In that compact, homeowners found not just the wealth embodied in home equity but an expression of the value and security embodied in property as a marker of class and racial status. The industrial garden in Alameda County thus rooted in place—indeed, literally in the *space* that city boundaries created—an ideological and political interest bound up in property markets. Homeowners in the suburban East Bay, like their counterparts throughout California and the nation, would act on that interest throughout the postwar decades to limit the financial burdens imposed on their property and to guard against threats—real, imagined, and manipulated—to the value of their property. In doing so, they participated in a regional and ultimately national redistribution of public resources and public responsibility. In simplest terms, the property tax base moved to the suburbs, indeed certain suburbs, while the greater proportion of social problems, and financial responsibility for them, remained in the central city. Suburbanization thus turned on the role of property and development in distributing a social surplus and social debt—the costs and benefits of capitalist economic growth.

Segregation was naturalized among white policymakers as a common-sense dimension of healthy property markets. At the level of federal policy, racial segregation was not understood as an end in itself. Rather, separation of residential districts by race was constructed as necessary to certain kinds of property markets: beginning in the 1930s housing legislation was always conceived as a program of economic stimulus. Equally important, despite the vast, even epochal, subsidies that the federal government poured into the housing market between the 1930s and the

1960s—primarily through the FHA and the VA, but also through tax abatement, interstate highway construction, education legislation, and other programs as well—housing was portrayed throughout the period as a classic free market, untouched by the hand of government. This structural and ideological rationalization of segregation encouraged whites and Anglos in the East Bay—as it did millions of Americans during the postwar decades—to argue that their actions were not *racist*, even as their individual choices and advantages represented, in sum, a version of apartheid with deleterious long-term consequences. The rhetoric of city building in the postwar years also encouraged homeowners to see property taxes as a division of social responsibility in which one's "fair share" was calculated according to local common-sense understandings, including the extent to which tax revenues were under the control of local authorities and subsidized by local industry. In this context, East Bay suburbanites began to develop in these years a neopopulist understanding of themselves and their interests. In subsequent years, this version of populism would be mobilized politically in ways that would perpetuate social inequality.[56]

This chapter has told two overlapping stories, each extraordinarily important to the postwar narrative of Oakland and the East Bay. In the first, suburban entrepreneurs created new investment markets with the assistance of the federal state. The spatial political economies of places like San Leandro, Fremont, and Milpitas were constructed to attract capital and growth—in the form of homeowners, industry, commerce, and the like. In the first two postwar decades, these places offered privileges and advantages to an array of groups, but especially to middle-class, white homeowners. Postwar suburbanization was driven by this development process, not by people "fleeing" Oakland. This East Bay story reaches beyond California to a national dynamic of the second half of the twentieth century: in the frantic competition for private capital investment, cities, trapped in the capitalist marketplace, entered into a savage rivalry with each other, the end result of which was the development of some places and the underdevelopment of others. Second, the postwar suburban compact among the federal state, city-builders, and homeowners lay the groundwork for the emergence of a political identity rooted in homeownership. This identity, and the ideological work done on its behalf, would emerge as a profound force in East Bay and California politics in the 1960s and 1970s. In those decades, that identity would become increasingly parochial and would be mobilized to preserve the suburban "good life" from a range of democratic challenges by excluded groups. Both of these stories take us back to Oakland, because the history and evolution of property markets ensure that as people and capital create places, those places in turn shape the possibilities and opportunities of other places.[57]

Part Two

RACE, URBAN TRANSFORMATION,
AND THE STRUGGLE AGAINST
SEGREGATION, 1954–1966

4

Redistribution

BECAUSE CAPITALISM demands that space be productive, Oakland's civic and business leaders, every bit as much as their counterparts in San Leandro, Milpitas, and Fremont, sought the "best use" of the city's land. "The choice is clear," a city of Oakland report warned in the early 1960s, between "a welter of obsolescence" and a "comprehensive program aimed at reinvigorating our economy and enhancing the livability of our community." Faced with an aging civic infrastructure, blocks and blocks of homes in disrepair, and a steep decline in property values in key parts of the city, Oakland planners and political leaders fretted over their competitive disadvantage with other cities. Beginning in the 1950s they saw in Oakland what Chicago architect John Fugard called a "no man's land which rings the central business district and forms a cancer which is slowly but surely gnawing away." Despite such pessimism, these same planners and politicians believed that the tools of postwar urban design—redevelopment, highways, industrial mechanization, office buildings—would resurrect their declining fortunes. To avoid "obsolescence" and to compete in the national marketplace for capital investment, Oakland's leaders turned to a modernist faith common in American culture in the 1950s and 1960s: a faith in the transcendent power of new technologies and efficiencies, remodeled neighborhoods, physical and social engineering, and management by large and specialized institutions.[1]

The legacies of their efforts can be traced by following the East Bay's new interstate highways, rail lines, and shipping corridors. Among the most visible of these was the Bay Area Rapid Transit (BART) system, a commuter rail line that linked East Bay suburban cities, downtown Oakland, and San Francisco. A resident of Fremont could board a train and arrive hassle free and ready for work in Oakland in thirty minutes, San Francisco in forty-five. Between the mid-1960s and the early 1970s, when trains began running, national periodicals proclaimed BART the apotheosis of modernity and progress. Urban planners showered applause. Journalists adored the sleek, jetlike car design. Even before trains began operating, BART lines cut channels of metropolitan development that defined the region's growth, especially in the suburban East Bay where the bulk of the system's tracks lay. But the biggest winner was downtown San Francisco, where property speculation soared and enormous office buildings rose in the Market Street corridor. San Francisco's emergence in the 1970s as a major West Coast center of banking, finance, and insurance was predicated on BART's capacity to carry thousands of workers from suburban cities to downtown. BART did far less for the working-class neighborhoods in Oakland over which its trains passed in daily commuter surges—surges that stood for the new locations of capital in the region.[2]

As capital and people were set into motion in Oakland and the East Bay in these years, a stunning fact of American political economy was always evident: restoring property values was easier, and a higher priority, than sustaining human communities. Powerful new institutions like BART ordered space in particular ways, but their actions were bound within a longer history of already ordered spaces. BART was one example among many. Beginning in the 1950s a new federal interstate highway system linked the East Bay suburban corridor, and its housing markets and labor pool, with Oakland and San Francisco. Urban renewal in downtown and West Oakland remade the city's oldest districts. Modernization of the port transformed the Oakland waterfront. Each of these features of the emerging Bay Area metropolis intersected with a history that magnified its consequences. Jobs, investment, and taxable wealth left the city. Redevelopment transferred property from residents to private developers. African Americans, displaced by urban renewal, moved into new neighborhoods. Tens of thousands of whites left for the suburbs, others remained in the city but moved away from their black neighbors. Oakland was remade in these decades. The transformation, however, led not out of the contradictions of American urbanism but ever deeper into them.[3]

Oakland was part of a national dialectic. Older American cities after 1945 faced their greatest historical challenge. They were reshaped demographically by the most extensive internal migrations in American history: the migration of southern African Americans to the cities of the Northeast, Midwest, and West and the mass movement of whites to suburban places. At the same time, economic transformation, especially deindustrialization and the rise of a service-oriented economy, eroded and destabilized the blue-collar job ladders erected during the first half of the century—the basis of the Fordist city. American cities adjusted to these multiple challenges by attempting to remake both themselves and their citizens. "Across the nation," *Newsweek* declared in 1959 with booster optimism, "the cities are rebuilding, refurbishing, marching ahead." There is nothing conscious or willful about a city, however. The actual efforts were the combined strategies of governments and property holders across both time and space. While the nature of efforts varied, they never strayed far from two elemental objectives: making property profitable and neighborhoods stable. Attempts to realize these objectives in most American cities, however, and Oakland was no exception, produced new forms of racial segregation and radically unequal patterns of capital investment. They were no accident of history. They were the product of shifting political interests and commitments at the federal, state, and local level and within the institutions that create the markets of urban capitalism. In the end, the power to reengineer the city was diffuse, but the levers remained in the hands of the owners of property.[4]

Urban reengineering redistributed more than jobs and capital; it redistributed social inequalities and the public resources with which to address them. This chapter is about the way Oakland city agencies, the national state, and neighborhood residents managed, ordered, and struggled over urban space after 1950 and the enormous redistribution of resources—people, capital, jobs, and wealth—that followed. Redistribution unites the elements of this chapter and provides a single frame through which to understand the complicated changes of this period. Beginning in West Oakland, the city's oldest neighborhood, we can trace the contours of this narrative and observe in detail the unfolding process of postwar American urban transformation, as declining industrial districts and their working-class residents experienced capital flight, urban renewal, new transportation corridors, displacement, and outmigration. From there, West Oakland offers a vantage on the city as a whole. At once the heart of Oakland's expanding African American community *and* a liminal space through which capital and people flowed to other places, West Oakland came to represent dramatic imbalances in postwar metropolitan development and the massive redistributions shaping the region.

Redeveloping West Oakland

Squeezed on all sides by the structural inequalities of the housing market, West Oakland received none of the enormous capital investment made in residential property in California between 1945 and the 1960s. Trapped on the margins of the private capital and federal subsidy pouring into new home construction, West Oakland's best hope seemed to lie in some form of urban renewal. Almost from the beginning, however, that hope proved ill placed and went unrewarded. In August 1949 West Oakland resident Lola Bell Sims wrote to Harry Truman. "Just now here in Oakland the colored people are much confused and very unhappy," Sims confided to the president, "thinking that they are going to lose their all and all by the U.S. government taking their property by force whether or not they want to give it up." African Americans in Oakland, Sims explained, had saved for years to purchase homes; soldiers sent home their paychecks during the war. And now it appeared that the city of Oakland and the federal government, in a partnership made possible by the Housing Act of 1949, planned to condemn their property, acquire it through eminent

domain, and redevelop vast stretches of the city's principal black neighborhood. To West Oakland residents like Ms. Sims, property ownership
represented "a home where they can have shelter in their old age," but
she recognized that postwar federal urban policy valued such property
insofar as it could be torn down and replaced with something else.[5]

In the decades after World War II, elected officials, downtown business
leaders, and urban planners across the United States turned their attention with renewed vigor to the fate of city centers. The attention gave
homeowners like Ms. Sims reason to worry, because she and a generation
of Jim Crowed African Americans owned or rented homes in the oldest,
most deteriorated sections of the nation's cities, now the targets of
renewal programs attached to ambivalent promises. In the latter half of
the 1940s, declining downtown property values, the effects of wartime
migration on urban services and quality of life, the expansion of neighborhoods identified as "slums" or "blighted," and decaying nineteenth-century
housing stock produced a burst of reportage nationwide calling for the
rehabilitation of American cities. Much of this was implicitly racialized,
as white mayors, city councils, and business leaders from Baltimore to
Chicago, Cleveland to Oakland, worried about black neighborhoods
encroaching on central business districts. At the same time, many white
officials were genuinely concerned with declining health, services, and
safety. Tuberculosis remained a stubborn problem in most poor urban
neighborhoods in the 1950s, many homes lacked proper running water,
and overcrowding, coupled with structural deterioration, made many
older buildings simply dangerous. Whether motivated by racial prejudice
or not, the remedies to which urban America and the federal government
turned in the late 1940s and 1950s, especially redevelopment, threatened
the delicate foothold that black communities had established in the nation's
dual housing market. "I ask you please let the good homes that are suitable
remain," Sims implored Truman, because "the colored people especially
here in Oakland some have their life earnings put in a home." In the remaking of the nation's postwar cities, working-class African Americans
would bear the heaviest burden.[6]

Since the early 1950s Oakland city officials and business leaders had
watched property values decline in the neighborhoods near downtown.
Retail stores lost customers. Poverty in West Oakland took hold of more
and more residents. Between 1955 and 1960 land values in the downtown's
core retail area and central business district declined by an astonishing
50 percent. New centers of shopping had emerged in East Oakland, San
Leandro, El Cerrito, Hayward, and Walnut Creek. Meanwhile, much of
West Oakland, downtown's logical immediate source of consumers, looked
like a slum, with dilapidated housing, overcrowded apartments, and
impoverished residents. "The purchasing power of the area is declining

each year," a banker told the City Planning Commission in 1962. From 1948 to 1962 the retail share of Oakland's downtown out of the East Bay as a whole declined from 18 to 9 percent. Its share of department store sales dropped from 40 to 20 percent. Overall, 24 percent of the city's land was blighted. Halting this centrifugal loss of capital, property value, and middle-income consumers preoccupied the city planning department and downtown property holders like nothing else in the 1950s. Downtown Oakland had been fighting to survive since the Depression, but it faced its fiercest economic threat in what were supposed to be the nation's boom times.[7]

Definitions and public discussions of urban decline, in Oakland as in the nation, were embedded in the history of racial segregation and in class-driven conceptions of urban space. Most local officials and business leaders understood decline as a physical and economic problem, what they termed "blight," rather than as a symptom of social inequality. In this view, blight did not originate in the racial segregation of housing and labor markets or in the unequal distribution of political and economic power, but in the deterioration of aging housing stock, overcrowding, and declining property values. Like cancer, to which it was often rhetorically compared, blight threatened the city as a whole, beginning with the financial interests of downtown property holders. For others, however, especially progressive political leaders, social workers, and liberal urban commentators, the problem was "slum landlords" who kept residents trapped in poor living conditions. For these reformers, urban improvements went hand in hand with public housing and other social services as twin answers to class and racial inequalities in local housing markets. Both understandings of blight and slums, and the deep contradictions between them, found their way into public policy. In 1949 the federal government and the state of California simultaneously passed major renewal legislation that provided funding for local projects and awarded cities broad powers to acquire property, while reserving additional funding for public housing and health and welfare programs. Oakland's Planning Commission designated *all* of West Oakland as "blighted," setting the stage for the city's reconstruction of this working-class, and increasingly African American, set of neighborhoods. Calling their "assault on slum conditions" a "war," Oakland officials sought to free the city from the economic restrictions of blight.[8]

To counteract blight, the Oakland city manager's office turned to a program prescribed nationwide in the 1950s by the federal government and professional urban experts: urban renewal. Renewal in theory embraced a broad set of efforts to revitalize older neighborhoods. In practice, renewal often meant *redevelopment*: denuding neighborhoods of low-income housing and small businesses for the benefit of industry and middle-class homes. City administrators spoke as if renewal and redevelopment were synonymous, but local residents knew the difference between low-interest loans and bulldozers: the former meant restoration and community improvement, the latter symbolized what became widely known nationwide as "Negro Removal." In 1959 the Oakland Redevelopment Agency unveiled its ten-year blueprint for West Oakland, the General Neighborhood Renewal Plan, described by City Manager Wayne Thompson as "the largest project city employees have ever embarked upon." Drawing almost entirely on federal and state funding, the plan promised to clear West Oakland's oldest housing, abandoned factories, and empty warehouses and replace them with middle-income homes and industry. It was to be Oakland's first attempt to remake the physical and social life of the city and its citizens.

Renewal plans drew on the optimistic spirit of the MOAP, but beneath the optimism lay persistent concerns about the city's economic viability in the context of East Bay metropolitanization. According to the Redevelopment Agency, West Oakland neighborhoods required "at least 1100 acres of new industrial land if Oakland is to maintain its regional industrial position, provide jobs for its citizens, and support its economy." Agency officials believed that West Oakland represented the heaviest drag on the city's economy and the logical location for new industry and middle-class housing, but these neighborhoods did not stand alone in renewal calculations. West Oakland redevelopment was one of a series of elaborate projects to rehabilitate the entire downtown area. Along with the Neighborhood Renewal Plan for West Oakland, the City Planning Commission and Redevelopment Agency undertook four additional projects between the late 1950s and early 1960s. East of Lake Merritt, the city would restore approximately fifty blocks of homes and build a new school in an area that was primarily white. West of the lake, the Planning Commission called for the construction of a new junior college. In downtown proper, where Chinese American merchants owned substantial retail property, a new "Chinatown" was planned. And in between West Oakland and downtown, the Corridor-City Center project devoted a seventy-block area to future interstate highway construction, underground lines of the Bay Area Rapid Transit (BART), and a massive office/retail/entertainment complex. This wholesale reinvention of the downtown cityscape—made possible by federal grants that ultimately funded two-thirds of all projects—drew on the financial interests of downtown property holders and the fiscal concerns of city officials, for whom property tax revenue remained the preeminent concern.[9]

According to the city planning department, a redeveloped West Oakland "should be a model of development for other parts of the city." In language reminiscent of the garden city, planners agreed that "the West Oakland

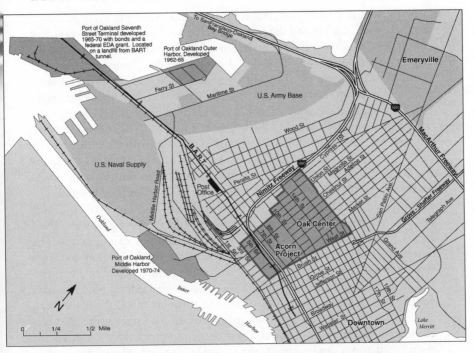

Map 4.1. The reengineering of West Oakland during the 1960s brought massive physical and social changes to the oldest neighborhoods in the city. Redevelopment, new interstate highways, rapid transit, and port modernization together remade the landscape of West Oakland. Cartography Lab, University of Wisconsin.

community should combine some qualities of both small town and large city." In the spatial narrative of the postwar East Bay, this turn to West Oakland as a paradigm for other parts of the city marked the beginning of city leaders' fifteen-year effort to reconstitute industry and residence there, in close proximity but not mutually invasive, supporting a vital working and middle class that shopped downtown. The logic seemed iron-clad in their eyes. Any money spent by the city, planners predicted, "can be repaid from taxes arising out of the increased valuation of the re-newed property." Endorsing the objectives of the Neighborhood Renewal Plan, the city council voted unanimously in early 1959 to pursue redevelop-ment in West Oakland (map 4.1). Among the first projects approved was Acorn, designed to tackle West Oakland's worst slum, the mixed-use indus-trial and residential area between Seventh and Fourteenth streets. Acorn's entire fifty-block redevelopment zone was condemned and scheduled for the bulldozer. Middle-income housing and new industry would complete the transformation.[10]

Blight was real. But powerful economic and racial preferences within the real estate market and the federal government's housing program, not simply age, produced the steep decline of West Oakland. Limited by the city's segregated housing in the 1930s and 1940s, black residents who could afford a down payment purchased older homes in West Oakland; others rented, often from the Euro-Americans who had preceded them. However, Euro-American whites could leave in large numbers for anywhere their incomes would allow. Blacks could not. West Oakland had enjoyed several decades in the first half of the century as a multinational port-of-entry for the nation's constant waves of immigrant and migrant traffic. By the late 1940s, however, it was on a steep path to total racial segregation. After World War II, when tens of thousands of black workers crowded into West Oakland's neighborhoods and absentee landlords accelerated the subdivision of apartments and two-story houses, local banks provided no loans for home improvement and maintenance. The designation of African American and mixed-race neighborhoods as "high risk" for loans inclined banks not to make capital available for home repair. Credit was simply unavailable. Further, the federal government's postwar housing program—administered through the Federal Housing Administration and the Veterans Administration—underwrote the purchase of new homes, not the restoration of older ones. Symptomatic of deep racial and structural inequalities, blight was real. The response to it, however, was directed by property and class considerations that endeavored to solve one set of problems, the most visible manifestations of slums, while ignoring or exacerbating others, the dense and tangled legacies of racial bias in the nation's property markets.[11]

The federal government gave major American cities the tools in the form of enormous grants to reengineer much of their aging downtown landscape. These efforts evolved in the context of national compromises over extensions of the New Deal state and debates about the government's postwar role in shaping urban areas. Congress's seminal renewal legislation, the Housing Acts of 1949 and 1954, bear the marks of these contests and compromises. Congress's 1949 bill, one of the only pieces of the Fair Deal to survive partially intact, emphasized low-income housing, both public and private, in the renovation of central cities. Drawing on Democrats' long-standing promise to guarantee the right of all Americans to a decent home, the 1949 act was inspired by the political appeal of housing for white urban workers, the core of the New Deal coalition. In 1954, however, a conservative Congress lobbied by an energized business community reconceived urban renewal as a means to spur cooperation between city halls and downtown developers. The acquisition and clearing of property was made easier, and Congress encouraged industrial, commercial, and institutional uses of redeveloped property. "Overemphasis on housing for reuse should be avoided," a congressional committee on urban renewal explained in its recommendations for the 1954 legislation. Renewal became a federal-local partnership in which the national state financed nearly anything local cities and developers wanted, a scenario in which downtown American business emerged to set the redevelopment agenda. Catherine Bauer, a University of California, Berkeley, professor and vocal critic of federal urban policy, charged that what had begun as a program to build new housing for low-income groups became "a program to rebuild downtown."[12]

Reflecting this complicated set of origins, redevelopment in West Oakland emerged as neither an enlightened model of progressive social planning nor the cynical business manifesto later critics charged. A range of contending forces and interests shaped its conception and implementation. Spurred by the new federal legislation, in 1954 Mayor John Houlihan, a former *Tribune* lawyer, appointed a redevelopment advisory committee dominated by the city's business and professional classes. Calling itself the Citizens Committee for Urban Renewal ("Oakland" was added a year later to form the acronym OCCUR), this group helped to draft the General Neighborhood Renewal Plan. They addressed the concerns of downtown business and the city council by emphasizing "strengthening the city's tax base" through the addition of new industry. "Urban renewal in West Oakland, to the extent possible, should reinforce the vitality of the downtown area," the plan explained, "creating new job opportunities and a new tax base." OCCUR viewed redevelopment in terms of economic revival, not as a means to solve social problems. At the same time, liberal planners and social service experts within the city redevelopment bureaucracy ensured that economic calculations did not overshadow human community in the renewal efforts. They wrote into the plan proposals for expanding DeFremery Park, center of Oakland's African American civic and recreation life, funding for additional new parks, and programs for addressing the health problems endemic to West Oakland's poorest sections, in all the ingredients for a better quality of life for local residents.[13]

Because of such possibilities, West Oakland's middle- and working-class African American communities initially expressed optimism about urban renewal. Most black residents favored some sort of housing rehabilitation, though nearly all opposed demolition of private homes as the instrument. As early as 1949 the Oakland NAACP appealed to the city council to address "Oakland's sorest blight problem," the rundown war housing in which many black families lived. In 1956 a group called the West Oakland Merchants—led by Thomas Anderson, an official of the Dining Car, Cooks, and Waiters Union—complained about "West Oakland's deterioration over the years." They were joined by other railroad and Pullman workers and independent merchants, many of them property owners and longtime residents of West Oakland (within the Acorn project area, just over one-third of the residents owned their own homes), who welcomed renewal but opposed demolition and removal. Other residents, too, favored rejuvenation of West Oakland, particularly the area between Seventh and Fourteenth streets northwest of downtown. Following the release of the Neighborhood Renewal Plan, a local survey revealed that two-thirds of those within the projected redevelopment zones wanted to rent or purchase a home in the renewed area. Even larger numbers rated local housing conditions as poor and complained of inadequate sidewalks, recreation facilities, and parks. African American residents of the planned redevelopment zones perceived overcrowding, crime, structural deterioration, and inadequate public facilities as threats to West Oakland's inclusion in the larger social and economic life of the city. However, black residents' desire not to be relocated or have their homes destroyed was ignored in the design of Acorn plans.[14]

Redevelopment undermined African American communities throughout midcentury urban America and positioned them in a particularly confounding double bind. Black residents of the oldest neighborhoods in American cities were forced to assert their right to participate in decisions that affected the immediate material conditions of their lives, and often to defend their right not to be relocated. At the same time, however, because mainstream white political culture linked African American neighborhoods ipso facto with decay, residents were compelled to profess over and over again that urban blight was not a condition of black life per se. Black residents of places like West Oakland had to assert both that neighborhood self-determination was a right and that blighted conditions were not a product of such self-determination. They were forced to negotiate this insidious double bind within a 1950s culture of race dominated by white assumptions that the continued migration of southern African Americans to northern cities was a *cause* of urban decline.[15]

That assumption, and the white prejudice and paternalism behind it, fueled the first large-scale public confrontation over postwar racial space in Oakland. As plans for the removal of residents in the Acorn area—more than 70 percent of whom were African American—proceeded in 1959, Tarea Hall Pittman of the NAACP issued a warning to city officials: "A majority of the families in this area are Negroes and their right to be relocated in decent, safe, and sanitary housing will be safeguarded by the NAACP." A few months earlier, the city council had denied NAACP members seats on a committee appointed to study public housing in Oakland, the first effort to reconsider that issue since the red scare elections of the early 1950s. Pittman, now the regional field secretary for the Northern California NAACP, and Reverend Solomon Hill, pastor of the First AME Church and the housing chairman of Oakland's NAACP branch, responded by announcing an independent study to monitor "the rights of displaced persons." Though embittered by the council's actions, Pittman and Solomon initially sought a middle ground on redevelopment. They attacked the city for ignoring the interests of West Oakland's African Americans. But they also encouraged the Redevelopment Agency to pursue Acorn, a project that seemed beneficial and possibly a key to reinvigorating the neighborhood if it were done well. To this end, the NAACP tactfully praised the agency and its work on the Acorn project. The possibility of cooperation, however, evaporated in the subsequent heat generated by the bigotry of city council members.[16]

Irreconcilable differences between the NAACP's and the city council's vision of West Oakland redevelopment emerged in early 1960 at a council meeting that revealed the racial prejudice at play in Acorn. In January the public housing committee appointed by the city council recommended building five hundred new low-income units, and the council as a whole voted to approve the new public housing construction, in part to accommodate Acorn displacement. At the same time, however, the council delivered a stinging and condescending rebuke of the NAACP in chambers packed with representatives of West Oakland's African American community. Councilmember Osborne, who voted against the plan, chastised NAACP members both for their behavior toward city officials — "minority groups have the obligation to assume duties as full citizens," he charged — and for their support of public housing. The latter, he observed, "leads some people to become blighted in ambition." "I believe there is a direct affinity between public housing and public welfare," Osborne continued, charging that the majority of welfare recipients "are from one minority group." Council meetings and other public forums in Oakland in the late 1950s had largely been spared such explicit racial slander. Osborne's words hung in the air in the council chambers and dissolved that false decorum. Reverend Hill shot back: "Erase 150 years of slavery, erase 80 years of low wages, segregation, and having doors slammed in your faces. Then you might find some moral reason for condemning instead of helping. But don't continue to push these people into a vicious circle and then blame them for being there." Osborne, whom the *Voice* reported to be "visibly reddened," said nothing and left the meeting. Having exposed the underlying cavity between council and NAACP redevelopment expectations, Acorn emerged for West Oakland residents as a glaring symbol of the open racial prejudice of some city officials, like Osborne, and the willful ignorance or apathy of others.[17]

Reverend Hill's anger was rooted in the ten-year battle to retain and improve postwar housing in the East Bay for the poorest black workers. In the early 1950s thousands of African American families lived, in larger proportions than whites, in public housing built by the federal government during the war in Richmond, Berkeley, and Albany, and in smaller projects scattered in West Oakland. All of them were segregated until 1952, when token integration resulted from federal law and pressure from local NAACP branches. When the federal government and East Bay cities agreed to begin destroying the housing in 1954, African American residents, with the assistance of the NAACP, contested the evictions and razing but lost. Displaced blacks poured into West Oakland. The closing of Cordonices Village in Berkeley, for example, sent 1,900 families in search of housing in the Oakland-Berkeley flatlands in 1954. Between 1945 and 1965 Oakland constructed only 500 new public housing units, those approved by the city council in the early years of Acorn planning, scratching only the surface of demand. In the face of white prejudice about blacks' "blighted ambition" and the vicious antihousing campaigns sponsored by the Committee for Home Protection and the California Real Estate Association, progressive housing advocates could generate neither public nor city council support in the 1950s for large-scale public building. Furthermore, Mayor Houlihan and the city council refused even to authorize a study of housing discrimination in Oakland until the federal government forced their hand by holding up six million dollars in redevelopment grants in 1961 until such a review was underway. For Hill and others among East Bay African American activists, the slights and indignities of ten years of housing fights fed their response to Acorn.[18]

The city council's embrace of redevelopment in the late 1950s was awash in hypocrisy. During the OVL campaigns for urban reform between 1947 and 1950, the *Tribune*, downtown business, and conservative city councilmembers had vehemently opposed public housing. The *Tribune* warned of "CIO communism" and raised the specter of state control of local affairs, but at the heart of its opposition was the fear, largely unspoken, that public housing construction would drive down values in the private real estate market. No such opposition to renewal and redevelopment ever materialized within the city's political and economic leadership, despite millions of dollars in federal subsidy, because such programs promised to *increase* private real estate values. One state intervention in the housing market was "communism," the other was good for business, and the *Tribune* praised redevelopment as unambiguously as it had opposed public housing and other social programs in the late 1940s. The federal government created value in urban real estate markets just as it created mortgage credit, and hence property value, for suburbanization. But it did so largely for commercial and business property owners, not for small homeowners and not for African Americans. Indeed, as an active manager of metropolitan space across the nation, the federal government in the two decades after World War II had become a major force in stabilizing real estate markets, protecting property value increases, and subsidizing the construction industry, all massive state interventions in the market.

Faced with a dramatic and potentially devastating redistribution of property and residents, activists in West Oakland developed two strategies of engagement with the city's redevelopment program. Both challenged demolition and removal. First, Wade Johnson, a Pullman porter, organized the United Tax Payers and Voters Union in 1960 to fight Acorn. Johnson owned two parcels of land in the Acorn redevelopment area and urged that the revitalization of West Oakland emphasize rehabilitation, not demolition. In 1962 he and twelve other residents filed suit in federal court, charging that no suitable plan had been developed to provide displaced persons access to housing on a racially open basis, a violation of federal law. By 1963, when the case appeared before the U.S. Circuit Court of Appeals, Johnson's challenge had gained national stature as a test of the racial dimension of urban renewal. Before the court, United Tax Payers and Voters Union attorney Benjamin Davis explained that segregation and discrimination, not renewal per se, made redevelopment a deeply destructive urban policy. The key question, Davis argued, was "to whom is housing available in Oakland?" Johnson ultimately lost before the U.S. Supreme Court, which found that Oakland's Redevelopment Agency was not in violation of either federal law or the Constitution and that its plan for relocating Acorn residents—a hastily assembled proposal to help people and businesses move, primarily to East Oakland—was sound. Ruling only in the narrowest sense on the agency's relocation efforts and declining to address the larger issue of segregation in Oakland, the Court's decision freed the city to redevelop the Acorn property.[19]

A second struggle over West Oakland redevelopment was more successful than Johnson's. The city had scheduled a parcel of land adjacent to and slightly larger than Acorn, fifty-six square blocks, for redevelopment, including massive demolition. Oak Center, as the neighborhood came to be known, contained a larger percentage of homeowners, fewer overcrowded and subdivided homes, and a much greater number of middle-income residents than Acorn. But, like Acorn, property there suffered from decades of neglect, due primarily to the indifference of lending agencies and the city. Fearing that they would face the same fate as Acorn, Oak Center residents organized. Lillian Love, Rose Sherman, Vivian Bowie, Missouri Riley, and a handful of other African American women created the Oak Center Neighborhood Association. "Living next to Acorn, what was going on was very vivid in the minds of the people," Love explained. "I was approached on many occasions by elderly people who said, 'We must do something to prevent this from happening in our area.'" Taking advantage of grassroots networks, Sherman and Love held a series of house meetings to inform neighbors of the impending destruction and

to discuss possible solutions. Rather than file suit against the agency—
Johnson's case was still pending, and Bowie was also a member of the
United Tax Payers and Voters Union—the Oak Center Neighborhood
Association pressed the Oakland Redevelopment Agency for negotiations.
After three years of diligent lobbying between 1961 and 1964, Oak Center
won a deal from the city permitting all property owners access to redevelopment funds for the rehabilitation and improvement of existing
homes, saving hundreds from demolition. It was a stunning and remarkable victory.[20]

Lillian Love's activism sprang from three decades of experience with
redevelopment politics in West Oakland. She lived with her family near
Peralta Street in West Oakland in the 1930s. Her first encounter with redevelopment came in the latter years of that decade, when the city cleared
land for a Depression-era housing project. "Our house happened to be
the last one to remain," she recalled, because her "father was determined
that he would not sign for his house to go." Unwilling to sell a house he
had worked years to acquire, Lillian's father went to court. "We stayed
there two years amid acres of cleared land," Love said of her father's
determination. Fighting eminent domain in the courts drained the family
resources, and the city won in the end. Two decades later, married and a
homeowner in West Oakland, Love again faced the city's bulldozer, this
time in the Oak Center Redevelopment Project. As determined as her
father to preserve her home, Love was instrumental in founding the Oak
Center Neighborhood Association and fighting for restoration rather
than demolition in her neighborhood—a fight that was the *second* for her
family in her lifetime. "When it comes time for them to take your property," Love learned watching the city over those twenty years, "it's very
expensive."[21]

Community organizing and determined local activists saved Oak Center
from the bulldozer. Acorn, however, was not so fortunate. Nat Frankel,
chairman of the Redevelopment Agency in the late 1960s, explained that
"the chief thrust, the chief interest" of Acorn property "is in industrial
reuse and commercial. This is attractive. This is marketable. You can
always sell it. It brings jobs, it brings money, it increases taxes." In these
terms, Acorn ultimately achieved moderate success, attracting more than
ten million dollars in private investment and twenty industrial firms by
the end of the decade, including Mack Trucks, Inc., the California Packing
Corporation, and the United States Plywood Corporation. But Acorn's
success in these terms illustrates how redevelopment embodied the calculable arithmetic of property values rather than the grammar of human
community. As late as 1969 not a single unit of housing had been built on
the Acorn site, and few West Oakland residents found employment in the
new industrial establishments—the job total was slightly less than the five

hundred predicted by the Redevelopment Agency, a "drop in the bucket," according to Frankel. "[W]hat really are we telling these people?" a member of the U.S. Commission on Civil Rights asked Frankel in 1967. "We are taking your home and you are not getting a job either?" West Oakland observers had already anticipated the commission's conclusions, seeing Acorn as a tax surge for the city at the price of hard-earned homes and neighborhood integrity.[22]

The history of redevelopment in West Oakland read like a morality tale by the early 1970s. Postwar blight threatened the tax base and downtown property interests. The reinvention of the downtown cityscape was the proposed solution, Oakland's first attempt to remake the social and physical life of its citizens. The concrete result was captured in the fate of Acorn. Redevelopment could erase buildings, but it was far more difficult to erase poverty and the structural racial inequalities built into federal housing policy and private housing and lending markets over decades. Oakland's public officials, including by the late 1960s many sympathetic ones, could do little to alter that legacy. There was plenty of blame to go around for the nationwide debacle that urban renewal had become, in city after city, by the early 1970s. Promises made had not been kept. Most were lucky if they received promises at all. Oakland's own story of failure was filled with less venality, for instance, than the exploits of Robert Moses in New York or Richard Daley in Chicago. But in Oakland no less than in other American cities, urban renewal constituted a massive redistribution of property and people in the name of saving downtown. In promising a staggering fifty million dollar increase in the valuation of taxable property at the completion of all of the Redevelopment Agency's projects, the city of Oakland neglected to explain (or to take responsibility for the fact) that at the heart of the plan was a redistribution of property from homeowners and small businesspeople to private industry and corporations and a redistribution of poor and middling homeowners and renters from one slum to another.[23]

At the Crossroads

Redevelopment was intended to increase downtown property values amid complex earrangements of capital and people in the 1950s and 1960s. These rearrangements were driven in large part by dramatic changes in Bay Area transportation. Regional and state engineers, with the endorsement of Oakland public officials, had by the mid-1960s constructed three major interstate highways and one rapid transit rail line across West Oakland. The Nimitz highway swept along the shoreline southwest of downtown, followed Seventh Street into West Oakland, and curved along

Cypress Street to join the Bay Bridge, moving traffic between South County and San Francisco. The MacArthur rolled down out of the foothills east of downtown and cut a swath between North and West Oakland before it, too, joined the Bay Bridge. A third, the Grove-Shafter, connected the Nimitz and MacArthur, passing between West Oakland and downtown. Construction of the Grove-Shafter remained in limbo until the mid-1970s, but much of the demolition required to accommodate it had been completed by the late 1960s as part of the City Center redevelopment project. Together, the three interstate highways laid the foundation for San Francisco–East Bay commuter traffic and interstate commercial trucking, which accompanied the expansion and modernization of the Port of Oakland. In addition, the BART system opened an above-ground rail line running from the southwestern edge of downtown to the bay.

This transportation network, the components of which met in West Oakland at the foot of the San Francisco–Oakland Bay Bridge, facilitated the regional dispersal of capital investment. But it disaggregated West Oakland neighborhoods and converted what had been an advantage for local residents—the area's transportation crossroads, waterfront, and rail lines—into a liability. New highways and light rail served downtown Oakland and San Francisco, suburban commuters, and the port, not West Oakland residents. Despite the General Neighborhood Renewal Plan's rhetoric about creating "a more desirable total physical and social environment for an existing and future West Oakland population," by the late 1960s West Oakland was a postindustrial transportation crossroads, not a thriving garden community. The costs to West Oakland residents—in the destruction of homes and commercial districts—were enormous. The three highways divided West Oakland into odd, incompatible units, isolated neighborhoods from downtown, and walled off the Acorn project behind two massive rivers of concrete. Construction of the above-ground portion of the BART line razed what remained of once vital African American commercial property along Seventh Street, former site of jazz clubs, barber shops, grocery stores, newsstands, and restaurants. And perhaps most consequential of all, unlike the Southern Pacific rail yards, station depots, and Pullman cars of an earlier transportation era, the emerging new systems created few jobs for West Oakland residents.[24]

The general outlines of highway planning had been known in Oakland since the early 1950s. Proposals for the MacArthur were first presented to the public in 1954, for the Grove-Shafter in 1956. Oakland planners thus knew that the Nimitz would come through West Oakland along Seventh Street, cutting through the heart of the Acorn project. The State Department of Public Works, the forerunner of the California Department of Transportation, designed the basic arterial flow and location of the highway system, but the Oakland City Council selected the exact final routes.

Figure 4.1. Construction of the Nimitz Interstate Highway through West Oakland in the late 1950s destroyed entire blocks of homes, sending thousands of people, the majority of whom were African American, in search of residence in other parts of the city. Courtesy of the *Oakland Tribune* Collection, Oakland Museum of California.

After a series of community meetings, the council had by 1958 approved all the highway locations for West Oakland. There is no evidence that the council intentionally undermined the Neighborhood Plan by approving the Nimitz, MacArthur, and Grove-Shafter, but such decisions were made easier by West Oakland's traditional role as the transportation crossroads of the East Bay, its depressed property values, and its African American residential population, which enjoyed no representation on the council. Whatever the council's thinking (the historical record contains few clues), the highway location decisions erected both literal and figurative barriers to reclaiming large parts of West Oakland for a thriving residential and commercial life.[25]

As a regional commuter system, BART was unlike anything else in California. Conceived in laborious planning sessions during the early 1950s, it was designed to serve downtown San Francisco and Oakland, linking the two cities with suburban Alameda and Contra Costa counties in a commuter network that would efficiently move workers and shoppers

Figure 4.2. An above-ground segment of the Bay Area Rapid Transit cuts through the middle of Seventh Street in West Oakland in the late 1960s. Two decades earlier, this section of Seventh was the heart of a thriving commercial and entertainment district, home to numerous black-owned businesses and other establishments that served the nearby black neighborhoods. Courtesy of the Dr. Huey P. Newton Foundation and the Department of Special Collections, Stanford University Libraries.

into and out of the central business cores. In the East Bay, BART would extend as far south as Fremont—bringing Oakland's suburbs more fully into the metropolitan orbit—as far north as Richmond, and across the Oakland hills eastward into Concord and Walnut Creek, professional-class bedroom communities. The BART district board was dominated by San Francisco interests who sought to make their downtown into the West's leading corporate headquarters. The project did just that, setting off a two-decade building boom in downtown San Francisco that produced thirty-four new high-rises and sixteen million square feet of office and retail space. BART did less for downtown Oakland, which now suffered from even greater comparative disadvantage: high-end shoppers could by-pass the city altogether in favor of San Francisco, an eight-minute train ride away, and San Francisco had more high-quality office space than Oakland. It did nothing to assist in the structural rehabilitation of West Oakland, now a throughway for transportation lines that carried people other places. Despite sitting at the center of two major new transportation networks, West Oakland had become cut off from an increasingly interconnected set of metropolitan spaces.[26]

While the California Department of Transportation and BART redesigned residential and transportation space in West Oakland's neighborhoods, the Port of Oakland transformed the adjacent waterfront. Between the early 1960s and the mid 1970s, Oakland overtook San Francisco and emerged as one of the busiest ports in the world. It became Oakland's dominant industry and a Goliath municipal agency that controlled hundreds of acres of land and the flow of millions of dollars of goods and services. Its modernization fulfilled the MOAP's dream of an Oakland-based transportation system preeminent on the Pacific Coast. In place of older terminals where longshoremen had unloaded cargo by hand, derrick, and dolly, the port erected a series of "container" cranes capable of unloading entire box-car-sized trailers that could be carried by diesel trucks. The port's modernization and mechanization took a decade and a half to complete, but its two principal projects—the Outer Harbor terminal and the Seventh Street terminal—coincided with other components of the physical remaking of West Oakland in the 1960s. The modernized port helped shape, through its intersection with new highways and its attraction of new investment, how people, goods, and capital moved through Oakland.[27]

Ports manage and organize space in obvious ways. Goods flow through them. Rail lines and highways connect them to hinterlands. Shipping lines link ports with cities on different continents. But ports manage and organize space in another, less obvious, sense as well. Ports manage properties for profit. Under the direction of Port Commissioner Ben Nutter, the port creatively reworked space, capital, and work. In the first stage of its redesign, port commissioners convinced the city to sell bonds to finance the program of mechanization that transformed the old docks near the Oakland Army Reservation into the automated Outer Harbor Terminal, completed in 1965. The port demolished warehouses in favor of a string of rail connections and broad streets linking the new terminals and automated berths with the Southern Pacific and Union Pacific rail lines and, more important, with the Nimitz and MacArthur highways. Second, Nutter and the Board of Port Commissioners won a federal Economic Development Administration (EDA) grant in 1966 to help finance a second containerized terminal, Seventh Street, as well as new facilities at the port-owned airport. The new Seventh Street terminal became the crucial bait with which Oakland lured two major Japanese shipping lines away from San Francisco in 1968. Finally, the port helped to shape the famous Mechanization and Modernization (M and M) agreement between the

Figure 4.3. In the late 1960s the Port of Oakland opened a new automated terminal on landfill extending from West Oakland into San Francisco Bay. This terminal, one of the first of its kind in the nation, gave Oakland an enormous advantage over competing West Coast ports in San Pedro (Los Angeles) and Seattle/Tacoma and represented a key element of the reengineering of West Oakland in the 1960s. Courtesy of the *Oakland Tribune* Collection, Oakland Museum of California.

ILWU and the Pacific Maritime Association, in which longshoremen sacrificed future job growth in the mechanizing industry for high pay rates and pension packages for existing workers. In sheer economic terms, the port emerged from the 1960s as one of West Oakland's few success stories, an enormous industry that, unlike much of the rest of the city, took advantage of, rather than lost ground to, the waves of economic restructuring sweeping through the East Bay in these decades.[28]

By 1970 the Port of Oakland was the second busiest container port in the world. Between 1965 and 1969 the cargo tonnage handled in Oakland waters increased *ten* times. In 1970 the port's tenants paid a total of $4.2 million in annual rents. This did not include the Oakland airport, which the port owned; Jack London Square, a redeveloped portside property designated for restaurants, convention space, and other tourist and leisure activities; and a 300-acre industrial park. In total, between 1955 and

1970, the port's operating income went from $742,000 to $6.5 million (in 1970 dollars). Over the same period, the port issued over $50 million in bonds, returning between 4 and 6 percent interest. Nutter and the port had demonstrated remarkable foresight, positioning Oakland to be the Pacific Coast gateway in a new era of international commerce in ways the MOAP architects dreamed. Much of the port's income, however, only indirectly benefited the city. Required by charter to reinvest income in port facilities, the new waterfront giant could not contribute money to the city's operating budget. Port bondholders, both individual and institutional, were scattered across the nation. Both conditions left the port oddly independent of the city that owned it, a fact that would frustrate a subsequent generation of Oakland activists.[29]

The reorganization of West Oakland in the 1960s left a complicated legacy. The federal government, the state of California, private capital, and the city reengineered the spatial integrity of Oakland's oldest neighborhoods. But the results were disastrous for West Oakland. On the one hand, the new highways, BART line, and containerized port looked toward an integrated Bay Area where transportation—between the metropoles of San Francisco and Oakland and between city and suburb—dominated the urban landscape. On the other hand, highways displaced residents and carved up neighborhoods. The BART line funneled suburban residents from the outlying cities to downtown Oakland and San Francisco but destroyed the Seventh Street commercial district and bypassed West Oakland's densest neighborhoods. Redevelopment subsidized private capital, which failed to employ local residents. Replacement housing took a decade to appear on the cleared Acorn land. And, most important, redevelopment and new transportation corridors failed to address, and indeed reinforced, the segregation of the city's real estate market. Far from engineering a new industrial garden, demolition in West Oakland reduced residential space and radically set people into motion. In all, West Oakland lost between 6,600 and 9,700 housing units in the first six years of the 1960s, forcing more than 10,000 people into motion in search of housing in other parts of the city.[30]

African American Narratives of Mobility

Oakland neighborhoods were not abstractions. They were not merely the products of economic restructuring and political decisions made at remove. Oakland and other East Bay neighborhoods mattered to the lives of the people who lived and constructed identities there. The corridor between West Oakland, North Oakland, and South Berkeley emerged in the 1950s and 1960s as the physical center of African American life in the

East Bay and the discursive referent when people, black and white, spoke of the "Negro" and later "black" community. These Oakland neighborhoods drew substantial numbers of southern African American migrants, beginning in the 1930s and continuing with greater pace in the 1950s. Migrants from places like New Orleans, Little Rock, and Muskogee, Oklahoma, established informal networks through which everything from child care to business deals passed. "Most of the people who lived in that neighborhood within a three or four block area were all from either Louisiana or Texas," Landon Williams said of his part of West Oakland. Tom Nash told interviewers that "there are so many Muskogeeans here that, you know, wherever I turn I'm running into one." Two of Oakland's most prominent professionals and civil rights activists in the 1960s and 1970s, Lionel Wilson and Donald McCullum, were from New Orleans and Little Rock, respectively, where they and their families had forged relationships with neighbors that carried over to Oakland. As friends and family from neighborhoods in the South sought to live near one another, and as work, commerce, leisure, and worship linked newcomers with longtime residents, African Americans in midcentury West Oakland refused to be defined solely by the city's red line.[31]

   Like their native-born and immigrant Euro-American counterparts, African American families sought the greater physical comfort, economic security, and class status that a move out of West Oakland afforded. People moved when they could. Until the mid-1950s, the paths out of West Oakland went north, along San Pablo Avenue, Market Street, and Telegraph Avenue into South Berkeley. "Half the Negroes in Berkeley in those days had just moved out of West Oakland," C. L. Dellums recalled. "As soon as they got on their feet and got jobs, they moved out." Berkeley's 21,850 African Americans in 1960 lived overwhelmingly in the southern part of the city, in areas contiguous with West and North Oakland's neighborhoods. Real estate interests and white homeowners maintained the color line at Telegraph Avenue. Neighborhoods northeast of Telegraph remained almost entirely white through the early 1960s, but African American homebuyers and renters faced significantly less opposition from west of there all the way to the industrial districts along the bayshore. Audrey Robinson recalled that her father, a redcap porter for the Southern Pacific, and her mother moved the family a number of times within these expanding African American neighborhoods. "The first home they owned was at Third and Market, and the next home they lived in was at Twelfth and Wood," in West Oakland. "And then they moved to Arlington Avenue just above San Pablo, and then they moved to Sixty-second and Colby, where they spent the remainder of their years," the latter in North Oakland, just below the Berkeley line. In those neighborhoods, as many as 86 percent of African American families in some census tracts were homeowners.[32]

West Oakland flourished in the middle 1940s, when wartime full employment, the booming nearby shipyards and military bases, and the heyday of American railroads combined to put money in the pockets of the city's white and black working class like never before. But it did not last. A decade after the end of the war, on the eve of redevelopment, West Oakland was a different place. The decline of rail traffic, for one, dealt a terrible blow. "When the Red Trains were taken off Seventh Street that just devastated the area," Vernon Sappers remembered, "people couldn't get there easily, and the businesses closed down, the streets looked shabby." The Seventh Street commercial and business corridor began its long decline when those Key System Red Trains stopped running, a process completed by highway and BART construction in the 1960s. The latter eviscerated what was left of Seventh Street, once the heart of the city's black business district and its eclectic immigrant shopping area. Dieselization of the nation's railroads in the early 1950s eliminated the need for the extensive maintenance facilities operated by the Southern and Western Pacific in West Oakland. In addition, as rail passenger travel waned beginning in the late 1950s, West Oakland lost more and more trains. In the early 1950s as many as forty passenger trains a day ran out of West Oakland. A decade and a half later, only three remained. By the late 1960s virtually all of West Oakland's once-dominant railroad industry lay quiet, thousands of jobs a memory. In a brutal final blow, containerization of the port stripped the waterfront of thousands of longshore and warehouse jobs in the 1960s. West Oakland had become, in Sappers' words, "eerie quiet."[33]

Memories of West Oakland were profoundly shaped by the rupture of redevelopment. "West Oakland was a beautiful place until the city with a decree to clean out West Oakland came through," Tom Nash, an African American reporter and newspaper publisher, recalled. "There was a lot going on. There were all kinds of businesses." In Nash's memory, redevelopment took large numbers of black residents and "scattered them." Landon Williams, born in West Oakland in 1944, "had a paper route down Seventh Street. . . . I can remember how vibrant Seventh Street was on both sides. I can remember a little cleaners, you know, meat markets, grocery stores, liquor stores, furniture stores . . . and they wiped it out and the ground lay fallow for like ten years." Redevelopment in West Oakland was one marker of change among many in the flatlands by the mid-1960s. The institutional and political isolation of African Americans had come to have spatial consequences in West and North Oakland, as redevelopment and aggressive policing disrupted life and cast city government as a hostile, invasive force. Coupled with the exodus of more and more whites, they rendered these flatland neighborhoods nearly unrecognizable to the generation who had lived there in the 1930s and 1940s, those who knew West Oakland in the words of one former

Figure 4.4. A Dorothea Lange photograph of young men in Oakland in the early 1950s. In their lifetime, these youths would witness increased segregation in the poorest parts of Oakland even as the African American middle class expanded and pushed for greater opportunities in the city. Copyright the Dorothea Lange Collection, Oakland Museum of California, City of Oakland. Gift of Paul S. Taylor.

resident as a "marvelous mixture" of nationalities alive with business and industry.[34]

Physical destruction for new transportation routes shaped people's mental and emotional maps of West Oakland. Landon Williams remembered "that putting in the freeway [Grove-Shafter] meant razing houses and destroying the neighborhood." The Grove-Shafter itself was not completed until the 1970s, but clearance for the project cut a swath of vacant land a block wide between West Oakland and downtown, a huge physical barrier in what had once been a walking corridor. For Vivian Bowe, BART stood out. "When they put BART above ground, that made a dump out of [Seventh Street]. Nobody wanted to go down there," she explained. They "wiped out the Barn, one of the finest. . . . soul food restaurants that we had down there," Tom Nash said of the changes along Seventh Street. "Johnny bulldozer," he continued, ran "through all of those homes that it took those people a lifetime to acquire." Josie de la Cruz recalled moving from West to East Oakland "because they were already buying the homes of the people that were living down there to build the freeway." West Oakland in the 1930s and 1940s had been, in Tom Nash's words, "a city within a city." In the 1960s large parts of it looked abandoned, forgotten.[35]

By the 1960s the elements of a new way of thinking about Oakland were in place. The physical destruction of black neighborhoods, the dislocation of West Oakland residents, and the systems of capital flow and transportation that bypassed African American communities gave people ample material with which to write new narratives of the city and its meanings. Residents knew that behind the physical changes lay economic and political power. Never in West Oakland's history had outside governmental institutions operated so visibly in the neighborhoods. The California Department of Transportation, which constructed the three interstate highways, the Oakland Redevelopment Agency, the Port of Oakland, and BART collectively spent a decade and a half reengineering West Oakland. These institutions were not distant bureaucracies to West Oaklanders. People knew them intimately. Neighbors had been relocated by them. Friends and relatives had their homes purchased under eminent domain. Residents drove past blocks of cleared land and concrete pillars rising from once bustling streets. Many in the West and North Oakland black community felt that their neighborhoods were under siege, that they were literally occupied. Among the generation that came of age in the postwar decades in the midst of this physical destruction, accompanied by the isolation of the black poor and the unprecedented abandonment of large parts of the city by whites, many began to distrust liberal platitudes about opportunity and progress. The city seemed a domain of power—sometimes raw, often capricious—not a landscape of openness and opportunity.

Race and Housing

Black Oaklanders faced numerous hazards and obstacles when the pursuit of homeownership led them across the accepted racial geography of the city. Housing segregation was bound up in a system of property values and rents in which homeowners, real estate brokers, and developers sought always to increase the net worth of homes and land. Within this system, prejudice, perceived racial hierarchies, and calculated self-interest reinforced one another, especially under the watchful eye of real estate agents and local real estate boards. "It is real estate brokers, builders, and mortgage finance institutions," the U.S. Commission on Race and Housing contended in 1958, "which translate prejudice into discriminatory action." Overall, a 1964 housing survey in Oakland found that by a margin of six to one the most common objection to mixed-race neighborhoods was "fear of economic loss." Here was segregation's consequence: racism rationalized as economic calculation. Further, structural inequalities of race and class—in home financing, insurance, and federal mortgage subsidies, among others—underlay the entire landscape of residential property, structural inequalities that even well-intentioned whites could do little to alter. The result was a decade and a half, 1955 to 1970, in which the city's racial residential patterns were constantly transgressed and renegotiated through the cultural and economic production of property. Less brutal and vicious than in many American cities—Oakland never experienced the levels of white violence common in Chicago, Detroit, Philadelphia, and Baltimore—this process yielded by the late 1970s one of the more integrated urban landscapes in the nation. Nevertheless, Oakland's experience with what contemporary commentators called "racial transition" exacted multiple individual costs that sorted the city by both race and class in ways that would have important and lasting consequences.[36]

Oakland's African American communities continued their expansion in the 1950s (maps 4.2 and 4.3). While the city as a whole lost 4 percent of its population between 1950 and 1960, the black residential population nearly doubled, from 55,778 to 100,000 (and to 125,000 by 1970). As the decade progressed, both recently arrived African American migrants and longtime black residents of the city looked to avoid or escape the overcrowded sections of West Oakland into which black workers had been forced during and immediately after the war. This was particularly the case for members of the black middle class, many of whom now sought to establish more comfortable residences in other parts of the city. For working-class black families, both middling and poor, the demolition of large parts of West Oakland, the lack of public housing, and the dearth of new housing units under construction in older parts of the city meant a wider search for available homes. Still, between 1950 and 1970, African American homeownership grew in every district in the city. In the process, both middle- and working-class groups pressed the older racial boundaries of Oakland neighborhoods.[37]

In the middle of the 1950s, African Americans began purchasing homes in parts of East Oakland, as the real estate industry slowly opened discrete neighborhoods for black buyers. "It would have taken an act of Congress to get east of Fourteenth then [1950s], but one of the members of my union, John Mabson, was among the first Negroes that got east of Fourteenth," Dellums told an interviewer of East Oakland's red line. "I had some members of my organization that had bought homes on Eighty-third and Eighty-fifth Avenues," he continued. Pullman porters, attorneys, physicians, and civil servants were among the first African Americans to purchase homes in far East Oakland, east of Fourteenth Street. In the late 1950s and early 1960s, Fourteenth Street was first a red line—between black and white—then a class boundary between middle-class black neighborhoods to the east and lower working-class black neighborhoods to the west. By the late 1960s that boundary had become an economic gradient: the neighborhoods below Fourteenth Street were trapped in tenacious forms of poverty and unemployment. Early in the decade, however, optimism for both sides of Fourteenth prevailed. "We were living on Church Street in East Oakland out around Sixty-ninth Avenue and East Fourteenth Street," Landon Williams remembered. "Because my mom, and the whole family was sort of like trying to be upwardly mobile. And at that time period, East Oakland was one of the areas where black people were going. That was a nice area." Describing the new Sears and Montgomery Wards stores that opened, Arthur Patterson, whose mother operated a boarding house in West Oakland, remembered of East Oakland that "the further you go, the better it got. Mama was looking and buying." He continued, "in the sixties you had this mass migration from West Oakland to East Oakland. The whites were giving it up out there."[38]

Bolstered by white community sentiment, the real estate industry had established a set of broad racial barriers across the length of the city. On the north and west sides of Oakland, and extending into Berkeley, Telegraph Avenue marked the line between the black west side and the white east side. By 1970 real estate brokers and agents had moved the line east to Broadway but maintained the Telegraph/Broadway corridor as a steep racial gradient. Broadway functioned as the de facto red line, because white property-owners and real state representatives wanted to preserve white racial homogeneity in the apartment district north of Lake Merritt and in the foothills surrounding Piedmont, the island city still famously occupied in the 1970s by the East Bay's elite. But a deeper legacy lay behind this geography: in a 1937 survey of Oakland for the federal government's Home Owners Loan Corporation, all of the neighborhoods north and west of Broadway were given a security grade of "red"—indicating high risk, racially mixed—the structural origins of the red line. In the city of Berkeley, Grove and Shattuck avenues, breaking away from Telegraph and heading due north through the center of the city, divided the black flatlands from the white foothills and hills, mirroring the racial geography

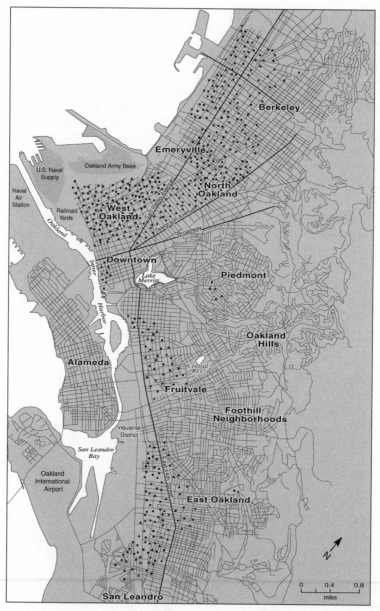

Map 4.2. Oakland's African American population in 1960. Each dot represents 200 residents. Note the dispersal of black neighborhoods along the flatlands north into Berkeley, as well as the developing black residential districts in East Oakland abutting the San Leandro city line. Cartography Lab, University of Wisconsin.

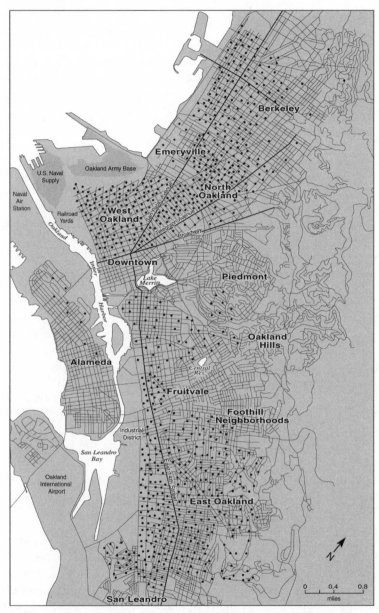

Map 4.3. Oakland's African American population in 1970. Each dot represents 200 people. Oakland and Berkeley had achieved a higher level of desegregation by the 1970s than most American cities. Note, however, the absence of African Americans in Alameda. Even as Oakland desegregated, suburban cities in Alameda County to the south remained overwhelmingly white. Cartography Lab, University of Wisconsin.

of Oakland. By the early 1970s black communities stretched from downtown through West and North Oakland along the flatlands in Berkeley north all the way to the Albany city line. But an interpenetrating combination of economic disadvantage and blatant real estate machinations kept the middle-class homes east of Broadway inaccessible to black buyers.[39]

A different pattern, with its own variations, emerged in Fruitvale and East Oakland. There, MacArthur Boulevard, and subsequently the MacArthur highway, divided the city into flatlands and foothills, stretching a racial barrier the length of the eastern two-thirds of the city. Three important exceptions stood out, however. First, white homeowners in what was known as the "Bible Belt" (initially for its large number of churches, later for its white racial conservatism) carved out a homogenous racial space in the flatlands between Fruitvale Avenue and High Street east of Fourteenth Street and kept black homebuyers out. Second, the municipal boundary with San Leandro, in far East Oakland, was a starkly drawn racial boundary that blocked the expansion of African American neighborhoods south into the suburban flatlands. Finally, between 1960 and 1970 a sizable ethnic Mexican community began to take shape in Fruitvale, a community that played an increasingly important and active role in the city's political culture as the 1960s progressed (map 4.4). Racial residential patterns thus followed an earlier class geography. The densest and most homogenous, and poorest, black neighborhoods lay closest to the bay. As one moved north and east away from the bay, neighborhoods of the black working poor gave way to black middle-class residential districts — areas with a few white, Japanese American, and Chinese American residents. Next, in flatland neighborhoods adjacent to the foothills, whites dominated, but significant numbers of African Americans (between 10 and 25 percent) lived there as well. Finally, the foothills and hillside districts were almost entirely white, with only a few professional African American residents. Thus, even as the city's racial composition changed remarkably, the older patterns of status embedded in the physical landscape and its geography of flatlands, foothills, and hills by earlier generations of real estate developers remained salient.

Achieving open housing in Oakland was a painful and tumultuous process, but African Americans there escaped the worst of the nation's postwar housing warfare. White homeowners associations in Oakland, with a very few exceptions, did not mobilize and organize against open housing neighborhood by neighborhood. Neither did whites resort to the unapologetic violence and antiblack public rituals that made many white neighborhoods not just unwelcome but unsafe for African Americans in the Northeast and Midwest. Nonetheless, discrimination was deep-seated, and within the city's neighborhoods less scripted, more variable dramas took place. The *Tribune* published "white only" real estate listings until

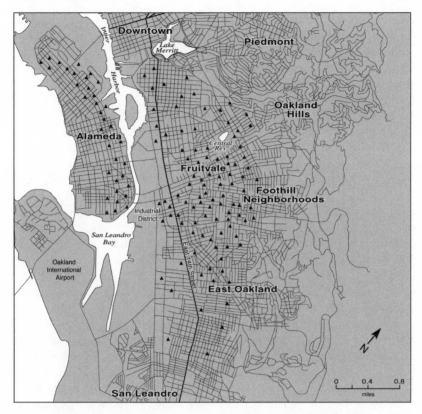

Map 4.4. The Spanish surname population of Oakland and Alameda in 1970. Largely ethnic Mexican, Spanish surname residents of Oakland were concentrated in Fruitvale. This population of Mexican Americans and Mexican immigrants increased dramatically in the 1970s and 1980s. Cartography Lab, University of Wisconsin.

1963, and in 1964 only 4 percent of real estate brokers in the city signed a fair housing petition circulated by the League for Decency in Real Estate. In many neighborhoods, real estate brokers manipulated the segregationist sentiment of white community members. "There is more trouble from real estate brokers in white areas than from the property owners," one informant told a housing researcher. In the hands of unscrupulous dealers, strategies designed to induce a panic among whites to drive selling prices down and buying prices up were common. "The real estate people moved the colored people in and made lots of money," one white Oakland resident told University of California researchers. "They hounded us to sell the house at that time so they could give it to the colored at about twice the price." And finally, poverty among African Americans restricted even further the kind and location of housing available in a city that had for decades refused to confront its housing crisis and had constructed few public housing alternatives. This combination of white opposition to desegregation and class inequality made the simple search for housing, whether for rental or purchase, a psychologically draining and financially taxing experience.[40]

The 1964 study of racial discrimination in Oakland housing revealed the extent of the financial penalties African Americans faced when purchasing property. In wide-ranging interviews with real estate agents, white and black homeowners, and informants inside the real estate industry, University of California Professor Floyd Hunter and the study's staff documented how industry representatives manipulated the market to disadvantage black buyers. The "Negro has to pay a higher interest rate," one informant explained. "Instead of 6%, he has to pay 6½ to 7%." Another observed that most banks would refuse to make loans for home purchases in certain areas of the city, typically those within formerly redlined neighborhoods. This forced "applicants to go elsewhere where interest rates are higher and more points are required." Furthermore, this informant continued, "Negro lending institutions, because of their more limited market and greater economic risk, require higher interest rates and more points on a shorter term." As for "block busting," one of the principal ways that the real estate industry turned an all-white neighborhood into an all-black neighborhood, one respondent said simply that "block busting is a way of making a fast buck—not motivated by the desire to help the Negro." These burdens were added to the widely practiced strategy of selling homes to black buyers for two, three, and sometimes four thousand dollars more than the original asking price. In all, African American home buyers in the 1950s and 1960s confronted not *merely* housing segregation but a far more elaborate and extensive structure of economic liabilities.[41]

At the same time, white Oaklanders left the city in impressive numbers. Between 1955 and 1960, 88,000 white residents moved out of the city. Between 1960 and 1966 another 75,000 left. They did so for an enormous number of reasons, only some of which had explicitly to do with race, but out-migrating white residents were overwhelmingly married couples with children—often families whose experience of desegregation was mediated by children and the social spaces of childhood: schools and recreation centers. "I wouldn't think of sending my kids to Castlemont High School. There are too many colored," an East Oakland resident told a University of California interviewer. For white residents who moved within Oakland, most sought housing in foothill neighborhoods and the Bible Belt. Indeed, white residents between 1960 and 1966 left North Oakland, East Oakland, and Fruitvale—all districts to which large numbers

REDISTRIBUTION 167

of black residents moved in the same period—en masse for central Oakland and the foothills. That students of Oakland housing in the 1960s found little evidence of massive organized resistance to black mobility is not surprising. With 150,000 whites leaving in the space of a single decade, in a city with a total population of just under 400,000, the social basis for such a movement had disappeared.[42]

Nevertheless, Oakland's opposition to open housing did not vanish entirely into the suburbs. Whites were not abstract bodies that moved like chess pieces from block to block. They were political beings. In 1964, one year after Byron Rumford had navigated the fair housing bill through the California Assembly, Oaklanders joined voters statewide in supporting its repeal. "A property owner has an inherent right to rent or sell—or to refuse to rent or sell—to whomever he sees fit," Oakland City Councilmember Osborne proclaimed at a fair housing session in 1964. Sentiment in Oakland and throughout white communities in California in 1963 and 1964 did not run far from Osborne's. When the Rumford Act, as the fair housing bill was known, passed after a bitter floor debate, the California Real Estate Association (CREA) vowed to offer California voters the opportunity to reject it. They did so with Proposition 14, a measure co-sponsored with the committee for Home Protection (CHP) calling for repeal of fair housing. By outlawing racial discrimination in both private housing and lending, the Rumford Act struck at the heart of residential segregation. Like the 1959 state fair employment law, it represented the culmination of many years of lobbying in the state legislature and was a cornerstone of the state's liberal legislative record. Proposition 14, the first evidence of an emerging white political backlash against the civil rights movement in California, struck back. The Proposition 14 campaign rhetorically linked property to freedom and permitted whites a public forum in which to express a segregationist politics in a language of private rights that most claimed had nothing at all to do with race.[43]

The CREA and Committee for Home Protection rarely discussed race in the Proposition 14 campaign. Instead, they resurrected the "creeping socialism" rhetoric of their mobilizations against public housing in the 1950s, calling the law "Rumford Forced Housing" and a violation of "the freedom to buy, rent, and sell." When the CREA did discuss race, it was to chide liberals for sacrificing "the American way of life" in what they considered a misguided and naïve social project. "Drop the cloak of minority civil rights," CREA literature proclaimed, "and there stands the police state in the name of social justice, with a dagger poised directly at the very heart of freedom." As the Proposition 14 campaign unfolded, however, little doubt remained that race was central to the CREA's efforts. Every civil rights and liberal organization in the state, including the AFL-CIO, opposed it. The Rumford Act's passage in 1963 had been California's major civil rights legislation that year. And the Proposition 14 campaign overlapped with the national presidential contest in which Lyndon Johnson defended the Civil Rights Act of 1964 against charges, echoed by the constituencies forming behind Barry Goldwater and George Wallace, that it sacrificed the rights of the majority to the rights of black Americans. On the eve of the election, in November 1964, polls showed that the CREA's rhetoric had found a sympathetic audience. A nearly 60 percent majority of Californians supported Proposition 14, and in Oakland the *Tribune* issued a full endorsement.[44]

The results of the 1964 election brought into stunning relief the extent of white California's resistance to desegregation. In an election in which over 60 percent of California voters cast ballots for Democrat Lyndon Johnson, 65 percent approved Proposition 14. The results in Oakland confirmed that large numbers of white homeowners opposed desegregation and racial liberalism. Though a lower percentage of Oakland residents (55 percent) voted for Proposition 14 than did so statewide, the election returns varied dramatically by neighborhood (map 4.5). The most heavily African American neighborhoods—those north and west of Telegraph and southwest of East Fourteenth—voted overwhelmingly against Proposition 14. Along the edges of these districts, where neighborhoods were most integrated—from Berkeley along Broadway into Oakland and across the city along MacArthur—the vote was much more evenly divided. More surprising was the massive vote in favor of Proposition 14 in the hillside districts, areas where in 1964 African Americans had made few housing gains and the real estate industry maintained racially homogenous neighborhoods. In these districts, along with the Bible Belt, Proposition 14 passed with more than 70 *percent* of the vote. The numbers suggest that the resistance to desegregation in Oakland did not come solely from an antiliberal white working class engaged in direct struggle with African Americans over jobs and housing, but arose equally among middle- and upper-class whites who understood property rights as sacrosanct expressions of their personal freedom and had little daily contact with African Americans.[45]

The dynamics of racial space in these years raised fundamental questions at the heart of Oakland's future: how would the city be managed, by whom, and in whose interests? By the end of the 1960s, African Americans constituted over one-third of Oakland's population and represented the city's fastest growing group. But the metropolitan growth elaborated in the MOAP had delivered benefits unevenly to black Oaklanders. Citywide, African American homeownership increased by 38 percent in the first half of the 1960s. About 25 percent of the city's homes were owned by African Americans in 1966, a proportion that lagged behind black representation in the population at large but was moving closer. At the same

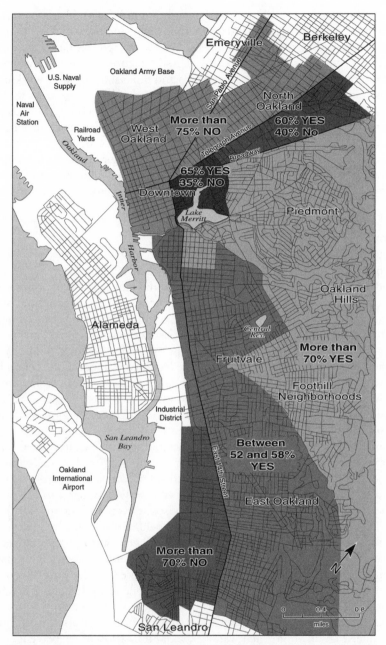

Map 4.5. Proposition 14 voting results in Oakland, 1964. Expectedly, African American neighborhoods in West and East Oakland voted against the measure overwhelmingly. The map is telling in two additional ways. First, it shows that in neighborhoods where blacks and whites lived in close proximity, the vote was either split or favored repeal of fair housing. Second, it shows that the foothill and hill districts, where very few African Americans lived in 1964, gave the strongest support to the anti–fair housing vote. Cartography Lab, University of Wisconsin.

time, however, the combination of demolition in West Oakland, patterns of white resistance to integration, suburban flight, and industrial restructuring threatened to reduce much of the city's working-class flatlands, west and east, to isolated racial ghettos. These "ghettos" were still dynamic communities with traditions of activism and thousands of stable working-class families, but they lacked the financial and political resources in the mid-1960s to press for greater inclusion in Oakland's economy and decision-making institutions. Middle-class African Americans may have benefited as a group from white abandonment of the city, but the vast social inequalities that accompanied industrial restructuring and deepening poverty now seemed ready to fall on that same class, who stood to inherit a troubled and eroding tax base and an entrenched employment crisis.[46]

Employment Crisis

People were not alone in motion across Oakland's landscape in the 1950s and 1960s. Capital and jobs, too, were on the move. The reorganization of capital in the East Bay brought yet another cycle of redistribution, one that by the early 1960s had produced a full-fledged employment and poverty crisis. In 1964 Oakland's persistent unemployment problem drew the attention of the federal government, which designated the city a "depressed area." The distinction made federal assistance with economic planning available to Oakland, but the larger meaning of the designation was not lost on city officials and community activists: in the midst of solid economic growth across the nation, and spectacular growth in California, Oakland had somehow been left behind, a "depressed" city. Oakland's predicament typified the decade for both medium-sized and large older U.S. cities, places clinging to an industrial infrastructure eroded by the flight of manufacturing to suburban places and the South and by the slow transition to a service economy. Peripheral to the economic engines that drove California's postwar economy—aerospace, information, and tourism—Oakland lagged behind places like Long Beach, Sunnyvale, San Jose, San Francisco, and Orange County in the competition for jobs and industry. Furthermore, like other second-tier industrial communities adjacent to major cities—places like Camden and Newark, New Jersey—Oakland labored in the shadow of a formidable civic neighbor, San Francisco. The East Bay's uneven metropolitan job growth in the mid-1960s, combined with both present and historical discriminations produced an unemployment rate in Oakland in 1964 of 11 percent and an African American unemployment rate of 20 percent.[47]

Never an industrial giant on a par with Detroit and Chicago, Oakland always depended on eastern and midwestern investment in branch plants.

In this sense, Oakland developed on the periphery of an earlier period of industrial decentralization from the Northeast and Midwest, beginning in the 1920s. By the 1950s and 1960s, operating expenses increased and older facilities in Oakland declined in profitability. Despite the precipitous drop in property values in Oakland, industrial land there was still far more expensive than in suburban cities, which encouraged plant relocation. In the early 1960s, for instance, the City of Oakland paid $179,000 for a single acre of land for a school and recreation center. At the same moment, land in suburban Alameda County was selling in some places for $8,000 per acre. General Motors, Dow Chemical, Shell Oil, Borden Chemical, and Trailmobile led the exodus of industrial employers from Oakland to new suburban plants in southern Alameda County and north in Contra Costa County. Between 1961 and 1966 Oakland lost 10,000 manufacturing jobs, the bulk of them in the transportation equipment sector. Oakland's share of production jobs in Alameda County dropped from 50 percent in the late 1950s to less than 30 percent in the early 1970s. Simultaneously, however, between 1951 and 1964 industrial investment in the county as a whole produced 41,000 new manufacturing jobs. The East Bay's industrial suburbs garnered most of Alameda County's growth in these years. A federal government survey in 1967 estimated that there were 185,000 total jobs, including 30,000 in manufacturing, in southern Alameda County, the Bay Area's fastest growing region in 1960s, which accounted for more than 90 percent of the East Bay's automobile, truck, tractor, and engine manufacturing by the end of the decade.[48]

Those groups of workers most vulnerable to cycles of unemployment and to various forms of discrimination—young African Americans of both sexes, black women of all ages, and, increasingly, Spanish-speaking youth and recent Mexican immigrants—found the regional dispersal of jobs unaccommodating. These workers overwhelmingly remained in Oakland. For them, municipal boundaries were theoretically porous to movement, but the social, familial, institutional, and ultimately linguistic networks through which most people acquired jobs did not extend broadly across space. The transformations in the East Bay economy unfolded unevenly over more than a decade, but they formed the structural background to the unemployment crisis—what mayor Houlihan in 1966 called "a problem of gigantic proportions facing Oakland." As industrial restructuring eroded the city's blue-collar opportunity structure and shifted working-class job creation into services, Oakland's workers struggled to keep pace. Unemployment, usually temporary but in some cases long-term, was the result. Oakland's overall unemployment rate ranged between 5 and 10 percent in the decade between 1958 and 1968 but varied dramatically within the city. In 1960, for example, in parts of East Oakland below Fourteenth Street, the city's emerging "second ghetto," unemployment ran between 25 and 30 percent and improved little over the course of the decade. Throughout the working-class flatlands—where, in 1960, the majority of the city's skilled, semiskilled, and unskilled blue/pink/white-collar workers still lived—unemployment ran between 8 and 15 percent.[49]

Economic and job growth did not come to a standstill in Oakland. But it changed directions. Service jobs replaced manufacturing jobs as Oakland assumed the role of the East Bay's administrative center and maintained its status as a retail hub through the early 1970s. Kaiser Industries constructed its world headquarters in Oakland in the early 1960s, employing 9,000 people in its new office building overlooking Lake Merritt. Montgomery Ward and Capwell's together employed nearly 5,000 workers as Oakland's dominant retail department stores. Safeway, Northern California's leading supermarket, maintained its regional headquarters in Oakland with a staff of 2,000. Overall, employment in services increased 32 percent in Oakland between 1958 and 1966; government employment increased 30 percent; and finance, insurance, and real estate employment increased 25 percent. Government employment, in particular, accounted for an enormous, and crucial, share of Oakland's economy. Together, Alameda County, the City of Oakland, the Oakland Army Base, the Naval Supply Center, the U.S. Naval Hospital, the Oakland School District, and the new U.S. Regional Post Office in West Oakland accounted for 24,000 jobs. In addition, just beyond Oakland's northern limits in Berkeley, the University of California employed over 12,000 people, and immediately across Oakland's Inner Harbor the Alameda Naval Air Station accounted for 10,000 civilian and military workers. Oakland remained in San Francisco's sizable shadow as a regional service center, but the city's transition away from manufacturing to services in the 1960s was unmistakable.[50]

The transformation from manufacturing to services as the core activity of the nation's economy in the postwar decades privileged sectors in the broadly defined area of "services" that had historically been resistant to hiring African American workers. At one end of the services spectrum were white-collar jobs that increasingly required college degrees—in financial, insurance, government, education, and information services. These jobs lay behind both class and racial barriers, because of educational requirements and the historic exclusion of virtually anyone not white (and, in many instances, not WASP). But even at the entry level, service employers were reluctant to hire African Americans, because of the historic front-of-the-house/back-of-the-house racial line, the perception that white customers did not want to interact with black employees, and a persistent white prejudice about black speech, decorum, and competence. In traditional "blue-collar" service jobs, in restaurant and hotels, for instance, African Americans had to struggle to open front-of-the-house jobs with lawsuits in the 1970s and 1980s. Similar patterns of struggle evolved in hotel and retail employment as well. Thus, the gentrification of the nation's urban job base, or more accurately its bifurcation into well-paying service sector jobs and low-wage service sector jobs, began in the 1960s and contributed as forcefully to the growth of poverty as manufacturing job loss.[51]

All workers, black and white, found themselves caught in the shifting labor markets of the metropolitan East Bay, but the dislocations associated with deindustrialization and the transition to services reverberated in African American communities with greater force than in white communities. The unemployment rate among Oakland's African American population was typically twice the rate among whites; in some years *four* times. Manufacturing decline hit black workers hard, to be sure, but many maintained their positions with large employers like General Motors and Ford. Far worse was the decline of employment in West Oakland, where the rail yards, docks, and warehouses once provided thousands of jobs for the community. Worse still was the decades-long exclusion of young African Americans from apprenticeship programs, the principal gateway to well-paying blue-collar jobs. The broad service sector remained starkly segmented by race, and many employers continued to refuse to hire blacks, especially in retail and wholesale sales, restaurant and hotel work, banks, and insurance companies. Only in government service, where fair hiring had progressed farthest by the mid-1960s, did black workers see significant job gains. Confined to a narrower range of employment opportunities, shut out of the southern Alameda housing and job markets almost entirely, buffeted by the capriciousness of discrimination among smaller employers, and often dependent on two incomes because of chronic underemployment, Oakland's working-class African American families on the whole had more experience with unemployment and economic marginality than did their white counterparts.[52]

Public discussions and political debates about unemployment in mid-1960s Oakland turned on the status of African American men. The focus on unemployed black males, however, obscured two central features of Oakland's new occupational realities. First, African American women had the highest rate of unemployment in the city. In 1966 more than half of the city's unemployed workers were women, and the unemployment rate for black women stood at just under 15 percent, the highest among any single group in Oakland. The numbers suggest that the region's emerging service economy was even slower in opening its doors to African American women than to men. These developments deepened the economic vulnerability of African American women, especially mothers without additional financial support, accelerated processes of class polarization within the city's black population, and increased the social service responsibilities of Oakland and Alameda County agencies—the latter an important dimension of the city's growing financial burden produced by increasing social inequality. The near exclusive focus on male unemployment shaped subsequent antipoverty efforts later in the decade. Despite the overrepresentation of African American women among the city's unemployed—and among its poor—antipoverty programs failed to make female joblessness a core issue.[53]

Second, even as unemployment emerged as an overwhelming problem in African American communities, class differentiation among black Oaklanders accelerated and the black middle class continued to expand. In 1970, for instance, more African American families had incomes above $10,000 (Oakland's median income was just over $11,000) than below the poverty line. A growing professional class, a new generation of black merchants, and government employment accounted for the gains. By the late 1960s, 29 percent of all employed African Americans in Oakland worked for some sort of public agency—from public hospitals and schools to state and county offices to the University of California and federal military installations like the Oakland Army Base, Naval Supply Depot, and the Alameda Naval Air Station. The homeownership rate among the black middle class was equal to or greater than rates among whites of the same economic status. Expansion of the black middle class could not, in a single generation, replace the taxable wealth lost in two decades of white suburbanization, but it nonetheless represented a spectacular increase from 1960. Growing problems with unemployment and poverty within parts of the African American community often overshadowed the extent to which the East Bay had developed by the mid-1960s a formidable black middle and upper middle class. The broad spatial and sectoral transformations within the East Bay economy had not affected Oakland's African American population evenly. Rather, industrial restructuring had begun to carve away a set of opportunities in semi-skilled and low-skilled blue-collar work, while the racialized job markets in services and skilled work narrowed new opportunities for working-class African American men and women. But the middle-class ranks of professionals, government workers, and small businesspeople had increased almost as dramatically.[54]

By the end of the 1970s, Oakland had undergone a stunning transformation. Its industrial and occupational base, civic infrastructure, and housing stock, its relationship to San Francisco and East Bay suburbs, and its racial patterns of residence had all been reconstituted. The process was characterized by epochal redistributions of people, property, and capital. Cycles of redistribution during the postwar decades were at once national and local, drawing Oakland into multiple, shifting currents. Nationally, nearly four million African Americans left the South for northern and western cities in the three postwar decades, and between 1950 and 1970 alone the suburban population of the nation doubled from thirty-six million to seventy-four million. Capital left central cities in enormous waves of industrial restructuring beginning in the late 1940s. In a political climate that celebrated "free enterprise," the freedom of capital to move at will was left unchecked. Across the nation, these shifts produced a massive redistribution of the property tax base: from city to suburb, old to new, industrial to postindustrial. At the same time, city leaders used federal urban renewal funds to remove aging infrastructure and housing stock near downtowns and replace them with "higher" uses, redistributing hundreds of thousands of acres of property from homeowners and small businesses first to city governments and then to private sector developers. Whatever benefits accrued to older core cities as a consequence of these dramatic changes lay in the shadow of a much more profound redistribution: of social problems, especially poverty, to the central city, and public resources, namely the tax base, to suburban communities.[55]

A plethora of new policies and institutions at every level of governmental authority steered economic development in specific directions in these decades. Prior to the 1930s federal involvement in urban affairs was minimal. But by the late 1940s the federal government had committed to an activist role in shaping metropolitan America, through housing policies that made places like San Leandro and Fremont possible and through redevelopment, highway construction, and other transportation subsidies that transformed central cities and suburbs alike. Left to the vicissitudes of the free market in the first half of the century, post–New Deal urban America came to rely on a variety of governmental strategies aimed at assisting economic development, part of the Keynesian consensus. Locally, quasi-governmental organizations like the Port of Oakland and BART coordinated the movement of goods and people across distances both proximate and vast. And a new generation of city agencies—especially those involved in redevelopment—and civic groups with governmental cover, like OCCUR, did the same. The complicated origins and interpenetrating influences of government-directed development should not obscure a fundamental feature of how Oakland, like most aging cities nationwide, accomplished their reinvention: with massive public subsidies that bolstered segregation and increased social inequality. Their strategies benefited some groups and disadvantaged others. Their strategies developed certain places and underdeveloped others. The latter increasingly included the entirety of the Oakland flatlands.

Intended to rescue Oakland from decay, urban reengineering in these years took the city ever deeper into the contradictions of metropolitan capitalism. In contrast to the modernist rhetoric of the city's property-holding faithful, no bright, sleek, redesigned future seemed on the horizon in the early 1960s. Even the normally boosterish national press had begun to take notice of the worsening state of the American urban landscape. Popular discussions of the nation's urban ills in the 1950s and 1960s featured phrases like "urban suicide," "the stricken American city," and "urban emergency." Questions like "Are American cities obsolete?" were common. In truth, cities like Oakland were neither dead nor dying, and proclamations of such in this era were more than tinged with white privilege and remove and an underlying antiblack reading of urban America. There was a profound urban crisis, to be certain, but both contemporary commentary and subsequent histories of this period have emphasized an outside-in view of its form and character. Metaphorically standing on the edge of cities, observers have peered into its tangled problems, encouraged either by a postwar social science that valued purportedly objective distance or by a media apparatus that issued sensational and too often Armageddon-like pronouncements. What has been missed in both cases is that the urban transformations of this period precipitated a vast rethinking of the social and spatial narrative of urban life in the United States from *within* the cities themselves. Redistribution shaped how Oaklanders understood the city and their place in it. This process of rethinking proceeded in the East Bay as contentiously as anywhere in the nation, and it helped produce political movements that rippled across the city in the decades of the 1960s and 1970s.

5

Opportunity Politics

IN THE LATE 1950s, urban renewal was still a gilded promise, not a catastrophe. Despite suburban industrialization, Oakland retained good jobs. The city still provided a meaningful "step up" for many families. And a revived liberal politics, both locally and nationally, seemed committed to extending opportunity across the social spectrum. But optimism and expectations were tempered by existing conditions and past experience, especially among the city's African Americans. "In many fields of work, the job opportunities for the Negroes among the high school graduates are limited solely by their race," Arthur Hellender of Alameda County's Central Labor Council told the Oakland press in 1958. "Their future as citizens and taxpayers suffers from this limitation. Our future as a prospering area also suffers." African American poverty and social inequality were increasing dramatically, threatening to engulf the better part of a generation. The contest over how to halt and then reverse this process shaped the city's politics as had nothing since the general strike in 1946. But no elections turned on these contests. Instead, they took shape on the terrain of culture, in street protests, and within the civic and federal institutions created in the liberal spirit of defeating urban poverty.[1]

Fighting poverty had long been an objective of African American leaders across the political spectrum. In the decades after World War II, especially, the broad civil rights movement stood for economic rights as much as for *civil* rights. The two were intertwined and to many activists inseparable. The desegregation of work, housing, and education, civil rights proponents held, would go far in destroying the artificial barriers that kept black workers trapped and poor. Desegregation was the remedy, progress the expected result. Oakland NAACP board member Clinton White explained this approach in personal terms in a 1965 address to a West Oakland African American audience. He recalled the time when parents "looked forward to the day that here in the United States, and even more so in the state of California," when your son "could say that he was a union member, and that he could make between four and five and six hundred dollars a month." Those same workers, White explained, could "take what their earnings are . . . save them up . . . go down and get a loan, because the federal government would back it up . . . buy a home and raise other children." With a reliable, well-paying job and a decent home, African Americans could "walk the earth with dignity."

Here White refined a key element of postwar civil rights liberalism to its essence: the concrete ambitions of a generation that believed that government protection of black economic rights, along with union wages and a strong economy, could be leveraged into upward mobility and a more secure future for succeeding generations.[2]

Both popular memory and academic scholarship have elevated the southern civil rights movement as *the* normative, paradigmatic postwar black struggle. According to the most influential version of this narrative, a liberal civil rights coalition was assembled in the decade between Montgomery in 1955 and Selma in 1964 with the goal of destroying southern Jim Crow. Then, northern violence and black power destroyed the coalition after 1965 by alienating whites and calling forth the wrath and backlash of mainstream America. While not wrong on some counts, that narrative errs in casting African American politics nationwide as reductive to the aims of the southern movement or, even more narrowly, to the aims of the Southern Christian Leadership Conference. Further, it overestimates the commitment of whites nationwide to black equality, even at the height of civil rights mobilizations in 1963 and 1964. A graver interpretive roadblock within the inherited narrative lies in its casting of the North and West, and subsequently black power, as the foil of the South's "beloved community." Black political and social movements in places like Oakland were influenced by southern protest, but their own logic and history cannot be reduced to an epilogue of a romanticized southern movement. Nor is it historically sound to frame all forms of black struggle in terms of their relationship to the southern variant. The postwar civil rights movement emerged within regional and local contexts across the country. In each, leaders and constituencies responded tactically to the obstacles and opportunities those conditions presented. In Oakland, this led the movement into a prolonged engagement with black employment opportunities, the processes of metropolitan development and underdevelopment, and the institutions and philosophical foundations of the federal War on Poverty.[3]

In Oakland, as across much of the nation, the two decades after World War II were defined by the struggle to secure fair employment and fair housing in major cities. That struggle reached a climax between the mid-1950s and the mid-1960s. These years saw the high-water mark of fair employment and fair housing liberalism: the political fight to secure civil rights laws at the federal and state level and the push to have those laws enforced. After the long struggle to win recognition for racial equality in the federal New Deal state and in California, making the legal architecture work remained the overriding objective of Oakland's African American leaders during this period. A second site of black organizing emerged after 1964 in the federal War on Poverty. Animated by liberal confidence that poverty could be effectively eliminated within a generation, the war brought dozens of programs and funding streams to cities across the country. Black leaders in Oakland hoped to use both the War on Poverty's institutions and its federal dollars to leverage greater economic opportunity for the city's African American workers, which they understood fundamentally as a civil rights aim. To consider either the civil rights movement or the War on Poverty at the national level alone, therefore, is to miss their primary arena of significance: their articulation in local struggles over fairness, economic opportunity, and power in places like Oakland.[4]

Civil rights liberalism in these years embraced two related but discrete approaches to African American economic rights and opportunity. One stressed fair employment and the hiring of black workers. Predicated on the gradual desegregation of the American workplace, this view held that in time, with the right pressure, employers would loosen the strictures on hiring and open all jobs to black workers. This approach emphasized the employer side of the economy. Fair employment practices remained the key. A second emphasized the workers' side. Here, reformers focused attention on African American educational disadvantage and underpreparation for the job market, the long legacy of slavery and Jim Crow. Equally predicated on desegregation, this view held that in time, with the right social programs, educational opportunities, training, and assistance, African American workers would find a secure place in the national economy. This view, which lay behind the War on Poverty, stressed that jobs were available but that underpreparation rendered them inaccessible. Both approaches found adherents in Oakland. Both sought social mobility for the black working class, the "step up" that middle-class African Americans had begun to enjoy. Neither was entirely distinct, however. In the cauldron of urban realpolitik and experience, each approach shaped the other.[5]

Between 1957 and 1967, as these dual efforts moved forward, a broad strategic and philosophical shift became apparent. The civil rights movement and the War on Poverty, sometimes in tandem, often in tension, sought to expand opportunity for Oakland's African American working class. The precepts with which these efforts began changed dramatically over ten years: from faith in law to faith in direct action; from faith in individualist remedies to faith in collective and community-based remedies; from faith in American pluralism to faith in black nationalism and radicalism. Judging liberalism and its promises of inclusion a failure, black leaders turned their attention to bringing political and institutional power to African American communities. To remake opportunity was to tackle, and attempt to counter, the social and spatial arrangements of the ghetto and the legacies of both slavery and segregation embedded in it.

In doing so, African Americans did more than engage in struggle. They called forth a deep philosophical debate about the meaning of the ghetto and by extension the city itself and the place of both African Americans and whites within it. That debate—and the vast grassroots mobilizations behind it—produced an extraordinarily rich intellectual and political ferment among African Americans that would shape the subsequent trajectory of black power and black liberation politics in the second half of the 1960s and first half of the 1970s.[6]

The Limits of Civil Rights Liberalism

In the 1950s and early 1960s, African Americans in Oakland, as in most northern and western cities, struggled above all for economic rights. It required waging fierce contests over access to jobs. Oakland's civil rights establishment had long fought to break the East Bay's Jim Crow labor market: from the Key System and shipyard battles of the war years, extending through the NAACP's "spend your money where you can work" campaigns and FEP legislative battles of the 1950s, and continuing with desegregation of the fire and police departments, municipal agencies, and large employers like General Motors. As deindustrialization, the growth of the city's black community, and the national civil rights movement accelerated in the early 1960s, those contests intensified. Civil rights activists and labor leaders saw the problem as blocked opportunity. Once opportunity was accessible—through fair employment laws, changes in hiring practices, and the elimination of union discrimination—the black community could expect a fair distribution of jobs according to the most optimistic adherents of this position. For them, at issue was the restoration of American capitalism's promised economic mobility—a restoration to be achieved by tearing down the barriers and obstacles in the way of black advancement.[7]

Black trade unionists in Oakland seized on momentum generated by A. Philip Randolph's ongoing campaign to desegregate the AFL-CIO to press these efforts forward. Speaking at the Negro American Labor Council's (NALC) second annual national meeting in 1961, Randolph inveighed against union discrimination, decrying Jim Crow unionism as central to the "discriminatory racial practices that force Negroes into a marginal position within the economy." Those practices, reasoned Randolph, were the foremost cause of poverty. Following the defeat of a series of resolutions to liquidate unions that maintained a color bar, introduced by Randolph in 1959 at the national AFL-CIO convention, he led the Brotherhood into open rebellion. Joining with the Trade Union Leadership Council, a caucus of African American autoworkers from Detroit,

Randolph formed the NALC as a permanent pressure group within the AFL-CIO. In Oakland, black trade unionists launched a local branch of the NALC. In its first two years, the Oakland NALC sponsored conferences on the state of African Americans in Bay Area unions and cultivated a small but active leadership among local union activists. In early 1962 these leaders decided to take advantage of union elections to publicize the issue of racial discrimination in the East Bay labor movement. Clarence Davis, president of the Oakland NALC and a member of Local 304 of the Hod Carriers Union, led the campaign. "In local 304," Davis explained as he announced the NALC membership drive, "there are about 3,500 members, seventy-five percent of whom are Negroes, yet it has no Negro officers as such. Results—only a favored few receive the jobs." Davis headed a "minority slate" of candidates for key union posts in the Local 304 elections.[8]

Invited to speak at a packed Oakland Auditorium the week before Local 304's elections, Randolph delivered his usual litany of charges against the nation's white labor establishment: segregationist unions were responsible for poverty; liberal leaders within organized labor had not evolved beyond racial paternalism; and the movement as a whole was hypocritical on racial matters. Local 304's reform slate, coupled with the appearance of Randolph, made for "the most exciting union election in local Labor history," according to the *California Voice*. In response, incumbent white officials in Local 304 accused Davis of "injecting the race issue" into the election. Davis replied that cronyism and union democracy, not race, were the crucial issues. His slate, Davis countered, represented the "rank and file" and would support "equality of treatment for all." In a surprising and disappointing conclusion to the dramatic public buildup, however, Davis and his slate lost the election to the incumbents by a margin of 2 to 1. Afterward, Davis attacked "the roots of white supremacy and race prejudice" in the labor movement. The *Voice* joined in, condemning Local 304's white leaders for using "red tape and the usual gimmicks" that over the course of six years had "stymied every effort to secure representation for the rank-and-file membership" in Local 304. Unable to secure a major victory in any local elections, and lacking a single worksite where black organizers could build support, the East Bay NALC enjoyed only a brief flowering, never becoming the prominent force in civil rights and trade union reform that Clarence Davis had imagined.[9]

The Oakland NAACP picked up where Davis and the NALC left off. In the early 1960s Donald McCullum, a prominent attorney and protégé of D. G. Gibson and Byron Rumford in the East Bay Democratic Club, led a reorganization and reinvigoration of the NAACP. The latter had begun to draw criticism for its cautiousness since C. L. Dellums' departure and the FEP victory of 1959. As president, McCullum helped imbue the organization with a new protest militancy and impatience with white Oakland's racial paternalism. Events in Oakland mirrored national trends, as NAACP branches across the nation reorganized under more militant leadership—the first real infusion of aggressive activists since the communist purges of the early 1950s. In the summer of 1963 the Oakland NAACP led a local coalition that mirrored A. Phillip Randolph's March on Washington Movement, bringing together the Congress of Racial Equality (CORE), churches, fraternal organizations, and ministerial alliances along with liberal white church congregations. Calling themselves the Civil Rights Coordinating Committee (CRCC), the coalition pressed the Oakland City Council for greater commitment to racial equality, especially the fight against employment discrimination. In a nine-point "program to end racial bias," the CRCC promised "direct action" if the city equivocated or refused discussion. "It is in the tradition of America," McCullum explained, "to attempt to negotiate while using the power of demonstration." CCRC pamphlets pointed to the "thousands of our citizens who are unemployed, underemployed, unable to procure housing, educated in segregated schools."[10]

The CCRC's program embodied reforms sought by the city's African Americans since the 1940s and reaffirmed a black political agenda that reached back to the United Negro Labor Committee's contributions to the OVL campaign of 1947. At the head of the list were demands that the city endorse fair employment and institute "an affirmative policy" of "increased involvement" of minorities in all city contracts and hiring. Affirmative action was not a new concept in 1963, dating under different names at least to the 1940s, but it had recently found official validation in a series of both local and federal initiatives, and its appearance here marks an important chapter in its long history in California. The CCRC program also called for a variety of city commissions and committees to study race relations and discrimination. Finally, two of the program's nine points stood out for their concern with the spatial isolation of Oakland's black community. CCRC leaders demanded that the city return to the district election of councilmembers, also an OVL holdover, bringing direct representation on the council to heavily African American West and East Oakland. Second, the CCRC proposed that the city spell out the "responsibility of satellite communities" for providing open housing after decades of segregated suburban development. Both points drew attention to the emerging racial geography of the East Bay, in which African Americans in Oakland were isolated and cut off from political power in Oakland, on the one hand, and economic opportunity in the suburban belt, on the other. Little save a war of words came from the CCRC proposals, however. Mayor Houlihan, who dodged and dismissed the committee's criticism, said that black leaders were behaving "as if Oakland is Birmingham."

The official attitude was epitomized by Councilmember Robert McKeen's condescending question to McCullum: would he entertain a statement of ways in which "Negro people could help make Oakland a better city? Would you object if *we* gave *you* a program?"[11]

On the heels of the CRCC campaigns, a second civil rights group, the Ad Hoc Committee to End Discrimination, joined the protests against job inequality in the East Bay. Formed by black and white college students, young activists, and CORE members from Oakland, Berkeley, and San Francisco, the committee adopted the civil disobedience tactics that had emerged in the early 1960s as the hallmark of new left protest. Their sit-ins in San Francisco automobile dealerships, the Sheraton Hotel, and restaurants in 1964 made them one of the region's most visible racial justice groups overnight. An offspring of the W.E.B. DuBois Club of San Francisco, an activist organization with strong ties to the old left, the committee emerged as the first significant local alliance between the white new left and young black activists, an alliance that would have a long and tense, but productive, career in Oakland and Berkeley. In the spring of 1964 the committee won an unprecedented series of meetings with *Oakland Tribune* publisher William Knowland by threatening demonstrations and sit-ins at the symbol of the city's conservatism, the downtown Tribune tower. Under Knowland, who had retreated from his 1958 electoral defeat to run his father's newspaper, the *Tribune* remained the cornerstone of racial paternalism in the East Bay, backing the city council in its deflection of the CCRC protests. A congenial exploratory meeting in early May with Knowland, the AFL Central Labor Council, and the individual unions that represented *Tribune* employees gave way to more bitter exchanges a few weeks later when the publisher refused to divulge the racial breakdown of *Tribune* employees. Knowland insisted that the newspaper practiced fair hiring and that he would submit such information only "to any agent of the state government or the federal government that feels they have a proper inquiry to make in this field."[12]

The *Tribune* and the Ad Hoc Committee stood on two sides of what had become a familiar divide in the early 1960s. Knowland took a legalistic position, arguing that the newspaper adhered to existing fair employment laws and union contract nondiscrimination clauses. The committee replied that obeying the law meant little if the end result was an absence of black employees. Less than 30 of the newspaper's 1,250 employees were African American, according to the committee. "I don't know of any organization or industry in the country who *admits* discrimination," committee member Michael Meyerson told Knowland. The only way to assess the problem, according to Meyerson, was to determine "how many Negroes work for a firm as opposed to how many others work for that firm." Outcome, not legalistic process, was the measure of fair employment. With little progress made over the spring and early summer, the committee threw a picket line around the *Tribune* building in down-town Oakland. In December 1964 the committee formed a human wall of more than four hundred demonstrators that blocked *Tribune* gates and prevented trucks loaded with morning papers from leaving. Eighteen committee members were arrested, and Knowland's resolve redoubled. He saw the demonstrators as a "threat to the entire community" and published in the *Tribune* a long defense of the newspaper's position. Pro-testers' momentum subsequently shifted to defending the eighteen in court, a long affair that diffused the on-site demonstrations.[13]

These and other large-scale protests and acts of civil disobedience, which grew in strength and numbers over the course of 1964, were little tolerated by the *Tribune* and the city's downtown business interests. "It is a new form of gangsterism," a *Tribune* editorial in early 1965 declared, "a thinly veiled attack upon the system of private enterprise." The largest antidiscrimination protests in the East Bay to date, with as many as six hundred pickets marching on weekends, the *Tribune* actions signaled the arrival of a powerful movement activism that placed both employers and politicians on the defensive. "How many people seeking to invest new capital, form new business enterprises, and employ additional workers will want to come here?" if protests continue, the *Tribune* asked in a caustic editorial. "It is time for the community to mobilize for counter-action." With those words, the *Tribune* staked out the ground on which it would stand for the remainder of the decade in the face of increasing grassroots organizing and direct action in Oakland. Knowland and the newspaper told protestors and activists again and again that their efforts kept businesses from locating in the city and hurt the economy.[14]

Following the *Tribune* campaign, the East Bay CORE extended the jobs struggle even deeper into the heart of the Bay Area's economy, chal-lenging a long-standing racial line defended by both employers and unions. Dismantling the "front of the house/back of the house" divide in service, restaurant, hotel, and retail work had been an objective of African Americans in both Oakland and San Francisco since the 1950s. Bay Area restaurants, bars, and retail stores had long supported unspo-ken rules confining black workers to unskilled jobs where customers could not see them, in the "back of the house." Such practices went far beyond personal insult. In all service work, especially in restaurants and hotels, the visible, public jobs were the most remunerative because they came with access to tip and commission money. African Americans could always get jobs busing tables, working in stock rooms, cleaning, and loading trucks, but almost never in the higher-status and better-paid jobs "out front." Drawing on student activists from the University of California in Berkeley, community organizers from West Oakland, and a group of men and women steeped in the activist tradition of James Farmer, CORE launched uninhibited and militant demonstrations. As pickets went up in front of Montgomery Ward, AGE (a large discount store in East Oakland), and restaurants downtown and in Jack London Square in 1964 and 1965, activists promised nonviolent direct action until employers agreed to negotiate with CORE activists.[15]

Oakland's service sector unions and employers ducked behind one another, diffusing CORE's pressure to integrate. The East Bay Restaurant Association blamed abysmal racial employment patterns—20 percent of busboys, but less than 2 percent of waiters and waitresses, were African American in a city now one-third black—on the city's cooks, culinary, and bartender unions. Restaurants, the association innocently claimed, employed only those workers who had union cards. CORE responded with a letter to the Central Labor Council. "CORE has found through past experience in employment projects," the letter read, "that it is the *employer* who bears the major responsibility for racial discrimination in hiring." Indeed, it was common practice among restaurant unions never to dispatch a black worker to a job unless the establishment specifically requested a "Negro," a rare occurrence. The East Bay Restaurant Association, CORE explained, had "tried to shift the blame for racism from the employers to the unions." When CORE looked to the Labor Council for assistance, however, the four major culinary unions balked, issuing a joint statement with restaurant management insisting that neither party was at fault. Because the industry's collective bargaining agreements stipulated that employers "shall not discriminate" and that unions "must refer all applicants to jobs on a nondiscriminatory basis," the statement explained, both employers and unions were innocent of charges of discrimination. Hiding behind contract language proved a successful sleight of hand, because it made CORE appear to be making unrealistic demands. But the real blow was the union's refusal to become an ally, even after CORE's solicitous request. Meanwhile, the racial line in employment remained intact. Not until 1972, when an African American waiter named James Gay, filed a federal class-action suit against one of the San Francisco culinary locals, did a court order force the industry to take meaningful steps toward desegregation and job equality. It remained one of the region's most segregated for another decade.[16]

The duplicity of Oakland's labor movement thus continued to undermine civil rights efforts. Liberal white AFL-CIO leaders like Arthur Hellender, Robert Ash, and Richard Groulx—all of whom came out of the left wing of the OVL coalition of the 1940s—spoke in favor of civil rights and against both union and employer discrimination. Alameda County's trade union leadership, along with San Francisco's, continued to anchor the Northern California Democratic Party, where the labor-NAACP alliance in the 1958 election had established an active and influential civil rights political bloc. But in the day-to-day business of dispatching, promoting, and organizing workers, most trade union locals in Oakland had shed only the outer trappings of their Jim Crow past by the early 1960s. Larger numbers of black workers now earned union wages, to be sure, but African Americans still found themselves confined to unskilled and semiskilled jobs by union tradition and seniority, and, in the case of the building trades and a number of service occupations, shut out of entire industries altogether. Whatever the AFL-CIO's abstract commitment to civil rights, trade union discrimination deepened the already multiplying problems of black poverty and unemployment and made the task of reconstituting ladders of African American working-class opportunity in Oakland more difficult. In the early 1960s overall union density in the six-county San Francisco–Oakland metropolitan area varied between 45 and 50 percent of the nonfarm workforce, and the wholesale and retail trade unions and the restaurant and hotel unions alone claimed nearly as many members (117,200) as all of the manufacturing unions in the Bay Area (121,100).[17]

Actions like those taken by the NALC, the CRCC, NAACP, CORE, and the Ad Hoc Committee at the *Tribune* embodied the liberal civil rights approach to jobs in the first half of the 1960s. To the leaders of these organizations and their constituents, jobs represented avenues of opportunity. But access to those jobs was blocked by patterns of discrimination that threw up obstacles in the normal paths of mobility for African American workers. The mechanisms of unemployment and poverty, in this view, lay in the economy and the set of white institutions responsible for erecting and defending the barriers. To remove those blocks, civil rights groups sought to pressure employers and unions to open the labor market to Oakland's black community—using a combination of moral suasion, direct action, and legal leverage. It was the intensification and expansion of a strategy that had occupied the city's African American activists to varying degrees since the end of World War II. But it was not working. Civil rights pressure worked most effectively in the early 1960s when the militancy of demonstrators compelled at least token cooperation by employers and unions. Such pressure did force some employers to negotiate employment agreements. But promises and agreements were often worth less than the paper on which they were printed, and job advocates had begun to realize that broad shifts in the economy could not be won small fight by small fight. As in the 1950s, civil rights advocates thus looked to the state—not to pass a fair employment law, but to make the existing law work. In the ongoing fight for jobs, the state of California still looked like a potentially powerful ally.

Fair Employment and Affirmative Action

Civil rights leaders had long sought a fair employment law to add leverage to their desegregation efforts. Fair employment legislation represented the great hope of African American and white liberals for dissolving Jim Crow in the workforce. When the Democratic electoral sweep of 1958 made the law a reality, Dellums, black labor leaders, and other civil rights advocates went to work to make the commission a lever of racial democracy in California. According to Dellums, who became the commission's first chairman, the state Fair Employment Practice law was to be the front wedge of an assault on hiring discrimination and Jim Crow unionism in California. It would ensure open and fair economic opportunity, what Dellums called the "unfinished task of democracy in industry." Governor Brown expressed similar optimism when he heralded the new law as "a historic step forward in the ages long battle against prejudice and discrimination." But California's FEP legislation neither anticipated nor could resolve according to its own precepts the structural legacies of racial exclusion in the state's labor markets. Sincere but toothless, the California Fair Employment Practice Commission stretched its meager resources across the state, case by case, in an attempt to outrun the rising unemployment rate among black workers. The double burden of a virtually unenforceable law and insufficient funding shackled the new commission, humbling its members and public supporters alike. To compensate for the law's weaknesses, the commission gradually and tentatively embraced affirmative action, helping to open a new era in California's employment history.[18]

The California FEPC's problems began in 1959, its first year of operation. Legally, the commission was empowered to investigate only complaints of discrimination filed by an individual, and the law made no provision for punishment other than requiring a guilty party to "cease and desist" the unfair or discriminatory practice. Class action was impossible; voluntarism the only remedy. Derived from New Deal labor law, the FEP required the plaintiff to prove the existence of discrimination. Forced to pursue thousands of individual complaints, and limited in each case solely to the individual worker named in the suit, the FEPC bogged down in what detractors called a "band-aid" approach: assisting a few individuals while broad patterns of discrimination persisted. Even in individual cases, discrimination proved difficult to establish. "I've had a lot of cases that I've firmly believed that the person was discriminated against," Dellums told an interviewer, "but I couldn't talk the employer into doing anything about it and we couldn't get any evidence that would justify a public hearing on it." The law was especially weak in addressing union discrimination. Most unions had nondiscrimination clauses in their constitutions by the early 1960s and kept few records of how membership decisions were made and no records of the racial composition of their locals. The law in which Dellums had placed so much hope now seemed a diversion for the civil rights movement.[19]

Weaknesses in the legal architecture of FEP led the commission to contemplate new strategies. Edward Howden, the commission's executive officer, told the U.S. Senate in 1963 that the "case-by-case method alone falls far short of solving the massive problem they [FEPCs in California and other states] face." The piecemeal approach authorized by the fair employment law had demonstrated, according to Howden, that "the traditional barriers to equal opportunity will not come down until large employers and unions, and whole industries and occupations, have been reached." Discouraged by the commission's ineffectiveness, and outpaced by CORE and the NAACP, which by 1963 had begun to negotiate employment agreements with Bay Area companies, the California FEPC turned to affirmative action as an antidote to case-by-case amelioration. In doing so, the FEPC ventured beyond the specific mechanisms of the fair employment law to, as Howden explained, "stimulate recruiting, hiring, and promoting of the best qualified personnel, inclusive of all groups in the population . . . carried out through cooperative surveys, research, planning." At the federal level, President Kennedy, under pressure from national civil rights leaders, had already taken the first tentative steps toward affirmative action in 1961 and 1963 with Executive Orders 10925 and 11114, which required federal contractors to make efforts to hire African American and Latino workers. Howden and the California FEPC, pushed by both local and national black activists, envisioned an even deeper and more sustained project of multiracial employment across the California economy: a full shift from antidiscrimination efforts, ensuring racially neutral hiring practices, to affirmative action, the purposeful pursuit of a multiracial workforce.[20]

Discrimination at the Bank of America, one of the state's largest private employers, emerged as the first major test of the FEPC's new approach. It began with protest. Early in 1964 CORE chapters in Oakland, San Francisco, and Los Angeles began picketing the offices and branches of the bank. CORE's leaders demanded that bank officials disclose the racial composition of its workforce and then enter into a "Fair Employment Process Pact" that would ensure fairness in all future hiring. CORE had won similar agreements with Montgomery Ward. Similar agreements had been forged by civil rights groups in the Bay Area with Safeway, the West Bay Association of Food Industries, and the San Francisco Retail Dry Goods Association. CORE protesters, riding the national wave of direct action in 1964, struck Bank of America hard. Picketers protested at bank branches throughout the spring and summer, embarrassing one of the state's oldest institutions in newspaper headlines and photographs throughout California. Unwilling to yield to CORE or negotiate with its representatives, the bank invited the FEPC to intervene in the dispute. The bank and the commission negotiated a "memorandum of understanding" outlining an affirmative action program. Initially suspicious of the pact, CORE finally withdrew its pickets three months after the memorandum was signed, concluding that in its most recent round of recruitment the bank had effectively "ended discrimination in the hiring of minority groups." CORE's San Francisco head, William Bradley, expressed optimism that the bank's "good faith" would continue to produce gains in black employment, where, he noted with emphasis, "Negroes still constitute little more than two percent" of the workforce.[21]

The Bank of America agreement became the affirmative action standard in California. It represented both the best and worst of these early, gradual, halting 1960s initiatives. Pressure from CORE had brought one of the state's most conservative employers into a public accommodation with the civil rights movement. Nonetheless, the FEPC–Bank of America memorandum of understanding was even more inoculated against enforcement than FEPC rulings. The agreement relied on voluntary compliance, because California law contained no mechanism to compel any private employer toward affirmative action, a concept and strategy just emerging. CORE had hesitated to end its picketing for three months precisely because its leaders feared that the FEPC-brokered agreement was the bank's way of maneuvering out from underneath public pressure. Activists worried that the FEPC's new level of involvement threatened to diffuse the burgeoning protest movement just then gathering strength in the Bay Area. After the Bank of America agreement, both CORE and the NAACP continued to pursue their own compacts with employers, turning to the FEPC principally as a mediator. The weaknesses of these early affirmative action agreements thus kept civil rights leaders wary and community organizers cynical, even as they constituted important early models for how the state might build a multiracial workforce.[22]

Affirmative action agreements in early 1960s California left a mixed legacy. Both the California FEPC and the federal Equal Employment Opportunity Commission (EEOC) continued to make voluntary compliance the basis of affirmative action. Such language reduced the agreements in the main to rhetorical documents alone. Construction unions working on projects for which an equal employment mandate existed, for instance, typically claimed that the contractual nondiscrimination clause itself, not the composition of the workforce, constituted their compliance. Such evasions gave African American leaders reason to be distrustful. At the federal level, changes in law and practice in the late 1960s and early 1970s, including the use of class action suits, marginally improved affirmative action agreements. In 1972 Congress gave the EEOC the power to initiate discrimination claims, substantially enlarging the commission's investigative and prosecutorial effectiveness. Nonetheless, enforcement of federal affirmative action agreements remained contingent on the agency involved, on political leverage, often on the discretion of the agency director, and on whether or not pressure could be applied by civil rights groups at the worksite. Affirmative action would prove effective in some arenas, such as education and government employment, where enforcement mechanisms and cooperative unions were strong. In much of the private economy, especially among small- and medium-sized employers, however, affirmative action remained in this era a weak, almost unenforceable, and completely voluntary policy.[23]

The formative period of affirmative action in California offers a vantage on national debates about workplace desegregation. The passage of fair employment laws in cities and states across the nation dominated the agenda of African American activists in the 1940s and 1950s. Employers and unions, however, quickly adapted. Adhering to the letter of antidiscrimination laws was easy, because once "white only" designations and other explicitly racist requirements were eliminated from job descriptions, discrimination was almost impossible to prove. In practice, the vast majority of employers in the private sector announced jobs through word of mouth and recruited new workers through existing employees. Unions, too, relied on recruitment networks composed of family, friends, co-workers, churches, seniority-based hiring halls, and the like. In law, such hiring practices did not constitute active discrimination. But they nonetheless produced striking employment segregation, because they were products of deeply segregated American life—in which white residential, social, and cultural circles never overlapped with those of African Americans—and a history of exclusion. Employers and unions thus accommodated civil rights demands in public while in practice they followed historical patterns of discrimination. Affirmative action emerged as a strategic compromise among activists, state fair employment agencies, and the federal government over remedies to this stubborn problem. But for black activists, both fair employment and affirmative action meant that employers would *hire* African American workers. The distinction was tactical, not philosophical or theoretical, because black activists had long insisted that the outcome, not the process, remained the measure of desegregation's success.[24]

Black and white liberals alike pursued affirmative action, but important distinctions remained between their approaches to economic opportunity in this era. Most African American liberals, from civil rights leaders to ministers, trade unionists, and politicians, stressed the *outcome* of fair employment—a fair distribution of jobs. Most white liberals, on the other hand, stressed the *process* of fair employment—ensuring that certain legal procedures were followed. In time, some white liberals would move closer to the outcome-oriented position, and for most white radicals outcome continued to define the appropriate measure of affirmative action. The basic differences between black and white liberals, however, would grow over the course of the 1960s, even as the Great Society emerged as the organizing framework within which both groups operated. This dynamic underscores the fluid, conflicted relationship that most black leaders had developed with liberalism, a relationship dating to the 1930s. As a loose set of prescriptions for an activist federal state intervening in the private economy on behalf of disadvantaged people, American liberalism since the 1930s had embraced individualist remedies and policies. As such, its capacity to solve broad social problems, especially the disadvantaging of an entire *group* across multiple sectors of American social and economic life, was always limited. Black enthusiasm for liberalism was thus conditional, never absolute.[25]

BART and Black Working-Class Opportunity

In the spring of 1966 construction of Bay Area Rapid Transit lines through Oakland brought the contest for jobs to an intense pitch. The adoption of affirmative action was a notable and important change in the civil rights language of employment, but in BART job protests an even more fundamental shift in rhetoric and strategy emerged: fair employment struggles gave way to a community-centered politics of place. In late April activists and pickets stormed a planning meeting of the BART board. "It's *your* problem to deal with discriminating unions," Tom Fike, co-chair of a coalition called Justice on BART (JOBART) told board members. Pushing past fellow protestors crowded together, Elijah Turner, a neighborhood organizer from West Oakland, followed Fike's remarks by shouting, "this is all white here that's making the decisions! You talk about FEPC, but that's run by fat cats like you." Turner gestured toward the board and added, "nothing I can do is as bad as BART." When questioned, BART representatives dismissed Fike, Turner, and JOBART as extremists. "Our contracts have a nondiscrimination clause, which is considerably beyond what is required by law," the transit district general manager told reporters. "Beyond that, we cannot legally interfere between our contractors and the unions." In a familiar scenario, BART's legalistic response permitted the appearance of rationality, while black activists were portrayed as making unreasonable demands. Meanwhile, construction had begun on the nation's largest regional transit system, the biggest jobs boom (eight thousand jobs promised) to hit the Bay Area since the massive

Figure 5.1. Elijah Turner delivering a speech in the late 1960s. Turner was a grassroots activist in West Oakland, a national leader in CORE, and along with Paul Cobb one of the chief strategists of community action within the city's War on Poverty program and later the Black Caucus. Courtesy of the *Oakland Tribune.*

bridge projects of the 1930s. No plan was in place to employ African Americans or ethnic Mexicans, and there was little agreement about how to conceive one.[26]

The long battle for access to BART construction and operation jobs lasted more than a decade, from 1965 through the late 1970s, testing approaches to black employment that had evolved in the fair employment struggles of the previous decade. Bay Area activists had proven in the early 1960s that public agreements on black hiring could be won, on however modest terms, with a combination of protest and negotiation. But as unemployment and poverty in Oakland's black communities grew worse, the victories to date seemed hollow, the promises of further gains empty, the affirmative action agreements worthless. Union and employer bias in the late 1950s and first half of the 1960s had decreased in measured degree and had produced some improvement in job equality in Oakland. Large parts of Oakland nonetheless remained untouched. The FEP model was a disappointing paper tiger and rankled many within the black community, especially community organizers like Elijah Turner. To activists like Turner and organizations like JOBART, the fate of the African American working class remained in the hands of people and institutions outside the community: white workers and unions, private business, the state, and even the FEPC itself. Rather than seeking remedies through such existing institutions, JOBART spoke the language of community power, a discursive and tactical turn that replaced liberal individualist legal remedies with place-based political organizing and action. The struggle over BART jobs thus not only tested the efficacy of different approaches to black employment but marked a deepening of the tension between FEP liberalism and a community-centered strategy of protest and confrontation designed to bring economic development directly to the working-class black community.[27]

Across the bay in San Francisco, preparations for BART protests had begun in 1965, when members of the San Francisco NAACP established the first incarnation of JOBART to press the transit district and the construction unions for a hiring program. After nearly a year of negotiations, San Francisco JOBART Chairman Arthur Lathan was exhausted and dispirited. "The apathy we have met among both the unions and at BART has been stunning," Lathan said. "Nothing is being done; nothing, it appears, will be done." Back in Oakland, where many of BART's above-ground tracks would require the clearing of housing and businesses, NAACP and CORE offices began fielding complaints that the transit district was forcing West Oakland homeowners to sell at below-market prices. "BART feels that the property owners should not expect very much money for their property because their neighborhood is run down," the grassroots newspaper *Flatlands* complained in 1966. The reality in

West Oakland, the paper continued, was that "fair market value can only be meaningless and cruel to a poor retired couple living in a mortgage-free $10,000 house which cannot be replaced for $10,000." The combination of BART's foot-dragging in job talks and the specter of more residential displacement compelled Oakland activists to call a community meeting at Beth Eden Baptist Church in West Oakland in early 1966. At the Eden meeting, organizers established an East Bay JOBART headquarters and broadened the group's agenda to include housing and business displacement. JOBART drew a diverse array of Oakland's religious, civil rights, and community organizations into a spacious coalition capable of mobilizing large numbers of people through a variety of leadership and organizational channels. The NAACP, CORE, and Wade Johnson's United Tax Payers and Voters Union joined the East Bay Conference on Religion and Race, the Baptist Ministerial Alliance, the Interdenominational Ministerial Alliance, and a host of other churches in JOBART.[28]

The coalition did more than bring together African American churches and civil rights organizations: it helped to change the language and philosophy of the local black struggle. In a series of open meetings that drew hundreds of community members to McClymonds High School in West Oakland, JOBART attracted a large contingent of grassroots activists and neighborhood organizers, people whose identification with West Oakland as a place was far stronger than their relationship to the city's middle-class black leadership. This was a self-selected group of men and women whose political consciousness had been forged in the "ghetto" or "community" where, working among considerable poverty and disillusionment, civil rights employment remedies seemed abstract at best and class-biased at worst. The group included African American grassroots activists, sympathetic white leftists, and a handful of ethnic Mexican organizers whose voices were growing more audible in the city's political culture. Speaking in the emerging language of community power, activists like Turner and Ralph Williams, one of West Oakland's longest-standing leaders, were searching for ways to connect West Oakland as a place to the social movement activism then sweeping through the East Bay. JOBART thus drew West Oaklanders into a coalition that embodied the style of liberal movement activism as well as the community orientation of new leaders increasingly dissatisfied with the legal gradualism of civil rights work.[29]

As JOBART representatives saw it, the future of West Oakland was at stake in 1966. BART itself could be a harbinger of that future. Resolving the dispute one way, the impact on the community was positive; resolved another, a disaster. "JOBART has remained firm in its position," an organizational newsletter explained, "of holding BART responsible for the problems created by the building of the rapid transit system." Distilled to essence, two major concerns occupied JOBART. First, BART was seen as the latest in a series of restructurings that had isolated West Oakland from the multiple centers of power and economic activity in the Bay Area. As a continuation of freeway construction and urban renewal, BART would accelerate the conversion of black neighborhoods into slums, places where jobs, income, and opportunity flowed out and away. "We've been bull dozed one time too many" was a typical west Oakland complaint. Second, JOBART wanted to force union discrimination into the open. Construction jobs were among the most visible in 1960s' Oakland, as redevelopment projects, new freeways, office buildings, and civic improvements provided a virtual jobs program in the central city for all-white trade unions. "Workers will be found when the time comes," JOBART representative Arthur Lathan insisted, "but they will be found by importing already trained people from outside the Bay Area. Thus our tax money will solve the unemployment problem of other areas." JOBART's demands ranged across the spectrum of social and economic dislocations produced by BART construction and sought to preserve West Oakland as a viable neighborhood, a "part of the city" as Ralph Williams would later say, rather than a liminal space on the margins of metropolitan life.[30]

Space itself was an important dimension of the exchanges between BART and the community coalition. BART General Manager B. R. Stokes insisted that the new transit system would permit West Oakland residents access to employment, shopping, and housing in outlying areas. "The non-white clearly needs mobility," Stokes noted, "the freedom to move out of ghetto life on a daily basis; for others, on a lifetime basis." Stokes echoed civil rights liberals' belief in the efficacy of unblocking exits to the ghetto. But his metaphor was mechanical, not social. Mobility was a physical problem, not a racial one. Other BART officials and regional opinion-makers argued that the system allowed "a person to live where he chooses and to work where he chooses anywhere in the metropolitan area." The *San Francisco Examiner* concurred, commending BART for knitting the region together as a "true metropolis—not a vast agglomeration of urban sprawl." JOBART's community coalition did not dismiss such optimism out of hand. Rather, community members demanded that BART provide direct economic benefits to West Oakland, much as the system had promised to downtown Oakland businesses and innumerable communities along the line's suburban route through Alameda and Contra Costa counties. If BART represented an economic boost for them, why not for West Oakland? JOBART stressed the need to rebuild the black community *in place* by using development money attached to major projects like BART. Both transit officials and JOBART embraced a metropolitan concept of the Bay Area, but each imagined West Oakland according to a different logic: BART as a collection of individuals who made free-market decisions, and JOBART as an organized community asserting a collective interest.[31]

The JOBART manifesto, issued in 1966, challenged the West Oakland community's isolation from the mainstream economy. The coalition wanted BART, but on terms that would benefit West Oakland rather than further marginalize it. They insisted that employees be recruited solely from current residents of the three transit district counties—San Francisco, Alameda, and Contra Costa—and that they include "significant numbers of minority group members." BART should provide employment to workers "who have previously received skilled training and have been unable to find employment in their trades because of historic patterns of discrimination," that unions "shall actively promote upgrading of workers," and that trainees should have "full union membership rights." Finally, JOBART addressed the larger question of political power, noting that "BART is a government agency—the government agency which is creating the social issues about which JOBART is concerned." "No BART contracts are valid," the JOBART manifesto declared, "which do not include the negotiated conditions of the JOBART proposals." To BART and Oakland's business class, this was the height of arrogance, but to the city's flatland residents it represented an important antidote to their historic disempowerment. It posited community control over the community's most precious resource, jobs. "There are eight thousand jobs that will be available with BART when the thing gets into full schedule," Rev. Alex Jackson told a West Oakland audience. "We feel that we should have our rightful share."[32]

The JOBART conflict stood at the heart of the second reconstruction in northern urban America. JOBART's coalition raised a set of questions that tested the black rights movement's purchase within both the local and national political culture. How should the African American community make claims on resources on the basis of historic patterns of discrimination and the new spatial reality of the ghetto? Could Oakland's black communities leverage the state—either through the California FEPC or the Civil Rights Act of 1964—to facilitate access to resources like jobs and training? Could "the community" metaphorically and actually insert itself into a contractual relationship between employers and unions and invalidate that relationship? In the mid-1960s the institutional architecture of U.S. labor and civil rights laws and state-level agencies like the California FEPC was underequipped either to answer those questions or to strike a substantial blow against broad patterns of employment discrimination. For their part, most labor unions were uninterested in, at best, and hostile to, at worst, fully desegregating the labor market. In response to such limitations, coalitions like JOBART sought community power, and subsequently self-determination, as means of achieving the access and freedoms that fair employment legislation had promised. JOBART represented one attempt to resolve an old tension within African American political movements between the push for desegregation and the goal of black economic development and community power. JOBART's coalition underscored that this tension was tactical, not philosophical: these were parallel, mutually reinforcing objectives, not competing or mutually exclusive ones.[33]

JOBART made some headway in securing black employment on the new transit system. On "Job Sunday" in early June 1966, JOBART led hundreds of marchers down Telegraph Avenue to a rally at Lake Merritt. Speakers attacked four "hard-core Jim Crow unions" (plumbers, electricians, operating engineers, and ironworkers) and the BART district, which "collaborated with and condoned discriminatory practices." Oakland Mayor John Reading dismissed JOBART's protests and tactics as unnecessary, but six months later he issued a surprising endorsement of JOBART's criticism of the unions. In a speech before dozens of the city's clergy, Reading accused the unions of promoting "discriminatory hiring" and using "various devices to screen out" African Americans and other workers of color. His decision was tactical. Reading knew that as BART made plans to seek federal grants, the agency's construction contracts would have to contain provisions ensuring the hiring of minority workers on a proportional basis. In addition, after the summer of 1966 Reading was desperate to accommodate the city's middle-class black establishment, which had become more important in the eyes of white city administrators as the rise of the Black Panthers introduced a new militancy into Oakland's working-class black neighborhoods. Reading could afford to risk losing the votes of those building trades unionists who still lived in Oakland if his concessions would mollify African American leaders. Though tepid and cautious, Reading's endorsement of affirmative action in BART contracts was the beginning of a community consensus around a BART employment plan.[34]

BART subsequently announced an affirmative action program in early 1967 designed to serve as a model for other federally financed urban projects. Brokered by the Department of Housing and Urban Development (HUD), the plan called for stepped-up attempts by unions to recruit minority apprentices, subcontracts for minority-owned firms, and outreach programs by BART contractors in Bay Area high schools to discuss employment opportunities. The plan incorporated some of JOBART's demands, though as expected neither BART nor the federal government pushed for more than voluntary compliance by the trade unions. The disappointing first year of the plan—black workers made up approximately 20 percent of the construction workforce, but were hired primarily as unskilled laborers and made up less than 2 percent of apprentices and less

than 5 percent of office workers in the first year of construction work—
reaffirmed for members of the JOBART coalition the tenacity of employment bias and the necessity of a prolonged engagement with both BART
and the unions. The struggle among BART, the construction unions, and
the West Oakland coalition over jobs, training, and community priorities
extended well into the 1970s. But the struggle's immediate legacy, the emergence of a community-centered model of organization, protest, and negotiation in West Oakland, would help change the shape of the city's politics.[35]

War on Poverty

Employment desegregation and the push for both equal opportunity and
a "fair share" of jobs, though thwarted in many instances, had begun to
yield results. Affirmative action agreements and pressure from protestors
and the state FEPC and federal EEOC had begun to pry open some previously all-white enclaves. Enforcement mechanisms remained weak, as
in the BART case, and the structural legacies of Jim Crow and the monopoly power of unions still blocked paths of economic mobility for
working-class blacks. But a decade of sustained pressure from civil rights
groups had at least worn away visible holes in those barriers. Such incremental progress, however, had done little for the city's poorest workers.
Poverty, unemployment, and underemployment remained Oakland's most
pervasive social problems. The city's overall unemployment rate in 1966
stood at 8 percent, 12 percent among African Americans. Worse, as many
as one-third of African Americans and Latinos in the city lived in poverty.
    When President Johnson and the Democratic Congress introduced the
collection of social programs that would constitute the nation's "War on
Poverty" in 1964 and 1965, liberal civil rights activists in Oakland responded enthusiastically. Superior Court Judge Lionel Wilson, a long-time
member of the East Bay Democratic Club and Oakland NAACP, declared
that Oakland would be "the first city in the nation to put planning for
human development on par with physical and economic planning." Two
other prominent East Bay Democratic Club members, Norvel Smith and
Don McCullum, echoed Wilson's enthusiasm. Smith told reporters that
the poverty war represented "new and inventive solutions to a big city's
socio-economic problems." McCullum added that the most important
problem "facing Negroes in the Bay Area" was "the lack of resources and
wherewithal to participate meaningfully in a money society." Wilson,
Smith, and McCullum urged the city's established professional black
leadership to embrace the War on Poverty as an extension of the fair employment and housing efforts of the previous decade. New federal antipoverty efforts seemed a logical extension of the civil rights movement

to include the most marginalized segment of the African American community. Smith headed the city's Ford Foundation programs in the early 1960s and went on to direct Oakland's Department of Human Resources, which oversaw local War on Poverty administration. McCullum directed the Adult Minority Employment Program and, along with Wilson, Clinton White, and Carl Metoyer, EBDC members all, sat on the city's OEO board.[36]

To understand the trajectory of Oakland's War on Poverty requires both a national and local frame of reference. Nationally, Johnson's war was one component of his and Congress's Great Society initiatives, a series of programs designed to erect a more stable economic foundation under the nation's middle class and to appeal to that class's cultural sensibilities. The Great Society included Medicare, Medicaid, federal subsidies for education, new urban renewal initiatives, expansions in Social Security, creation of federal arts and humanities endowments, and improved national park and highway programs, to name only the major programs. As a fresh-faced New Deal, and Johnson's effort to distinguish his liberalism from Franklin D. Roosevelt's, the Great Society's foundation was an optimistic theory of American society: opportunity existed for those who, with the government's assistance in education and welfare, were willing to look for it. "A generation ago," Walter Lippman wrote on the eve of the War on Poverty, "it would have been taken for granted that a War on Poverty meant taxing money away from the haves and turning it over to the have nots." But, he continued, "a revolutionary idea has taken hold" in which "the size of the pie can be increased by intention" and every part of society rewarded—an extension of the growth liberalism of which California was the preeminent national example. The central War on Poverty legislation, the Economic Opportunity Act, established the Office of Economic Opportunity (OEO) on the heels of Johnson's 1964 inaugural address. Congress approved a dizzying array of programs and grants between 1965 and the early 1970s aimed at eliminating poverty in the country's two most publicized deindustrialized spaces: central cities and the rural counties of Appalachia. The bulk of these programs, including the Manpower and Development Training Act (MDTA), the Comprehensive Employment and Training Act (CETA), and Model Cities legislation, provided education and training. Programmatic diversity characterized the federal government's antipoverty initiatives, but two fundamental concerns united them: holding Johnson's middle-class political coalition together and attacking poverty through education and other social services.[37]

Locally, the federal War on Poverty intersected in the East Bay with the political terrain shaped by the broad social movement of civil rights and community activists. That movement was ideologically manifold, multigenerational, and rapidly shifting, but in 1965 its most visible texture was a growing rift between the liberal professionals, African American and white, on the one hand, and the mobilized grassroots, on the other. Longtime NAACP and East Bay Democratic Club members Wilson, Smith, and McCullum each headed a major antipoverty agency or program in Oakland. They, and the East Bay Democratic Club leadership more generally, were positioned in between the established white downtown business interests who still ran the city and a loosely organized, but vocal and catalyzed set of community organizations and grassroots activists. The latter included veterans of CORE and the Civil Rights Coordinating Committee, West Oakland groups like the United Tax Payers and Voters Union, new coalitions like the East Oakland Parish, JOBART, and Spanish-Speaking Unity Council, and a host of organizations and spokespeople concerned directly with neighborhood needs. The community organizers who represented this broad and diverse population believed that antipoverty efforts had to be remade by grassroots struggle, because the war itself was an extension of a liberalism that by the middle 1960s they judged a failure. Pressing the city's middle-class black leadership as well as conservative white elites from below, grassroots activists raised fundamental questions about and challenges to reigning antipoverty philosophy. How would poverty and the poor themselves be defined and represented? Could the *war*'s emphasis on education and training make a difference in an economy still permeated with the legacy of Jim Crow? Rather than unblocking ghetto exits, should not antipoverty efforts be used to bring power to the ghetto? In this political terrain, antipoverty efforts were far more than an alphabet soup of federal programs. They constituted a discrete phase in the evolution of black political capacity in the East Bay and in the transformation of Oakland's political culture.[38]

Most of Oakland's OEO programs—the cluster of direct services to the poor that Americans associated with the War on Poverty—evolved directly out of a Ford Foundation grant the city received in 1961. They reflected Ford's emphasis on addressing the underpreparation that poverty warriors had come to associate with poor communities. Holding to a fundamentally optimistic view of the American economy and the place of an individual worker within it, the OEO addressed poverty through the preparation of workers for existing jobs. Oakland's OEO programs, like those throughout the nation, stressed educational reform: public school in-service training for teachers, summer school programs for remedial education, improved family planning and greater access to health-related information, and neighborhood youth programs. These services improved the lives of individuals and made life for those on the margins of the economy measurably better and more sane. Programs such as Head Start, Remedial Instruction, Elementary Summer School, and Neighborhood Legal Services seemed to promise the "human development" that many among the city's middle class, white and black, believed the ghetto lacked. "New economic opportunities were meaningless for the poor," Oakland's antipoverty agency declared in 1966, "unless the latter could take advantage of them." Many of OEO's programs brought undeniable benefits to poor people, but how far they would go toward eliminating, or even diminishing, poverty was another issue.[39]

Oaklanders thus vigorously pursued OEO funding and sought to make the city a model in the building of the Great Society. The city's OEO grants were among the largest in the nation: calculated on a per capita basis, Oakland received twice as much OEO money as Los Angeles and led all West Coast cities in the size of its federal antipoverty largess. The OEO divided Oakland's flatlands into four target areas—West, North, and East Oakland, and Fruitvale. In each, an Area Services Center coordinated job placement, vocational training referrals, adult education, legal assistance, and a host of other health and educational services. Job placement and training referrals, in particular, represented important initial steps toward the creation of career and educational pathways historically denied African Americans in white Oakland. Head Start, the OEO's most celebrated contribution to national efforts to assist poor communities, was also an important War on Poverty development.[40]

But philosophical and financial shortcomings overwhelmed these contributions. Philosophically, the OEO addressed poverty as a problem of individual development and the social disorganization of poor communities rather than as a function of the distribution of existing jobs or employment segregation. Moreover, the War on Poverty accelerated a profound shift that had been underway in antipoverty research and policy since the 1930s: from a focus on structural reform of the economy to a focus on managing and shaping the supposed "pathological" behavior of individuals. The OEO's emphasis on education and pathology had two advantages within the Great Society context: (1) it did not threaten middle-class assumptions about success, and (2) it presumed the existence of almost unlimited opportunity for those willing and able to seize it. These philosophical shortcomings were joined by financial ones. For instance, Oakland Family Planning Clinics received a 1965 OEO budget of $29,000, Head Start just over $90,000, and other preschool education programs $71,000. The $167,000 budgeted for "planning, coordination, and evaluation," the second largest budget line, did little to answer War on Poverty detractors who claimed the OEO mostly fed local bureaucracies and provided jobs for social workers and other "helping" professionals. Like most cities, Oakland found that its OEO funding declined sharply after the first two years, as Congress cut social programs in the wake of accelerating American involvement in Vietnam and the backlash against the OEO's empowerment of grassroots and black power political movements. Even those OEO programs with real potential did not last long enough to make a measurable difference in the lives of flatlands residents.[41]

Programmatic limitations of the War on Poverty were not unique to Oakland. The same summer in which Oakland launched its OEO programs, 1965, NAACP Labor Secretary Herbert Hill issued a stinging indictment of federal antipoverty initiatives. "We must shed the illusion that there is a war against poverty," Hill told delegates at the association's annual meeting. "The pattern of discrimination in employment" and "the racism of the American economy" were the principal causes of poverty among black workers, Hill said, not social disorganization. Calling the federal government's new programs "white paternalism," the NAACP warned the nation's black leaders to be wary of the co-opting power and seductive rhetoric of President Johnson's liberalism. Many in Oakland's African American community agreed, but the community participation mandate of federal legislation, the lure of federal funding streams, and a desire to assist poor neighborhoods in *some* way nonetheless gave Oaklanders reason to invest time and energy in the War on Poverty. Still, the growing criticism could not be dismissed. In time, a steady stream of black leaders, from Martin Luther King, Jr., and Bayard Rustin to Stokeley Carmichael and Huey Newton, would question the sincerity and efficacy of the nation's antipoverty efforts. In 1967 King told a Los Angeles audience that in Vietnam "we spend $322,000 for each enemy we kill, while we spend in the so-called War on Poverty in America only about $53 for each person classified as poor." Eldridge Cleaver added his own inimitable version: "We don't need a War on Poverty. What we need is a war on the rich." King, Whitney Young, and A. Philip Randolph had all by 1968 announced their own formal proposals calling for massive public expenditures to attack black poverty—far more than anything the federal government had contemplated. In cities across the nation, the War on Poverty had done less to eliminate poverty and blocked opportunity than to raise questions about and public battles over political power, economic development, and the nature of social mobility and racial marginalization.[42]

The OEO's most important legacy in Oakland, as in most cities, was not the arsenal of individual programs it unleashed but the "community participation" mandate of the antipoverty legislation. By requiring the "maximum feasible participation" of the poor in the administration of OEO programs, the federal government created a noble, but inevitably contradictory, set of requirements and expectations. Poverty warriors envisioned the participation mandate as both a philosophical and bureaucratic safeguard against their programs dictating to local communities, reinforcing the pathological dependence and disorganization the OEO was supposed to remedy. By participating in the running of the OEO programs, the community would, according to the most idealistic of Johnson's advisors, organize itself. That the community's principal problems were structural and political, rather than behavioral, and that the participation mandate could evolve into a vehicle for community mobilization to challenge local political officials, did not entirely escape the architects of the OEO in 1964. But they included the participation mandate in the OEO legislation nonetheless, seeing in the Community Action Programs (CAP) primarily an opportunity to, in the words of Johnson aid Charles Schultze, "talk to poor people to find out what their problems are." However, the liberals who designed the OEO underestimated the divisions in urban America and oversimplified the legacies of Jim Crow. To them, community participation was in the main a psychological, sociological, and behavioral issue, not a political one. The history of Oakland's War on Poverty would prove them wrong.[43]

Community participation in Oakland's OEO programs initially followed the Ford Foundation model—control by professionals. Mayor Houlihan appointed twenty-five people to serve on the Oakland Economic Development Council (OEDC), the policy-making "poverty board" for the city. All members of the Citizens Advisory Committee, which had overseen the Ford gray areas program, were invited to sit on the OEDC in anticipation of a smooth transition from one antipoverty effort to the next. In addition, the city's Department of Human Resources organized a series of community meetings in the poverty target areas to explain the OEO programs, to establish neighborhood advisory committees, and to provide for the selection of "target area representatives" to serve on the OEDC. These tangled schemes of representation ultimately evolved into a remarkably democratic set of antipoverty institutions. In 1965 the mayor and city council envisioned the OEDC as an arm of the municipal bureaucracy. Federal OEO money would come to Oakland's OEDC, and a small group of handpicked mayoral advisors would decide which antipoverty programs to fund. As a concession to the city's African Americans, Houlihan appointed a number of liberal middle-class black leaders, including attorneys and East Bay Democratic Club stalwarts Clinton White, Smith, McCullum, and Wilson, to sit on the council as representatives of the community. In a remarkable coup, White, McCullum, and Wilson helped to lead a quick reorganization of the OEDC that left civil rights activists, social workers, and black professionals in control of the council after only its second meeting. Wilson was elected chairman, replacing the self-appointed Houlihan.[44]

A far more fundamental and long-lasting challenge, in which neighborhood activists pressed the OEDC for greater democratization, came quickly on the heels of the liberal coup. Community activists demanded, and eventually won, "51 percent control" over the poverty board. In doing

so, they shifted the center of gravity of the War on Poverty and transformed the OEDC from an extension of the city's service bureaucracy
into a potential center of political opposition. The challenge from the
neighborhoods involved more than power politics, however. It represented
an ideological conflict over the nature of War on Poverty liberalism.
Members of the OEDC, particularly the East Bay Democratic Club contingent, initially envisioned the city's antipoverty efforts as a chance to
improve the life chances of poor people while strategically pushing the
city as a whole toward greater responsiveness to the growing African
American population. They hoped to, in the words of Norvel Smith,
"give poor people a way to express themselves, ever so unsophisticated
for the time being, at the places where decisions are made." Carl Metoyer
added that "this program, with the cooperation of industry, of city government, of county government, all people of good will, may very well
make a strong inroad on poverty in Oakland." The community activists,
organized in what were called Neighborhood Advisory Committees, made
two counterarguments. First, they claimed that middle-class African
American and white OEDC members did not "represent" the poor and
could not speak for them. Second, they argued that the War on Poverty
should deliver concrete jobs to the neighborhoods, not an expansion of
existing social services. These calls for community power increasingly defined the battle lines within the city's poverty program.[45]

Despite the initial objections of Metoyer, Wilson, McCullum, Smith,
and others, the OEDC gradually moved toward accommodating the
neighborhood demands. When told at a planning meeting that middle-
class African American OEDC members did not "represent" the poor
and could not speak for them, Lionel Wilson, visibly insulted, shot back
at community members that his own experience as a poor black man
growing up in West Oakland during the Depression more than qualified
him to speak about poverty. "[I]t smacks of, to say the least, impertinence
for any social worker to tell me that I am a person of no understanding
of the poor," Wilson countered. McCullum questioned the presumption
that the neighborhood committees represented the poor at all: "Who is
the advisory committee? Are they the poor? Are they someone else?" Encouraged by the language of OEO legislation and the emerging bureaucratic face-off, the "neighborhood representatives" came to stand for "the
poor." "We're the most important people—the poor—and we come as citizens, hoping to formulate our own programs," Ralph Williams, a West
Oakland advisory committee member, told the OEDC. Williams had both
numbers and federal legislation on his side. Two events proved crucial in
moving the OEDC toward an accommodation with community activists.
First, the neighborhood advisory committees, the grassroots power base,
walked out of a March OEDC meeting. Without their participation, the

city's OEO programs faced chaos. Second, Wilson, as chairman of the OEDC, learned that neither the OEO's Western Regional Office nor Sargent Shriver in Washington, DC, would back the OEDC in its stand-off with the advisory committees. In a series of reconfigurations of the OEDC in late 1966, the city's poverty board officially endorsed the "51 percent control" and transformed the poverty board into a neighborhood-centered institution.[46]

As in the Bank of America affirmative action dispute and in the debates over BART construction jobs, community activists pressed from below for more sweeping changes than those envisioned in the reigning liberal orthodoxy. Taken together, the Bank of America, BART, and OEDC episodes in quick succession delivered a powerful message both to the city's Republican establishment and to the East Bay Democratic Club's African American leadership. A new politics of community empowerment—based on the overlapping influences of liberal civil rights politics, black nationalism, grassroots radicalism, and old-style urban interest-group politics—had taken root in Oakland. It was on the rise, and its rhetoric, tactics, and demands could not be ignored. Because Oakland's governing elite had not sought the broad incorporation of working-class votes, black or white, into the "trenches" of urban power, the city never developed anything resembling a patronage system. Local Republican merchants and their political allies kept African Americans, especially, at arm's length. The city's African American middle class, despite its sizable presence in the municipal bureaucracy, thus had few political favors to distribute and no real means of co-opting neighborhood politics. This made for a strikingly fluid, contentious, and variable political terrain in mid-1960s' Oakland in which a vocal, organized grassroots could exert considerable influence, even if it never achieved formal political standing.

Oakland's Not For Burning

No Great Society program in the East Bay opened with more fanfare in the mid-1960s than the Economic Development Administration's Port of Oakland project. Coincident with the formation of the OEDC, the EDA promised work for Oakland's unemployed. It seemed the ideal complement to the city's new education and training programs, because here was the promise of actual and enumerated jobs. Enormous expectations accompanied the project's opening in the spring of 1966, when Governor Pat Brown announced at an Oakland press conference that the city would receive $23 million in public works grants and loans for two major construction projects: an aircraft maintenance hangar at the Oakland Airport and a second automated terminal for the port's West Oakland operations. Brown's presence in Oakland signaled more than just the un-precedented size of the federal commitment—at $23 million, it was nearly ten times the city's OEDC budget. Oakland was also among the first cities in the United States to receive EDA funding, the first post-Watts experiment in direct urban job creation. Brown called it "a massive experiment in solving the principal urban problem, unemployment."[47]

National and local urban realpolitik, however, not a genuine concern for Oakland's poor, shaped this new program. Oakland's EDA project was born at the crossroads of two powerful forces: the concern among federal poverty warriors and local observers of "another Watts," and the development agenda of the Port of Oakland. On the heels of the stunning Watts uprising in Los Angeles in August 1965, federal policy makers and California officials feared that Oakland was next in line, a "potential powderkeg" and "racial tinderbox" in the words of a front-page *Wall Street Journal* article. In the aftermath of Watts, the *Journal*, *New York Times*, *Time*, and *Newsweek* each carried stories in which Oakland appeared prominently as the next city that could "spark an explosion." Desire to prevent further riots spurred federal interest in funding urban job creation programs (critics called them "riot insurance") and hastened the development of Johnson's Great Society initiatives. Playing on this fascination with urban unrest, the book that traced the EDA's involvement in Oakland was entitled *Oakland's Not for Burning*. This post-Watts scrambling at the federal level dovetailed with the Port of Oakland's ongoing search for creative ways to finance its modernization. When EDA grants became available in the months following Watts, Oakland's port commissioners proposed an ambitious expansion plan, arguing that a new harbor, industrial park, and expanded airport capabilities would dramatically increase the city's ability to recruit and hold new industry and to create jobs for the city's unemployed. Delighted that a major institution such as the port would manage the development funds, the EDA promised the city $23 million on the condition that jobs reach underemployed black and ethnic Mexican communities in the flatlands. The central irony of the port's proposal—that port modernization was, in the short term, costing jobs, not creating them—was lost on EDA officials.[48]

As a riot-prevention strategy assembled in the flurry of federal activity after August 1965, the EDA brought to Oakland an approach distinct from other War on Poverty agencies. Unlike the OEDC, the EDA programs did not evolve from Ford Foundation beginnings, nor did they share the emphasis on urban community pathology or skills deficits. The EDA simply promoted job creation. In April 1966 EDA director Eugene Foley brashly promised Oakland three thousand new jobs, one-third of which would go to minority workers, among them the "hard-core unemployed." Oakland's local EDA administrator, Amory Bradford, nonetheless anticipated problems reserving jobs for the unemployed and underemployed. In the early spring of 1966 he proposed, and Foley approved, an employment plan that Bradford believed would ensure that the EDA project translated into community jobs. "It's the first time that this sort of requirement has been made," an EDA staff member optimistically told the *Wall Street Journal*. But Foley and Bradford were in complicated waters. No consensus existed among EDA staffers and administrators on the employment plan; many assumed, based on the agency's previous experience primarily in rural areas, that economic growth would eventually benefit "the community," even without a strict employment plan. The issue of training further complicated things. Bradford and other EDA staff members anticipated that the city's new Skills Center would be able to train many of the incoming workers and that employers would train the remaining. But the EDA could guarantee neither the employment plan nor the necessary training, because the Skills Center and private employers had their own agendas.[49]

The burden of training the unemployed fell to the Skills Center, another federal antipoverty initiative underway in Oakland. Like the OEO programs, the Skills Center project held two assumptions: that the principal problem in urban labor markets was a skills deficit, and that

Figure 5.2. A sign reading "New Jobs for Your Community" delivers the eternal 1960s promise in West Oakland. Despite a massive federal grant of $23 million, the Economic Development Administration's Port of Oakland project did not solve the city's deepening unemployment problem. Courtesy of the Bancroft Library, University of California, Berkeley.

opportunity existed for those with the proper training. The center's development in 1965 put both assumptions to the test. The U.S. Department of Labor selected Oakland as one of six cities nationwide to receive MDTA funding for an industrial training center modeled on a successful program in Detroit. Labor Department representatives promised training for fifteen hundred unemployed or underemployed workers to compensate for African Americans' historic exclusion from trades and apprenticeships. Norvel Smith, director of Oakland's Department of Human Resources, welcomed the Skills Center as "a significant new resource in the War on Poverty," and the *Voice* hoped that it would "strike a blow at racial imbalances in the East Bay workforce." The center promised two things that both Smith and the *Voice* thought essential to a meaningful employment program in Oakland: it would provide training to a wide variety of workers, including the so-called hard-core unemployed, and it would be outside the direct control of the trade unions. Union opposition to the Skills Center materialized nonetheless. "There'll be no jobs for these people," Central Labor Council Assistant Secretary Richard Groulx warned, "until employers and unions agree through collective bargaining agreements to make them available." "We're not going to be a party to this kind of operation," Building Trades business representative J. Lamar Childers added. "We've been in the business of apprenticeship training for 100 years and we don't need anyone from the Department of Labor or the State Department of Employment to tell us how to do it."[50]

The "skills deficit" that the East Bay Skills Center sought to address was real. Denied apprenticeship training and meaningful employment above the lowest occupations, many African American workers, both longtime Oakland residents and recent southern migrants, found themselves trapped at the economic margins. Despite its limitations, the Skills Center offered one avenue to accumulating the education and training required to break into the East Bay's job market. Skills Center advocates claimed that by providing this service they could substantially reduce unemployment, underemployment, and poverty. Critics, however, charged that the program suffered from both practical and philosophical shortcomings. The Skills Center, for instance, emphasized blue-collar jobs in an increasingly white-collar labor market. Moreover, even the minimal cooperation with trade unions, achieved in the twelfth hour, did not guarantee graduates jobs. Nor could the Skills Center overcome existing entrenched patterns of racial discrimination in local labor markets simply by providing larger numbers of trained workers. Further, the involvement of federal, state, and local bureaucracies (the center was administered by the Peralta Junior College District) in the center's funding and management, in addition to the local MDTA advisory committee, brought far more interests and agendas to the table than could be accommodated.[51]

A weak Skills Center added to the EDA's larger shortcomings. By the early 1970s many East Bay observers had labeled the EDA project a disaster. After four years and a stunning lack of success at employing poor workers, the project, both federal officials and local commentators admitted, had done far more for the port's economic viability than for the city's hardest hit black neighborhoods. The EDA project had helped to make the Port of Oakland one of the richest, busiest industries in the Bay Area, but neither the port nor World Airways lived up to its commitment to the original employment plan. In a scathing letter to the Port Commission in 1969, Ross Davis, head of the EDA (Foley had resigned in late 1966), warned that "the agency is not in the business of building aircraft hangars or other facilities for port authorities or business firms. . . . EDA is in the business of creating jobs for the unemployed, the underemployed, and the poor." Funding for the World Airways project was withheld for several years because of the company's recalcitrance on the issue of minority hiring, but in the early 1970s the money was finally released. Bradford, Foley, Davis, and Oakland's EDA staff had not anticipated the extent of noncompliance with the employment plan, and when the port and World Airways remained intransigent, the federal government was faced with either canceling the project altogether or funding economic development with no affirmative action mechanism. The government chose the latter. By the early 1970s the EDA's most generous reports counted a mere two or three hundred jobs that project funding had helped to create for the city's black community.[52]

Over time, the failures of programs like the Skills Center and the EDA project convinced a growing number of African American antipoverty activists and program administrators of the need for a black "power base." Liberal hopes that federal antipoverty and employment programs would create economic avenues out of poor neighborhoods yielded increasingly to calls for power and community self-determination. In early 1968 Percy Moore, executive director of the OEDC and nominal head of Oakland's War on Poverty, stood before the city council and said two things. First, he assessed the first three years of the War on Poverty. "The emphasis has been on fitting people into the existing structure," Moore explained. "We are training many people for whom there are no jobs. In doing so we have spent millions of dollars." Second, he said something that many did not expect. "The present problem isn't lack of jobs," Moore observed. "The problem is the way jobs are distributed across the community." That unequal distribution was, in Moore's eyes, a consequence of some groups having power while others did not. Employers and unions had a "monopoly" on jobs, and they "use it to their own advantage." Don McCullum had arrived at a similar position. McCullum, a one-time civil rights liberal, member of the East Bay Democratic Club, and early

War on Poverty advocate, joined Moore in seeking a concrete form of community power. "The only thing that will be understood by business is the same thing as with unions, a power base," McCullum told an audience of the city's antipoverty administrators and activists in 1968. Moore and McCullum embodied an ideological and strategic shift away from Great Society liberalism and its opportunity politics. In the late 1960s that shift transformed Oakland's antipoverty programs and, ultimately, the city's political culture.[53]

New Spaces, New Language

Disappointment with the War on Poverty emerged in a larger context. As Oaklanders measured the programmatic shortcomings of federal antipoverty efforts, they did so against what in the 1960s was a booming regional economy. Unemployment and growing poverty in Oakland appeared all the more dire because the metropolitan East Bay as a whole looked like the growth machine predicted in the MOAP. "We have failed in the ghetto," John George, an Oakland attorney and political leader, lamented in 1967. Declaring the "old tradition of upward mobility at an end" because there were "no unskilled jobs to provide the first exit out," George epitomized the declining faith in the liberal dream of social mobility. When George and others from his generation, including members of the East Bay Democratic Club, looked at parts of West and East Oakland in the late 1960s, they saw a telling inversion. Instead of the incubator of the middle class they had sought to create, they believed that the ghetto had become a social trap, a sink of downward mobility. George recognized that the causes were multiple and complex, the remedies equally so. As he and others came up against Oakland's limits, they looked for new languages and new strategies. More and more Oaklanders did the same. For many, the search would hinge on a new vision of black empowerment and a turn from desegregation to anticolonial liberation as the paradigm of struggle.[54]

White and black Oaklanders drew from a wide range of interpretations and experiences to fashion conceptions of themselves and their place within the city. At the same time, those conceptions developed in complicated fields of meaning and struggle that extended well beyond the boundaries of Oakland into national and international channels. In the second half of the 1960s, operating together, local transcripts of meaning among African Americans and an emerging national and international dialogue about colonialism began to shape a remarkably new, extremely influential, and powerfully persuasive language of the city. It was not unique to Oakland, but Oakland offered as fertile a place as any in the nation for its emergence and refinement. Eldridge Cleaver would rechristen the old FHA red line the "racial Maginot Line" to emphasize both whites' unwillingness to desegregate and his conception of the city as a constant, irresolvable power struggle—a conflict "between the white mother country of America and the black colony." Paul Cobb would call West Oakland an "urban plantation." And the Black Panther Party likened Oakland to "the colonial cities of Asia or Africa . . . except in Oakland's case the colony is the poor community in the heart of the country itself." Influenced by anticolonial struggles for national liberation in Africa and Asia, this emerging language intersected in the 1960s with an older discourse within the United States in which city and suburb stood in elemental opposition—the machine and the garden. The synthesis constituted a rejection of liberal explanations of the American city and their promise of equal opportunity and constant progress toward dismantling segregation.[55]

George Clinton's 1975 recording "Chocolate City" narrated, with high irony, the political transformation of urban America. "We didn't get our forty acres and a mule," Clinton sang, "but we did get you, C.C. [Chocolate City]. . . . God Bless C.C. and its vanilla suburbs." The emergence of "chocolate cities" in places like Newark, Washington, DC, Philadelphia, Detroit, Atlanta, and Oakland and their "vanilla suburbs" in the 1960s gave rise to a new language of urban space, race, and opportunity in American political culture. In Clinton's playful version, the failure of Reconstruction and the resurgence of white racism in the nineteenth century received their answer in the advance of black political power in "chocolate cities" in the twentieth. The metaphor, however, could serve the part of tragedy as easily as irony. Don McCullum testified to the U.S. Commission on Civil Rights in 1967 that "[h]ere in Oakland . . . we are ringed by a white noose of suburbia." In McCullum's version of metropolitan America, the white suburbs drew jobs and the tax base away from the core city, then sought a form of "regional government," which promised to drain political power away from the central city as well. Whether one saw the suburbs playing a benign, and boring, "vanilla" to the urban "chocolate" or playing the lyncher's noose to the strangled urban core, the new language of black-white/city-suburb dominated discussions of American cities by the mid-1960s. In Oakland and Alameda County, that language turned on the contrast between the industrial garden developing in the cities south of Oakland and the industrial slum that large parts of Oakland increasingly resembled.[56]

When African American leaders placed Oakland and the suburbs in conversation, their metaphors increasingly went to power, liberation, and colonialism. In the 1967 hearings before the Civil Rights Commission, Don McCullum gave fullest expression to an emerging critique of metropolitanization by elaborating on the notion of the white noose. "A payroll

212

CHAPTER FIVE

tax would be getting at the heart of what I am crying about," McCullum told the commission, expressing his frustration with "the people who come here and make the money and take it back to the suburbs, and they are the ones that have us enslaved. We are their colonies." Two years later McCullum argued that "Oakland is manipulated and run by absentee landlords and power brokers who live in Piedmont, Orinda, and Castro Valley—the white suburbs." Searching for a new language to describe the alignments of power in the region and believing that the liberal dream of an open society had been dashed, McCullum, like many others in Oakland and the nation, turned to the politics of anticolonialism for analogies. McCullum's casting of the ghetto as "colony" captured and bundled in powerful rhetoric the observable spatial realities of the new Oakland. Across the border from East Oakland in San Leandro, McCullum told the commission's members, lay "a city that any white person would be very happy to live in, and any black person, if they could get into it." San Leandro has, McCullum continued, "a very substantial industrial base. They have very good schools. They don't have the problems of overcrowding." By 1967, the contrast between East Oakland below Fourteenth Street and San Leandro, just across the Oakland city line, had become the paradigmatic example of the close spatial coincidence of poverty and affluence, black industrial slum and white industrial garden. In seizing upon that contrast, McCullum hoped to press his larger case that African American poverty, and the civil and economic rights of black people more generally, should be understood in a metropolitan context.[57]

Oakland in the 1960s was no longer the city of C. L. Dellums's generation. It had become a different place—and a new generation was emerging to define its politics. Dellums's generation envisioned the gradual erosion of racial segregation under the influence of liberal politics, protest, and legislation. This vision of the city, and its promise to secure the "step up" for working families, had hardly disappeared. Indeed, it remained stronger than ever and was enthusiastically championed by most middle-class and many working-class African Americans. But it was joined in this era by a new vision that reimagined the city as a colonized place from which the black nation—with its homeland in the ghetto—could fight for and win liberation. The failure of the War on Poverty, the deepening of black social inequality, and rapid suburban economic development in the mid-1960s fueled this new vision. But to understand Oakland and the nation fully in this period, we must resist the temptation to see whites as merely bodies that left and African Americans as a reservoir of romanticized community. The new colonial language of the city was fraught with its own paradoxes and new challenges, even as it offered a picture of urban space that closely corresponded to a generation's experience of the city. It was, like all sociopolitical formulations, an attempt to answer a set of questions and to solve a set of problems. But whether or not the colonial metaphor gave black activists purchase on urban problems remained a deep, troubling, and unresolved question. How and whether that language, and the metaphors it evoked and on which much of its explanatory power rested, could be mobilized into an effective urban politics remained to be seen.

The battle for jobs in 1960s Oakland left both liberal civil rights and antipoverty theories and assumptions battered. Even as civil rights groups managed to open some parts of the economy to black workers, large segments of the East Bay labor market remained closed—often because of direct racial discrimination, just as often because historical patterns of access, education, and residence had worked to marginalize African American workers. Antipoverty programs had failed to alter more than superficially the racial calculus of opportunity for most workers. Neither the civil rights strategy of pressuring employers to open jobs to African Americans nor the War on Poverty's education and training seemed capable of creating the kind of opportunity observers believed Oakland's ghettoes required. In his "state of the city" address in the early weeks of 1967, Oakland Mayor John Reading told the East Bay press that unemployment remained the city's most pressing problem. "Despite the city's attacks on unemployment," Reading observed, "recent figures indicate that we have had but little success in cutting the overall unemployment rate in Oakland." Reading's words were disappointing, but they did not surprise many Oaklanders. After a decade of high-profile efforts to address the city's unemployment and underemployment, there were few encouraging results. Indeed, by the time Reading had given his measured assessment of the city's lingering predicament, many people in Oakland, African American and white, had grown skeptical of existing strategies for attacking joblessness and poverty. Oakland was increasingly providing a home for blacks and a place of work for whites.[58]

The War on Poverty came of age philosophically in the late 1950s and early 1960s, evolving from theories of social disorganization that stressed community pathology much more than segregation, discrimination, or the class-based distribution of wealth. But the federal government's antipoverty theories and programs did not enter a vacuum. They descended on cities like Oakland at the historical crest of the civil rights movement, at the exact moment when the battle for jobs in urban America had reached its most intense pitch, when affirmative action programs and the notion of access to jobs as a "right" were being tested as political strategies to democratize the economy and reconstruct opportunity for the black working class. Many civil rights leaders, as well as community activists, poured money, energy, and resources into the War on Poverty, hoping that the new federal commitment to training and education would prove to be an effective arm of the larger black liberation struggle. But as they watched the programs evolve and tested the results against both their ambitions and the poverty warriors' promises, they could not help but be disappointed. Their conclusions and their politics would over the next decade turn back to the economy and back to power. The calls for self-determination and black power emerged from the main currents of American political life, from the tensions and contradictions within liberalism, on the one hand, and the enormous opposition to full desegregation, on the other.[59]

Part Three

BLACK LIBERATION AND SUBURBAN REVOLT, 1964–1978

6

Black Power

"THE TIME HAS COME for a declaration of independence in West Oakland," Paul Cobb told an Oakland audience in 1968. "We live on an urban plantation. We have to plan our liberation." Cobb, the son of an Oakland longshoreman and one of the city's leading community organizers in the late 1960s, drew his metaphor from a language of anticolonial struggle that had become the dominant lexicon of black political movements by 1968. In that penultimate year of a decade of global uprisings against colonial rule, from Algiers to Prague, Luanda to Hanoi, African American intellectuals and activists in the United States cast the urban ghetto as an exploited colony, the liberation of which required new tactics. They moved away from the desegregation and opportunity politics of their forebears in search of a framework and a discourse to capture both the persistence of racial segregation in American cities and an affirming message of community empowerment. They found it in the spatial situating of black power and identity in the ghetto itself and in the political imagining of a nation within a nation. With this new lexicon of liberation came an economic and political agenda that called for black control over community job distribution and municipal levers of power—from the mayor's office and city council to the school board and recreation department. The nation had to understand, to borrow Eldridge Cleaver's formulation, "that it is a reality when people say there's a 'black colony' and a 'white mother country.' . . . that there are two different sets of political dynamics now functioning in America."[1]

Histories of post-1965 African American politics have long treated *black power* in terms of charismatic figures and ideological pronouncements said to mark a distinct, even fatal, break with the civil rights movement. This interpretation typically rests on the differences between Malcolm X and Martin Luther King, Jr., splits within the Student Nonviolent Coordinating Committee (SNCC), the rise of the Black Panther Party, and the declarations of movement media icons like H. Rap Brown. Civil rights and black power have come to represent the divergent histories that are told about black-led political movements in the second half of the twentieth century. Civil rights is nonviolent. Black power is violent. Civil rights is normative, black power an aberration of late 1960s' hyperradicalism. Civil rights was a long struggle, black power a brief and disastrous moment. But in their artificial halving of black politics and its ideological and strategic spectrum, these inherited narratives flatten and distort the richness, complexity, and continuities of twentieth-century African American social and political movements. And in their conflation of black power, black nationalism, black radicalism, and violent urban rebellions and riots, they leave us bereft of the meaningful distinctions that provide a guide through a tangled and tumultuous period. For in truth, black power stood in the main currents of American politics in the 1960s and 1970s. As a product of liberalism and its failures, it represented a poignant effort to advance a political strategy beyond desegregation. Black power was a creative outgrowth of earlier efforts, not a radical and failed break from them. "[B]lack people must organize themselves without regard to what is traditionally acceptable, precisely because the traditional approaches have failed," Stokeley Carmichael insisted in his 1967 book, *Black Power*.[2]

As a political and a cultural credo, black power was an extraordinarily plastic concept. It meant everything from revolution to electing African American school board members to wearing a dashiki. Maoist revolutionaries and liberal reformers alike embraced its cultural purchase. Its flexibility was part of its attractiveness. Its adaptability to multiple contexts rendered it at once a potent discursive and psychological force and a generic and sometimes diluted cliché. However, black power has been deployed as an analytical category by scholars and observers more frequently than it was actually used by activists and leaders themselves. Black power in popular and many scholarly accounts of the 1960s and 1970s has obscured both the continuities within the postwar African American struggle and the key differences among ideologies and tactics as they developed over time. We need therefore to reclaim black power as part of the periodization of postwar African American political struggle and simultaneously to parse its varied meanings and diverse applications. Black power was merely one dimension of a broad terrain of ideological and strategic approaches to the urban problems of the 1960s and 1970s, especially to persistent patterns of economic disadvantage that liberal social policy had done little to alter or had exacerbated. All of those ideological and strategic dimensions, black power included, are central to narratives of postwar urban history.[3]

In Oakland, African American leaders used the term "black power" sparingly, and many black leftists avoided the phrase because of its nationalist overtones. African Americans in the East Bay spoke of the "white power structure" and "the people" or "the community" more often than they spoke of "black power." Their language was equally filled with references to "rights," "revolutionary struggle," "colonialism," "liberation," "control," and "the poor," among many others. The Black Panther Party's famous slogan, "all power to the people," signaled their self-identification as leftist revolutionaries for whom "the people" represented a broad array of colonized communities, and their allies, in the United States and abroad. Indeed, the Panthers' history underscores that one of the most important developments of post-1966 African American liberation politics was activists' self-conscious embrace of an internationalist language. In this context, "self-determination," as much as black power, emerged as an organizing framework. "In the U.S. the primary struggle is a revolutionary struggle," Eldridge Cleaver explained in 1970, "but at the same time we have to deal with the specific conditions of oppression of Black people."[4]

In cities across the United States, calls for self-determination emerged in the late 1960s primarily as a response to police brutality, the failures of Great Society liberalism, and the uneven economic development of the American metropolis. Black power and community empowerment grew up together as concepts in this period as challenges to local political elites and the federal and municipal bureaucracies that controlled civic resources. In Alabama and Mississippi, Stokeley Carmichael's famous summons—"I say we need black power"—resonated with a generation of civil rights activists facing the massive resistance of southern white society. But in Oakland and dozens of prominent cities in the urban North and Pacific Coast, calls for self-determination had roots in a set of institutional failures and the political-economic geography of the new city-suburb conglomerate. The War on Poverty and dozens of other federal antipoverty and jobs programs had foundered against intransigent municipal governments and the stubborn legacies of Jim Crow in the economy. Fair employment and housing laws had done little to remedy segregation, discrimination, and black poverty. At the same time, nearby all-white suburban communities diverted tax revenue and private capital away from older core cities. Advocates of self-determination in this context offered a critique of the whole of metropolitan development since World War II. Drawing on a spatial definition of community, the ghetto, they asserted a neocolonial relationship between African Americans and other spatially designated sites of power, downtown and the suburbs. But far from rejecting their predecessors in the civil rights movement, these activists revived an agenda that harkened back to the 1940s: defending the community against outside violence, delivering jobs, services, and economic development into the community, and using black solidarity as a springboard to gain local political influence.[5]

Between 1966 and 1972 two principal political strategies thus evolved in Oakland under the broad rubric of African American self-determination: Black Panther Third World nationalism and War on Poverty grassroots community empowerment. Both groups drew for their political language on metaphors of decolonization. Oakland's ghetto stood for "the community" and, more expansively, the black nation. Jobs, political power, and other resources that should have by right been located in the community itself had been stripped from it by outsiders. The answer was liberation. According to this view, the liberal politics of desegregation had advanced the black struggle as far as the logic of those politics allowed—that is, until they came up against the underlying resistance of the white "power structure" and, especially for the Panthers, the structural inequalities and exploitation inherent in capitalist imperialism. Both groups saw the city's African American community locked in a struggle against Oakland's largely white business and political elite, as well as the white suburban "noose." But in practice, black power and self-determination politics never worked out so neatly. They always contained contradictions of class, struggles over leadership, and broad ideological conflicts that divided African Americans as much as the symbolic notion of community united them. This period was also about coming to terms with that proposition. Both strategies politicized, rather than accepted as natural, patterns of East Bay metropolitan development and inaugurated a period of struggle more intense than any in Oakland's history since the 1940s.

Self-Determination and the Rise of the Black Panther Party

On a May afternoon in 1967, the slap of Panther leather echoed against the granite steps of the state capitol in Sacramento. Armed but peaceful, a contingent from the recently formed Black Panther Party for Self Defense entered the building, read a brief statement before the press, spoke with reporters, and left, rifles in full display. Images of the event ran on the evening news across the country and made headlines around the world. "The power structure depends upon the use of force," Huey Newton wrote that year, "in order to get rid of the gun it is necessary to take up the gun." Five months later, in the early morning dark, an Oakland Police officer named John Frey pulled over Newton driving in his girlfriend's Volkswagen in West Oakland. A scuffle ensued in which Newton and Frey exchanged shots. Frey was fatally injured. In jail for the remainder of the decade for Frey's murder, Newton emerged as the nation's most celebrated prisoner—"Free Huey" became an instant mantra—his cause a potent symbol of the end of decades of anguished acquiescence to indiscriminate police power. The following spring, on an April evening two days after Martin Luther King, Jr.'s assassination in Memphis, Oakland police shot teenage Panther Bobby Hutton in the back during an ambush intended for Eldridge Cleaver. The killing of Hutton once more focused national attention on Oakland. It occurred at the height of the Free Huey campaign and signaled the beginning of uninterrupted police warfare against the Panthers on the streets of Oakland.[6]

Figure 6.1. A "Free Huey" rally outside the Alameda County courthouse in Oakland, 1968. Rallies were held frequently throughout that year and provided an important meeting ground for a range of activists from Oakland, Berkeley, and San Francisco, black and white. Courtesy of the *Oakland Tribune* Collection, Oakland Museum of California.

The events of 1967 and 1968 marked the ascendance of the Black Panther Party to a national stage. The party's synthesis of radical nationalism and Maoist condemnation of capitalism took its place alongside the manifestoes of SNCC, Students for a Democratic Society (SDS), and the Revolutionary Action Movement in the evolution of 1960s' new left political discourse. The Free Huey campaign made headlines and network television news, while Panther uniforms—leather jackets and black berets—redefined black chic. Party boldness in its dealings with police inspired a nationwide movement against police brutality. Inheritors of the discipline, pride, and calm self-assurance preached by Malcolm X, the Panthers became national heroes in African American communities by infusing abstract nationalism with street toughness, joining the rhythms of black working-class youth culture to the interracial élan and effervescence of Bay Area new left politics. Black Panther Party chapters opened monthly in city after city during the last years of the decade, and letters streamed into Panther headquarters from African American communities nationwide on a scale associated with rock stars. One young follower in Charlotte, North Carolina, wrote to Newton hoping that he "would write back . . . and if you would, send me a picture of you." She concluded her letter by stating "I'm in the eighth grade and very proud that I'm *black* (and I love you too)."[7]

But there was a local meaning, a local story, behind the rise of the Panthers. As much as they operated within the larger national theatrics of the late 1960s, the Panthers emerged out of, and played a critical role in, the milieu of African American struggle in North and West Oakland. Huey Newton and Bobby Seale launched the party in 1966 amid a rich and contentious period of debate and conflict over the direction of the African American community in Oakland and its relationship to the larger city. Oakland's future hinged on these debates. Over the second half of the 1960s and first half of the 1970s, African Americans from diverse backgrounds and political affiliations were determined that they would shape that future. The party came to play an immensely important role in these efforts.

In 1962 Don Warden, a law student at the University of California at Berkeley, established the Afro-American Association, the West Coast's first indigenous black nationalist organization. With the assistance of Berkeley undergraduates—including at various points Paul Cobb and Ron Dellums, nephew of C. L. Dellums—Warden promoted cultural nationalism on Bay Area college campuses in an era when the national media and even some civil rights organizations preached accommodation to white institutions and culture. Warden and the Afro-American Association embraced a nationalism that fused black capitalism, Afro-centrism, and Garveyite self-help. Stressing education and skill acquisition as the foundation of African American economic power, Warden inspired a small but dedicated following in the East Bay through a weekly radio program. If people "aren't in church," Warden said, "it's through the disk jockeys that they have to be reached." Along Grove Street in front of Merritt College, North Oakland's public junior college, Warden was the most popular political speaker, remembered by Bobby Seale for his "artistic oratory" and the "laughing acceptance" he elicited from black audiences with his observations about black people going "to white people's schools to learn about white people." Warden's Afro-American Association and the emerging black studies courses at Merritt and the University of California at Berkeley began to circulate an eclectic collection of texts among black students in the East Bay flatlands: James Baldwin's *The Fire Next Time*, Jomo Kenyatta's *Facing Mount Kenya*, Kwame Nkrumah's *Neo-Colonialism: The Last Stage of Imperialism*, E. Franklin Frazier's *Black Bourgeoisie*, classics by W.E.B DuBois, the revolutionary writings of Che Guevara and Mao Zedong, and Franz Fanon's *Wretched of the Earth*. "They got me caught up," Bobby Seale said of the intellectual and political atmosphere in North Oakland. "They made me feel that I had to help out, be a part and do something, to help out in some way." By 1966 Newton and Seale had both been students at Merritt and members of the Afro-American Association. They frequented reading groups as well as the ubiquitous street-corner rap sessions at Merritt and along Bancroft Avenue adjacent to the Berkeley campus, a short drive or bus ride up Telegraph Avenue from North Oakland.[8]

The long corridor from West Oakland north through South Berkeley to the University of California campus, between San Pablo and Telegraph avenues, formed one of the most vibrant political landscapes anywhere in the nation in this period. Intellectual, social, and physical geographies intersected here in powerful combination. Home of the East Bay's largest African American community—representing all ages and classes—as well as thousands of white Berkeley college students, in these neighborhoods a quarter century of American labor and civil rights movement politics and the burgeoning student and antiwar movements overlapped with some of the poorest districts in the East Bay. Birthplace of the East Bay Democratic Club and the home of both the Brotherhood of Sleeping Car Porters and the East Bay International Longshoremen's and Warehousemen's Union, the African American triangle between West and North Oakland and South Berkeley remained the center of black life in the Bay Area. By the mid-1960s the East Bay student new left also flourished here: the Free Speech Movement was born near the corner of Bancroft and Telegraph, and the Vietnam Day Committee, the Peace/Rights Organizing Committee, and dozens of other white-led new left organizations met and organized in these neighborhoods. In early October 1966, the same month that Newton and Seale wrote the party's Ten Point Program, "What We Want, What We Believe," ten thousand people organized by the Vietnam Day Committee marched down Telegraph from the Berkeley campus to the Oakland city line to protest the war and the draft.[9]

More than coincidental, the proximity of old left and new meant that red diaper babies met the sons and daughters of longshoremen and Pullman porters; black and white members of the DuBois Club met SNCC veterans and white college students from around the country; and anti-capitalist, anti-imperialist readings circulated in ever wider networks. Free Huey rallies at the Alameda County Courthouse regularly attracted hundreds of demonstrators, drawing as many whites as blacks and large numbers of Chicanos as well. Beginning in 1964 and continuing through the early 1970s, this corridor was home to some of the most creative and inspired political projects on the American scene. The flatlands were no utopia of racial egalitarianism and intergenerational rapprochement, but they nonetheless formed a physical world where political milieus intersected: Berkeley emerged as the center of the white new left in the East Bay (and nationally), while Merritt College and North Oakland emerged as the center of African American radicalism (soon, also, nationally).

Drawn to the revolutionary political theory they were reading at Merritt, Newton and Seale initially sought to blend Maoist socialism with the cultural nationalism of Warden, all the while recruiting into their circle what Newton called his punks and thugs from the streets of North and West Oakland. "The street brothers were important to me," Newton wrote, "and I could not turn away from the life shared with them." But the Panther founders did not last long in the Afro-American Association, both because the "bourgeois" Warden resisted the street code of physical confrontation that Newton admired and because the cultural nationalists' belief in the redemptive power of Africa rang false to him and Seale. With its embrace of African folk culture, religion, and moral authority, cultural nationalism seemed to Newton and Seale divorced from the grittier realities of their flatland lives. They left the Soul Student Advisory Council at Merritt College—a cultural nationalist organization under Warden's guidance—in 1966 after Newton had failed to produce the desired ideological reorientation. The cultural nationalist "college boys," as Seale called them, "jiving dudes who articulate bullshit all the time and don't ever want to get into the real practice of revolutionary struggle," had neither a style nor a program that Newton and Seale respected.[10]

Instead of cultural nationalism, Newton and Seale, joined subsequently by Eldridge Cleaver, rendered a version of Marxist-Leninism from an eclectic range of sources. Much of the immediate inspiration for and discourse of the early Panthers came from Frantz Fanon's *Wretched of the Earth*, which Seale had read and encouraged Newton to look at in 1966. This treatise on the French colonial regime in Algeria helped to transform the nationalism of Warden, less the romanticized Africa, into a spatially situated revolutionary community ideology. Behind the guns— literally, as Newton often quoted Mao—lay an elaborate analysis of the black nation as a colony, exploited by an imperialist class system. Colonizers included city hall, white businessmen, the suburbs, and the police, the "pigs of the state." Following the example of the Revolutionary Action Movement, which had preceded the party by half a decade, the Panthers turned to Mao for their basic revolutionary lexicon. Mao's notion of a united Third World aligned against the colonial West and his program of moral self-improvement and revolutionary ethics inspired the Panthers' internationalism as well as their internal program of personal discipline. Like Malcolm X, whose legacy the Panthers self-consciously embraced, Panther ideology stressed black self-determination and the necessity of armed resistance to "the brutal force used against us daily." Yet unlike the Nation of Islam, and Malcolm X until the final months of his life, the Panthers never adopted a separatist language or line, believing

Figure 6.2. Following the teachings of Mao Zedong and Malcolm X, Black Panther Party members modeled discipline and calm self-assurance in their public appearances. The leather jackets and berets also helped to define a kind of black power chic. Courtesy of the Dr. Huey P. Newton Foundation and the Department of Special Collections, Stanford University Libraries.

that alliances with sympathetic anticolonial whites, as well as Chicanos, should remain a fixture of the black liberation movement.[11]

The Panthers gave concrete, radical expression to two currents of thought circulating in North and West Oakland's African American community in the 1960s: black pride and community defense. The vital seeds of the party came from the 1966 summer youth program at the West and North Oakland poverty centers. There, Seale and Paul Cobb taught black history to teenagers, while Newton worked as an organizer in the North Oakland War on Poverty office. The writings of Fanon, Malcolm X, Che Guervara, and Mao Zedong made the rounds among the youth instructors at the poverty center. This fertile intellectual environment, nurtured by Cobb and Seale, produced two organizations: the McClymonds Youth Council, which focused on educational and social activities that stressed black history, and the Black Panthers. "My objective in the program was to teach Black American history if I could, and teach them [young people] also some community responsibility . . . in terms of their own people living in the neighborhood," Seal wrote in his memoir, *Seize the Time.* "I knew there was a way to reach these brothers because I wasn't too much different from them." Cobb and the Panther founders took divergent paths after 1966—Cobb into academia, political organizing, and journalism—but their relationship in the summer of that year was more than coincidental. All three were trying to work out, as were many others in West Oakland, a postliberal philosophy of black liberation capable of inspiring a new phase of struggle.[12]

Newton's application of Fanon, Mao, and the colonial analogy to the American ghetto enjoyed a resonance and explanatory power that other formulations, especially the liberal faith in desegregation and equal opportunity, could not match by 1968. The Panthers' colonial analysis was highly impressionistic and derivative of a much deeper set of inquiries made by other groups and institutions—namely, as we will see, War on Poverty activists and radical social scientists. Neither was it entirely original, based on variations of nationalism that ran from Harold Cruse and Malcolm X back through the midcentury Popular Front and black Communist Party activists, among others. But the Panthers brilliantly combined a theatric *performance* of radical Maoist nationalism and one of its central promises, speaking "truth to power," with an elaborate metaphysics that captured both the crisis-driven cynicism endemic to American cities in the 1960s and the optimism that had run as a steady stream through African American political culture and resistance since at least Nat Turner. Such a combination resonated in Oakland in particular because the black community was so thoroughly marginalized from the political life of the city, and because West Oakland had endured so many years of virtual occupation by outside agencies reengineering the neighborhoods—BART, the Oakland Police Department, California Department of Transportation, and the Redevelopment Agency. The Black Panther Party advanced the language and strategies of decolonization further within the American polity than any other group in the late 1960s, bringing to African Americans a public language of resistance and action almost entirely outside of liberalism.[13]

Combining revolutionary nationalism and male street bravado, the Panthers defined an actual and metaphorical space the defense of which had become their mission. During the fall of 1966, mostly in the poverty program offices, Newton and Seale put together the Black Panther Party Platform and Program, "What We Want, What We Believe," which became a seminal document of postliberal African American political ideology. Along with full employment, decent housing, and black history in the schools, the Panthers demanded an end to police brutality and committed themselves to "defending our black community from racist police oppression and brutality." Newton and Seale wrote of the "black colony" and "black colonial subjects" as they drafted a "declaration of independence" calling for revolution. Newton proved willing to act on the program, bragging that the party's eagerness to turn words into actions distinguished them from other street corner orators and black revolutionary groups. After opening the Black Panther office at Fifty-sixth and Grove, a block from Merritt in the heart of North Oakland in January 1967, Newton, Seale, and new Panther recruits began "patrolling the pigs," tracking police cars as they made rounds through black neighborhoods in the flatlands. Openly carrying guns, party members also toted statute books and legal manuals in their Volkswagen Beetles and Ford Falcons, often reading the Constitution, citing court decisions, and enumerating rights for blacks detained by the police. "The main function of the Party is to awaken the people and teach them the strategic method of resisting," Newton wrote in the Black Panther, the party's newspaper. Over the course of the spring and summer of 1967, "patrolling the pigs" came to embody the tool of that instruction as well as the Panthers' assertion of community power within North and West Oakland. The Black Panthers "talk about liberation of the black community," Bay Area labor and civil rights activist Percy Moore observed. "They talk of politicizing the community. They talk of coalitions with radical white organizations . . . and that ain't where the black man's place is supposed to be." But, Moore stressed, "that's the risk a man has to take."[14]

The party's public performance on the streets of Oakland embodied the spirit of black empowerment, while "What We Want, What We Believe" drew together political demands that stretched back to the 1930s with a postcolonial agenda of self-determination and reparations. This Panther syncretism represented a creative, fluid engagement with decades of African American struggle. Their calls for "full employment for our people," "decent housing," and "an immediate end to police brutality," among the first seven demands of the Ten Point Program, had been central to various Popular Front, labor, and liberal civil rights political platforms in the 1930s and 1940s. The final point, "we want land, bread, housing, education, clothing, justice, and peace," strongly echoed the internationalist African American left of midcentury—men and women like William Patterson and Charlotta Bass. At the same time, their calls for the "power to determine our own destiny" and "a United Nations–supervised plebiscite to be held throughout the black colony" reflected an immersion in postcolonial discourse and politics. By demanding an "end to the robbery by the capitalist of our black community" and "freedom for all black men held in federal, state, county, and city prisons and jails," the party implicated capitalism and the federal state in the historic subjugation of black people. Sympathetic to the desegregation efforts of local black leaders like C. L. Dellums and Tarea Hall Pittman, as well as national leaders like Martin Luther King, Jr., and Bayard Rustin, the Panthers nonetheless asserted that such efforts could not ultimately deliver liberation.[15]

Desegregation efforts suffered from another misapprehension, according to the party. In their admittedly raw anticolonial analysis, the Panthers contended that persistent white-enforced segregation had actually delivered to black people a measure of power. That power lay in spatial confinement, the concentration of African Americans in urban centers, where poverty and hopelessness had created a "lumpen proletariat," ignorant but teachable, the core of a revolutionary movement. This did not excuse segregation. But like their counterparts in colonial resistance in Africa, the Panthers emphasized that the structures of colonial rule (i.e., the ghetto) could be turned against the imperial nation by creative leaders and appropriate tactics. The Panthers rose from the crossroads of West and North Oakland, where a particular kind of street culture met Garveyite notions of self-help, the radical internationalist black tradition, the socialist laborite culture of Oakland's waterfront unions, and the armed community defense strategies of people like Malcolm X and Robert F. Williams. This eclectic mix, stirred equally by Newton's idealism and megalomania, emerged in the late 1960s as one of the nation's most elaborate and inspired attempts to reread the nature of American cities and the place of black people within them.

Panther memoirs offer compelling testimony to the complicated layering of violence within the party's milieu, a violence that should neither be ignored nor be romanticized. The party issued a rallying cry for a generation of sincere young black intellectuals and political figures as well as street toughs. After that first summer, the street violence that had shaped the background of many party members on occasion blurred the line between radicalism and extortion. When local stores refused to donate food and other resources to their social programs, Panther members often threatened violent retaliation. On May 10, 1969, a group of Panthers firebombed a convenience store on San Pablo Avenue in North Oakland because the store owner refused to donate more than a dozen eggs to a breakfast program. In 1971 the Panthers staged a massive boycott of California's largest black-owned liquor distribution network, Cal-Pak, to force its members to make cash donations to the party. "I was angered and amazed because I had never heard anybody publicly threatened like this," Albert McKee, a black real estate broker, said of Newton's behavior at one of the Cal-Pak meetings. "Some of us were fighting against racial injustice when Newton was running around barefoot," McKee added. Accused in dozens of other incidents, the party faced increasing criticism from both white and black leaders for its alleged involvement in illegal markets in weapons and drugs. For Newton, Fanon's *Wretched of the Earth* provided the final justification for translating the street violence and underground economic entrepreneurship of his adolescence into political resistance: the proletariat was the legitimate agent of revolution in anticolonial struggle. In their hands, guns were justified. Newton deployed Fanon's notion of a revolutionary colonized proletariat to explain organizing "the brothers on the block" rather than the black bourgeoisie. But these "brothers" included some of Oakland's most alienated youth whose inclinations ran more toward firebombing than toward building an alternative vision of African American progress.[16]

The Party indulged in inflammatory speeches and at times provided cover for a violence not related to the legitimate defense of community. But such judgments are applicable to the white-led police and FBI Counter Intelligence Program (COINTELPRO) operatives as well, who met the Panthers with their own brand of violence and subterfuge that crossed both legal and moral boundaries. None of the Panthers' alleged connections to illegal activities justified the swift and terrible repression they encountered. The Oakland police department, long a bastion of both racial paternalism and virulent racism, responded to the Panthers with nothing short of guerrilla warfare—no less than three black men were killed by Oakland police in the spring of 1968 alone. For his part, FBI Director J. Edgar Hoover called the party "the greatest threat to the internal security of the country" and supervised an extensive program of counterorganizing that included surveillance and eavesdropping, infiltration, harassment, false testimony, and a laundry list of other tactics designed to jail party members and drain the party of resources. In 1976 a Senate report on COINTELPRO operations charged that the bureau had "engaged in lawless tactics and responded to deep-seated social problems by fomenting violence and unrest." By the end of that decade, 233 out of 295 total FBI counterintelligence operations directed against black liberation groups across the nation were aimed at the Black Panther Party. The murder of Fred Hampton, leader of the Chicago branch of the party, by the Chicago police remains one of the signature political assassinations of the decade, but it was only the most extreme example of systematic efforts by local cops and federal agencies to harass and disrupt the party. State repression of the Panthers, along with the long FBI campaign against Martin Luther King, Jr., stands among the darkest and most cynical acts of American officialdom in the 1960s.[17]

At the same time, at some remove from these struggles, grassroots Panther activists brought a romantic idealism and practical agenda to their work in Oakland. As the party's leadership battled the city of Oakland in the courts and newspapers, fought a near-constant war with the FBI, and watched many of its principal figureheads, including Newton, Seale, and David Hilliard, go to prison, Panther recruits established a host of social programs for the East Bay's poorest African Americans. Beginning with their free breakfast for school children program in 1968 and stretching through a 1974 free ambulance program, the party introduced to Oakland

Figure 6.3. Children giving the black power sign at a grocery give-away sponsored by the Black Panther Party. The Panthers stressed black pride and black history, especially among young people who attended the party's Liberation Schools. Courtesy of the Dr. Huey P. Newton Foundation and the Department of Special Collections, Stanford University Libraries.

some of the most interesting and audacious community welfare experiments of the decade. The free breakfast program was followed in 1969 by the founding of Liberation Schools, which taught children "about the class struggle in terms of black history." The Intercommunal Youth Institute and the People's Free Medical Research Health Institute were founded that same year. A free clothing program followed in 1970, and the Sickle Cell Anemia Research Foundation, which provided free sickle cell anemia testing, came a year later. By 1972, when Panther rallies at DeFremery Park became larger and more numerous as components of their various political campaigns, a free food program, in which bags of groceries were given away, was added. While some of these programs were conceived and directed from the top of the Panther hierarchy, others, such as the Liberation Schools, were initiated by rank-and-file members, testifying to the relative openness and degree of experimentation possible within the interstices of an otherwise centrally directed organization.[18]

The breakfasts in particular embodied the Panthers' notion of practical revolutionary activity. Along with free sickle cell anemia testing and other periodic food giveaways, the breakfasts formed the core of what became known as the party's Survival Programs. By "helping the people survive," the breakfast program allowed the children of West Oakland's poorest neighborhoods to eat a healthy meal in a safe, supportive environment. Those among the Panthers who worked most closely with the program, particularly women, made sure that the free breakfasts offered concrete assistance to the city's poor while dramatizing a powerful symbol of racial injustice and ghetto marginalization in America: childhood hunger. Free breakfasts were both practical and idealistic in their commitment to ameliorating this social wrong. An important historical companion to Head Start, initiated by the federal government in 1965, the free breakfast program also stood as a powerful reminder that Title I funding under the 1965 Education Act should directly benefit poor schoolchildren, not middle-class school districts. It would be a decade or more before free breakfasts would become almost universally available to poor children, in no small part because of the party's ambitious example.[19]

Beyond their immediate material impact, the Survival Programs aimed at deeper spiritual and ideological transformations among the neighborhood men and women whom the party hoped to mobilize. A self-conscious model of black self-determination and pride, the programs combined self-help and education in revolutionary diction, with the free-spirited, animated public displays of political commitment that had become the sine qua non of left culture in the Bay Area. Schoolchildren at the party's breakfasts sang in uproarious tones, with their female teachers, "Black is beautiful, Free Huey!" Grocery giveaways and sickle cell anemia testing attracted large crowds to DeFremery Park in West Oakland, where party

Figure 6.4. Families like this one were the intended beneficiaries of the Black Panther Party's Survival Programs. Those programs had multiple goals: to draw community members to political rallies; to dramatize social inequality; to provide needed community services; and to educate people in the ideas and program of the party. Courtesy of the Dr. Huey P. Newton Foundation and the Department of Special Collections, Stanford University Libraries.

stalwarts gave speeches about black pride. Like "patrolling the pigs," which Seale described as "bringing them [local residents] basic things in everyday life about the law," the Survival Programs positioned the Panthers as a vanguard party and a vehicle of consciousness raising. The party had long held that "the people can't understand and progress to the stage of communists right away because of abstract arguments." Community programs, rather than the elusive grammar of radical politics, would win broad grassroots support for the party's political objectives. At the same time, the Survival Programs solidified the party's standing in the larger community. Many people in West and North Oakland, especially older adults, knew Newton when he was a C student and a bully. The party's daily presence in the neighborhoods with breakfast, child care, sickle cell anemia testing, and other food programs changed this impression among people who knew him and, among those who did not, raised the Panthers' profile as community leaders, not gangsters.[20]

The Panthers produced the late twentieth century's most powerful and subversive articulation of revolutionary nationalism. Their notion of defending the community, embodied in the visible arming of party members and confrontations with the police, became a militarized, performative expression of community power. But their importance to urban and African American history is far deeper than merely resistance to violence. They envisioned a reawakened ghetto, alive with possibilities, confident and assertive of a newfound capacity to shape the world. In their hands, the call for self-determination, the gesture associated with post-1965 African American movement politics, was joined to a spatial critique of urban America that deployed the ghetto to stand for the black nation. If the colonial analogy could be diffuse at times, it could also be trenchant. "We recognize the national character of our struggle," Eldridge Cleaver wrote in the *Guardian*. "We have to deal with both exploitation and racial oppression, and we don't think you can achieve a proper balance by neglecting one or the other." By reawakening and reclaiming the tradition of black radical internationalism that the Cold War had suppressed, the Panthers staked out an enormously broad terrain both for subsequent African American political projects and for evolving understandings of the relationship of urban black communities to the postwar American metropolis.[21]

The War on Poverty and the Rise of Community Politics

The Panthers drew international media coverage to Oakland in the late 1960s, but they were not the city's only advocates of black self-determination. Others labored in comparative national obscurity but were much closer to the actual workings of civic authority in Oakland. In particular, a group of civil rights activists, grassroots community organizers, and social work professionals involved in the War on Poverty and other Great Society programs emerged in the middle 1960s to challenge the conservative political class that ran the city. Attempting to provide meaningful political content to the loose and formless black power credo, this group turned federal antipoverty boards and agencies into a set of autonomous institutions from which to lead political campaigns against city hall. Between 1965 and 1971 the Oakland Economic Development Council, the city's "poverty board," evolved from an appendage of the mayor's office into an independent, community-controlled body dedicated to "organizing the poor." The community action mandate of federal antipoverty legislation, which created an opening for the OEDC, helped to establish a new constituency for activists who attempted to mobilize the ghetto with a populist version of black self-determination. Less Marxist-Leninist than urban grassroots insurgency, this variation on black power stressed the return of power to local communities (the "people" or "the community") from the hands of an assortment of outside institutions that included private capital, business, the state, and the suburbs—the "power structure."

Unlike the Panthers, these community activists would never make news beyond Oakland, rarely appear on television, and never become heroes to millions. But they were as central to Oakland's political life and its emerging discourses of black liberation and self-determination as the far more celebrated and iconographic Newton, Seale, and Cleaver. Community politics in Oakland during the second half of the 1960s, however, was just that: politics. Even as grassroots leaders emerged, they faced a patchwork of conflict within the neighborhoods themselves. Middle-class African Americans, poor flatland residents, community organizers, liberal whites, and Mexican American leaders did not share a single vision of "the people" nor did they always present a united front against the white "establishment." The late-1960s' eruptions of community politics within the institutions created by the War on Poverty allowed grassroots activists to move into positions of authority, but their leadership was contested from all sides, even as they identified the "power structure" as their principal antagonist.

In building a mandate for community participation into the federal legislation that created the Office of Economic Opportunity, President Johnson's advisors and the Eighty-ninth Congress laid the groundwork for a revival of neighborhood-level politics. Self-conscious, if paternalistic, about helping the poor "enhance their confidence" and "improve their circumstances," federal poverty warriors improvised "maximum feasible participation": encouraging poor people to participate in the design and implementation of antipoverty programs. In Oakland this window for local input would be forced open as wide as possible. The OEDC never administered immense amounts of federal dollars—about $5 million in 1968, for instance, an amount equivalent to just under 10 percent of the city budget—but control of the council came to have a symbolic importance far out of proportion to its influence. As a concept, community participation in antipoverty programs seemed tailor-made for Oakland. West Oakland alone boasted dozens of grassroots organizations active in everything from school desegregation to economic development, child care, and public health. A short list would have included the Ad Hoc Committee on Quality Education in Oakland (responsible for an African American school boycott in the mid-1960s), Organized Negro Women of the East Bay, United Tax Payers and Voters Union, Oakland Direct Action Committee, Conference on Religion and Race, Fair Housing Committee, Blacks United Mobilizing for Progress (BUMP), the Western End Help Center, and the West Oakland Citizens Committee, in addition to the Urban League, CORE, and the NAACP. Not all of these organizations opposed the city's political status quo with equal fervor, but they stood ready in 1965 to take up the mantle of "maximum feasible participation," to breathe life into an abstraction penned by federal poverty warriors.[22]

Community participation took on a vigorous life of its own nationwide that far outdistanced anything imagined by Great Society liberals,
Lyndon Johnson, or his poverty chief, Sargent Shriver. In cities across the
country, mayors, city councils, business interests, and neighborhood groups
contended over control of federal dollars and, behind the money, political leverage. Despite changes at the federal level intended to depoliticize
antipoverty programs in 1965, Oakland's neighborhood activists pushed
the War on Poverty's political potential as far as any group in the nation.
As we saw in the last chapter, community organizers in Oakland wrestled
control of the poverty board, first from the mayor and city council, then
from liberal black professionals. The OEDC community insurgents, like
the Black Panther Party, cast the defense of community—and its corol-
lary, community empowerment—as a new authenticity. Steeped in the
language of anticolonial struggle, these community leaders proposed to
"offer our assistance to any indigenous group seeking funding for its
program," which purposefully did not include the bourgeois OEDC
board. Pressed from below, and from the left, middle-class black leaders
on the OEDC were forced to change their politics or risk being outrun by
emerging neighborhood radicals. At the same time, some of those black
leaders—Don McCullum and Clinton White, in particular—had begun
to embrace black power discourses and style because of their own frustration with intractable white elites and the failure of their liberal politics
to change conditions in Oakland. McCullum had risen to become chairman of the NAACP's West Coast Region and was contemplating a run
for Oakland mayor in 1968, but his views on politics and economy were
increasingly moving to the left. Thus, once the OEDC and the Neighborhood Advisory Councils had negotiated the compromise "51 percent"
control, the city's poverty program moved forward with the productive
tension between grassroots community activists and professional leaders
as its defining characteristic.[23]

This was the dominant, but not only, fault line in the emerging poverty
program. To prevent their marginalization in the contest over the resources
of the federal War on Poverty, Oakland's Spanish-speaking community
also organized. Numbering between twenty and thirty thousand in the
mid-1960s, Oakland's Spanish-speaking residents, primarily Mexican
Americans and Mexican immigrants, resided principally along Fruitvale
Avenue between the tidal canal and the foothills in central East Oakland.
As early as 1965, leaders of the Community Services Organization (CSO)
and the Mexican American Political Association (MAPA) challenged the
dominant conception of the city's War on Poverty as a remedy for black
disadvantage. "We must categorically state our objection and opposition
to the program proposals submitted by the City of Oakland," a coalition
of leaders from the Mexican American community wrote to Sargent Shriver

on the eve of the poverty program's first round of grants. "Neither in conception, planning, nor in its content will the needs or problems of the Spanish Speaking, Oriental, Filipino, or American Indian communities be taken into consideration." Bert Corona, a longtime labor activist and leader of both the California CSO and MAPA, along with James Delgadillo of the Oakland CSO, and Evalio Grillo, a Cuban and prominent member of the East Bay Democratic Club, helped to organize the Spanish Speaking Unity Council (SSUC). The SSUC in turn established the Spanish Speaking Advisory Council, based in Fruitvale, to advocate for antipoverty programs aimed at the city's ethnic Mexican residents. Between 1965 and the early 1970s, the SSUC and the Spanish Speaking Advisory Council were the pivots around which Oakland's Mexican American community organized both social programs and neighborhood politics. They challenged the OEDC's African American leadership and pushed the city's poverty programs and its Anglo elite to draw Mexican Americans more fully into political power sharing.[24]

These efforts bore fruit, but they never succeeded in transforming Oakland's War on Poverty or the city's essentially biracial political culture. In 1966 Jack Ortega of the SSUC appealed to Lionel Wilson and others on the OEDC to "resolve the problems of communication and cultural differences that are peculiar to the Spanish-speaking people of this area." In addition to a long history of entrapment at the bottom of California's dual-wage economy, the ethnic Mexican community confronted issues, as Ortega put it, "peculiar" to them: the need for bilingual education, language translation for job applicants, a more streamlined and democratic citizenship for immigrants, and a variety of programs that took into account the linguistic and national complexity of a working-class community long central to California's economy but consistently marginalized and taken for granted. By 1969, following three years of struggle with the OEDC, the SSUC sought and gained an independent status that allowed it to receive grants directly from the federal government and private foundations. This laid the groundwork for the more comprehensive development of both social programs and political organizing within the city's ethnic Mexican community during its rapid growth in the late 1970s and 1980s. With African American majorities in all of the city's other poverty "target areas," however, the SSUC in the 1960s could not dramatically shift the War on Poverty's existing programmatic and political emphasis.[25]

The widespread break with liberal fair employment premises among African American leaders in the years between 1964 and 1968, rooted in their experience of early War on Poverty programs and the civil rights push, forced them to consider new strategies and to search more creatively for leverage in what was increasingly seen less as a war against poverty than a war over jobs. In the mid-1960s, black Oakland's most pressing problem remained the lack of accessible jobs. "When we consider matching men with jobs, we must ask, 'what jobs?'" J. M. Regal said upon leaving the city's Department of Human Resources in 1967. "Spending thousands of dollars on programs to motivate people to accept jobs which are not being offered is a shameful waste of human resources," he continued, a sentiment that neatly summed up a generation's flagging faith in federal antipoverty programs and their emphasis on preparation. In the OEDC's first year, the majority of War on Poverty money mostly supplemented the budgets of existing city agencies. To the leaders of the Advisory Committee revolt, this seemed both wasteful and irresponsible when the clearest need remained changing "the way jobs are distributed across the community." Don Warden spoke at a summit of East Bay African American leaders in 1967 of the "need to control our own work projects," a notion that would in time attract many War on Poverty activists. McCullum, once an enthusiastic supporter of the War on Poverty, had also become critical of its underlying assumptions. He began to favor "massive employment programs, massive rehabilitation of our cities, massive make-work projects" to create the needed jobs.[26]

While the debate over how to create or redistribute jobs raged, the OEDC and Mayor John Reading engaged one another in an increasingly bitter contest over the degree of the War on Poverty's independence from city hall. Reading never accepted the Advisory Committee's "51 percent" control and still resented the OEDC's revolt against city council authority. Retaining nominal oversight over Oakland's antipoverty programs, the mayor pressed when he could. After a trip to Washington, DC in the early summer of 1967, he demanded that all "directives and administrative data" as well as funding be sent through "existing administrative channels." But activists pushed the OEDC further away from city hall, not closer. When Norvel Smith departed as executive director of the OEDC, board members and the board chairman, Lionel Wilson, sought their own hand-picked executive director and the authority to develop independent antipoverty programs without city council veto. The mayor and council refused, and after two months of complicated negotiations the OEDC formally dissolved its relationship with city hall. Now called the OEDCI (for "Incorporated"), the city's poverty board had become an independent, nonprofit organization no longer subject to city council veto—an unprecedented level of independence. Under federal law, the mayor still appointed twelve public officials to the thirty-nine-member OEDCI, but for all intents and purposes the poverty board belonged to the community. Divorced from the city, the OEDCI hired Percy Moore as its new executive director. Moore recognized the potential of the board's new liberty and its grassroots base in the Neighborhood Advisory

Committees. Calling on the city's African American leaders to "organize the poor" and "unite for power," Moore brought a combative, community-centered agenda of jobs and political power to the OEDCI.[27]

That agenda met with hostile opposition from city hall. Mayor Reading maintained that the key to reducing unemployment in Oakland was to raise the skill level of the city's workforce. But the OEDCI controlled most of the city's resources to do that. Moore and the OEDCI, alternately, sought ways to redistribute jobs to community residents, the closest thing possible to Warden's "control of our own work projects." Training was important, but secondary, in their view. In addition, Moore had come to believe that the problems of the black poor would never be resolved until the African American community exercised real local political power. Reading and the federal OEO opposed both positions. "They want absolute political and economic control of the entire city," Reading told the *Oakland Tribune*. "They" were "a militant, extremist Negro minority" who had "seized leadership of the black community from more moderate leaders," according to Reading. As Moore and the OEDCI moved ahead on both jobs and politics, Reading's opposition grew more determined.[28]

The OEDCI could not create jobs, but it tried to shape how jobs were distributed. With the unemployment rate among African Americans stubbornly high in the late 1960s (often reaching above 20 percent), and the service sector slow in opening to black workers, the problem remained, in Norvel Smith's words, "that in Oakland we still don't have a genuine commitment from the private sector to share in the risk of employing marginal people. . . . the private sector just doesn't want to get involved." When the federal government awarded the OEDCI local sponsorship of the Concentrated Employment Program (CEP) beginning in 1968, the poverty board hoped to turn the new federal training dollars into leverage against local employers. One of the central issues, Percy Moore believed, was that too many people from outside Oakland held jobs in the city. Outsiders held half of all jobs in Oakland, Moore explained, and 75 percent of jobs paying $10,000 or more—in 1966, two years earlier, a major federal survey had placed the figure at 41 percent of all jobs. To remedy the imbalance, in 1969 and 1970 Moore proposed, and the OEDCI approved, plans for the direct control of jobs by neighborhood councils. "If black folks don't work in Oakland," Moore proclaimed, "we can say nobody works in Oakland." In one program proposed by Moore, the OEDCI would approve and provide job training once employers committed to hire people living in the neighborhood where the jobs were located. In a later, more radical draft, the poor would be organized into neighborhood-level "central labor committees," according to the OEDCI proposal, quasi-hiring halls that would have "first call" on all job openings referred through state and federal employment agencies.[29]

The OEDCI's community jobs plan ran headlong into a quagmire of resistance. Mayor Reading had opposed the OEDCI's control of CEP funds from the beginning and spent most of 1969 and 1970 trying to have the OEDCI's budget cut completely. "I washed my hands of that organization some time ago because of the way it was run," Reading said in late 1970. "My sympathy goes wholly with the poor of this city who are being cheated by the maladministration of the OEDCI." He had washed his hands of dealing with the OEDCI, not of fighting it. In a series of letters to California Governor Ronald Reagan, Vice President Spiro Agnew, and the Western Regional office of the OEO, Reading charged that the OEDCI was corrupt, irresponsible, and an explicitly political body. Even without Reading's intervention, however, it is unlikely that the OEO would have approved the OEDCI's jobs plan. The kind of community control proposed by Moore went beyond even the most radical notions of "maximum feasible participation" and "community action" envisioned by federal OEO liberals, not to mention the Nixon administration officials charged with retrenching the War on Poverty. Moore's proposal for a proto-union of Oakland's poor pushed the boundaries of the Great Society and challenged its assumptions that gradual desegregation, education, and uplift were sufficient to ensure economic opportunity and development in impoverished black communities. In a city where more than half of all jobs were held by whites who lived outside Oakland, these assumptions had come to seem naive by the early 1970s. But community-controlled job distribution was never put into effect precisely because its break with Great Society liberalism was so profound, as was its challenge to white control over jobs.[30]

Its jobs plan stalled, the OEDCI drafted a report in 1970, widely publicized and distributed, that criticized Oakland's political and business establishment in the language of anticolonialism. Indeed, the report emphasized that colonial or neocolonial structures preserved economic segregation and uneven development between black and white communities. The *Tribune* called it an "outsized, artistic political propaganda booklet." The booklet, entitled "Discover Oakland—The Friendly City," set quotations from Jack London alongside photographs of the city's contrasts: wealth and poverty, power and despair, white and black. London had lived in Oakland during much of his life and remained an iconic figure of the East Bay left, old and new. "Discover Oakland" articulated an anticolonial critique of Oakland's poverty—emphasizing the police as an occupying force, the white monopoly on jobs in Oakland, and the political clique, backed by the *Tribune*, that ran the city—in playful mockery of the "city-beautiful" style of chamber of commerce promotion. It castigated the city council for destroying housing in West Oakland, railed against large tax subsidies to corporations, and condemned such high-profile projects as the Oakland Coliseum, which "contains enough electrical cables to wire housing for 115,000 families." The *Tribune* and the city council came in for especially vitriolic criticism. It was, in total, a powerful visual elaboration of the OEDCI's critique of the city's "ruling class." Its broad indictment captured much that was true in Oakland's postwar development, but its polemical tone suggested that the OEDCI had given up on working with or within the existing political channels in the city. The OEDCI had openly declared its outsider political standing. "Discover Oakland" further alienated Reading, who redoubled his efforts to strip the OEDCI of funding.[31]

On the heels of the publication of "Discover Oakland," the OEDCI promised to make the poverty board a political "power base" for the city's African American community. Moore announced that he would use OEDCI funds to support the 1971 city council campaign of Stephen V. Brooks, OEDCI's community services director. In what seemed to Moore like the logical next step in the OEDCI's ongoing war with Reading and the city council, the poverty board defied federal regulations that prohibited local agencies from engaging in political activity. As much as Moore hoped and believed that he had transformed the OEDCI into a bastion of community power, however, the federal government still held the purse strings. Events moved quickly following Moore's announcement. Governor Reagan, who had been urged by Reading for years to act against the city's poverty boards, denied OEDCI funding. The Oakland city council endorsed Reagan's actions. By April 1971 the federal OEO had joined them, sinking the OEDCI. Moore and the poverty board had stretched the political capacity of the War on Poverty to its limit.[32]

When the OEDCI's end came, it did not tell a single story. There was no easy lesson. Wilson, one of the city's most highly regarded civil rights figures, and the man who had hired Moore, publicly warred with him and resigned from the OEDCI before its collapse in 1971. McCullum stayed on for a time, but he too resigned before the 1971 campaign. More broadly, there was a growing sense, especially among the city's African American East Bay Democratic Club leadership, that Moore had taken the OEDCI too far, even in the hostile and polarized political climate sustained by Reading and the *Tribune*. Moore was defensible to a point, but no further. By 1970 Moore was under attack from two directions: the OEDCI board and, ironically, the Neighborhood Advisory Committees, Moore's supposed constituency. Representatives from the latter accused Moore of the "gradual and near disastrous elimination of ongoing programs," a "total disregard of rules and procedures set forth

Figure 6.5. In the late 1960s community activists hoped that the federal War on Poverty could become an effective platform for black self-determination in Oakland. That hope went largely unrealized, but a new generation of grassroots leaders, like those pictured here, nonetheless kept the problems of racial injustice, poverty, and exploitation before the public and challenged liberal assumptions that social inequality would ultimately disappear. Courtesy of the Bancroft Library, University of California, Berkeley.

by the duly designated OEDCI corporate body," and "the blatant and outrageous involvement of political issues without justification" in the poverty programs themselves. Whatever his initial intentions, it does appear that Moore and his OEDCI staff increasingly operated with heavy-handed calculation, alienating many of the same neighborhood activists who had championed his hiring.[33]

Yet Moore made sense to many people, black and white. Involving "the community members themselves" in antipoverty programs "automatically becomes a more affirmative action," Moore explained in early 1969. Given the battles over jobs during the previous five years, giving neighborhoods some say in who got to claim jobs did not seem entirely unreasonable. After the problems with EDA and BART, Mayor Reading's insistence in 1968 that local employers simply needed more encouragement to hire black workers sounded insensible, a retreat to the ineffectual gradualism that had failed so spectacularly over the course of the decade's intense fights over jobs. While Moore took the blame in some eyes and Reading in others for the OEDCI disaster, the poverty program's collapse into internal struggles over leadership should not obscure its more essential fault lines: access to jobs as real ladders of economic mobility versus underfunded training programs for a handful of people who may or may not be hired. In retrospect one thing is clear. The Great Society's commitment to grappling with the legacies of segregation, with black poverty and unemployment, and with the sinking fortunes of almost an entire generation of working-class African Americans was weak and philosophically flawed from the beginning. Its structure and funding streams encouraged a civic struggle over meager resources: between the existing municipal bureaucracy and neighborhood activists and among various neighborhood constituencies, such as the long and often bitter contest between the Spanish Speaking Advisory Council and other, black-dominated councils in West, North, and East Oakland. When faced with its own internal failings as well as determined local opposition in cites like Oakland, it collapsed altogether.[34]

Model City in West Oakland

By seeking control over federal employment funds for community-controlled job placement, the OEDCI challenged existing job distribution mechanisms. In addition, OEDCI Advisory Committees helped to mobilize a new group of leaders, often called "indigenous" in the language of anti-colonialism. The two principal demands of the OEDCI—jobs and political representation for African Americans—marked and politicized the spaces of the metropolitan region. As in the Black Panthers' Ten Point Program, the ghetto stood for the black community. The defense of that territory, and the redirection of capital, jobs, income, and authority to black communities, had become the new project. OEDCI leaders like Moore imagined themselves at the head of a unified "community" against an ancien régime, the white "power structure." But who got to claim authenticity in that community, who got to speak for it, remained constantly contested. The colonial analogy had produced a powerful critique of the distribution of resources across space and race in the new East Bay metropolis. But its suggestion of an offensive strategy—liberate the community in the name of self-determination—posed as many difficult questions in the context of urban American political economy as it answered.[35]

The challenges of forging a liberation politics surfaced in even greater relief in a second, nearly parallel, War on Poverty arena in the late 1960s—Oakland's Model Cities program. Negotiations over control of Model Cities, like the OEDCI struggle, posed the African American community against city hall and drove debates about black power to the heart of the city's decades-old plans for remaking West Oakland. A late-1960s' revamping of federal antipoverty strategy, Model Cities attempted to correct the shortcomings of national urban policy by restoring community control to neighborhood renewal projects. Model Cities legislation targeted federal grants at specific neighborhoods for a variety of job creation, small business, and social service programs, funded through the newly created Department of Housing and Urban Development. Most important, Model Cities sought to overcome the neglect of impoverished neighborhoods that liberal federal poverty warriors had come to associate with many city governments by channeling funds through nominally independent community agencies. Locally, Model Cities promised both new infusions of capital into West Oakland and a second community-centered administrative apparatus independent of city council control—the West Oakland Planning Committee (WOPC). Both possibilities raised expectations in West Oakland and drew neighborhood activists into the larger civic conversation about renewing and remaking the city.[36]

Before embarking on specific projects, the WOPC had to settle two highly charged issues in its relationship to city hall: the extent of WOPC authority and the geographic scope of the Model Cities program. Each issue went to the core of how power and resources were distributed in West Oakland and across the broader metropolitan area. Resolution of the first issue required six months of negotiation between the city council and the WOPC, the latter led by Ralph Williams, Paul Cobb, and Elijah Turner, three West Oaklanders who had helped to secure "51 percent" control of the OEDC for the neighborhoods. In a compromise plan, the city council and WOPC agreed to share power, each retaining a veto over proposed programs. The second issue was more complicated and represented a far more fundamental challenge to the balance of power in the city. Williams and Cobb pressed the city council for veto power over all federal programs and agencies with federal funding operating within the Model Cities boundaries. This would have included, among others, the Port of Oakland, BART, the EDA, and, depending on how the physical boundaries of the Model Cities area were drawn, the proposed downtown City Center, a hotel-retail redevelopment project that promised more than five thousand jobs. After a bitter fight with the city council in April 1968, the WOPC softened its position and accepted the best it could get: veto power over Model Cities projects only.[37]

The WOPC sought broad authority over federal projects in West Oakland because those projects represented concrete jobs. By mid-1968 Williams, Cobb, Turner, and other WOPC leaders had grown cynical about the War on Poverty's underlying premise: federal funds were allocated to services that, in the words of one WOPC memo, merely "maintain the status quo." The EDA, BART, Port of Oakland, and the City Center project, however, contained funding for *actual* jobs, what nearly every observer of Oakland during this period counted as the city's most pressing need. Like Moore's plan to secure community control over job distribution through the OEDCI, WOPC leaders hoped to leverage Model Cities into a power base from which to exercise control over job distribution. To men like Williams, Cobb, and Turner, such a move seemed natural, because in their view the city's black neighborhoods had been marginalized by the economic and political power structures of the city and the surrounding suburbs. To secure jobs, this institutional form of black power was essential. Mayor Reading and the city council, however, opposed what they considered blatant and irresponsible grabs for power that failed to recognize "legitimate" political channels.[38]

These early struggles over Model Cities were complicated in May 1968 by a series of police actions against the Black Panther Party that began with the killing of Bobby Hutton. Protest politics and the War on Poverty became even more firmly linked, as African American activists, including Cobb and others involved with the WOPC, redoubled their efforts to stop police violence and defend neighborhood institutions from city council encroachment. In the week following Bobby Hutton's death, a half dozen former CORE members, many of them now working in War on Poverty agencies, formed the Black Strike for Justice Committee to reclaim control over what Paul Cobb called "community domain." Three of the five principal figures on the Black Strike for Justice Committee, including Cobb, were members or staff of the West Oakland Planning Committee. In early May the committee called for a boycott of Housewives Market, a major downtown retail store—an appealing target because of its substantial African American clientele and connections to the city's political establishment. Black Strike for Justice Committee members threw a line of pickets around Housewives Market and demanded the indictment of police for the murder of Bobby Hutton, "an end to police harassment and brutality," the "decentralization of the Oakland Police Department," and "community control of policy and administration." In total, the committee listed eleven demands for police reform and a variety of neighborhood-level checks on police authority.[39]

Negotiations between the Black Strike for Justice Committee, the mayor's office, and the downtown merchants—facilitated by a group of liberal whites called Community Organization United for Progress (COUP) and a number of the city's prominent churches—broke down repeatedly. As the rhetorical exchanges escalated on both sides, Knowland's *Tribune* stepped into the fray. For one week in late May, every issue of the *Tribune* included a full-page advertisement featuring a disembodied, gloved hand pointing a revolver directly at the reader. In his accompanying editorials, Knowland called the Housewives Market boycott "extortion." He suggested that "Negro militants" were holding the city hostage. The advertisements, widely supported by the downtown business community, shocked both African Americans and liberal whites, who accused the *Tribune* of irresponsible propaganda and fear mongering. In response, the Black Strike for Justice Committee expanded the boycott. Meanwhile, bodies accumulated. At least three young black men were shot and killed by police between Bobby Hutton's death in May and the first of July. The last, Dallas Charles, was shot in the back.[40]

Cobb pushed for inclusion of the City Center and the Port of Oakland in Model Cities at the same time that he was leading the Black Strike for Justice Committee. "If these tactics and totally irresponsible demands are any indication of how they intend to run the Model Cities program— then we should forget it," Reading scolded West Oakland activists in the paternalist tone he increasingly took in public forums. At the heart of those tactics, Reading charged, was "a social revolution, a political battle for political control of the community." "As long as the WOPC is controlled by these three or four people [he meant especially Cobb and Elijah Turner]," Reading continued, "we are not going to see the Model Cities program come to fruition." By mid-July, however, the Downtown Retail Merchants Association had relented, coming out in support of eight of the committee's eleven demands for police reform. Cobb met separately with Reading and Knowland, and the *Tribune* posturing temporarily ebbed. This series of compromises, in which Cobb, Reading, and the chief of police each stepped back from the brink of their most extreme positions, preserved a semblance of working harmony between the WOPC and city hall. Cobb and Williams, however, had failed in their bid to have the City Center and port included in the Model Cities project.[41]

The battle over the inclusion of the port, BART, and City Center in the Model Cities proposal reignited debate about the meaning of black liberation in Oakland. Reading accused the WOPC in general, and Cobb in particular, of manipulating events to amass "political muscle." There is little doubt that Cobb saw the War on Poverty as a vehicle for black political power. In the midst of Model Cities negotiations, Cobb issued his "declaration of independence" for West Oakland and its "urban plantation." At the same time, both Cobb and Williams identified black political power with the fate of the city as a whole. Williams said repeatedly, as he told the *Oakland Tribune*: "we're not trying to take over anything . . . we're trying to be part of the city." Privately, Cobb might have admitted to having more ambitious aims for African American political leadership than Williams, but he shared the latter's deep and sincere concern for the welfare of Oakland. What Reading interpreted as irresponsible grabs for power, Cobb explained as attempts to ensure that the city's most underprivileged group, African American workers, had concrete opportunities opened up to them. Because Cobb saw the black working and middle classes as Oakland's future, his understanding of black power and the critical need to redistribute jobs reflected a deep regard for the long-term health of the city, not merely a self-interested run at power. In the hyper-politicized environment of 1968 nurtured by the aggressive and reactionary *Tribune*, however, such subtleties, and their echoes of deep traditions in urban interest group politics in the U.S., were lost or ignored.[42]

Oakland's War on Poverty activists politicized the city's socioeconomic institutions and neighborhoods, enlarging both the conceptual and the ideological scope of the black liberation struggle. Conceptually, these African American leaders drew all of the city's major institutions, as well its adjoining suburbs, into the orbit of political contest and rhetoric: the Port of Oakland, the City Center, BART, the Redevelopment Agency, all active federal programs, and even such notoriously white suburbs as San Leandro and Fremont. Ideologically, Moore, Cobb, McCullum, Turner, Williams, and others insisted that black power embrace specific objectives: the establishment of an African American political presence in the city, the redistribution of jobs, and the reordering of civic priorities around the neighborhoods, at the expense of the downtown oligarchy. One of the central projects of black self-determination in northern cities like Oakland was the creation of an "imagined community," a politically self-conscious nation, defined by race and place. The narrative of Oakland's War on Poverty exhibits this complicated dynamic, as black power advocates spoke *for* a putatively united community, even as they struggled to define the spatial and ideological context in which such a community existed. Neither Moore nor Cobb ever won the kind of control over job distribution they believed necessary, but their efforts to provide programmatic content to the call for black self-determination had begun to remake Oakland's political culture and to construct a language, style, and set of institutions through which to mobilize Oakland's heretofore disengaged grassroots black electorate. "The real issue is not me and it is not the mayor," Cobb explained to the *Tribune*. "The real issue is the economic development and advancement of the black community in Oakland."[43]

The Black Caucus

As the OEDCI and WOPC pushed against the boundaries of War on Poverty institutions, Paul Cobb founded the Black Caucus. Independent of Great Society funding streams and city hall, the Black Caucus was designed to unite Oakland's black voters around a political agenda and a series of candidates for local office. The *Tribune* would later demean it as a "gadfly," but Cobb had larger ambitions for the organization. The Black

Caucus brought together dozens of African American organizations in Oakland, from the NAACP and CORE to JOBART, merchants groups, and the smallest block clubs and revolutionary sects. It thrived for three years, parallel in structure to the WOPC but more inclusive geographically, taking in North and East Oakland as well as the new Model Cities area. Because it did not depend on federal funding for legitimacy, it could operate with an independence not possible for the OEDCI and WOPC. By providing a unique forum for people and organizations unaccustomed to being taken seriously in Oakland politics, the Black Caucus gave the grassroots mobilization already underway in the poverty program another institutional expression. The Black Caucus embodied dramatic changes in the tenor of African American political organizing in Oakland and the nation since the height of the desegregation fights only half a decade earlier. Previous coalitions of African American organizations in Oakland—the CRCC of the early 1960s, for instance—had sought either to pressure the city's leaders into dismantling Jim Crow with moral suasion or to force businesses and government to comply with the state's fair employment and housing laws by threatening legal action. The Black Caucus sought local political power.[44]

Under the leadership of Cobb and Elijah Turner, chairman of the Oakland CORE, the Black Caucus hoped to solve the decades-old problem of Oakland municipal politics: the lack of a mechanism for mobilizing grassroots voters and making city politics more than a strictly middle-class endeavor. Citywide voting for council seats still crippled black electoral ambitions. However, the Black Caucus developed an alternative formula of civic engagement—demand that city agencies become accountable to the African American community, raise a key set of issues, and hope that black unity could galvanize the community into a voting bloc that could swing elections. In the summer of 1969 Cobb initiated the strategy when he brought three hundred people to a meeting of the Board of Education and requested a citizens committee to involve the black community in upcoming decisions. Without such a committee, Cobb insisted, "the Oakland Black Caucus has no alternative other than to initiate elections to recall individual board members to accomplish its ends." At another meeting, the Black Caucus issued a request for $25 million from the Oakland business community and federal government for economic development. It also attacked the Port of Oakland for its poor record of employing the city's black and ethnic Mexican workers and for recognizing no citizen input into the port's decisions, especially personnel decisions. With thirty-eight member organizations representing sixty thousand individual members, the Black Caucus in a short period emerged with a confident political voice. But when it came to translating that voice into electoral politics, it was less successful. Keeping its promise to run candidates for local

offices, the Black Caucus backed Lawrence Joyner, vice president of the
OEDCI, for mayor and Booker Emory for school board in 1969. Both
lost. Cobb had established the Black Caucus as a formidable new presence in the city's political culture, but it had yet to develop a consistently
mobilized electorate or a strategy capable of overcoming the disability of
the city's governing structure.[45]

The leaders of the Black Caucus invoked as their adversary the city's
traditional power "elite," the *Tribune* and the Knowland family. The latter had come to symbolize, much as they did to the generation of labor
activists of the 1940s, Oakland's tight-knit conservative economic and
political interests. Like their insurgent predecessors in the OVL, Black
Caucus leaders hoped that a barrage of public attacks on this "elite"
would unite an opposition and rally people to the polls. Beyond political
calculation, they were also simply furious at the city's leadership class.
Exchanging the 1940s-era language of "downtown interests" for the
1960s' "power structure," Cobb and the Black Caucus identified a familiar set of villains in league with the *Tribune*—the mayor and city council,
the Downtown Merchants Association, and the Chamber of Commerce.
The mayor in particular came in for steady criticism. In late 1968 and
early 1969, when Reading broke with the OEDCI, the Black Caucus
rushed to Percy Moore's defense and attacked the mayor's office. In a
characteristic pronouncement late in 1969, the Black Caucus described
upcoming Neighborhood Advisory Committee elections as "a contest between the establishment, headed by John Reading, and the poor of the
city, headed by Percy Moore" for which they distributed a pamphlet entitled "Get Busy—Let's Defeat the Mayor." The *Tribune* also drew the
Black Caucus's fire because the paper's editor, William Knowland, had
defended Reading in editorials, accused civil rights and black power advocates of disturbing "law and order" in the city, and responded to the
lawful boycott of Housewives Market in the summer of 1968 with the in-
cendiary revolver ad.[46]

Oakland's political class in the 1960s was unsuited to dealing with the
emerging grassroots political movement and resistant to a full power
sharing with the city's black community. The notion of a "power structure"
or "power elite" holding the city in its grip may have been exaggerated,
but opponents played on the quite real perception that this was the case.
The charges came from a variety of sources, from academic studies to
personal observations. In the early 1970s a University of California political science professor, Edward C. Hayes, published *Power Structure
and Urban Policy: Who Rules in Oakland?*. Hayes confirmed that Oakland
had been run for many years, to its detriment, by and for the interests of
downtown property owners. Between 1929 and 1945, he argued, the tax
assessments on all major downtown properties had declined precipitously,

gifts to retailers, banks, and hotels from the business-dominated city council. This had been one of the central issues of the labor-led OVL campaigns of the 1940s, but Hayes brought his story of the "power structure" into the 1960s as well. He showed that OCCUR, the organization responsible for designing much of the city's early redevelopment priorities and nominally a "citizens committee," was composed of, and controlled by, members of the "power structure"—the Oakland Real Estate Board, Homebuilders Association, Downtown Retail Merchants Association, and Chamber of Commerce. This corps of economic interests, Hayes claimed, maintained tight control of city politics because the *Tribune*, the chief downtown booster, ran the city's Republican Party and dominated city council elections.[47]

Hayes was not alone. Oakland's critics carried on a running dialogue over this "power elite" throughout much of the 1960s. Among outsiders, the Ford Foundation commented extensively. David Gordon, a Ford field representative, wrote that a "large part of the explanation [for problems with race relations in Oakland] lies in the so-called power structure, the attitudes of which are fully as backward as many claim. . . . And there's little doubt that Oakland is a much worse city in which to live because of the predominance of that elite." In the same year, 1966, Warren Hinckle wrote a story for the new left magazine, *Ramparts*, castigating "the elite group which makes 99 percent of the decisions in Oakland." Hinckle portrayed the city's "power elite" as a group of frightened oligarchs afraid to descend from the Oakland Hills to face the "people" in a truly democratic city. Hinckle's claims were thick with the hyperbole of late 1960s new left political discourse, but they captured the essential reality of twenty years of postwar politics in Oakland.[48]

Mayor Reading, the city council, and the political "establishment" envisioned the world differently and refused to adjust their views over time. Reading entered public office with a more sincere desire to tackle the city's social problems than any postwar mayor. In 1966, his first year as mayor, he announced that "the wall around city hall must come down" in order for civic leaders to communicate with the African American community. But by 1968 he was primarily concerned with keeping the city from burning—with preventing the kind of riot in Oakland that had ravaged so many cities between 1965 and 1968. He believed that black leaders were obligated to tone down their rhetoric and cooperate with the city's white officials. "For every headline produced by groundless charges," Reading told the U.S. Commission on Civil Rights, "there are a dozen unwritten stories of progress. For every militant spokesman who seeks to justify the allegiance of his followers by issuing scorching demands, there is an army of patient builders constructing improvements in our city." Reading was not, nor were many city officials, a one-dimensional representative of an abstract "establishment," bent on controlling the city's black population. But he conceptualized the new grassroots African American politics in terms of the "good" patient builders and the "bad" militants. It was an assessment that rendered him ineffectual and hostile in relating to leaders like Cobb, Moore, and Turner, and eventually to moderates like McCullum and Wilson.[49]

Reading and the city council did not understand or appreciate the complexity of African American politics. In the middle of the summer of 1968, Reading gave an interview to the *San Francisco Examiner* in which he complained that when he had come into office three years before, black people wanted civil rights, equality, and jobs. Now, he said, they want nothing short of absolute political control of the city. The *Oakland Post* rebutted, accusing Reading of defining leadership in terms of militancy, then tautologically identifying the militants as the black community's leaders. "This interview with the mayor does a disservice to the black community and its leaders," the *Post* observed. "The black community has many members they look to and follow." From the Black Panthers to Democratic politicians to black ministers, the *Post* continued, black leadership fell across a range of styles and issues, "each in his own bag." A militant, the *Post* insisted, is simply someone "dissatisfied with the status of the Negro and uses all his abilities to correct this evil." The *Post's* comments cut in two directions. First, the *Post's* editors, in this piece and in previous editorials commenting on Model Cities, hoped to stir the city's black middle class into greater political involvement while carving out legitimate space, in the minds of African American readers, for those "middle-class leaders." Second, the *Post* wanted to discredit Reading (the "cry baby mayor"), whom its editors saw as crippled by his misapprehension of black political struggle. Either way, the *Post* marked out a more complicated map of African American politics in the city than Reading or any mainstream white leader was prepared to admit.[50]

Despite these complexities, representatives of the Black Caucus were not shy about speaking for "the black community," especially when the target was Reading. But, as events between 1969 and 1971 revealed, it was a hoped-for but unrealized unity. Cobb's aggressive stance with city agencies and the "power structure" inspired many African Americans, because he raised issues in public forums with a directness rarely seen in Oakland politics. That same aggressiveness, however, alienated others and helped to precipitate a split in the city's African American political forces. The result was a complicated set of political maneuvers over the course of three years, in which the OEDCI, the WOPC, and the Black Caucus contended over the direction of the new grassroots movement. By 1971 the contests had strained the unity of the city's African American community while producing few concrete electoral or policy victories.

In the first phase of these political battles, Wilson, McCullum, Ralph Williams, and others involved with the OEDCI grew weary of Moore's aggressive and overblown rhetoric and his heavy-handed exercise of personal authority. Moore faced accusations on many counts: that he misused funds; that he forced his proposal for new employment plans through the OEDCI without proper democratic procedures; that his use of anticolonial discourse diverted focus from "the poor" and kept white liberals from assisting the poverty programs. Williams attacked Cobb and the WOPC on similar grounds. In November 1969, after seeing the WOPC through its most difficult first year, Williams resigned from the committee. Of the WOPC and OEDCI, he said: "The poor have not really been helped. They are more divided now than have been in the whole history of Oakland." At the same time, Booker Emory resigned as chairman of the OEDCI's West Oakland Advisory Committee, charging that the Black Caucus, which supported Moore strongly in 1969, was determined to take over the city's poverty board. He added, echoing Williams, that the poor had not been helped by the OEDCI but were "in the same fix as when it came." Williams and Emory subsequently worked together in the latter's organization, BUMP. Their charges and defections undermined the unity within black communities that both Cobb and Moore had worked to cultivate.[51]

Subsequent developments in these political scuffles focused on Cobb and Moore. Both men had advanced an anticolonial philosophy and rhetoric through the OEDCI, WOPC, and Black Caucus. Despite their similarities, however, Cobb and Moore struck people in quite different ways. Cobb, an accomplished scholar and political theorist (he would later turn down a Kennedy Fellowship to remain active in Oakland politics), grounded his politics in thoroughly researched and sophisticated arguments. Personally, he was affable, articulate, and studious. In contrast, many found Moore to be more chaotic and unpredictable, taken to political posturing but not schooled or disciplined in the art of politicking. The two men had extraordinarily different styles. Still, they remained allies through the summer of 1970, when they appeared together to call for Reading's resignation. They split almost immediately, however, over who would receive the support of the Black Caucus in the upcoming city council elections. Moore lost and resigned from the Caucus (or was ousted, depending on the version). The Cobb "bloc" and the Moore "bloc," thus divided, launched parallel campaigns for four open council seats in early 1971, driving a deeper wedge into African American political unity. In the campaign, Wilson, Williams, Turner, and McCullum all supported Cobb, their alienation from Moore seemingly final. Indeed, on his resignation from the OEDCI in late 1970, McCullum said that Moore "has been isolated by a coterie of sycophants" and was no longer operating the poverty program in the legitimate interests of the city's residents. What were normal political divisions within a complicated set of communities became—because of segregation, black underrepresentation in local government, and the city's voting system—a liability. Unity seemed a prerequisite to political influence, but it was not easily found.[52]

Cobb's city council campaign was important, however, because it provided a bridge to much of the political activity that was to follow in the 1970s. Cobb was officially endorsed at a community meeting attended by nearly a thousand registered voters at Technical High School in North Oakland. He joined other candidates backed by what organizers called the Oakland Coalition, a group of liberal whites and African American activists who joined together in 1971 to launch a slate of reform candidates for municipal offices. Many of the candidates came from the Black Caucus, including Cobb, Alphonso Galloway (who ran for the Peralta Community College Board), Rev. Frank Pinkard (who ran for the at-large city council seat), and Doug Jones (city council). But Oakland Coalition members did not draw candidates solely from the Black Caucus. The coalition was fueled equally by a liberal resurgence among whites that, as we will see in a subsequent chapter, helped to transform the city's politics in the early 1970s.[53]

The central message of Cobb's campaign came directly from his colonial analysis of Oakland. His campaign highlighted the spatial distribution of resources in the city, drawing from his experiences with the OEDCI, WOPC, and the Black Strike for Justice Committee. It represented a culmination of the spatial critique of Oakland that had been generated by the eruption of grassroots community politics during the previous four years. He focused on the Port of Oakland and the distribution of jobs in the East Bay. According to Cobb, "the Port has over $100 million cash flow annually, but 78% of the people who work for the Port don't live in Oakland." Indeed, as Cobb would tell reporters and audiences, more than half of the city's government and school employees did not live in Oakland; more than half its police force lived outside the city; and only 39 of the city's 725 police officers came from minority groups. Cobb proposed an alternative: a formal affirmative action policy for the City and Port of Oakland, a program through the Redevelopment Agency to encourage African American and other minority residents to become owners and managers of housing; and an affirmative action policy for the new City Center and the businesses that located there. Cobb proposed to rebuild the city's working and middle class through the redistribution of new and existing jobs, the cornerstone of the OEDCI and WOPC agendas since 1968. Though his campaign generated a good deal of attention, particularly among East Bay liberals, he lost in the primary to the incumbent, Raymond Eng. Cobb's campaign for city council in 1971 drew considerable attention and widespread support (he garnered 36,000 votes out of 84,000), but the rending of the political consensus of the poverty program forces was the bigger story that year. Moreover, the old nemesis of neighborhood politics—at-large voting—meant that Cobb's enormous support in West Oakland was diluted and inconsequential. What had looked like an emerging new political movement with a grassroots base and dedicated leaders fizzled out in the spring of 1971.[54]

In the waves of neighborhood-driven and self-determination politics that swept over Oakland in the decade between 1967 and 1977, the year 1971 represented a lull, a moment in between two relatively distinct periods. Cobb's defeat, and the defeat of every Oakland Coalition candidate, marked the end of the War on Poverty's central role in the city's political culture. The black power, revolutionary, and reform currents of thought lifted into the city's political mix by the OEDCI, the WOPC, and the Black Caucus lost the vital institutions and leaders that had carried them through the late 1960s and the first two years of the 1970s. The OEDCI was without Lionel Wilson, Don McCullum, Ralph Williams, and Paul Cobb and would soon be without funding. The WOPC was without Williams and Cobb, its most dynamic leaders. The Black Caucus folded. Those institutions, and that leadership combination, had proven unable to win the local political offices that activists believed necessary for the city to solve its problems. But the door on Oakland politics had not been closed, and no one walked away permanently. The subsequent phase would see the resurgence of the Black Panther Party and the return to local politics of the East Bay Democratic Club, the thirty-year-old brainchild of D. G. Gibson. First as opponents, later as allies, both would work to bring the city's African American communities fully into civic power sharing.

What at first appeared like a useful route to power, the various War on Poverty programs, boards, and committees, ultimately proved to have limited potential. The city's conservative political class resisted the challenge of these federally sponsored seats of neighborhood power and ultimately annulled the program altogether. Advocates of self-determination ironically had come to rely on the federal government as an avenue to local political influence. Black nationalism and radicalism in Oakland had limited political success in the late 1960s, but they had invested African American political struggle with a set of issues—affirmative action, jobs, social services—and symbols—the port, City Center, police, and suburban power—that would come to dominate the city's political culture in the 1970s. In linking the larger African American rights movement to mobilizations in the name of the black poor, community organizers in Oakland had taken steps similar to those of national civil rights leaders. The 1968 Poor People's Campaign, under the leadership of Martin Luther King, Jr., was the best-known example of this trend, but Whitney Young of the National Urban League and George Wiley of the National Welfare Rights Organization, among others, linked antipoverty work to black struggle and the fight for political power. Skeptical that "affluent, middle-class Americans are going to move over and share their wealth and resources," Wiley did express hope "if the poor people who have the problems can organize, can exert their political muscle." The failure of Oakland's War on Poverty mobilizations, and the mixed successes in cities nationwide, demonstrated that finding a home for liberation politics would not be a simple task.[55]

Nationally, too, calls for power were fluid and came from multiple courses. Bayard Rustin, who would never have identified himself with a phrase and cultural style he abhorred (he called black power "a psychological solution to problems that are profoundly economic"), wrote in 1964 that a "total program" of black liberation could only be achieved "through political power." In 1965 Adam Clayton Powell introduced in Chicago a seventeen-point program entitled "My Black Position Paper for America's 20 Million Negroes." Black Americans must seek "audacious power," according to Powell, who called upon the movement to "shift its emphasis to the two-pronged thrust of the Black Revolution: economic self-sufficiency and political power." Eldridge Cleaver told an interviewer in 1969 that blacks "didn't choose to be packed into ghettos, but since that's where we are, we're not going to get any real power over our lives unless we use what we have—our strength as a bloc." Indeed, in U.S. urban historical context, the call for black power echoed both a long tradition of interest-group claims on political authority and newer efforts to find an ideological and strategic position for black liberation that did not rely on the assumptions and institutions of midcentury liberalism. That is, "black power" could relatively easily translate for liberal politicians into a convenient interest group claim. But in the hands of others, it could also mean a far more radical politics aimed at social transformation and international solidarity among colonized peoples. It was precisely this combination, and the tension among its various elements, that made the post-1966 era so rich and its legacy for urban politics as a whole profound.[56]

We can appreciate that legacy by following continuities between the left and liberal generations of African American activists emergent in the 1940s and the subsequent nationalist and radical generations of the 1960s without downplaying the real differences between the two. Such an effort helps to contextualize the emergence of black power within the longer sweep of urban history and political economy in the twentieth century. Historians and popular critics alike have devoted insufficient attention to the evolution of black power and self-determination politics out of earlier liberal efforts, have downplayed the effective grassroots organizing undertaken in the name of black power, and have too often marginalized a broad and diverse set of strategies and analyses in favor of tropes of violence and alienation. For some black people, black power symbolized their alienation from racist mainstream America. For many more others, however, it symbolized their profound engagement with the institutions and traditions of American political culture and intellectual life. Some of those traditions were liberal, in their calls for political representation and reform within an interest-group framework. Others were traditions of African American radicalism, like leftist internationalism, that the Cold War had forced underground. Seeing through the latter lens provides an important counternarrative to accounts of black power as an emotional, rhetorical, and ultimately marginal and self-destructive political phenomenon. Its continuities with previous African American political traditions notwithstanding, in the longer sweep of twentieth-century urban history, advocates of black power and self-determination articulated a profoundly important rereading of the landscape of metropolitan America. Their penetrating insights would shape debate over American cities for more than a decade. Oakland stood out in this national context. The Black Panther Party and the loose network of War on Poverty activists and social program advocates infused their calls for black self determination with a critique of metropolitan America and its legacy of development and underdevelopment that reformulated the class and racial politics of the New Deal and World War II era by indicting liberalism for its complicity in racial segregation, black poverty, and disfranchisement.

7

White Noose

THE SUBURBAN "white noose" surrounding the urban black community stood metaphorically for metropolitan inequality and segregation. Unwelcome in the South County (Southern Alameda County) suburbs, African Americans in Oakland were denied access to the region's fastest growing employment and housing markets. Suburban Alameda County, from San Leandro through Fremont (and across the Santa Clara County line into Milpitas) *was* closed to black homebuyers in most important respects through the middle 1970s. But the denial of access was only one story. It must be joined to others. Suburban homeowners shaped regional distributions of opportunity and resources in more ways than just policing racial boundaries. Indeed, by the 1970s white East Bay homeowners were more interested in reducing taxes than in managing race. But unequal metropolitan development meant that fighting taxes represented the reproduction of racial disadvantage by other means—and therefore the reproduction of race by other means. In the 1960s and 1970s the suburban politics of property were an extension, under changing economic conditions, of the processes that underlay city building in the 1940s and 1950s. Even as they remained major beneficiaries of public subsidy, South County suburban homeowners nonetheless claimed that they were under siege and victimized. In their view, the industrial garden had begun to show signs of wilting, the suburban dream signs of malaise. Keeping it alive and flourishing remained their overriding objective.[1]

The pace and reach of postwar suburbanization had transformed California in a single generation. Between 1950 and 1970 the state's population doubled, from just over ten million to just under twenty. Men and women from every state, Mexico, and, after 1965, Southeast Asia poured into California in these two decades, dwarfing even the enormous World War II migration. To accommodate them, three and a half million new housing units were built—double the number that existed in 1950—in a twenty-year construction bonanza of enormous scope. The new population was overwhelmingly young. As the median age in the state dropped from thirty-two to twenty-seven, the percentage of people over sixty-five years of age fell from 8 to 3, and the percentage of school-age children shot up from 17 to 25. In all, the number of California school-age children quadrupled in two decades. Population growth and development fed a real estate boom in which the median home price jumped by 50 percent—and it would increase even more dramatically during the 1970s. In the space of twenty years, California had become the nation's economic engine and population magnet.[2]

In the late 1960s the East Bay suburban corridor, from Oakland to San Jose, looked like much of postwar California. Two decades of industrial-garden city building had made the "Metropolitan Oakland Area" one of Northern California's leading poles of growth. A forty-mile river of concrete, the Nimitz Interstate Highway, spanned its length and stitched together the landscape in linear regularity (map 3.2). South of Oakland, Nimitz exits led first to San Leandro and its booming industrial districts. Fifteen thousand blue-collar workers labored here, at Caterpillar Tractor, International Harvester, National Can, Frieden Calculators, Simmons Mattresses, the Latchford Glass Company, and dozens upon dozens of small, ten- and fifteen-employee machine shops and light assembly plants. They drove to work on the Nimitz and parked on vast asphalt acreages. Others arrived on surface streets through San Leandro neighborhoods, patchworks of ranch homes and stucco bungalows that looked much like Oakland's. Outside the city limits lay San Lorenzo, one of the largest subdivisions in Northern California, five thousand wartime ranch homes on unincorporated county land with a population of seventeen thousand. Filled with World War II veterans turned machinists, welders, teachers, civil servants, clerks, and salespeople, San Lorenzo's government was its homeowners association, its downtown the Bayfair Mall in San Leandro. Here, and in neighboring Castro Valley, racial segregation was a given, and homes appreciated ahead of inflation every year.

Further south, exit ramps led east into Hayward, by the late 1960s a city more than double its prewar physical size. Ethnic Mexican *colonias*, once on marginal land, had been incorporated through annexation, as had acres of Anglo tract homes. Near Hayward's prewar downtown, the giant Hunt Foods canneries hummed with seasonal activity and four thousand workers. Hunt's large ethnic Mexican workforce lived in *barrios* in Hayward, Union City, Milpitas, Alviso, and even on San Jose's Eastside. Surrounding downtown and the canneries were new subdivisions with names like Fairway Greens and Holiday Estates, and new shopping malls indistinguishable at a distance from factories and warehouses with their low-slung, horizontal design and gargantuan parking lots. In Hayward, Okie and Arkie migrants and their descendants lived in close proximity to Mexican migrants and their families, with multiple subdivisions of white-collar WASPs in between, in a city that symbolized the sudden and often jarring confluence of an agricultural past and a suburban future. Hayward was the most eclectic South County suburb, a mish-mash of working-class and ethnic cultures stirred together with an ascendant managerial and commercial Anglo middle class.

Leaving Hayward, the Nimitz passed quickly through Union City and then into the largest municipality in Northern California, Fremont. In the 1960s Fremont's population more than doubled, from forty-three thousand to just over a hundred thousand—within corporate limits larger than either San Francisco or Oakland. Horizontal, diffuse, uncentered, Fremont lived up to America's suburban clichés. On the far south side of town, Nimitz traffic buzzed along within a hundred yards of the sprawling General Motors plant, set in near-perfect industrial garden coincidence against the vacant, verdant hillside. Back in the city proper, wide boulevards criss-crossed one another in a broad latticework that linked each new subdivision to the next. Nearly devoid of any pre–World War II structure, Fremont boasted the newest housing stock in the county, cul-de-sac after cul-de-sac of ranch-style homes set back behind front lawns and rows of freshly planted maple trees. By far the greenest South County suburb, Fremont's parks, lake, nearby hills, huge blocks of undeveloped land, and plentiful crabgrass on both public and private property, along with the ubiquitous sunshine common in the southern part of the Bay Area, gave the city literally the feel of a garden. Past Fremont lay the autoworker suburb of Milpitas and San Jose's sprawling Eastside, the center of Mexican and Chicano life in Northern California.

The Nimitz provided one possible viewing frame of this emerging landscape. By the 1970s, BART offered another. With its multiple stops along the length of the East Bay, BART took managers to work in Oakland from Fremont, but also autoworkers to Fremont assembly lines from Oakland. Nurses at Kaiser Hospital in Oakland or San Francisco traveled from their homes in Hayward. Seasonal cannery workers in Hayward commuted from their homes near the Fruitvale stop in Oakland. Workers passed back and forth across one another's paths in a complex set of daily migrations that did not always correspond to the organization man model—commuting to central city jobs from bedroom suburbs. Two long bridges across San Francisco Bay in South County, intersecting with the Nimitz at Hayward and Fremont, respectively, multiplied the commuting combinations. They made it possible for aerospace engineers at Lockheed in Sunnyvale or electrical engineers at the Stanford Industrial Park to live in Fremont, which many did. The bridges also carried ethnic Mexicans from the barrio in Redwood City south of San Francisco to work in Hayward or Union City or, by the 1970s, at General Motors in Fremont and Ford in Milpitas. Black autoworkers Jim Crowed out of Fremont and Milpitas in the 1960s lived in East Palo Alto, at the foot of the Dumbarton Bridge. Shopping malls and factories on the fringe, multicity commutes, and vast subdivisions spread life, labor, and leisure horizontally across the spaces of the flatlands.

The most powerful frame in which to understand South County, however, remains property. Underneath the commuting, subdivisions, and

Figure 7.1. Suburban tract housing in San Lorenzo, just outside the city limits of San Leandro. Though many white Oaklanders fought fair housing and advocated lower taxes, the strength of Northern California's opposition to desegregation and support for tax reform came largely from postwar suburban communities like this one. Courtesy of the *Oakland Tribune.*

development lay a history of property markets and the politics that shaped them. The expectations of racial segregation and low taxes produced in suburban South County after World War II could not be contained by the boosters and public officials who helped to construct them. They would take on a life of their own. Homeowners in the 1960s and 1970s remained focused on how property would be developed and taxed, how space would be mobilized for social and political ends. That concern, animated by the homeowner populism that was a foundation of suburban city building in the 1950s, precipitated a series of suburban counterrevolutions in these two decades that lay the groundwork for the so-called tax revolt of 1978. The price of California's extraordinary growth had to be met, but not, if suburban homeowners had their way, by them. On three key issues—racial segregation, affordable housing, and taxes—suburbanites in the East Bay joined with their counterparts statewide in a political retrenchment with far-reaching consequences. Suburban homeowners in Alameda County presented themselves as protecting their economic future and preserving the promises of the industrial garden, but their actions, embedded in already skewed metropolitan structures of opportunity, continued to shift a disproportionate share of the costs of postwar capitalism to Oakland. Furthermore, they participated in the creation of a narrative of victimization, which appealed to increasing numbers of homeowners over these decades, that may have reflected genuine feeling but belied the enormous privileges they enjoyed. The suburban break with liberalism, so evident in the East Bay by the late 1960s, changed California politics within a decade and national politics within another.[3]

The Suburbs in Black and White

In November 1964 tens of thousands of southern Alameda County suburbanites drove to the polls. They voted in overwhelming numbers for the figurehead of mid-1960s liberalism, President Lyndon B. Johnson, while casting ballots in equal proportion against one of California liberalism's signature achievements, fair housing. Two million Californians statewide joined in this performance, making a contradictory case to the nation about where the state stood on race and equality. But the results likely did not appear contradictory to residents of South County, because they had come to understand the limits of liberalism and the American welfare state through the lens of property. Property and homeownership organized a set of primary concerns and issues for suburban voters. It also structured the mechanics of political participation—who was heard and which groups defined the debate. Homeownership dominated the framing of social and political questions. But homeowners were not alone in setting forth these parameters. Leaders of the real estate industry—at every level, from local to national—kept watch on the California housing market, one of the most dynamic and profitable in the nation, carefully and deliberately. That industry's investment in residential racial segregation had ebbed little by the early 1960s. In 1964 no threat to property markets seemed greater to either homeowners or the real estate industry than the Rumford Fair Housing Act, passed in 1963 after a decade of work by Byron Rumford, the East Bay Democratic Club, and the statewide liberal coalition.[4]

The California Real Estate Association (CREA) brought Proposition 14, repeal of the Rumford Act, before voters in 1964. Part of the CREA's broad antiliberal agenda, Proposition 14 made California "a battleground for a national showdown on housing legislation," in Byron Rumford's phrase. One of the most important social movement organizations in the postwar United States, the CREA organized people on the presumption that property, as space that produces capital, is the highest social good and should remain the least regulated, most "free," arena of human activity. The CREA campaign in 1964 emphasized the sanctity of private property and its centrality to Americanism. "I want to talk about the preservation of this *real* American," a CREA representative explained in 1964, "an individual who, at least up until now, has been endowed with personal freedom as to choice." Co-opting the rights language of the national black liberation movement, the CREA and its political supporters aggressively shaped public discussion of fair housing. "If we believe in the American democratic system," a Republican state senator explained, "we must acknowledge that it is the right of the people to tell the government what to do." He concluded his defense of Proposition 14 by warning that "[w]hen the government tells the people what to do and think, we have a dictatorship." In place of the "traditional right" of property ownership, the president of the National Association of Real Estate Boards asserted, the Rumford Act supposedly established "a new so-called right for individuals of a minority group."[5]

This individual rights language represented a profound dissembling on the part of real estate interests. Industry leaders had long shaped segregation with institutional bulwarks and market manipulation. Through its buying and selling policies, the CREA controlled local real estate boards and set standards for segregation in hundreds of local communities statewide. The Southern Alameda County Board of Realtors, a CREA member, determined, for example, which homes in the East Bay would be advertised as "white only." Prior to 1948 the CREA used racial covenants to prevent the sale of homes to "non-Caucasians," and after 1948 it endorsed "corporation contract agreements" like those used in the East Bay by M. C. Friel to keep communities white. The CREA also maintained a powerful presence in the state legislature in Sacramento, where it influenced property tax legislation, state building codes, and a host of other property-related matters. Indeed, the CREA remained a more consistent reservoir of conservative politics in 1960s' California than the Republican Party and stood as the principal force in the state opposing liberal or social democratic claims on private property. On the eve of the 1964 election, the CREA had 2,600 member realtors in Alameda County and a statewide grassroots network of realtors, realty boards, and business connections that rivaled any political party. A late-1960s report by the California Committee for Fair Practices estimated that "the California Real Estate Association is, among profit-making trade groups, without parallel in power and prestige."[6]

Proposition 14 passed in southern Alameda County by an overwhelming margin (see map 7.1). In an election in which Lyndon Johnson won the county by a margin of two to one, and voters returned Democrats to seats in the state legislature and U.S. Congress, Proposition 14 received

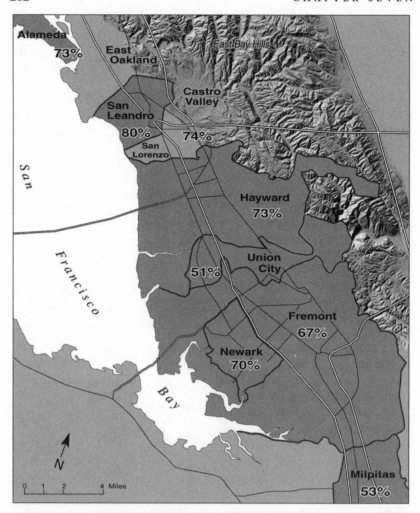

Map 7.1. Proposition 14 voting results in Alameda County, 1964. The repeal of fair housing legislation had overwhelming support in most South County cities. Only Union City and Milpitas proved exceptions. In Union City, the large ethnic Mexican vote against Proposition 14 helped narrow the margin, and in Milpitas, Ben Gross and UAW Local 250 campaigned vigorously against Proposition 14. Cartography Lab, University of Wisconsin.

a stunning endorsement. San Leandro, for instance, voted to repeal the Rumford Act 80 percent to 20 percent while endorsing Johnson over Goldwater nearly two to one. In Hayward, three-fourths of the voters favored repeal, with two to one margins for Johnson as well. Only in Union City, where the Mexican American community remained a near majority, and in Milpitas (in Santa Clara County), where Ben Gross and the UAW campaigned relentlessly against Proposition 14, was the vote against fair housing reasonably close; however the proposition still won in both cities. The San Leandro–Oakland municipal border offered the most striking instance of Proposition 14's intersection with local racial segregation. In San Leandro precincts along the Oakland city line, Proposition 14 passed with slightly more than 80 percent of the vote—in three precincts it was as high as 85 percent. In parallel precincts directly across the city line, African American neighborhoods in East Oakland voted *against* Proposition 14 by more than 92 percent—in one precinct the vote to defeat the referendum was 204 to 3. Such patterns, and the remarkable totals for Alameda County as a whole, belied the CREA's insistence that Proposition 14 was a race-neutral issue of "freedom." South County voters endorsed the CREA discourse of property rights as a rhetorical stand-in for resistance to desegregation. Byron Rumford lamented that "the whole proposition was built on fear and discrimination and racism," such that even "those who expressed themselves as liberals" believed they needed Proposition 14 "in order to protect their homes." Nationally, Proposition 14's victory was widely regarded as a severe blow to the civil rights movement, what "No on 14" advocate Edward McHugh called "the severest setback to the forces of fair housing since the current phase of the civil rights struggle began."[7]

Homeowners, however, were not Proposition 14's only constituents, nor was the measure a transparent expression of homeowner political objectives. In Alameda County, as in all developing localities in California and nationwide, dense home finance and construction networks linked a variety of individuals and institutions to the process of community building. Land speculators and developers, as well as the banks that lent them money, were in this group. Real estate brokers and home mortgage brokers, as well as the banks that lent them money, were in it too. The process of home building, from the subdivision planning stage to the handshake over the final sale, involved attorneys, title companies, professional planners, and a host of other subsidiary planning and finance institutions. These multiple constituencies symbolized the range of both personal and structural investments in segregation. At the same time, the uproar over the Rumford Act was ignited and fueled by the CREA and the National Association of Real Estate Boards, not by a spontaneous homeowner revolt. Both the CREA and the NAREB had been fighting fair housing in the California Assembly and promoting segregated communities for decades. When the Rumford Act passed in a close vote in 1963, CREA representatives, not homeowners' organizations, were on hand in Sacramento to declare their intention to repeal it. Proposition 14 *engendered* a grassroots response, with hundreds of thousands of homeowners enthusiastically championing the campaign. But the campaign itself was organized and directed by the CREA and its affiliates."[8]

Indeed, if there was a grassroots dimension to the 1964 campaign, it came from Proposition 14's opponents. The measure passed in South County despite enormous public efforts to defeat it. "The 'No on 14' campaign," according to one postelection assessment "was strongly endorsed, relatively well financed, and backed by a hard-working army of volunteers." Outside of San Leandro, which remained the most segregationist city in the county, virtually every major public official—from state legislators to mayors and city council members—opposed the measure. "In the interests of justice and common decency, it should be defeated," declared the Tri-Cities Committee Against Proposition 14, a group that included the mayor and city council of Fremont, South County's congressional and assembly representatives, and Union City's major public figures. Another prominent member added that the referendum "would create a new kind of right—alien to our state and not found in any other state, including Mississippi . . . the absolute right to discriminate." Governor Brown called it "the segregation initiative" and referred to it as "legalized bigotry." Californians Against Proposition 14, the umbrella organization for the anti-14 forces, drew on the same grassroots networks of churches, labor unions, and civil rights organizations that had come together to defeat the right-to-work measure in 1958. Proposition 14 "would erect a Jim Crow Wall around the ghettoes of California," opponents of the measure emphasized. In press releases, public debates, radio announcements, and innumerable public meetings and information sessions, Alameda County's political, religious, and business leaders vigorously opposed Proposition 14. Only realtors and homeowners associations were absent from the No on 14 coalition. But they, operating through institutional networks cultivated over two decades of city building, proved far more able to convince and mobilize voters than the county's political leadership.[9]

The CREA framed Proposition 14 as a decision between "freedom of choice" and "forced housing" and asked California homeowners to choose segregation under a different name. Naming was especially important in the election. Opponents of the Rumford Act rehearsed in California a well-worn rhetorical strategy that would become increasingly popular in national conservative circles in the late 1960s and early 1970s: employing a putatively race-neutral civil rights language. The Rumford Act's detractors discussed race only to place liberal supporters of fair housing on the defensive and accuse them of "naiveté." Encouraged by the CREA, those aligned against Rumford used a discourse of property rights to argue that the law "forced" property owners to rent or sell to a specific group, namely, African Americans. Further, the CREA claimed in public that they had no influence over housing markets and could not control the racial preferences of property owners or renters. "When one of the so-called minority groups moves in, the majority group moves out," Oscar Brinkman, a lobbyist for the National Apartment Owners Association and its California affiliates, told the House Judiciary Committee in 1963, "and the end result will be financially calamitous to an owner who had no racial prejudice of his own." While such claims may have contained an element of truth, given the segregationist prejudice of most whites, their larger duplicity was evident. After decades of lobbying both state and federal governments against fair housing, and decades of promoting segregation in local communities, representatives of the real estate industry then claimed that they were merely looking out for the "rights" of their constituents and were innocent of any complicity in discrimination. This purposeful deception underscored the lengths to which industry representatives would go to preserve their control over one of the most lucrative real estate markets in the nation.[10]

That control had three principal dimensions. First, since well before the New Deal, NAREB and the CREA had segregated property markets using racial covenants. This allowed the industry both to manipulate the racial prejudice of home buyers and to create predictable markets. The real estate industry wanted reliable control over any market fluctuations created by white prejudice. This emerged as an even more pressing issue within New Deal housing policy. Under Home Owners Loan Corporation (HOLC), FHA, and VA guidelines, the most profitable real estate strategy was to treat black and white housing markets as entirely distinct entities. There was a second, related dimension. Open housing threatened real estate industry control because it raised the possibility of chaotic market fluctuations. Rapid white turnover and property devaluation, wholesale white abandonment of rental properties, or the refusal of developers to build or banks to finance mixed-race developments, to name a few select fears, introduced market factors that undermined steady, predictable, upwardly trending property valuations—the real estate industry's chief concern. Finally, there was a third dimension to industry control. African American residential mobility was always understood in negative terms, because it forced ever wider readjustments of property values in white neighborhoods. Among other factors, white home values were affected by their proximity to African American neighborhoods. Containment is not too strong a word for the industry's desire to minimize these readjustments. In all, the real estate industry came to see the promotion, preservation, and manipulation of racial segregation as central—rather than incidental or residual—components of their profit-generating strategies.[11]

To dramatize the industry's promotion of segregation in suburban Alameda County, in the summer of 1963, a year before Proposition 14,

African American leaders from Oakland had appealed to suburban Alameda County in an effort to dramatize suburban segregation and lay the groundwork for application of the Rumford Act. They delivered prescient warnings of impending social distress in Oakland and pleas for justice in the language of liberalism and progressive Americanism. In a major speech before the Southern Alameda County Bar Association, Don McCullum explained that the condition of impoverished black Oaklanders was made worse by the "rigid housing discrimination in Southern Alameda County—beginning at the San Leandro city limits." "This is not good—not good for America, not good for yourselves individually or for your children," he continued. He related his own frustration at being turned down by South County housing developments in a three-year search for a new home. "The minority people cannot break out of the city because of the irresponsibility of the suburban areas," he told the audience of journalists. Clinton White, an Oakland attorney and NAACP official, also toured South County communities urging residents to accept integration. "Fairness in jobs, housing, and education can give Fremont a 'welcome wagon' appearance," White told the Fremont Council of Social Planning in the summer of 1963. That same summer, Berkeley and Oakland CORE chapters staged "Operation Windowshop" in East Bay suburbs, demonstrations in which black home buyers strolled through all-white neighborhoods where homes were listed for sale. In these and other instances, beginning in 1963 and continuing well into the 1970s, South County communities were under constant pressure from Oakland's black leaders to open housing to African American buyers and, in a more general sense, to improve their relationship with African American Oakland.[12]

Black leaders from Oakland could reprimand and cajole suburban residents and appeal to what McCullum called the "responsible white community," but moral rhetoric was virtually their only leverage. McCullum could insist that the notion of property rights articulated by the CREA preserved segregation and trampled on the rights of African Americans, but he and the community he represented were positioned at great remove from the levers of municipal power in places like San Leandro and Fremont. Here was the national civil rights dilemma writ small. The geographic concentration of the African American political community and the structure of American political authority—around municipal, state, and federal, but not regional, poles—made addressing regional problems extraordinarily difficult. State laws like the Rumford Act and federal civil rights legislation represented the best hope that these political boundaries could be superceded. In places like Oakland, there was a constituency for civil rights legislation, especially for the federal Civil Rights Act of 1964, every bit as large, vocal, and determined as in Birmingham and Selma, a constituency that hoped to turn moral suasion into political leverage. But their adversary was not "massive resistance," the South's campaign against desegregation. It was sunbelt metropolitanization and its structure of property markets, homeowner politics, and segregated municipal enclaves.[13]

Resistance to open housing in southern Alameda County rested simultaneously on both willful action and a rhetoric of innocence. Willful acts included Proposition 14, homeowners association agreements, and, prior to the 1960s, all of the architecture of suburban apartheid recounted in chapter 3. These cleared the way for inaction, including homeowners' protestations in 1963 and afterward that no "civil rights problems" existed in South County suburbs. In San Leandro, for instance, when Democratic Mayor Jack Maltester proposed a Committee on Human Rights and Responsibilities in the civil rights heat of 1963, he was stonewalled by the city council. The council, controlled by the city's homeowners associations, three separate times refused to create such a committee, the last two after direct appeals from Don McCullum. "I feel that the great majority of the residents of San Leandro feel that we have no problem that requires the establishment of any committee on human rights," a typical letter to the editor read. Indeed, when David Creque, a San Leandro resident, spoke in support of establishing the civil rights commission, the homeowners association of which he was president quickly dismissed him, claiming that his statements "do not necessarily reflect the views of the board of directors." Homeowners contended that the absence of African Americans meant the absence of a "civil rights problem," much as an earlier generation of whites had denied complicity in a "Negro problem." Such willful inaction and its rhetoric of innocence underscored the physical and social remove that were the privileges of San Leandro's whiteness as well as the power of segregation to perpetuate racism and false consciousness among whites. Combinations of action and inaction sustained suburban segregation in the East Bay for two postwar generations.[14]

Homeowners were not innocent. In conjunction with their real estate industry patrons, they participated in the construction of a new white racial ideology with sweeping implications. Across the middle of the twentieth century, classic forms of white supremacy in the United States slowly gave way in public forums to a right-based language of individualism and freedom. The discourse was not itself new. It had been used for at least two centuries to buttress private property claims, including those of former slaveholders in the postbellum South and those of homeowners who placed racial covenants on their property in cities like Chicago, Detroit, and San Francisco in the first half of the twentieth century. But the aggressive assertion of this rights language as the dominant discourse through which white racial privilege was articulated was new. The Proposition 14 campaign in California played an important role in this larger, mid-twentieth-century development. On the eve of the 1964 election,

California Assemblyman Robert Stevens gave voice to this language in a television debate. Claiming that prejudice and discrimination were "not the issue before us," Stevens likened the Rumford Act to the "witch hunts" of early colonial times, insisted that it denied "freedom of choice," and asserted the primacy of "the right to acquire and protect property." Labeling white resistance to open housing in the 1960s a "backlash," as many historians and other commentators have done, distracts attention from the central fact of that resistance: it took the form of rights-based counterclaims. These claims were intended to inoculate segregation and white privilege against charges of racism through appeals to hallowed American rights traditions. Homeowners in California in 1964 helped to advance this project, one that would increasingly come to shape how racial equality was debated and contested in the national political culture.[15]

The California Supreme Court declared Proposition 14 unconstitutional in 1966, but desegregation advocates had lost three years fighting the CREA. Finally enforceable, the Rumford Act eventually became a critical tool for equal rights in California. But lost time, coupled with the long legacy of housing discrimination, meant that change came slowly. In 1971 a national report brought South County's history of racial exclusion to the surface. That year, the National Committee against Discrimination in Housing (NCDH) published the results of a study warning that "developing Bay Area suburbs will be racist enclaves in the image of San Leandro if the segregated housing development and marketing policies are not reversed." Focusing on San Leandro, the NCDH report blamed federal housing policy, homeowners associations, the city government, and the county real estate board for racial restriction, the familiar cast of characters in what NCDH Chief Executive Ed Rutledge called "typical of the situation across the nation." "The Veterans Administration guaranteed more than $1.6 million in home loans" in San Leandro, the report observed, "while the Federal Housing Administration insured more than $1.7 million in home mortgages." All went to white buyers. Those loan guarantees became, in the hands of real estate brokers and homeowners associations, bulwarks against desegregation, subsidized apartheid. In the 1970 census more than three quarters of Oakland census tracts along the San Leandro city line had a black majority. San Leandro itself was less than one-tenth of 1 percent African American. Here was a racial gradient as steep as any in the nation, preserved deep into the 1970s by both custom and structure.[16]

Segregation in suburban housing markets raised concrete economic questions about how resources were distributed in the divided metropolis. "Ironically," sociologist Wilson Record wrote in a 1963 study, "San Leandro may get [industrial] plants which, if located in Oakland, would provide the tax base upon which Oakland needs to draw in order to service the Negroes excluded by San Leandro." A major study of California housing in the early 1960s predicted that segregation would ultimately force older cities like Oakland "to look largely for their revenues to poorer groups of taxpayers who will require higher outlays for social services." Advocates of racial justice made their case against suburban segregation in these concrete economic terms. Trapped in declining cities, they argued, poor African Americans required a greater share of public resources but received a lesser. "Our cities are already virtually bankrupt," Whitney Young, executive director of the Urban League, wrote in his 1969 *Beyond Racism*, citing "the mushrooming demand for costly social services required by the impoverished slums" as the principal reason. Of all the consequences of unequal metropolitan development, the redistribution of the tax base was ultimately one of the most severe and consequential. Even as housing and employment barriers lifted in degrees after the 1960s and metropolitan boundaries became more porous for African Americans, property markets changed slowly. Property value differentials hardened across space, and gaps between the urban and suburban per capita revenue from municipal property taxes widened, creating vast inequalities that functioned to reproduce racial disadvantage—especially in key property tax–supported urban services like education and health and welfare.[17]

Exclusion and containment kept African Americans from making substantial inroads in South County housing markets through the 1960s. Black workers enjoyed slightly more success in obtaining employment in the suburban East Bay, but these gains were limited to the General Motors and Ford plants in Fremont and Milpitas and the U.S. Naval Air Station in Alameda. In the late 1960s the GM plant was thought to employ between 1,500 and 2,000 black workers out of a fluctuating total employment of between 5,000 and 6,000. The Ford plant employed a similar figure. Both hired large numbers of Mexican Americans as well, increasingly so during the 1970s. The Naval Air Station employed between 1,600 and 1,800 black workers out of a total work force of about 8,000. Outside of the automobile factories and the Naval Air Station, however, black workers could be found in only a few corners of the suburban East Bay labor market. A Federal Civil Rights Commission study of San Leandro in 1967 revealed that only 5 percent of employees in the city's industries were black. A similar study for Fremont, Union City, and Newark found 6 percent. Both studies, however, were limited by their reliance on companies required to file reports with the Equal Employment Opportunity Commission. Companies outside of the EEOC's purview may well have employed even fewer African American workers.[18]

Employment discrimination against black workers in the East Bay was capricious and demoralizing. In blue collar fields, East Bay suburban communities were dominated by a few medium-sized employers—like GM and Ford, but also Trailmobile, Caterpillar Tractor, Pacific States Steel, Peterbuilt, and International Harvester—and an enormous number of smaller companies, plants, and establishments that employed less than one hundred workers. For black job seekers, the mixed-industrial landscape envisioned by both the MOAP and suburban city-builders could be almost impossible to navigate. Local offices of the California State Employment Service, for instance, filled jobs in Fremont, Union City, and other South County cities with local residents first. Only then were unfilled jobs forwarded to offices in Oakland. For those who could not afford an automobile, suburban work was especially difficult to secure, because the tasks of finding an opening and appearing for an interview required transportation. After finding a job announcement and driving (or taking BART or a bus) into a suburban city, an African American applicant still might be told that the position had been filled. Race entered the decisions of managers, employment agencies, owners, and others in control of hiring in unpredictable ways. Furthermore, Bay Area employment in the manufacturing, transportation, and wholesale trade sectors was highly unionized, over 90 percent in many industries. In general, African Americans fared best in those sectors of the suburban labor market where they had gained a foothold in plants previously located in black population centers— Ford in Richmond and GM in Oakland, for instance—and in federal military installations.[19]

Between 1963 and 1970, after a decade of attempts to reclaim and revitalize Oakland's neighborhoods, African Americans there looked outward. They turned toward the East Bay suburbs, the lengthy residential and industrial landscape stretching from San Leandro to Milpitas, McCullum's white noose. "The flight to the suburbs is the highest form of social irresponsibility," McCullum charged in 1969, in his most stinging indictment of suburbanization. The metaphor of white strangulation of the black city was powerful precisely because it reduced the complexity of metropolitan patterns of residence and industry to an essential trope of American race and cast the metropolis in black and white. In instances like Proposition 14, the noose seemed very much in evidence. But the trope itself raised questions about how best to address regional racial inequality. Was it a product of overt racism, market economics, or both? Would appeals to suburban whites make a difference? How could African Americans develop a regional program to change the distribution of resources while remaining politically isolated in Oakland? Searching for the answers would occupy Oaklanders for a generation.

With remarkable speed in the mid-1960s, the city-suburb dualism replaced the bigoted southern sheriff, the lynch mob, and the lunch counter as the archetypal national symbol of American racial inequality. Oakland experienced this shift in metaphor and language with the nation. Beginning as early as the 1950s, northern civil rights, nationalist, and grassroots radical leaders alike had adopted variations on the city-suburb contrast in their speeches, writings, and interviews. The center of these efforts was initially battles over open housing in the industrial Northeast and upper Midwest, where indices of segregation were higher than anywhere in the nation. Confined largely to local political arenas in the 1950s, by the mid-1960s these voices found a national stage with two dramatic episodes in California. The first was Proposition 14. The second came the following summer, with rebellions in Watts in Southern California. Though African Americans across the nation had been pointing to the destructive effects of white suburbanization and the hardening of segregation in "second ghettoes" since World War II, the national press was slow to take the issue seriously. Indeed, as late as 1960 the *Saturday Evening Post* was writing of the "great human tides, made up of middle-income Americans . . . flowing out of the cities. Into the cities, to take their place, dark tides were running." Such rhetoric not only buttressed segregationist thinking ("dark tides running"), it also reinforced the widespread white interpretation of black migration as a cause of urban decline. Not until Proposition 14 and the eruption of violence between 1964 and 1968 did either the national press or the federal government begin to discuss with some seriousness the postwar trend toward metropolitan segregation.[20]

Between 1961 and 1968 official white circles slowly took notice of this segregation in ways that black leaders had been urging for decades. In 1961, reports of the U.S. Commission on Civil Rights used the term "white noose" to describe suburbanization, introducing that term into white policy arenas for the first time. Four years later, when the McCone Commission report on Watts in 1965 blamed African Americans for instigating the violence and made no mention of the Proposition 14 election from the previous fall, African Americans in California and elsewhere scathingly criticized the commission. A near total "whitewash," in the words of one local black critic, the report was also criticized by white federal officials. The U.S. Commission on Civil Rights called it "elementary, superficial, unoriginal and unimaginable." Though weak-kneed and retrograde, the McCone report had the effect of generating a national discussion among both whites and blacks over the segregated metropolis. In 1968 the report of the Kerner Commission (National Advisory Commission on Civil Disorders), the federal government's official interpretation of the urban violence of 1967, appeared. The commission's indictment of white America—"[w]hite institutions created it [ghetto], white institutions maintain it, and white institutions condone it"—represented what African American leaders in major cities had been saying for decades, but it took Proposition 14, four summers of violence, the glare of national publicity, and multiple government reports to reorient white discussion of civil rights to a metropolitan (and northern/western) context.[21]

For white East Bay suburban homeowners, Proposition 14 represented the early phases of a long engagement with the changing nature of California. That engagement only occasionally took explicit racial form, though race was nonetheless embedded in every stage. The rhetoric of Americanism and "free" property encouraged by the CREA thinly veiled a resistance to desegregation. More typically, homeowners joined causes that kept racial assumptions and prejudices at a greater remove even as their politics reverberated with profound racialized consequences. Ensuring ever rising property values while keeping other housing costs, especially taxes, as low as possible in the midst of the state's convulsive growth remained homeowners' dominant political objective. In the name of that objective, they collectively resisted the broad structural changes necessary to desegregate the housing market, and they fought other claims on the financial resources of their segregated communities.

On the Suburban Margins

Every morning between 1969 and 1972, workers in Union City hustled to frame houses. Developers were busy opening new subdivisions with names like The Tropics, Casa Verde, Central Park West, and Town and Country. In these three years, Union City's population increased from fourteen thousand to twenty-four thousand, and its number of housing units doubled. It was an astonishing pace. Like most postwar subdivisions in the East Bay, those going up in Union City contained exclusively single-family homes in the middle price range. For many, however, the new construction was little cause for celebration. As places like The Tropics and Casa Verde continued to make homeownership accessible to a broad white middle class two and a half decades after the war, they pushed to the suburban margins large numbers of working families who could not afford even modestly priced new homes. Hardly unique, Union City typified suburban South County, where politically powerful homeowners kept high-density, multifamily housing—such as apartments, duplexes, and condominiums—and low-priced new homes out of their communities. In doing so, they struggled to maintain a segregated suburban landscape by keeping from these new cities an older logic of American urbanity and civic culture in which homeowners and renters from a range of economic stations, races, and nationalities could live in close proximity.[22]

In the East Bay, suburban homeowner politics did not exist solely in black and white terms. Within these cities themselves, class power kept a range of low-income people—Anglo/white, ethnic Mexican, and African

American—at bay. Homeowners monitored and shaped development with an eye toward property values and quality of life, translating their private concerns into public policy. But homeowners were not only concerned with keeping places white. Homeowners wanted homeowning neighbors. More specifically, they wanted cities free of low-income renters, of any racial background, and the social and financial burdens understood to accompany them—poverty, welfare, and low property values. The politics of property *within* suburban communities took many forms across South County, but a good beginning is Union City, where the development of new subdivisions squeezed an existing Mexican American community as Anglo homeowners organized politically against low-income residents. It is a useful starting point for understanding larger countywide patterns.

By the late 1960s over one hundred thousand Spanish-speaking people, the overwhelming majority of whom were ethnic Mexican, lived in Alameda County. More than half lived in emerging suburban cities like Union City and Hayward and in the unincorporated interstices of county land lying between and around those cities. Ethnic Mexican communities, colonias, had rural roots, often existed on the periphery of new suburban cities, and contended constantly with what Ernesto Galarza called "the super-urbanization of America." Metropolitan growth moved toward them, not away from them. The status of the region's ethnic Mexican communities varied. In Hayward, an established Mexican American middle class enjoyed political and economic influence beginning in the late 1950s, obtaining civil service jobs and construction contracts, while the working class supplied essential labor for the city's canning industry as well as its growing manufacturing sector. In smaller, more isolated communities in Russell City, Union City, and across the Santa Clara County line in Alviso near Milpitas, however, ethnic Mexican power to shape suburban growth was negligible, as neighborhoods fought to obtain even basic municipal services such as running water and underground sewers. Ethnic Mexican colonias faced a double bind in the suburbanizing East Bay. On the one hand, remaining in unincorporated parts of the county made the securing of essential urban services difficult. On the other, incorporation into a larger municipality generally meant displacement, as economic and political interests from encroaching cities redeveloped colonia property for industry and middle-class housing.[23]

In the period before World War II, colonias were intimately connected to the local agricultural economy. Residents worked as field laborers or in canneries, entrepreneurs built businesses, a small professional and civil service class developed, and a handful of laborers broke into the ranks of the skilled crafts, all within or serving the needs of rural agriculture. Though colonias retained their close ties to the rural economy in the postwar years, they increasingly served as places of residential and occupational transition between the rural-agricultural and urban-industrial economies of the East Bay. As such, they functioned in three crucial ways: first, as places where seasonal farm work and part-time craft and industrial work were readily accessible and often interchangeable; second, as dense residential communities where middle-class property accumulation and political participation was a possibility, if usually a distant one; and third, as stepping stones in a ladder of rural to urban migration that frequently began in Mexico, or the Central Valley, and ended in major cities like Oakland, San Francisco, and San Jose. Colonias shared a good deal in common with black communities in Oakland, but ethnic Mexican enclaves in Alameda County nonetheless represented a distinct spatial formation: in industrializing cities with a high tax base and high property values dominated by middle- and upper-income housing. Throughout the 1950s and 1960s, colonias remained prominent, if precariously situated, components of the emerging East Bay suburban landscape and its rapid reconfiguring of residential and industrial space.[24]

Emerging housing markets shaped colonias in divergent ways. For many ethnic Mexican communities in the East and South Bay, suburbanization represented an invasion, a disruption of existing rural patterns of work and residence. That invasion could be both beneficial and destructive. For instance, Ford's move to Milpitas, near the heart of the Bay Area's largest ethnic Mexican district on San Jose's Eastside, provided new industrial opportunities for working-class Mexican Americans for whom autoworker wages, even in the lowest-paid occupations, were considerably better than any local alternative. By 1970 nearly three thousand ethnic Mexican adults lived in Milpitas, out of a total population of twenty-seven thousand. More than half had family incomes above $8,000, a solid, if not generous, figure that brought Milpitas's modest housing within reach. Housing discrimination against people of Mexican descent persisted, but was not as vicious and widespread, nor as vigilantly enforced by white/Anglo homeowners, as that against African Americans. Emerging suburban communities like Milpitas often served to improve the housing and employment options for ethnic Mexicans, providing a kind of class mobility unavailable within the rural economy.[25]

At the same time, however, suburbanization could wreck havoc with colonias, upsetting the stability of existing ethnic Mexican communities and unsettling the lives of residents. Alviso, for example, a small unincorporated colonia on the west side of Milpitas, was a refuge for ethnic Mexicans displaced from the agricultural economy in the 1930s and 1940s. Like many relatively poor local colonias, Alviso functioned as a residential space of transition for workers and their families adapting their labor and other economic activities to the decline of regional agriculture and the rise of manufacturing and construction industries. But as potentially valuable industrial property, it was also attractive to San Jose civic officials, who made three bids to annex Alviso during the 1960s. Knowing that annexation meant the destruction of their community for new housing developments or industry, Alviso residents twice defeated San Jose's efforts in high-profile elections. They could not do so a third time, and in 1968 San Jose annexed Alviso, cleared the land of homes, and zoned it for industry, displacing over a thousand ethnic Mexican residents. Alviso's history was not unlike that of other semirural East Bay colonias faced with an aggressive and encroaching urban/suburban landscape extended into new regions by public officials in search of taxable property and developers in search of profit. As these islands of affordable housing became casualties of rising property values and the new uses of industrial suburbs, working-class ethnic Mexicans were forced to fend for themselves in inflationary housing markets.[26]

This combination of industry, new housing, and older colonia became a significant feature of suburban formation in the Bay Area, and California generally, in the 1960s. In the East Bay, Hayward, Union City, and Milpitas were typical examples. Of these, Union City best embodied the marginalization produced by the overlapping geographies of the colonia and the Anglo suburb. Union City was born of two logics. One was the older logic of the colonia and its network of relationships to the rural economy. The other was the newer logic of the Anglo industrial garden and its patterns of residential and industrial property values. The two were not antithetical, but neither were they entirely compatible. Union City's incorporation was driven in the late 1950s by an alliance between homeowners in two small towns, Alvarado and Decoto, and the Southern Pacific and Western Pacific railroads, which owned considerable property in the area. Together, they resisted Hayward's annexation attempts and formed a city modeled on San Leandro: a broad economic base of small-scale industry with housing developments predominantly in the middle range, accessible to an array of white/Anglo professional, managerial, craft, and service workers. Throughout the 1960s the city's civic and business leaders implemented that vision. Residents of Union City's new housing developments came from the broad middle: two-thirds were skilled craft workers, semiskilled operatives, professional, managerial, and service workers. Ninety percent commuted outside of Union City to work. This typical East Bay suburban formation in which industry supported the municipal tax base but did not employ city residents developed around the existing colonia in what had been Decoto.[27]

Union City's spectacular growth in the late 1960s brought Anglo newcomers who demonstrated little respect for colonia residents. As the city council contemplated redevelopment for Decoto's aging and dilapidated housing, older members of the Mexican American community who had purchased homes and accumulated modest equity feared they would be pushed out. With the lessons of other bulldozed colonias fresh in their minds, residents predicted that redevelopment would force retired home-owners to sell below market, leaving them without the resources to re-main in a city overrun with new subdivisions. Younger ethnic Mexicans were in no better position. With most new housing priced beyond the reach of low-income workers, residential mobility seemed increasingly unavailable to many young families in Union City, most of them on low budgets. Crowding within the neighborhoods of the colonia threatened to perpetuate a downward spiral of home values and housing conditions there. A planning report submitted to Union City by an outside consult-ing firm in 1967 recommended that the city encourage a large-scale pro-gram of multifamily housing construction, particularly to accommodate existing low-income residents rather than newcomers. Spurred by the re-port, the Southern Alameda County Spanish Speaking Organization (SASSO), an OEO-sponsored community action group, conceived a plan for low-income housing and sought federal assistance to purchase land for a multifamily development in Union City.[28]

Mexican Americans in Northern California were politically organized. Groups like the G.I. Forum and, in the 1960s, the Mexican American Po-litical Association were important architects of Mexican American civil rights in California. The state's most dynamic ethnic Mexican alliance, however, working across both class and nationality, was the Community Services Organization. Founded in Los Angeles in 1947, the CSO was at the forefront of efforts to improve the housing, health, and education of the state's Mexican American and Mexican immigrant population. These ef-forts often focused on pressing local governments to bring basic services— such as running water and underground sewers, sidewalks and paved streets, public transportation, and better housing and recreation—to ex-isting colonias and ethnic Mexican neighborhoods. Because California's ethnic Mexican population was entangled in two overlapping urbanizing processes in the postwar decades—the expansion of cities into and around existing colonias and the oversupply of rural labor, which pushed migrants into urban areas—the CSO linked civil rights, citizenship, cul-tural pride, and Mexican nationalism to urbanization and neighborhood improvement. Outside of Oakland, the county's CSO membership lived primarily in Union City and Hayward, largely in colonias established prior to or during the war. In the 1960s the CSO's combination of civil rights, cultural nationalism, and neighborhood politics fueled the War on Poverty activists who founded SASSO.[29]

In 1968 SASSO secured an option to purchase twenty-three acres in Union City for a development of 280 low-income, multifamily housing units. Before construction could begin, the city council had to vote to rezone the property for this high-density use. However, residents from Westview Estates, a three-year-old Anglo subdivision adjoining the SASSO property, pressured the city council to delay a rezoning ruling and to appoint a special commission to consider the issue. When the council appointed a majority of Anglo Westview Estates residents to the new commission, SASSO and the Decoto Residents Association, a predominantly Mexican American neighborhood organization, went back to the city to request immediate action on the rezoning proposal. Facing public charges that both the city's actions and the Westview Estates protests were racially motivated, the council approved the rezoning. Westview Estates residents were livid. They responded by organizing the Citizens Committee for Referendum in order to place the rezoning decision on a special citywide ballot. "Where is the city council's concern for *us*?" homeowner Gene Doty, co-chair of the committee, asked. Doty organized a self-styled "grassroots campaign" to fight the SASSO plan. In a result widely interpreted as a revolt of Anglo newcomers against the established colonia, Union City residents voted to repeal the council's zoning decision and return the property to its previous low-density designation. With a majority of the city behind them, Doty then extended a disingenuous olive branch. "Now we're going to show that we're not the racists they said we were," he told the local newspaper.[30]

Whether or not Doty and his homeowner populist compatriots in Westview Estates were racists, the Westview Estates campaign revealed how thoroughly Anglo homeowner populism supported a suburban geography of segregation. When Anglo newcomers voted to stop a low-income housing project planned by and intended for Mexican Americans, the racial implications were not hard to decipher. "Where I can afford land, people won't let it be built," SASSO Director Ramon Rodriguez explained of his two-year search for property on which to construct affordable housing. Rodriguez added that "lack of sophistication and social awareness of the suburbanite" translated into "criticism from very uninformed people." In response to the citywide vote, SASSO, with the assistance of the National Committee against Discrimination in Housing, filed suit in federal court. In a case that became part of a string of lawsuits nationwide in the 1970s against suburban communities that refused to build affordable housing, SASSO and the NCDH contended that restrictive zoning violated the equal protection clause of the Fourteenth Amendment, because it interfered with the lawful development of property by low-income advocates. The flesh and bone of the case, however, was SASSO's assertion that the effect of the citywide vote "was to perpetuate residency for an ethnic minority in a slum area."[31]

In *SASSO v. Union City* (1970), the U.S. Circuit Court issued a conflicted ruling. It denied SASSO an injunction against the referendum vote,

allowing the Westview Estates victory to stand. But the court simultaneously ruled that "the poor, most of them minority citizens, cannot be excluded from the benefits of local land use planning." Additionally, the
court strongly implied that the consequences of local land use policy, not
the intention of its authors, were the measure of discrimination and that
Union City should proceed as quickly as possible to eliminate any unfairness. The court declined to specify how, however. Faced with these
legal ambiguities, SASSO and Union City returned to litigation in late
1970 and early 1971, now with interested local and national audiences.
Burdened by legal expenses, Union City relented in the spring of 1971,
agreeing to a settlement that NCDH Co-Director Edward Rutledge
called a "landmark" statement of the "responsibilities" of local communities. In the agreement, SASSO was allowed to develop half of its initial
280 high-density units, the other half devoted to single-family homes.
Thirty percent of those would be occupied by low-income families subsidized by federal support. Buoyed by Union City's decision to settle, the
NCDH announced the agreement as "a significant demonstration of what
local suburban communities can do to meet the housing needs of poor and
minority citizens." Nevertheless, neither the SASSO case nor a parallel
suit in Mt. Laurel, New Jersey, provided the broad federal ruling the
NCDH believed necessary to prevent low- and moderate-income families
from being zoned out of new suburban communities.[32]

At the center of the SASSO-Union City conflict was property and its
role in different visions of community. SASSO raised a version of the
question of civic responsibility that McCullum and White had put to
their suburban audience: suburban communities were obligated to prevent the machinery of local government from becoming an instrument of
particular economic and racial interests. They were obligated to desegregate. The SASSO-Union City housing dispute had public drama and national implications, but it was only the most visible example of a much
broader countywide pattern of excluding affordable housing and high-
density neighborhoods. In planning commission hearings, city council
chambers, and municipal referendums across the East Bay, homeowners
turned back proposal after proposal for multifamily housing of all
types—low- and moderate-income apartments, duplexes, and condominiums—while approving redevelopment plans that threatened older,
affordable neighborhoods. A typical example was the 1965 effort of the
West Castro Valley Homeowners Association to block a seven-acre
apartment complex in the unincorporated, but highly developed, Castro
Valley area southeast of San Leandro. Declaring that "Castro Valley
homeowners need representation at the County Planning Commission,"
organizers assembled four hundred homeowners to protest at a County
Board of Supervisors meeting. A parade of Castro Valley residents went

Figure 7.2. The main commercial thoroughfare in Hayward in the 1960s. More than people came to suburban communities in the postwar decades. Investment came too. Banks, insurance companies, the real estate industry, retailers, merchants, and all kinds of industry helped to shift patterns of investment within the metropolitan region, creating development in some places, underdevelopment in others. Courtesy of the *Oakland Tribune*.

to the microphone where they pleaded with the board to reject the project. "It is against the public interest to zone for apartments in this predominantly single-family area," Joe Van Noy, West Castro Valley chairman told the board. Van Noy and his compatriots evinced little difficulty in equating the "public" interest with their own, as homeowners. The facility with which Doty made that equation is a powerful representation of the total eclipse of any idea of a broader social collective by the private individualism of homeownership—the product of a generation of suburban segregation in which the "public interest" was defined entirely in terms of white homeowners.[33]

Across Alameda County in the 1960s, suburban homeowners kept vigilant watch over the class homogeneity of their communities. They inveighed against multifamily housing with a wide range of rationales. In 1968 the residents of Mulford Gardens, a subdivision in San Leandro, blocked a density rezoning proposal in order to, in the words of the Mulford Gardens Improvement Association, preserve "beautiful estate-type homes surrounding the golf course." Bay-O-Vista subdivision homeowners fought

280

a condominium project the following year because "a single-family home developer will be reluctant to invest as long as there may be a possibility of higher density development," according to the homeowners association. In the Warm Springs area of Fremont, homeowners battled to prevent low-cost and multifamily subdivisions that threatened to extend the integrated autoworker community of Sunnyhills in Milpitas north across the city line. Starlite Hills residents signed petitions claiming that a high-density development there would destroy the rural atmosphere of Fremont and attract transient residents who would not properly maintain the property. In Alameda, the city closed its World War II–era Estuary Housing Project in the early 1960s and refused to construct replacement low-income housing because it was too expensive for the city to run. In a letter to Governor Brown, the Alameda Citizens Committee for Low-Rent Housing complained that the "high rents and high housing costs" in Alameda amounted to a "vicious form of financial discrimination" against people who had lived in Estuary for twenty years. Solely because of their low incomes, "families are being uprooted from their homes and forced to leave the city," the letter continued.[34]

Opposition to multifamily housing was both an assertion of the class power of homeowners and a reaction to the perceived erosion of that power. Homeowners were on the defensive in part because multifamily subdivisions and projects had actually become more common in South County. East Bay suburban homeowners had long opposed multifamily housing, but in the 1960s and especially the 1970s they were placed on the defensive by developers convinced of the profitability of apartment complexes. Diversifying the production of home types worked for developers as it worked for other manufacturers: providing them with consumers at a wide range of incomes. In the 1960s and 1970s this logic led to sharp increases in multifamily housing construction. In every major East Bay suburban community between 1960 and 1980, the number of renter-occupied housing units increased. In Hayward, for instance, the homeownership rate dropped from 75 percent in 1960 to 55 percent in 1980. In Castro Valley, the rate fell from 81 percent to 69 percent. If homeowners felt themselves under siege by multifamily housing construction, they were in part reacting to this tangible shift in the proportion of suburban renters.[35]

The intensity of homeowner opposition to multifamily housing reflected a desire to preserve the quality of life residents believed they deserved as homeowners. "Everyone except the man who owns a home is trying to affect the future of that home," the chairman of West Castro Valley complained in 1965. "Protecting the single-family areas from turning into a hodgepodge of apartments and other uses," as the *San Leandro News Observer* put it in 1964, was understood as an extension of both the economic and moral value people invested in their home. Property values remained paramount among homeowner concerns, but a host of other fears motivated their politics: school overcrowding, increased traffic, degradation of parks and other public spaces, crime, and increased social service burden, to name the most prominent. In short, suburban homeowners hoped to exclude the complicated social life they associated with large cities. For two decades their collective efforts generated a constant debate over housing, with homeowners claiming that they were being "overrun" with multifamily units and others, primarily developers and public officials, asserting that the East Bay suburbs faced a profound housing crisis in the midst of one of the largest construction booms the nation had ever seen. Both positions could marshal evidence for their claims. Developers had begun to fill available land between and around single-family subdivisions with apartments despite homeowner resistance. At the same time, the suburban housing crisis remained quite real.[36]

Hundreds of thousands of migrants poured into California from all over the United States and Mexico during the 1960s, but in places like the East Bay suburbs their search for housing was frustrated by class and racial segregation. The reluctance of East Bay homeowners to embrace less privileged neighbors relegated large numbers of working-class families to the suburban margins. The combination of federal mortgage guarantees, new housing production techniques, and relatively inexpensive suburban land brought homeownership to historically unprecedented numbers of white/Anglo people in California and the nation in the two decades after the war. But in the San Francisco-Oakland area in the early 1960s, no FHA homes had reached the lower third income group, and only 16 percent had reached the lower half. The majority of such homes were purchased by the top 30 percent. Moreover, in 1960, already one in five renters was paying more than one-third of household income for housing. For many, the suburban housing market was not the symbol of democratic access idealized by boosters. It was an example of skewed opportunity structures that favored middle-class whites. Barreling along in the 1960s, California's economy attracted migrants and helped homeowners to build wealth, a process that obscured but could not hide these deeper contradictions.[37]

Prelude to the Tax Revolt

The most lasting and far-reaching suburban retrenchment in the East Bay involved taxes. In the late 1940s homeowners in places like San Leandro, Milpitas, and Fremont had elevated low taxes to a civic creed within a populist politics centered on the "small taxpayer." In the late 1960s and early

282 CHAPTER SEVEN

1970s a resurgence of these politics was fueled by incremental increases in tax rates, property valuation, and government costs that, in sum over a decade, amounted to a hefty burden on what tax reform advocates called the "average homeowner." Tax revolt politics would not crest until 1978 with the statewide passage of Proposition 13, the nation's first property tax limitation measure, but the grassroots tax reform movement began in earnest a decade before. "It won't be long before the average working man in California—particularly Alameda County—cannot afford to own a home," the president of the American Taxpayers Union of California told the Alameda County Board of Supervisors in 1967. Between 1945 and the early 1960s property tax politics had been local. In the 1960s they became a statewide obsession. Tax politics in this decade were about far more than the financial solvency of the "average working man," however. They centered on the social question of who would bear the costs of California's spectacular, but uneven, growth. Like the issues of fair housing and multifamily home construction, property tax struggles drew homeowners into an alliance based on their class interests and the metropolitan distribution of public resources.[38]

Between 1965 and the early 1970s property taxes increased in two ways in California. Tax *rates* went up as municipalities, counties, and school districts faced rising costs, and property value *assessments* rose in a real estate boom tied to the state's extraordinary postwar growth. In different ways, each contributed to a modest but steady escalation of the tax load on individual homes. In the two decades between 1950 and 1970, as California's population doubled and the number of school-age children quadrupled, the number of people living in poverty rose to over one and a half million. These jumps were dramatically ahead of the nation at large. New populations placed heavier demands on government services, and local leaders responded by raising tax rates—for cities, counties, school and hospital districts, junior colleges, municipal utilities, flood control, and transit districts, to name the most common. At the same time, California's booming real estate market made for higher and higher home valuations, which, too, translated into a higher tax bill for homeowners. Median housing prices in Castro Valley and Fremont, to take two examples, increased by 22 percent and 19 percent, respectively, between 1960 and 1970, then jumped a phenomenal 63 percent and 79 percent between 1970 and 1980. Overall, East Bay suburban homes increased in value far ahead of inflation in the 1960s, then exploded during the 1970s.[39]

It is difficult to exaggerate suburban East Bay booster hyperbole in the 1960s. Hawking, selling, and boasting were a relentless fact of public life. Every factory dedication became a public performance, a celebration of progress. Proof of the region's awesome potential, according to civic boosters, was everywhere in evidence. "Fremont is our kind of town," the president of General Motors declared during the 1964 christening of its new plant. "Workers here have country living at their factory doorsteps," Fremont's newspaper added in a special 1964 edition dedicated to GM and the city's mushrooming subdivisions. Proclaiming its city a "go-go machine," the San Leandro Manufacturer's Association bragged in 1965 that industry brought "international acclaim to the city" and made it a "prosperous, well-balanced, on-the-move community." Major newspapers in San Leandro, Hayward, and Fremont published annual "year end progress" editions that embodied this genre of booster fawning. Photo spreads featured aerial shots of new growth; industrial "box scores" listed the jobs created and capital invested in industry; economic leaders and politicians testified to the low taxes and excellent business climate; and a general modernist faith in bigness and permanent expansion pervaded every feature. But not far underneath the constant celebration of growth lay a pervasive homeowner ambivalence in the face of California's unprecedented economic expansion. Pleased with growth and increasing property values, homeowners were determined that they not bear too much of the costs such prosperity would inevitably bring.[40]

Those costs added up quickly in suburban Alameda County, where the consequences of California's growth in the 1960s were magnified. During the first half of the decade, Alameda County had the highest average tax rate in the state—based on the sum of county, city, and district tallies. Each city confronted a unique set of local conditions, however, and responded in ways shaped by local political culture. In San Leandro, the mayor and city manager kept the municipal tax rate low, even as other taxes, primarily county, increased. In 1966 San Leandro lowered its municipal rate for the nineteenth consecutive year. "We're keeping the faith," Jack Maltester, the city's longtime mayor, declared as he promised that the cut (six cents on every hundred dollars of property valuation) "gives back to the people all the tax money that would result from the recent reappraisals." Three years later, Maltester again appealed to his homeowner constituency. In the past, he explained, the city had often lowered its tax rate "for the national recognition." But in 1969, he stressed, "the main decision is how do we show our concern for the people who have received huge assessments." Maltester's "concern" translated once again into a slicing of the municipal rate—for the "twenty-first straight year," the newspaper boasted—in an attempt to keep the total homeowner tax bill as low as possible. By the late 1960s San Leandrans faced large property reappraisals as well as an escalating county tax rate, but Maltester and the city manager, keeping a bargain with homeowners that stretched back to the election of 1948, did their best to deflect these increases by continuing to lower the city rate.[41]

Tax cuts in San Leandro were possible because industry continued to underwrite much of the municipal budget. Indeed, the city's industry showed no signs of slack during the 1960s. The fifteen thousand industrial jobs and $130 million in capital investment San Leandro had gained during the 1950s kept the local economy strong throughout the succeeding decade. In 1966 San Leandro industrial employers paid 57 percent of city sales taxes and 45 percent of city property taxes, totals matched in few residential suburbs statewide, much less in Alameda County. San Leandro's "healthy industrial climate," the city's newspaper asserted in 1965, meant that officials always gave "consideration to the taxpayer who must meet the bills" when calculating the municipal tax rate. Calling its readers' attention to the other "seven taxing agencies in San Leandro—including the county and school district," the editor asked rhetorically "how many of these agencies can point to cuts in their tax rates?" None, the editorial replied. "Actually, their rates go up every year." Indeed, taxes outside the purview of city officials continued to increase. The city could not add property to tax rolls and boost municipal revenues indefinitely, especially with available land exhausted. The tactic of lowering municipal tax rates to compensate for the mushrooming demand on the homeowner from other sources would inevitably encounter limits. In the larger metropolitan and statewide contexts, San Leandro officials hoped to stay ahead in their cycles of adjustment—but how long could they do so?[42]

Demands on the industrial garden's tax structure were even more visible in Fremont and Milpitas, which did not enjoy San Leandro's vaunted capacity to lower taxes. Municipal tax rates increased in those cities every year, and their leaders desperately sought new industries to shoulder a larger share of the property tax burden. Half of Fremont's 1970 population of 100,000 residents were under the age of twenty-one, an enormous school-age population. School district tax rates increased in proportion. New public transit costs necessitated higher taxes as well. In 1957, just after incorporation, Fremont had the lowest total tax rate in Alameda County after Emeryville. By 1967 Fremont taxes were fourth highest in the county (appendix table 6). "You can have all the improvements this city needs now," Fremont City Council candidate Hugh Block said in 1966, "but with no industry you will add tremendously to the already exorbitant tax rate." Living in the fastest-growing city in Alameda County during the 1960s, Fremont residents had begun to pay for their "country living" and dependence on General Motors. Milpitas grew more slowly than Fremont—the city population was just under twenty thousand in 1966—but it too saw enormous increases in school-age children and costs for basic city services. And Milpitas, too, remained wedded to a single large employer, Ford. "Cows don't pay taxes!" the *Milpitas Post* admonished its readers in 1966, as the city faced an important bond election. "Let's convert our pastures to dollar producing commerce and industry," the *Post* encouraged on the eve of the bond vote. The bonds, dedicated to new infrastructure to attract investment, passed, and the following year the city's tax rate was $1.66 per hundred dollars of property value, two-thirds higher than the rate in San Leandro.[43]

As property taxes rose across Alameda County during the 1960s, suburban East Bay residents seized on a number of causes, but one of the most conspicuous and frequently cited culprits was "welfare." By the end of the decade, welfare had become firmly lodged in the California tax debate, not as a symbol of shared wealth assisting the needy, but as the embodiment of wasting taxpayer money and draining the "average" homeowner. Concern in the East Bay began in the early 1960s, when county budgets began to bulge with annual increases dedicated to direct payments to welfare recipients and salaries for administrators, the largest share of both in Oakland. Aid to Families with Dependent Children (AFDC), also known in California as Aid to Needy Children (ANC) and "welfare" by colloquial tradition, was a federal New Deal program that California expanded in the late 1950s and early 1960s. County governments paid about one-third of the total welfare budget, state and federal sources the remainder. In a series of state legislative hearings in 1960, opponents of ANC rehearsed hoary American attacks on social programs and cast "welfare" as an unfair imposition on upstanding, financially solvent homeowners. Contra Costa County's district attorney called ANC a "social monster" that "threatens the moral and financial well-being of the citizens of this state." The hearings were followed carefully in the East Bay, where residents increasingly resented their financial contributions to Oakland welfare recipients.[44]

Concern about welfare in South County built slowly but steadily over the course of the decade. In 1964 Alameda County declared its intention to fight state rules earmarking higher payments to welfare recipients. The new rules, according to the *San Leandro Morning News*, would raise the county's $50 million welfare budget by more than 10 percent. The newspaper lamented the "continual drain on the tax dollar for welfare purposes." Three years later, when welfare costs jumped another $15 million from the previous year (a 23 percent increase), county officials warned that "welfare is threatening to burn a hole right through the Alameda County taxpayers pocket." Already the state's most taxed county, Alameda County saw its rates increase by as much as 20 percent per year in the second half of the decade. Rising county welfare costs were especially resented in San Leandro, where the tradition of reducing the city property tax rate every year conditioned residents to expect low taxes. Because county welfare budgets were determined by the state, local residents in places like

San Leandro cast themselves as victims of two outside forces: welfare recipients in Oakland and the overgenerous, liberal legislature in Sacramento. East Bay suburban homeowners disparaged welfare recipients, but their public rhetoric and political energies were equally directed at state government "bureaucrats."[45]

The combination of rising property assessments and increases in property tax rates produced the state's first major tax reform movement in 1968. The story stretches back to 1965, when a scandal centered in San Francisco opened the state's property assessment system to public scrutiny. The bribery trial of San Francisco tax assessor Russell Wolden revealed that elected officials regularly received campaign contributions in exchange for favorable assessments and lower taxes on business properties. Implicating San Francisco's business elite, including the city's leading hotel and retail establishment, Wolden's trial uncovered for the public the mechanism by which politically connected property owners could dodge taxes, while homeowners received ever increasing bills. In addition to the assessment scandal, the trial also uncovered hundreds of millions of dollars in business inventory that annually went unreported and untaxed. Beginning in San Francisco, the scandal rippled outward statewide in 1965 and 1966 as cities across California came under review for their assessment practices. By 1967 an outraged public and a chagrined state legislature were prepared to overhaul the state's property tax system in total.[46]

Legislation designed to address the assessment scandal, passed by the state legislature in 1967, created its own ripple effect, ironically sending homeowner tax bills climbing even higher. The culprit was what commentators called "equalization." As one consequence of the Wolden trial and subsequent reportage, legislators and tax reform advocates learned exactly how "unequal" property assessment standards were from property to property within a single jurisdiction, as well as from community to community. In San Francisco, for instance, a downtown hotel might be assessed at one standard, a private home in the Mission District another, an auto repair shop south of Market another, and a furniture warehouse in Chinatown still another. Moreover, no single regime of rules governed comparable properties across the state, leading to dramatically different assessments from community to community: beachside houses in Malibu, Santa Barbara, and Half Moon Bay, for example, would each be assessed for tax purposes according to a local formula, producing dramatically different value ratios. With the news of such disparities plastered in front page headlines around the state, legislators faced enormous pressure to "equalize" assessment standards, to establish a single bar by which every property would be evaluated—in effect, to take politics and local formulas out of the mixture. The legislative solution, however, Assembly Bill 80 (A.B. 80), had enormous unintended consequences. The bill required that communities across the state reassess all property at 25 percent of market value within three years. From then on, localities were required to conduct frequent reassessments to ensure that the ratio remained intact. The result was an explosion of taxable property value among homeowners and an even higher tax bill.[47]

Equalization boomeranged to deliver an unexpected blow to California taxpayers. The San Francisco assessment scandal had exposed businesses that bribed elected officials for low property valuation, but in most communities statewide business and industrial property was typically assessed at a higher ratio of market value than single-family housing. Businesses paid a greater share of property taxes than homeowners. Application of the uniform ratio of 25 percent meant that in many instances business and industrial assessments actually decreased while single-family home assessments increased. This was the case across the suburban East Bay. In Alameda County, A.B. 80 forced the assessor's office to increase residential and agricultural property from 21.6 percent to 25 percent of market value, while reducing commercial and industrial property from 28 to 25 percent. When news of the assessment ratios became public in the early summer, county taxpayer organizations began a petition drive that collected eighty thousand signatures within a month. "We're going to concentrate on winning greater individual and organizational strength throughout the county and state to fight this tax situation," the president of the American Taxpayers Union of California told his Alameda County constituents. Overwhelmed with requests for hearings to protest the new assessments, the Alameda County assessor's office moved slowly, prompting the Taxpayers Union to threaten a lawsuit. "There will be fireworks," union representatives predicted.[48]

Reactions across the length of the East Bay suburbs to A.B. 80's consequences ran from shock to outrage. In Fremont, UAW Local 1364 organized a protest campaign, employing a sound truck and door-to-door canvassing to reach taxpayers. Working closely with the American Taxpayers Union, a surprising if not entirely implausible ally, Local 1364 helped to lead Fremont's campaign against high property taxes, what the union called a bane to the "working man." In the spring of 1968 East Bay homeowners packed into the Alameda County assessor's office in a major protest of high assessments. The *San Francisco Chronicle* reported a scene "overwhelmed with mad people, trying to get into the assessor's office." Robert Hannon, chairman of the Alameda County Supervisors, and Nick Petris, a state senator from Oakland and one of the co-sponsors of A.B. 80, engaged in a verbal feud over the new tax structure. "Five percent of the county's population is getting the exclusive use of 52 percent of the budget!" Hannon declared in a "plain talk" speech to the San Leandro Chamber of Commerce. Hannon blamed A.B. 80 and, with greater vigor, welfare rolls for unfairly burdening suburban homeowners. "These welfare payments aren't something the county controls," Hannon continued, "the state tells us what we must pay and it's up to the county to pay it." Petris responded with a defense of A.B. 80—labeling Hannon's complaints "political mumbo jumbo"—and pointed out that the county's new sports coliseum, where the Oakland A's and Oakland Raiders played baseball and football, had for several years "somehow avoided being assessed," implying a county effort to protect its pet project from taxation. "Who had been paying the difference before?" Petris asked. "The taxpayer, that's who." With county tax rates increasing in the late 1960s and with assessments on the rise as a result of A.B. 80, Alameda County homeowners and their political patrons contended over who best represented "the taxpayer."[49]

The A.B. 80 assessment boom led to a ballot measure calling for tax relief. Los Angeles County Tax Assessor Philip Watson sponsored an initiative in 1968 requiring that property taxes pay only for "property-related services," such as water, streets, fire and police, maintenance, and the like. Other "people-related services," such as education, health, and welfare, would become entirely the state's responsibility. The measure also required that taxes not exceed 1 percent of a property's current market value. Fearing that Watson's initiative would cripple the state and lead to massive cuts in services, leaders of both parties, including Republican Governor Ronald Reagan, opposed it. Reagan, just then emerging as a tax-relief politician, hoped to head off support for Watson with a more modest tax reduction package. His plan, which offered homeowners an average of $70 in tax relief, sailed through the legislature prior to the November 1968 election. With a tax reduction in their pockets and dire warnings coming from state officialdom about dramatic service reductions and an unprecedented budget crisis, voters overwhelmingly rejected the Watson initiative, defeating it statewide by a margin of two to one. Nonetheless, the crisis was far from over, and the groundwork for a much larger and more powerful tax reform movement was just then being laid. The effects of A.B. 80 would continue to ripple through the state, as localities rushed to meet the three-year deadline. "A taxpayers revolt threatens California unless a more equitable distribution of the tax load can be made," Casper Weinberger, state director of finance under Governor Reagan, told a San Leandro audience in 1969, a prescient observation a decade before Proposition 13.[50]

The tax reform push of the late 1960s drew together a wide range of resentments that fueled a resurgent suburban homeowner populism. In the subsequent decade, these resentments—against rising welfare costs, state bureaucrats, county assessors, inflation, and rising service and education costs—fused and hardened into a broad, multipolar tax revolt. And in city after city across the state, tax reformers propelled their cause with a rhetoric that cast suburban life as increasingly unfair to homeowners. Promised low taxes and ever higher living standards in the city building of the 1940s and 1950s, suburban homeowners, including large numbers in the East Bay, reacted to the rising costs of the late 1960s and 1970s by building the basis for political counterrevolution. They lay the groundwork for the massive tax revolt social movement of the ensuing decade. Proposition 13 originated in the widespread frustration with unprecedented property value increases in the middle 1970s, but tax politics in that decade must be understood in the longer sweep of the state's postwar suburban history. In that history, the 1978 tax revolt, about which chapter 8 will have more to say, marked the resurgence of a populism based on the "small taxpayer" that had been building for decades.

The strength of the "white noose" trope was its symbolism. It stood for segregation's power to shape opportunity and access in the postwar metropolis by strangling a disadvantaged black community. Its weakness was a reductionist logic that collapsed contingency and politics into frozen categories. Accurate in important ways, McCullum's metaphor was an incomplete guide to the larger field of politics in the East Bay suburbs. Those politics embodied white resistance to desegregation, as in Proposition 14, but just as often they expressed a dissatisfaction with commissions, developers, and the property tax system itself. Moreover, the presence of ethnic Mexican colonias in the suburban East Bay belied the bi-racial viewpoint typical of both black and white observers in Oakland. To these communities, suburbanization was not "white flight" or a "white noose," but an invasion, a massive migration of Anglo newcomers into an existing landscape of work, commerce, and residence. Nevertheless, even as its shortcomings become clear, there is reason to return to the "white noose" metaphor with which the chapter began. The racial geographies of the East Bay may have been more complicated than Oakland-based critics allowed, but the central premise of their observations, that suburban development disadvantaged Oakland and represented state-sanctioned racial segregation and uneven development, could not have been more true. As suburban voters worked to limit their financial and social responsibility for California's growth during this period, they forced places like Oakland to assume an ever greater share of that burden. With each passing year, the noose seemed to tighten.

Even as California homeowners insisted on their individual rights, they acted collectively as a class or group to disadvantage other segments of society. The suburban retrenchments of this period were based on economic individualism and dismissing collective claims of all sorts. Homeowners looked out for themselves in a not-in-my backyard elaboration of a politics of "no." But the effect of such individualism was the emergence of a regional—indeed, a statewide—political movement that positioned the interests of older central cities against the state's vast new suburban developments. Suburban homeowners had no regional social or political strategy, but their power was regional, crossing multiple municipal boundaries. The opposite case prevailed for Oakland's African American leaders. They had a regional analysis but no regional power. As black Oakland looked toward the suburbs in the 1960s to explain the city's problems, regional strategies consistently fell short—the state's fair employment and housing laws were widely judged a failure, and judicious speech-making and small-scale demonstrations had little effect on suburban Alameda County's racial composition. Political concentration in Oakland in this instance worked against African Americans. The fracturing of local state power into innumerable municipalities, coupled with segregation and the relative weakness of counties as political bodies, produced a political space remarkably underequipped to serve the needs of central cities. Within that spatial-political structure, white homeowner "individualism" constituted a broad, pervasive, and powerful political force.[51]

8

Babylon

"IF WE GIVE freedom to ourselves right here in Babylon," Eldridge Cleaver told an audience in the late 1960s, "we will give freedom to the world." For Cleaver, Babylon was America. But the Black Panther Party increasingly cast California, and Oakland itself, in this role. Oakland stood for the national condition of black America: a colonized nation living in an underdeveloped urban ghetto amidst an inaccessible regional and national prosperity. In the decade between 1968 and 1978 these meanings acquired even greater resonance. During these years African Americans in Oakland, led first by radicals and subsequently by liberals, looked to transform local politics and guide the city out of the mire of its unemployment and disinvestment crisis. Simultaneously, white homeowners, largely though not exclusively in suburban cities, again took up the cause of tax reform and helped to fuel one of the most far-reaching conservative political movements of the twentieth century: the so-called tax revolt that resulted in the passage of Proposition 13 in 1978, the nation's first property tax limitation measure and national harbinger of a new and mobilized politics on the right. Thus, in the late 1970s two of California's most enduring and significant postwar political cultures met and clashed—in the real world of East Bay politics as well as the metaphorical world of Babylon, the corrupt and declining imperial city that symbolized both decadence and the possibility of rebirth. In the decade after 1968, both black power and white homeowner politics reached their historical crest in California.[1]

These developments echoed the political battles of the 1940s but turned the pivotal question on its head. In those immediate postwar years, East Bay politics centered around how to divide the potential benefits of metropolitan growth. In the 1970s East Bay politics had come to focus on how to divide the *costs* of metropolitanization. Oakland's predicament was hardly unique. By the 1970s, declining middling industrial cities like Oakland, as well as massive Fordist ones like Detroit and Chicago, confronted the economic and social legacies of segregation and uneven metropolitan development at the historical juncture when they could devote the fewest resources to those problems. Moreover, most cities devoted fewer resources than they could have. After two generations of shifts in postwar wealth, property value, and employment away from core cities, followed by the near wholesale abandonment of urban policy by the federal government in the 1970s, fiscal limits defined the new reality for urban America.

Oakland, like dozens of American cities, faced these limits as the long postwar economic expansion drew to an unmistakable close, its vast social costs standing in plain view.[2]

Urban voters across the country responded to the metropolitan predicament of the 1970s by electing new municipal regimes that fell broadly into two categories. In one, liberals, including many African American–led coalitions, came to power promising greater attention to neighborhoods, new approaches to poverty, and an expansion of social services. They hoped to satisfy their grassroots electoral base and to sustain traditions of urban liberalism that stretched back to the New Deal. In the second, business-dominated coalitions came to power—or fended off liberal challenges—promising retrenchment: social service and welfare cutbacks, attacks on union contracts, and fiscal conservatism. Both kinds of administrations came to power in cities that by the 1970s had the largest African American populations in history: cities like Detroit, Newark, and Atlanta had black majorities; cities like Oakland, Camden, New Orleans, and Baltimore had African American populations just under 50 percent; and in cities like New York, Chicago, and Los Angeles, African Americans constituted a critical political mass of between one quarter and one third of the population.[3]

The political terrain of urban America in the 1970s, however, was not occupied solely by liberal and conservative variants of the nation's twentieth-century political archetypes. There were radical alternatives. In Detroit, the League of Revolutionary Black Workers asserted both on the shopfloor and in city politics a radical alternative to liberalism. In Newark, Amiri Baraka and the Modern Black Convention Movement pioneered a creative and open-ended experiment in urban politics that combined elements of cultural nationalism with radical political economy. At the 1972 National Black Political Convention in Gary, Indiana, delegates from around the nation put together a broad political agenda of black liberation and urban reform. And in Oakland, the Black Panther Party offered voters an elaborate and compelling version of the political agendas developed within the OEDCI and the Black Caucus in the late 1960s and early 1970s. Combining their colonial analysis of black America, revolutionary Maoism, and the long-standing critique of Oakland's uneven postwar development into a political-economic analysis of the East Bay, the party provided an alternative to either liberal or conservative positions in major municipal elections in 1973 and 1975. The Panthers' radical alternative, however, was largely absorbed into, and demobilized by, the liberal Democratic Party in the second half of the 1970s, a process that raised profound questions about the ultimate influence and staying power of black radicalism.[4]

At the same moment, and in stark contrast, suburban East Bay homeowners increasingly cast *themselves* as the victims of metropolitanization.

Their communities had grown more expensive, their social burdens heavier. Spectacular property value inflation in the first half of the 1970s, combined with a sluggish economy, increasing welfare costs and the perception of educational waste, and the effects of 1960s tax reform convinced vast numbers of California homeowners that their lifestyle, and their homes, were under siege—even as their wealth, embedded in property values, increased to unprecedented levels. In their minds, the postwar metropolitan ideal had been compromised, and it required their efforts to reinvent it. In the tax revolt of 1978, voters in the East Bay and across the state registered with historical force what had long been an operating assumption in California: the single-family home was the preeminent site of political interest and commitment. Voters demonstrated that they were prepared to sacrifice vital public services and traditions of liberal social welfare and ultimately to institutionalize the fiscal advantages that suburban segregation afforded. Thus, in the late 1970s California's two most enduring postwar political cultures met in Babylon, each hoping that they held the secret to renewal. The spatial history of the East Bay metropolis had produced this moment: a black power political movement in Oakland and a tax reform political movement in the suburban surroundings. These were interest-group political projects in the traditional American sense, but they were products of and profoundly shaped through the spatial history of the postwar city.

Liberal Reawakening

The political and institutional mobilizations of the War on Poverty activists had done little to displace the *Tribune*-led downtown interests that still ran Oakland. With African Americans 40 percent of the city's population in the late 1960s, and still hamstrung by an at-large election system, black Oaklanders needed allies. Eldridge Cleaver said in 1968 that "black people can't do it by themselves. It's going to take white people who recognize the situation that exists in this world today to stand up." By the early 1970s the War on Poverty fights had indeed convinced a large number of whites that the city's future was inextricably linked to dismantling the ghetto and establishing a more democratic system of representation in city hall. These groups sought to open Oakland's corridors of power to black and white liberals and, under their control, black radicals. Standing in their way, as in the 1940s, was a conservative Republican city council whose strong ties to the downtown business community and to the city's major real estate interests had changed little in three decades. A few moderate Democrats had made their way to the council by the late 1960s, but four Oakland districts with overwhelming Democratic majorities were represented by Republicans. Citywide elections, voter apathy, and the *Tribune*'s influence in local political circles continued to undergird a municipal political system in which conservative Republicans governed a city with a growing majority of registered Democratic voters.[5]

More was at stake than a few city council seats in Oakland, however. For in Oakland, as in innumerable cities across the nation, municipal politics in the 1970s opened a larger debate about what post–Great Society liberalism would look like. The question was not only whether liberals and radicals, both black and white, could find common ground against formidable political foes. The question remained how the range of issues, political causes, and strategies of the previous decade would be incorporated into urban regimes actually coming to power. How would the critique of unequal metropolitan development translate into a local political agenda? How would affirmative action, racial nationalism, and anti-imperialism translate in municipal campaigns? Could the black-white, bi-racial paradigm of urban politics include the city's burgeoning ethnic Mexican population? Would the class-based issues of poverty and underdevelopment be lost in the ascension of a middle-class politics? These questions were more open in the early 1970s than they had been in Oakland politics since the 1940s.

Reformers in Oakland had long complained that the city's political structure rendered progressive change impossible. Incumbents dominated every election, backed by the *Tribune*'s endorsement. After 1968, liberal activists in Oakland made reforming that system a priority. The liberal challenge did not come from labor, however, as it had in the 1940s, but from a vocal group of middle-class whites drawn into Oakland politics by the vicious battles over the War on Poverty and the arrests and murders of Black Panther Party members in the late 1960s. Replacing at-large voting with a district, or ward, system, they argued, would enable the working class and poor residents of the flatlands to elect councilmembers to pursue needed reforms of the police department and the school system. In the summer of 1968, during the tense negotiations between the Black Strike for Justice Committee and the city, the League of Women Voters packed the council chamber with supporters of a district election system. "Large numbers of Oakland residents with particular problems are inadequately represented by councilmen whose election depends on political and financial support of the city as a whole," a league representative explained. Dozens of others testified in favor of the league's proposal in a massive display of public disaffection with existing political arrangements.[6]

Pressure from the League of Women Voters placed Mayor Reading and the council in an awkward position. Already accused by African American activists of ruling like oligarchs, the council could not afford to dismiss the League's proposal out of hand. They compromised by placing Proposition

M, mandating district election of council members, on the city ballot in 1968, confident that they could orchestrate a campaign to defeat it. The League was nevertheless optimistic and assembled a coalition to campaign for the measure. They kept their message deliberately simple: district elections of council members would mean a more responsive, democratic city government. The coalition brought together the city's most visible liberal organizations: the Alameda County Labor Council, Mexican American Political Association, Oakland Council of Churches, NAACP, and Catholic Interracial Council, among others. Coming on the heels of the volatile summer of 1968, liberal activists endorsed Proposition M as a necessary first step in loosening the stranglehold conservatives had on city government. The opposition to Proposition M, led by the *Tribune*, included all of the city's major property-owning groups: the Alameda County Taxpayers Association, Oakland Real Estate Board, Alameda County Industries Committee, Alameda County Apartment House Association, and Oakland Property Owners Association.[7]

Proposition M divided the city by race and class and did little to dispel the image of a conservative, cliquish "establishment" controlling Oakland politics. Charles Kehrlein, chairman of the committee created to fight Proposition M, warned that the proposed system would return Oakland to "the dark ages of politics" and inaugurate a period of "special interest spending beyond the control of the taxpaying majority." Anti-M forces desperately feared that council members from poor neighborhoods would raise property taxes to help bolster the city's depleted social services budget. Knowland and the *Tribune* led a full counterattack to head off such a result. In the week before the November 1968 election, the *Tribune* openly blasted Proposition M, calling it "the desire for neighborhood boss control." In a series of hyperbolic campaign ads, the newspaper then turned the events of that summer against reformers: photographs of demonstrations overlaid with the words "No on Militants, No on Mob Rule, No on M" appeared in the pre-election editions of the *Tribune*. District election of council members, the *Tribune* suggested, would bring the city under the control of the same militants who had threatened Oakland the previous summer—antiwar protestors and black power advocates. Aided by the *Tribune*'s opposition, Proposition M went down to decisive defeat. In unsurprising returns, Proposition M passed overwhelmingly in West and East Oakland and failed in every other part of the city.[8]

A second campaign stirred Oakland's liberal political activists two years later: the candidacy of Ron Dellums for U.S. Congress. Dellums, nephew of C. L. and a protégé of D. G. Gibson's in the East Bay Democratic Club, had been a member of the Berkeley City Council since 1967. Dellums had been raised in West and North Oakland, had attended both McClymonds and Oakland Technical High Schools, and had joined Don Warden's

Afro-American Association while a student at Berkeley in the early 1960s. Under Gibson's wing in the second half of the decade, Dellums had successfully weathered the left-of-center political storms in Berkeley, where radicals, liberals, and nationalists fought one another within the Democratic Party, and sometimes, as with the Peace and Freedom Party, outside it. Berkeley's city council races in the late 1960s were heavily contested across the breadth of the city's progressive political spectrum. In this environment, Dellums had made a name for himself as an outspoken critic of the war in Vietnam and as a spokesman for black nationalism who could effectively speak to, and work with, both radical and liberal whites. The rise of Ron Dellums demonstrated that East Bay politics was rapidly shifting to the left of the Great Society and that the East Bay Democratic Club remained adept at fashioning a capacious liberalism that could draw nationalists into its fold and engage with both old and new left radicals.[9]

By the late 1960s the Seventh Congressional District, which encompassed most of the East Bay flatlands from West Oakland to North Berkeley, was one of the most heavily antiwar districts in the nation. It was also home to the majority of East Bay African Americans. Democrat Jeffrey Cohelan represented the Seventh District in Washington, DC. Cohelan, a former teamster and member of the OVL coalition in the 1940s, had settled into a moderate Cold War liberalism. Supportive of civil rights laws and the War on Poverty, Cohelan successfully channeled federal poverty and redevelopment funds to the East Bay. But as a vigorous supporter of President Johnson's Vietnam policy, he increasingly found himself at odds with his district. In the eyes of many Oaklanders he had come to represent the establishment. Robert Scheer, editor of the new left magazine *Ramparts* and an antiwar stalwart, ran against Cohelan for the Democratic nomination in 1966, forcing the issue of Vietnam into East Bay politics. Two years later, Cohelan's opponent for the Democratic nomination was John D. George, an Oakland lawyer and former NAACP president. Scheer made a relatively small dent in Cohelan's support in 1966, but George, running on a platform that linked the antiwar struggle with efforts to eliminate unemployment and empower black residents, pushed Cohelan hard in 1968 before losing. Though unsuccessful, both Scheer and George had revealed the incumbent's weaknesses. In a newly politicized environment, where Vietnam and black power were the salient issues, Cohelan, a reliable and solid old-line liberal, had come to seem anachronistic.[10]

Following Scheer and George, Dellums declared his candidacy for Cohelan's congressional seat in 1970. Vowing to run against the incumbent's "expedient liberalism," Dellums undertook the challenge of grafting West and North Oakland's African American vote onto the largely white antiwar vote, concentrated in Berkeley. It was a task for which he proved especially capable. Dellums linked imperialism in Southeast Asia with racism and poverty at home. Poor and working-class West Oakland African Americans were initially suspicious of a black candidate running primarily on the white student antiwar issue, but Dellums explained the connection—40 percent of the deaths in Vietnam, he told audiences, "come from two ethnic minorities in this district and in the country." In black neighborhoods, Dellums called for greater community control of police, a program to address racism in American cities, and a withdrawal of troops from Vietnam, rhetorically linking the ghetto and Vietnam in his basic stump speech. Many of his positions on issues in the African American community were more generic than his antiwar views, but black voters responded enthusiastically. It certainly did not hurt Dellums that his family name was as familiar to East Bay African Americans as was Martin Luther King, Jr.'s, and equally a part of the civil rights pantheon. Moreover, Dellums' appearances with Huey Newton after the latter's release from prison gave the Democrat a radical and street credibility that he might not otherwise have enjoyed.[11]

Dellums' congressional campaign helped to redefine liberalism in the East Bay. In doing so, Dellums followed Scheer and George, but also the Black Panthers and a host of African American activists in West Oakland and Berkeley, whose politics stressed anti-imperialism abroad and political cooperation with radical and liberal whites at home. By 1970 the antiwar struggle had moved close enough to mainstream Democratic liberalism— with Richard Nixon in the White House—that Dellums could successfully run as a liberal while simultaneously attacking the Cold War liberal zeit-geist from the left. Radicals still eschewed the Democratic fold. Stinging from their 1968 setbacks, the Peace and Freedom Party ran a candidate against Dellums. But Dellums was able to win enough trade union and middle-class support to construct a traditional liberal coalition, albeit one put together in the left-of-center political hothouse of Berkeley and West and North Oakland. In Oakland, the largely white organizations leading the liberal revival in city politics, especially the League of Women Voters, the Citizens for Responsive Government, and the Community Organization United for Progress, enthusiastically endorsed Dellums. With Dellums' victory in November, the Seventh Congressional District Caucus, a crucial local branch of the influential California Democratic Central Committee (CDC), was captured by a group who carefully blended black nationalism, anti-imperialism, and traditional liberal social and economic views.[12]

After 1968 the collection of liberal reformers, African American and white, who had pushed for Proposition M and worked on the Dellums campaign turned to Oakland city politics. They worked through a variety of private and semipublic organizations that included the Citizens for Responsive Government, COUP, the Committee for Change, the East Oakland Caucus, OCCUR, and the New Oakland Committee. But as liberals laid the groundwork for future black-white cooperation in electoral politics, they simultaneously created dilemmas for black radicals and grassroots activists. Would such coalitions marginalize African Americans and silence radicals, as had the white-led liberal coalitions of the 1940s? Would alliances with the emerging black and white liberal mainstream in the East Bay force African American radicals and nationalists to submerge their critiques of class power and to compromise their political aims? The questions were not rhetorical, because so much of the political energy in Oakland between 1968 and 1972 had drawn on profound disillusionment with liberal remedies and pieties.[13]

The Political Turn of the Black Panther Party

By the 1970s, the Black Panther Party was both a worldwide media phenomenon and a local touchstone of black power. Huey Newton's release from prison in 1970 brought ten thousand well-wishers streaming into the streets of Oakland. Dozens of interviews with journalists, national and international, followed. But all of the media attention that year, as in the life of the Panthers more generally, obscured as much as it revealed about the actual life of the party and its leadership. Just prior to Newton's release, David Hilliard offered a more telling assessment in the party's paper, the *Black Panther*. "February Seventeenth is Huey's birthday," Hilliard wrote. "The passing of one year finds Huey still in jail, and much more. Bobby Seale is also incarcerated. Eldridge is exiled in Algeria. Dozens of Panthers have been murdered. Over 350 Panthers have been arrested on major charges, though hardly any of them have been convicted of anything." With the party leadership in jail, murdered, or in exile, the Panthers appeared to be held together through court appearances, press releases, and the *Black Panther*. Whether the party had an organizational life outside of that discursive existence was difficult to assess, because the media's exaggerated Panther narratives tended to focus on legal troubles and periodic declarations by Newton, Eldridge Cleaver, and Bobby Seale. Even in the East Bay, it was often difficult to distinguish Panther iconography from the actual organization.[14]

Away from the radical-obsessed late-1960s media glare, however, the party enjoyed a vibrant life at the grassroots. Having expanded to dozens of cities nationwide by the early 1970s, the party claimed more than a national following; it had a national infrastructure. Panther-run Survival Programs thrived in Los Angeles, New York, New Haven, and Chicago, among other cities, and party chapters around the country worked creatively within their local political contexts on police department reform, prisoners' rights, welfare rights, and a host of other issues relevant to urban black communities. The *Black Panther* had emerged as one of the most important new left organs in the country with a wide national distribution. Emory Douglas, for instance, working in the *Black Panther* from his home in the Bay Area, influenced the Black Arts movement with his "protest aesthetics" in posters, cartoons, and sketches.

Despite this long reach, Oakland was still home. There, the Pantherite blend of revolutionary idealism, practical social programs, and street bravado enjoyed enormous popularity. By the early 1970s Oakland's Survival Programs included day-care centers and the Panther Liberation Schools, free breakfasts for children, sickle cell anemia testing, shoe and clothing programs, health clinics, and massive grocery giveaways. The *Black Panther* itself was published and distributed by a dedicated local staff, who increasingly understood themselves as journalists as well as revolutionaries and polemicists—but not, as they wrote idealistically in 1970, like "the bourgeois press, to be read once and then discarded in the nearest trash can." The party's upper leadership echelon was, as Hilliard's assessment revealed, disconnected from its base because of jailings, trials, and, even more consequentially and tragically, murders. But the Panthers remained organizationally viable through the labors of young men and women whose commitment was profound, even if they remained far outside a media spotlight that sought out only protests and radical chic.[15]

Following Newton's release from prison, the party transformed itself. In that transformation, ideology and grassroots politics would play equally significant roles. Reading the ghetto as a colonized space and mobilizing the flatlands politically in the 1970s remain the Black Panthers' most important local legacies. After his release, Newton and the party reorganized around three important new objectives focused on Oakland. First, they emphasized greater alliances with mainstream black institutions, especially the church and the East Bay Democratic Club. Second, they closed the party's chapters in most other cities, moved many of the far-flung leaders to Oakland, and announced that Oakland would become the party's practical demonstration of "revolutionary intercommunalism." Oakland would be the sole "base of operation." Third, the Panthers committed to formal electoral politics. All of this, largely directed by Newton in the tradition of Panther decision making, followed quickly on the heels of Newton's split with and subsequent ouster of Eldridge Cleaver. The latter, exiled in Algeria, wanted the party to retain its internationalist orientation and anticolonial guerilla tactics. These moves closed one era of the party's history and opened another. If the Panthers were to succeed at building a revolutionary movement in America, it would happen in Oakland. And at the heart of the movement would be an expanded analysis of Oakland as a colonized space—the platform behind their entrance into formal electoral politics.[16]

The Panthers announced their new revolutionary approach in the summer of 1972 with a headline in the *Black Panther* that read "Oakland—
A Base of Operation!" "In this interest," the newspaper explained, "each
week the Black Panther Intercommunal News Service will publish a sup-
plement examining one aspect of the city of Oakland in the hope that this
information can be used to turn a reactionary base into a revolutionary
base." "Intercommunalism," as the new efforts were called, represented
an elaborate positioning of Oakland within an international revolutionary
narrative in which Oakland's contribution was to be something like socialism in one city. But the base of operation was not a city on a hill. Oakland was the starting line in a revolutionary distance race. Once Oakland
had become a "people's base" through the electoral victories of the party,
the revolution would move to other cities. Anticolonial political struggle
in Oakland would yield rearranged political, social, and economic priorities as an example to the remaining "colonized world." It was simultaneously practical, because specific to Oakland, and ambitiously utopian.
It represented the Panthers' complicated fusion of liberation politics and
geography, in which historical racial oppression was linked to the specific
injustices of a capitalist metropolitan order that developed certain places
and underdeveloped others.[17]

The Panthers' critique began with the physical destruction of West
Oakland and moved, in an ever widening arc, to encompass the principal
contradictions of the East Bay economy as a whole. "Oakland is unique
in its particulars," Newton wrote, "a city with a small-town face doing
big-time business." Using the publications of the Oakland Project, the
University of California's multiyear study of Oakland, the results of the
federal government's 701 housing survey, and various reports and research papers produced by the University of California's Survey Research
Center, the *Black Panther* documented the demolition and redevelopment
of West Oakland. Here were the familiar culprits: BART, the new interstate
highways and federal post office, the closing of public housing projects,
massive delays on West Oakland's biggest housing project, Acorn, and
residential displacement. "BART has spent over 20 million dollars," the
newspaper cited as an example, "has literally dislocated thousands of
people in West Oakland, offered few of the promised jobs to Blacks, and
has the nerve to make one stop in West Oakland." The *Black Panther*
published special editions on the cost of living, public housing, imbalances
in urban and suburban public school budgets, urban renewal, and unemployment. In each, attention focused on the spatial contradictions of
late-twentieth-century capitalism and urbanity: poverty amid wealth, the
prevalence of violence in the urban landscape, a declining urban tax base
inside a ring of comparatively affluent suburbs, and a colonized black
nation living within an imperial state. It was a remarkably coherent body

of critical journalistic work, concluded after its first year, 1972, with a special issue entitled "Our Challenge for 1973." The latter became the political platform on which Bobby Seale and Elaine Brown ran for political office.[18]

The base of operation campaign provocatively reconceived the spatial logic of the Metropolitan Oakland Area Program. In the MOAP, Oakland was the "center" of a new metropolitan order in which progress came with ever expanding industrial and residential markets, enriching suburban areas but redounding to Oakland as well. The party constructed a vision of social advancement with Oakland "at its center" as well, but what was naturalized in the MOAP was political in the base of operation. Oakland *should* be located spatially, according to Panther logic, but on a global grid of power in which centers and peripheries had different meanings: centers were developed colonial powers and peripheries undeveloped subject people. In the example of the Port of Oakland, for instance, the city's most visible industry, the Panthers politicized the way capital and people moved through the city. The disembarking of troops heading for Vietnam from the Oakland Army Base, the siphoning of tax dollars into port redevelopment while West Oakland's unemployed stood literally two blocks away, and the port's enormous cranes that lifted commodity-filled containers onto the city's streets—all were powerful spatial metaphors for the dramatic coincidence of wealth and poverty in Oakland. There was nothing natural about the way property and goods changed hands through the port, the Panthers suggested. The exchanges benefited some and exploited others. In this analysis, Oakland was both center and periphery, home to both colonizers and colonized.[19]

The base of operation series reflected two important branches of ideological evolution within the Black Panther Party. The first, intercommunalism, represented subtle but important changes in party ideology. Intercommunalism defined the world as a collection of communities dominated by the United States and its global allies. Ongoing struggles against oppression worldwide need not be tightly coordinated, because most faced a common set of constraints and enemies. Liberation at any point would serve the larger cause. African Americans, in this view, were particularly well placed to lead global opposition to imperialism and neo-imperialism, because they had more than three hundred years of experience in dealing with European racial oppression and two hundred years of experience with the state apparatus of the United States. "We black people have always lived under this threat in our communities inside the United States," Newton wrote in 1971. "United States control of our communities is not difficult to understand." The analysis led to an optimistic conclusion. "We can transform these circumstances to our benefit: Revolutionary Intercommunalism." After his release from prison, Newton had taken Panther delegations to Africa and Asia, meeting with Mozambique President Samora Moises Machel and Chinese Premier Zhou Enlai. These sessions with international leaders influenced the development of intercommunalism. Back home, the party's grassroots strength in Oakland and its evolving commitment to global counterimperialism made their home city a natural choice for the party's revolutionary demonstration.[20]

Second, the base of operation embodied Newton's notion of advocating practical revolutionary activity to which people could relate. In a long dispute with the Revolutionary Action Movement (RAM), Newton and the Panthers insisted that revolutionary action take place "above ground," in visible public space—hence, "patrolling the pigs" and all of the other Panther public activity. The leaders of RAM, on the other hand, argued that revolutionary organization should remain underground, beyond the long reach of the state police and surveillance apparatus. But Newton and other party insiders had long believed that the principal problem with late-twentieth-century radicalism was it abstractness and distance from the material experience of ordinary people. Fomenting violence from "underground," as other groups like the Weathermen had done in the late 1960s, only served to alienate any potential revolutionary constituency, according to Newton, because people feared the violence and did not understand its political relevance. The base of operation, coming on the heels of the successful local survival programs, embodied the party's effort to educate the public in a revolutionary language by developing a practical political agenda people could find relevant to their daily lives. It was not simply about giving out free bags of groceries and then asking people to listen to a few revolutionary speeches. It was more fundamentally about making capital, power, and injustice visible and real—to politicize what most people, ordinary black folks and white folks, took for granted as natural.[21]

Like Paul Cobb and the West Oakland Planning Committee before them, the party seized upon the Port of Oakland as a symbol of the city's failed priorities and the deep contradictions within local economic development. "While the Port thrives, Oakland stagnates," read the headline in a special edition of the *Black Panther* in 1972. "Its spiraling growth, which began a few years ago, has not brought about the same kind of increase in employment for Black and poor people in Oakland." While the Port of Oakland had become the West Coast's busiest and largest, doubling its annual income between 1968 and 1972, according to the Panthers "the city gets little in return: no jobs and no access to Port income at a time when Oakland city government flirts with bankruptcy." In fact, the party contended, "tenants get special tax privileges to lower their property tax bills, and in some instances the Port actually pays their property taxes." The Panthers highlighted the odd independence of the port.

Its Board of Commissioners was appointed by the mayor, but city hall had little other official control over port activities and revenue. It remained a public entity, technically owned by the city, but its operations and revenue were virtually untouchable. As the *Black Panther* observed, this arrangement meant that when public tax dollars were invested in the port—as had happened during its phenomenal growth—the proceeds benefited private shipping companies, not the residents of Oakland. In all, the party argued, the port's operation was another example of the city's "behind the scenes deals for millions of dollars, money that is never used to benefit us [Oakland citizens]."[22]

The party's two-year base of operation campaign mixed its older anti-colonial discourse with this new attention to local political and economic arrangements in Oakland. The party emphasized the enormous percentage of the city's white workforce that lived outside of Oakland (more than 50 percent by some estimations), particularly members of the municipal police force and fire department. Party journalists wrote countless articles on the failure of federal redevelopment and urban renewal projects to provide opportunity for local residents while nearby industrial suburbs boomed with new factory and construction jobs. In 1973 the Panthers urged a full reassessment of the city's tax structure and advocated raising taxes on the long-sheltered downtown properties and reducing the property tax burden on small businesses and residents in the neighborhoods. In preparation for the 1973 municipal elections, the party prepared a detailed analysis of past Oakland voting patterns, exploring divisions between white and black neighborhoods on such issues as public housing and Proposition M. West Oakland "ranks among the lowest in registered voters, and is consistently the lowest in votes and voter turnout," according to the party. This was true despite the fact that it "shows the greatest united support for Black and poor people's candidates and issues." Such analysis confirmed what the party suspected: apathy and lack of political consciousness among the poor, as much as the *Tribune*'s political monopoly, prevented progressive change in Oakland.[23]

Panther writers envisioned the base of operation as a means of educating the city's African American and Latino residents in preparation for political action. The party's central leadership, especially Newton, Seale, and Elaine Brown, understood that large-scale reform in Oakland was impossible without electoral power and public office. In Oakland, even the highly publicized struggles over community control of the various poverty programs had not produced much change in voter turnout. "In the last elections, 25,000 Black people were removed from the register rolls because they did not vote in the general election," the party's writers claimed. "Our community cannot afford to repeat this mistake." The Panthers took on this considerable challenge in 1972 and 1973, determined through the

Figure 8.1. Bobby Seale and Elaine Brown on the campaign trail in 1973. Though neither Seale nor Brown was ever elected to city office, both proved to be effective grassroots campaigners who brought the Black Panther Party's message of new economic priorities to tens of thousands of Oaklanders. They helped to make the city elections of 1973 and 1975 among the most interesting in Oakland's history. Courtesy of the Dr. Huey P. Newton Foundation and the Department of Special Collections, Stanford University Libraries.

education drive of the *Black Panther* and the sheer strength of their reputation to mobilize the city's poor voters. Electoral action lay behind the base of operation program from the beginning: the *Black Panther* would expose the city's failed priorities, while simultaneously promoting Seale and Brown for public office. Newton had declared Bobby Seale a candidate for Oakland mayor and Elaine Brown a candidate for city council nearly a full year in advance of the spring 1973 elections. They were to run on the base of operation platform, campaigning against the "establishment" on such issues as the port, the City Center, unemployment, and what they called a new "Revenue Raising Plan." As a warm-up, the party ran a slate of candidates for the West Oakland Planning Committee's governing board in the late summer of 1972. At the polling places, party members passed out free bags of groceries and new women's shoes to voters, winning six seats. It was a small victory, but core party regulars, of whom there were approximately 150 by this time, interpreted the success as proof that the combination of Panther popularity and their new platform was a potent electoral mix. After the WOPC elections, the party devoted all of its resources to the candidacies of Seale and Brown.[24]

Bobby Seale and Elaine Brown cast the 1973 municipal election as a contest between the community and the "establishment." According to the Panthers, the "conservative majority which has dominated the Oakland city council for more than thirty years" was beholden to the publishers of the *Tribune*, the attitudes of which "ranged from outright neglect to direct racist provocation." "The struggle of Black and poor people in Oakland to seize control of their own lives and realize political power in the city," the party continued, "will inevitably lead to a confrontation with the *Tribune*." Such a characterization reflected the civic polarization and rhetorical excesses of the late 1960s and early 1970s, but beneath Panther diatribes lay important truths about the kind of closed civic political culture that had persisted in Oakland for decades. Knowland was widely known to have handpicked the city's previous three mayors—Clifford Rishell, Houlihan, and Reading—and Houlihan had been a *Tribune* attorney for many years. In addition, the *Tribune* had been responsible for escalating conflict during the spring and summer of 1968, when the paper ran the series of provocative ads portraying the boycott of downtown retail stores as radicals holding the city hostage at gunpoint. And finally, *Tribune* editorials praising Richard Nixon, J. Edgar Hoover, and the Vietnam War, as late as 1973, seemed to mark the city's "establishment," even in the eyes of moderates, as reactionary, entrenched, and determined to maintain a cliquish control over civic affairs.[25]

Seale and Brown did not rely solely on protest banner logic in their contest with "the establishment," however. In addition to the Base of Operation series, which carefully documented how decisions about economic development in the city had been made, who had benefited, and who had borne the costs, the party undertook a massive voter registration and grassroots organizing drive. "We must first organize the block, then the neighborhood," the party announced, "gradually expanding to the city." By some estimates, they had registered more than twenty thousand new voters by early 1973. Between 1972 and 1973 the party divided Oakland into a dozen sections and assigned teams of workers to each section. Each team, in turn, broke its section into manageable neighborhood units, where party workers sold the *Black Panther*, registered voters, met with community leaders, and stumped informally for the Base of Operation campaign. A typical day in the life of a section worker went something like the following, from a 1973 report to Newton: "We opened the office at 9:00 a.m. Patti did registration at the Welfare Dept. until 2:00 and then did door to door registration in Section 1. Steve registered two people on call. . . . went to see Charlie Fair about the use of his van. . . . 53 people were registered." In effect, the party created through its own initiative something resembling a ward system, with section leaders held responsible for the party's presence, strength, and effectiveness within their bounded area. It was a creative response to the city's lack of a true political apparatus in the neighborhoods, and by all accounts it worked extremely well.[26]

Seale and Brown hiked, stumped, and handshook their way across the city in the first truly grassroots municipal campaign Oakland had seen since the late 1940s. Community control of the port and City Center, affirmative action, residency requirements for employees of the city police and fire departments, and a new "revenue-raising, revenue-sharing" plan designed to redistribute the tax burden from the neighborhoods to downtown topped their list of proposals. Not unlike the OVL platform of three decades earlier, the Panther candidates called for a more equitable distribution of the city's tax burden. Seale proposed a 1 percent tax on private stocks and bonds and a 5–10 percent tax on capital gains. Small businesses, Seale emphasized, would be excluded. The Panther leader also proposed a residency requirement for members of the Oakland police and fire departments, 70 percent of whom, Seale claimed, lived outside the city and had no contact with its residents except during patrol hours. Both "Bobby" and "Elaine," as they were affectionately known to party faithful, carried the message of the "People's Plan" to Oakland voters. Brown, a tireless campaigner with an extraordinary speaking voice, explained the party's "revenue raising, revenue sharing" plan to countless audiences. Refusing to run simply on name and reputation alone, both Brown and Seale worked Oakland's streets like true grassroots candidates. As the April 1973 election neared, their message became simple and focused: the city's existing priorities "reflect the needs of the city's business community," while Seale and Brown would take the first steps toward "the construction of a people's economy."[27]

To gain the support of the city's liberal mainstream, Seale and Brown had to prove that their campaign was more than an extension of the fiery Panther rhetoric of the past. Everyone connected to the party's campaign conceded that its fortunes hinged on middle-class African American and white voters, liberal Democrats who favored fundamental changes in the way Oakland was governed but were reluctant to endorse the Panthers. Many liberals believed that the Panthers were as responsible for the rhetorical escalations and street confrontations of the late 1960s as Reading, Knowland, and the *Tribune*. Seale had for many years been the party's principal speaker. His vigorous strides to the podium and electrifying Maoist speeches were well known in Oakland, and they gave him a reputation for excess that proved to be a political liability. But Panther notoriety also gave Seale an advantage. Local media treated the mayoral election as if it was solely a contest between Reading and Seale, marginalizing a number of other candidates, including Otho Green, an African American businessman, liberal Democrat, and former assistant to the city manager in Berkeley. Seale and Brown attracted considerable attention everywhere they went during the campaign months of early 1973. The attention was good for the campaign, but constant questions from the local and national press dogged them. How could the Panthers expect to govern a city in which they had created so much tension? How effective could a self-proclaimed radical group be in building a workable coalition in city government? Would the fiery rhetoric of the past give way to organization and action?[28]

The Panthers led a broad field of radical and liberal challengers to Mayor Reading in 1973. Seale and Brown expectedly garnered the "radical" label, but all of the candidates on the left included in their platforms issues and themes that dated back to the Black Caucus, the WOPC, and the OEDCI of the late 1960s. Otho Green, for instance, stressed unemployment and taxes as the critical campaign issues (he also included crime), noting that "half the people who work in Oakland live outside; 22 percent of Oakland resident are unemployed." John Sutter, a mainstream white liberal, ran on the promise to "reorder our priorities in favor of the neighborhoods as compared to downtown interests. . . . Reading's policy has been to ignore the neighborhoods." Though neither Green nor Sutter proposed as radical a set of new taxes as Seale did, both men stressed the need to distribute the tax burden more evenly between downtown and the rest of the city. Green's and Sutter's candidacies made clear that the neighborhood-first politics of the late 1960s and early 1970s, the community-driven reorientation of civic priorities around ghetto rehabilitation and the health of Oakland's living spaces, had moved to the center of politics in the city. No candidate hoping to occupy a position anywhere from moderate to radical on the political spectrum could hope to run successfully in Oakland without championing the neighborhoods.[29]

Voting returns in 1973 revealed a startlingly good showing for the Panther political novices. Brown received nearly 35,000 votes in her council race against the moderate African American Republican incumbent, Josh Rose (Rose won 55,000 votes). Brown's showing convinced her to make a second run in 1975. Seale fared well, though in a complicated three-way split of the liberal-Democratic vote, he garnered only 21,000 votes in the primary. Still, it was just enough to force Reading into a runoff election in May. In the subsequent race, Seale's Panther past haunted him. Though he gained important endorsements from the city's liberal community, none was enthusiastic. The memory of his recent jail sentence, the violence of 1968–1971, including his arrest and trial stemming from demonstrations at the 1968 Democratic National Convention in Chicago, and continued rumors of Panther involvement in local illegal activities hamstrung Seale's efforts to bill himself as a candidate acceptable to black and white moderate

Figure 8.2. The Black Panther Party registered thousands of new voters in the early 1970s. These volunteers, and hundreds like them, gave Bobby Seale and Elaine Brown broad grassroots support. Courtesy of the Dr. Huey P. Newton Foundation and the Department of Special Collections, Stanford University Libraries.

liberals among the city's crucial swing voters. Reading demolished him in May, winning with 77,000 votes to Seale's 43,000. However, his candidacy generated unparalleled political involvement and enthusiasm in the city's poor and working-class African American communities. A stunning 70 percent of registered voters turned out for the May 1973 runoff between Reading and Seale, a nearly unprecedented total in Oakland. And though Reading defeated the Panther handily, Seale showed impressively for a political novice running a grassroots campaign dogged by a complicated past. Seale demonstrated, particularly in the month-long campaign between the primary and the runoff, that he could quickly and deftly transform himself into a political figure capable of running with what the *Oakland Post* called "composure and dignity," even against long-time foe Reading. But it was not enough to overcome the suspicion and distrust of the city's moderate middle third. Seale declared a symbolic victory and promised that the party would fare better in 1977.[30]

Oakland's political culture had begun to turn on a new axis. The Black Panther Party's foray into electoral politics and political education was an important component of this turn, joining the OEDCI, the WOPC, and the Black Caucus in creating new poles of politics in the city's African

American community. The political culture called forth by these institutions and the various leaders who passed through them and used them included three central elements. First, metropolitan space, and the relationship between Oakland and its nearby suburbs, had become the definitive political issue in the city. A politicized metropolitan space was not new in Oakland politics, of course. But unlike the Metropolitan Oakland Area Plan, 1970s' politics questioned rather than celebrated suburban progress. Second, race and the "community" had emerged as poles around which the political culture organized authenticity. This, too, had spatial elements, since to live in the community was also to be of the community, something a good many African American liberals could not say by the 1970s. Third, politics had come to be associated with the provision of concrete jobs. This was true, not in the older sense of political patronage, but in terms of how jobs in the private and semipublic sectors were distributed. Here, the port and City Center were the most important symbols, and here too there were the familiar spatial elements. This new political alchemy reworked both class and race in important ways, revealed in the years following the Panthers' initial foray into electoral politics. The party may have been naive about the realpolitik behind urban policy, but the position that they had staked out, in the larger conversation with integrationist African Americans and liberal and conservative whites, marked them as a potent political voice with a concrete vision of Oakland's future.

Return of the East Bay Democratic Club

The Black Panther Party had become a major political force in the city, but Seale's loss in 1973 demonstrated that Panther candidates discouraged as many votes as they mobilized. Elaine Brown, however, almost single-handedly kept the Panthers' 1973 agenda before the public and the city's leaders. More than any other individual, she constructed a bridge between the Panthers and the liberal community, black and white. Between 1973 and 1977 Brown moved out from under the long shadow of Seale, her former Panther boss, and Newton, her famous companion. She claimed a public space and voice for both radical and feminist politics unlike anything the city had ever seen. Originally from Philadelphia, Brown had come to Oakland in the early 1970s from Los Angeles, where she was a veteran of the party's renowned clashes with the cultural nationalist Ron Karenga and his organization, US. In Oakland, she edited the Panther newspaper and served on the party's central committee. In 1974 Newton, in exile in Cuba, appointed Brown chairperson of the Black Panther Party. Brown became one of Oakland's most important leaders and a spokesperson for the left wing of the city's progressive forces. Her capacity to discuss local issues and her never-ending networking among black leaders, including representatives of the church and Democratic Party establishments, earned her a reputation unique among Panthers. At a national Urban League conference in San Francisco in 1974, Brown spoke forcefully about guaranteed full employment, a guaranteed minimum income, and how effective community organizing can deter crime. Adding "I think it would be better if we saw a lot more women here [at the conference] speaking on a lot of things," Brown signaled her efforts to reform the party's gender codes and to place a new public face on the party's politics.[31]

In 1975 Brown made another run for the Oakland City Council. It was a second test both of the Panther vision for Oakland and, perhaps more consequentially for political calculations, the Panthers' ability to work with other African American leaders and to attract liberal whites. Brown put together a campaign that reflected her considerable coalition-building skills and established a working partnership between the party, the emerging political apparatus under Ron Dellums, and the community leadership of West Oakland. Brown's campaign manager was Beth Meador, a prominent organizer for Dellums; her executive chairperson was Dorothy Payne, former head of the West Oakland Planning Committee; and her co-chair was Otho Green, who had run against Seale in 1973. It was a potent combination, because Brown had tapped the two most important liberal-progressive political networks in Oakland—Dellums' Democratic Party organization and the West Oakland planning community—while reaching out to mainstream black businesses and the middle class through Green. Brown was determined to run as much behind this kind of political savvy as on the Panther name and radical platform.[32]

Brown ultimately lost in a close election, but her campaign coalition anticipated the combination that would elect Lionel Wilson mayor two years later. And Brown herself exemplified what many people felt was the best of the decades-long grassroots and black power movements in Oakland. She ran as the candidate of "multi-ethnic Oakland," promising the city's African American, Latino, Asian, and white voters "a new day in Oakland." She also drew large numbers of women into the campaign, breaking the Panther gender division of labor by selecting women for the top strategy positions on her team. For the first time in Oakland politics, a candidate for major local office spoke of the feminization of poverty, a process that had been eroding the city's neighborhoods for nearly two decades. "The women of the city of Oakland, over half the population," Brown declared at the event officially announcing her candidacy, "suffer job discrimination in city agencies, unequal pay plans, and lack of child care plans." In addition, she echoed her and Seale's platform from 1973, em-

phasizing the lack of accountability of the port, the unequal distribution
of taxes, and the lack of neighborhood priorities in the city budget. Mod-
erating the radical language of Oakland as a revolutionary base rewarded
Brown with key liberal endorsements from the Alameda County Democratic Party Central Committee, the Alameda County Labor Council, the
Teamsters, the United Autoworkers, and virtually all of the city's neighborhood Democratic clubs. Brown had, like Dellums in his congressional
district, forged a coalition with roots anchored in black radicalism and
anti-imperialism that simultaneously attracted the traditional liberal base
of the Democratic Party.[33]

The Panthers' "revolutionary intercommunalism" had been an attempt
to forge a left politics outside of Cold War liberal philosophies and institutions. Indeed, "revolutionary intercommunalism" charged that American
imperialism abroad had a domestic cognate—segregation and the underdevelopment of black America—that compromised every national institution, including both major political parties. As Brown moved the
Panthers into closer alliance with the East Bay Democratic political
establishment after 1973, the fate of the party's radicalism remained an
open question. Would that radicalism encounter an inevitable demobilization as Panther activists sought a place in the mainstream political process?
Would self-determination as a political credo—along with the radical
critique of political economy advanced by Seale and Brown—be either
sacrificed to or rendered empty and hollow by the necessary alliance with
liberals? The possibility after 1975 of African Americans achieving real
power in Oakland—and the promise that African American leftists would
be part of that coming to power—made these questions far more than
hypothetical.[34]

Both Brown and her ardent supporter, Ron Dellums, understood the
possibility that a left African American politics could gradually erode under strong pressure from middle-class black liberals. "Simply changing
white faces for black faces," Dellums explained at a rally for Brown in
1975, reinforces "the same materialistic, empty, plastic values that we've
come to know as middle-class America." He further warned of covering
over "reactionary politics with black rhetoric." Instead, Dellums and
Brown argued that year, East Bay African Americans should pursue a
class politics in which black leaders would reform, rather than simply
take the reigns of, the local political economy. Radical African American
activists and political leaders around the country faced a similar dilemma,
as they watched black power rhetoric increasingly serve the interests of
liberal and moderate blacks—who, once elected to municipal or legislative
posts, isolated or marginalized radicals and other leftists. Amiri Baraka's
complaints about "bourgeois black nationalism" had begun to resonate
among East Bay activists who believed that the black revolution stood for

something greater and more transformative than simply electing black faces to public office.[35]

Nevertheless, the powerful gravity of the political middle exerted a steady pull on these activists. Following Elaine Brown's run for city council in 1975, the city's left-liberal coalition was led by Brown, Paul Cobb, Elijah Turner, Don McCullum, white veterans of OCCUR, and African American veterans of OCCUR and the WOPC. This group drafted Lionel Wilson to run for mayor in 1977. The former chairman of the OEDCI and one of the most popular leaders in the city, Wilson was a fiscal conservative and social moderate who had steered relatively clear of the black power disputes of the late 1960s. The first African American Superior Court Judge in Alameda County, Wilson had managed a successful career in law while making clear his political differences with Mayor Reading and the city council. He seemed an ideal candidate to chart a liberal middle course between the city's radical left and its professional and business establishment. In 1972 Reading had appointed Wilson, along with McCullum, Cobb, and Turner, to serve as black representatives on the New Oakland Committee. Formed to appease Black Panther radicals like Seale (and, then, Brown), the New Oakland Committee was charged with designing long-term plans for retaining existing employers and attracting new ones to the city. Wilson's rapid ascension in the years after the Seale and Brown campaigns marked the triumphant return to Oakland politics of the East Bay Democratic Club, D. G. Gibson's thirty-year-old stronghold of African American liberalism. And it marked the incorporation of both Black Panther radicalism and West Oakland's blend of nationalism and grassroots populism into the EBDC's political orbit.[36]

The mayoral election of 1977 thus represented a test of two major political strategies that had emerged within African American Oakland since World War II. First, 1977 was a test of the EBDC's decades-old coalition-building strategy: of working with white-dominated groups from positions of strength in the black community. It stretched back to Byron Rumford's first campaign for the California assembly in 1948. The EBDC had lost its working-class base in the Brotherhood of Sleeping Car Porters and among other railroad and dock workers in West Oakland, but its strength was now solidly rooted in the city's sizable black middle class and among civil servants and African American blue-collar workers in labor unions like the ILWU and the Service Employees International Union Local 250. The EBDC would need to join these constituencies to the liberal and moderate white vote in order to elect Wilson. The second test would determine if Brown, Cobb, and Turner could successfully push the emerging coalition from the left, forcing the cautious and deliberate Wilson into more radical positions on key issues. For Brown and her Panther cohorts, the latter included at least progressive reform of the city's

tax system, including a payroll tax to offset the suburban exodus of income, as well as an aggressive affirmative action program in city hiring.
Brown especially imagined that having Wilson's ear—he had supported
her in 1975 and actively sought her assistance in 1977—would allow her
to influence the direction of the potential new administration. Historically,
these were crucial tests. The *California Voice* put it this way: "Four years
have passed since Bobby Seale, former Chairman of the Black Panther
Party, forced John Reading into a runoff for the office of mayor of Oakland, Calif. During these four years, Oakland has been marking time on
a treadmill leading nowhere."[37]

Despite the presence of many radical and community activists on his
campaign staff, Wilson ran as a moderate liberal who wanted to increase
social welfare without alienating business, emphasizing both fiscal conservatism and the expansion of social services. Unemployment, public safety
(crime), and the "eroding tax base" were his principal stump issues. With
virtually the city's entire liberal base behind him, a campaign manager
from Ron Dellums' office, and Reading having decided not to run again,
Wilson ran a cautious, but confident, campaign. He proposed an "urban
bank," funded through the federal government, to be used to attract new
businesses to Oakland. He promised an expansion of virtually all city
services, from police protection to care for the elderly and public housing. He pledged to improve and promote the port as the city's most vital
industry, while simultaneously harnessing its resources more directly to
the city budget. In an optimistic campaign moment prior to the 1977
election, Wilson told a crowd of well-wishers that Oakland had "the human, economic, and environmental potential to develop into a Renaissance city" and that his bid for mayor was "a catalyst, a conduit, through
which we can express the needs that we have as a people in this city." He
was celebrated in the African American press as "the first black mayor of
Oakland" well before the election, but Wilson publicly downplayed the
"first black" dimensions. He lamented and pledged to end minority unemployment, but his messages of "Oakland first" and "we have to learn
to live together" stressed the liberal unity Wilson's team believed necessary to win against a weakened, but determined, conservative establishment. Appalled that so many Oakland workers lived outside the city, he
nonetheless opposed a payroll tax (that would tax those workers' incomes before they could leave the city) because he found it "regressive"
and because it would create a disincentive for businesses to locate in the
city. Most importantly, he refused to make that issue an explicitly racial
one, preferring to stress Oakland's relationship to surrounding suburbs
in the abstract.[38]

In a close election, Wilson won. Elaine Brown remembered that she
and her cohorts "fielded every Panther and every other campaign worker,

on foot, in cars, and on buses, to drag those black registrants to the polls. The streets of Oakland were being harvested." Nonetheless, voter turnout in the flatlands was disappointing, below 50 percent in most precincts. The election had not produced the enormous participation rates that Seale's candidacy had generated in 1973. It would later appear that white swing voters, Democrats who had voted for someone other than Wilson in the primary, had made the difference. They were as crucial to his victory as were the Panther streets. Black Oakland celebrated. "We can look forward now," the *Voice* editorialized, "to Black people beginning to be represented adequately at decision-making levels in all areas of city government there, and we note with approval that, even in the few public statements he has made since the victory, Judge Wilson has shown his commitment to the Number One social priority, not only in Oakland, but throughout the rest of the nation as well—jobs."[39]

Wilson's victory was part of a nationwide pattern. In the 1970s, in urban centers across the United States, African Americans achieved civic power in unprecedented numbers. In 1973, black mayors were elected in 48 U.S. cities. Another 268 came in the next decade and a half. All told, it represented one of the postwar half-century's most remarkable and sweeping political changes. White suburbanization, the War on Poverty, three decades of black political coalition-building, and the civil rights/black power movement all contributed to the enormous shift. In addition, the ascendance of African American-led coalitions to civic power reflected a reenergized urban liberal agenda. Even as liberalism was in decline in national politics and its virtual death was declared in much of the nation's suburban areas, urban voters overwhelmingly supported a wide range of liberal candidates and programs. Inheriting cities in decline—the "hollow prize" described by one contemporary commentator on the surge of black mayors—however, was nothing if not an ambivalent victory, and there was no better instance of this stark ambivalence than Oakland.[40]

Wilson advanced to the city's mayoralty confronting profound predicaments that were the product of three decades of metropolitan history in the East Bay and California. Oakland's experiences with capital investment since the mid-1960s had convincingly demonstrated that competition with the nearby suburbs was a zero-sum game. Almost in direct proportion as San Leandro, Fremont, Hayward, and Milpitas gained jobs and investment, Oakland's tax base declined, its major industries fewer and fewer. Left with an enormous population of relatively poor people to support with city services, Oakland increasingly lacked the tax base to support those services. The kinds of proposals designed to guarantee new jobs to Oakland residents—as in affirmative action at the City Center and the port—had the potential to generate new sources of employment for historically oppressed communities. But without economic growth, the city

Figure 8.3. Lionel Wilson at a press conference in the late 1970s. With him are representatives of the two strategic forces behind his campaign for mayor in 1977: the East Bay Democratic Club and community activists from West Oakland. To Wilson's right is John George, a member of the state legislature. To his left are, in order, Doug Jones, Paul Cobb, and Elijah Turner. Cobb and Turner had been leading activists in West Oakland grassroots politics since the early 1960s. Courtesy of the *Oakland Tribune.*

would ultimately lose more jobs than it created. The more radical proposals for dealing with the urban-suburban competition and the shrinking city budget—such as the Panthers' system of redistributing the tax burden—threatened to make Oakland an even more unfriendly place for businesses to invest than it already appeared to be to outsiders. Thus, whatever group of leaders Oakland's residents and neighborhoods selected to run the city, those leaders were trapped in a spatial class system in which competition for economic investment placed the city's future as much in the hands of outside capitalists and investors as in politicians, neighborhoods, and anything resembling "the people."

Wilson and Oakland simultaneously had to contend with tax reform. The California tax revolt, driven by conservative activists in Southern California but eagerly embraced by homeowners in the Bay Area, represented the most far-reaching spatial predicament of the postwar generation.

In an earlier era, control of city politics in Oakland would have meant a great deal, but in the thirty years since the close of World War II, power and civic authority in the East Bay had dramatically decentralized. A populist political movement in suburban Alameda County, as in suburban counties statewide, could limit and constrain the power of Oakland, a contradiction of both capitalist development and metropolitan governance with enormous consequences for Oakland's residents. This was confounded by the massive retreat of the federal government from urban policy in the 1970s and the consequent contraction of federal money. The demobilization of federal urban policy had begun under President Richard Nixon, whose distaste for the OEO and War on Poverty were well known, but it continued apace throughout the decade. The federally funded job training, support for public schools, and public housing that Wilson knew the city so desperately needed were increasingly unavailable. The combination of Proposition 13 and the federal retreat from urban policy in the late 1970s dealt a heavy blow to Oakland and places like it, a blow that would ripple across the subsequent decade.[41]

The Tax Revolt and the New California

At a conference on California's Proposition 13, the nation's most far-reaching property tax limitation measure, Bay Area Urban League representative Percy Steele explained that "although the initiative does not appear to have an overt racial implication, any cuts in service delivery or any employment layoffs will have an adverse impact on the minority community." Later, at the same lectern, Paul Cobb put the situation more bluntly. "Proposition 13 was white folks' message to us that we are going to have to do it ourselves." These pessimistic assessments came so quickly on the heels of Lionel Wilson's election in 1977 that a sense of tragedy descended on Oakland's African American leadership. California voters, including a large majority in Alameda County, approved Proposition 13 in June 1978, one year after Wilson's victory and only a handful more removed from Elaine Brown's campaign for a "people's economy" in Oakland. Few Californians explicitly racialized Proposition 13—Steele was correct—and the campaign was spared the backlash rhetoric of Proposition 14, the 1964 measure that repealed the state's fair housing law. But Cobb was not wrong. For in 1978 it appeared that urban African American California was once again peering across a spatial-political divide at suburban white California. Clayborne Carson, a professor of history at Stanford University and former SNCC activist, accused white suburbanites, the widely recognized grassroots base behind Proposition 13, of being "less interested in tax and government reform than in declaring their unwillingness to pay for public facilities and services that are needed for central cities."[42]

Proposition 13 grew out of an existing, quite real crisis in the state's system of taxation. The political resolution that it imposed, however, deepened a more profound crisis in the political economy of California's metropolitan areas: a spatial political economy in which vast differences in the levels of development within a single metropolitan region were not merely tolerated, but encouraged and subsidized. Proposition 13's principal support came from postwar suburbs like San Leandro and Fremont, places where a low tax populism was nurtured in postwar city building. The measure's principal opposition came from the statewide liberal coalition that, too, was a product of the postwar decades. African Americans, especially, opposed the measure in larger numbers and with greater voice than any other single group. In this sense, Proposition 13 represented the kind of standoff that Carson described: between revenue-starved older cities, where the majority of African Americans and other communities of color lived, and revenue-rich suburban communities dominated by white-Anglo homeowners. It was a political confrontation produced by the state's uneven postwar metropolitan development and the racial and class segregation built into postwar federal housing policy and private housing markets. As such, the 1978 tax revolt cannot be reduced to a transparent rejection of liberalism by ideologically driven and reflexively antistatist conservative voters. Its causes and sources were more complex, and ultimately enframed within the spatial and political history of California's property markets, postwar suburbanization, and urban underdevelopment, the longer story told in this book.[43]

The 1978 tax revolt was the product of three intersecting developments. Each played a crucial role in shaping both the election's outcome and how that outcome would be interpreted and mobilized on both the left and right—in the East Bay, in California as a whole, and subsequently across the nation. First, tax reform in the 1970s was a response to the real increase in taxes paid by individuals in California compared with those paid by corporations and other businesses. In Oakland the Panthers had made this an issue for the progressive left, arguing for higher corporate and business taxes. Statewide, however, the issue was captured and advanced politically by the right. This linked to the second development. Tax reform in the late 1970s emerged as one component of a larger attack on liberalism. This attack's reliance on a rhetoric of unfairness and a broad-brush denigration of government ("bureaucrats") only thinly veiled its complete incorporation into a long-standing conservative political opposition to the welfare state and the social wage. But that same rhetorical framework allowed tax revolt proponents to appear as populists defending the "little guy" against a flawed government bureaucracy. Third, the tax revolt voting returns strongly suggest that California's legacy of residential segregation—and the segregation of wealth and political interest within spatially distinct urban and suburban enclaves—profoundly affected how individual Californians had come to understand the mutual obligations between state and citizen. In this regard, it is clear that even among people who did not oppose government programs and who were not ideologically opposed to the welfare state in the abstract nonetheless voted for Proposition 13 because their immediate concerns remained local and property-centered. The tax revolt likely would not have been successful absent any one of the preceding three components. It is thus best to understand the tax politics in late 1970s California as both an indication of growing opposition to liberalism and a structural product of segregation, including suburban overdevelopment and urban underdevelopment.

Tax reform politics in California in 1978 were an extension of efforts that had been underway since 1966. In that year the California legislature passed A.B. 80, requiring assessors to evaluate all property in the state at 25 percent of market value. As we saw in chapter 7, this had the effect of shifting the overall property tax burden from business and industrial property to individual homeowners. The bill had the desired result of reducing assessor fraud, but the legislation had imposed a much more regressive tax structure on California. Under the 25 percent rule, local governments had little freedom to adjust property valuations to reflect the mix of industry and residence in their locale and no ability to provide homeowners with relief—the sort of tax relief that municipal regimes in cities like San Leandro had used so effectively in the 1950s. The only option available in most counties and municipalities was to increase tax *rates* and to impose new special assessments or to raise sales taxes. The result was an even greater burden on individual homeowners—or on other residential property owners, who passed their higher costs on to renters. In a metropolitan region like Alameda County, all homeowners and renters experienced this financial pinch. But it hamstrung older, economically depressed cities like Oakland—with higher social service burdens and greater demands on public services—more than suburban cities like San Leandro and Fremont.[44]

The contradictions within the postwar development strategies of places like San Leandro were laid bare in the 1970s. In the 1950s and 1960s cheap land, federal mortgage subsidies, a booming industrial economy, and racial segregation combined to permit San Leandro's leaders the luxury of manipulating property taxes both to attract industrial investment and to maintain a political consensus among homeowners. Though successful for a time, this strategy always contained within it two regressive tendencies. The first we have encountered numerous times—suburbanization of this kind had the effect of segregating wealth and development by race and class. The second, however, was less obvious. Keeping property taxes low as a development tool, especially taxes imposed on business property, placed a constant pressure on local municipalities to redistribute the tax burden away from businesses. In a competitive capitalist marketplace in which cities across the state were competing for business investment, this pressure on individual cities had the cumulative effect of increasing the regressive nature of the tax structure.

California's spectacular property market inflation during the 1970s amplified this already regressive system. Until the early 1970s, property values in California consistently rose between 4 and 5 percent annually. By the late 1970s, however, inflation was as high as 14 percent. This translated into as much as a tripling of an individual homeowner's tax bill. To make matters worse, between 1967 and the late 1970s, California had gradually increased its reliance on income taxes as a source of state revenue. By the later years of the decade, the per capita state collection of income taxes was rising at a rate of about 20 percent annually. Inflation combined with a state tax structure that burdened homeowners more than business and industry meant that individual Californians experienced dramatic increases in virtually every form of taxation across the decade of the 1970s. The fabulous land price increases that boosters and developers had so praised in the 1950s and 1960s as the key to California's prosperity had now boomeranged to strike back at homeowners.[45]

In this political economic context, antistatist conservatives, rather than liberal or left leaders and activists, emerged to set the tax reform agenda. Proposition 13 was conceived by two conservative political activists from Southern California, Howard Jarvis and Paul Gann. In his post tax revolt memoir, entitled *I'm Mad as Hell*, Jarvis cast himself in the mold of the American populist. "The brains and capacity of the citizens of the United States are invariably greater than the brains and capacity of the bureaucracy," he rhapsodized. Jarvis, an apartment house owner and longtime anti–New Deal Republican, loudly and passionately proclaimed Proposition 13 to be the "people's" revolt against incompetent spendthrift politicians and their profligate welfare state. Gann was a former realtor and also a longtime political entrepreneur on tax reform initiatives. Though he did not share Jarvis's crusader-like voluntarism nor his quest for the spotlight, he was nonetheless a staunch political opponent of liberal social policy. Jarvis's and Gann's political orientation and the alliances on which they drew were important, because they framed tax reform as an oblique attack on the liberal state. Rather than arguing for tax reform as an effort to correct the regressive nature of the state's tax system—as the Panthers had done in Oakland—Jarvis and Gann approached the tax question from the right. They thus combined two political positions that did not necessarily converge: tax reform and antiliberalism. It was, however, a powerful combination that gained appeal month after month in the first half of 1978. Jarvis and Gann shaped the state's political discourse around a broad rejection of the political establishment and government "bureaucracy."[46]

Jarvis and Gann were figureheads, but tax reform remained a mass grassroots social movement organized and led by hundreds of local groups across the state, coordinated in the late 1970s by the United Organizations of Taxpayers. The social basis for what became known as the "Jarvis-Gann," or simply "Jarvis," initiative lay in the postwar logic of California suburbanization and in a political culture that elevated home-ownership and property itself above all other social goods. Two generations of Californians had come of age politically in a suburban world in which low taxes, moderately increasing property values, and minimal fiscal and civic connections to core cities and their social problems could be taken for granted. Moreover, the various institutions that required public revenues—especially the state's immense college and university system, local public schools, and diverse social services and social wage programs—were more burdened than ever by the dramatic expansions of the state's population in the 1960s and early 1970s. Since 1966, when tax reform politics first emerged as a compelling statewide issue, the California legislature had done little to ease the burden on the "average home-owner," by then the most important political interest and ideological identity in the state. What relief legislators had offered, as in A.B. 80, deepened the crisis.[47]

One of the major problems with Proposition 13, in 1978 and since, was its misrepresentation of how taxes in the state were divided. Local governments and agencies received nearly all of their funding through property taxes. Fifty percent of all local public school budgets, for instance, were funded with property tax revenues, 40 percent of county budgets, 27 percent of city budgets, and 90 percent of fire department budgets. State government, however, was funded overwhelmingly by other kinds of taxes: especially those on personal income, retail sales, transportation, banks, and corporations. Spectacular property-value inflation, especially in the three years between 1976 and 1978, had pushed property taxes into public consciousness. However, the equation between property taxation and wasteful state bureaucracy was entirely ideological, because property taxes had (and have) little to do with state government financing. Only county government contributions to certain federal- and state-mandated social insurance programs linked property taxes with state government. Proposition 13, then, stood to do far more damage to local services than state government and promised, because the state would presumably have to find other revenue sources, to shift further the state tax burden onto individuals—through income and sales taxes, for instance.[48]

In suburban Alameda County, the tax revolt of 1978 was an extension of the tax reform efforts that had begun in 1966, fueled by the same mixture of populist resentments and property politics. At the top of the list of complaints lay California's welfare state. In a series of letters to the editor leading up to the June 1978 election, the *San Leandro Daily Review* gave voice to these concerns. The "frills and exorbitant wastes" of state government, according to one letter writer, had forced homeowners to go on "strike" against the state bureaucracy. After all, he noted, "our civil workers have made demands beyond the negotiable amounts offered by their supervisors," which constituted a "strike against the taxpayer." Another cited the "overpaid political hacks" ensconced in state government who constituted an assortment of "gluttons at the public trough." A third declared that "the initiative is the last barricade the taxpayer has to rock some sense into these reckless officials." In Fremont, where the debate over Proposition 13 was as fierce as anywhere in the state, one letter to the editor summed up this position: "The taxpayers' enemies are the free-spending politicians who approve the mounting budgets at every government level." No observer of Alameda County in the decade before 1978 could deny that the tax burden on small homeowners had increased—indeed, opponents of the Jarvis initiative often rushed to make this admission in order not to seem insensitive—but the ferocity and scale of attacks on state government shifted debate from how best to correct an uneven tax structure to the broader social legitimacy of liberalism and state social policy.[49]

Proposition 13 proposed an enticing, superficially simple resolution: limit the taxes levied on any piece of real property and require a two-thirds vote of the state legislature to increase any other tax. Coming on the heels of failed property tax limitation measures in 1968 and 1973, the Jarvis initiative purposefully streamlined its formula—property taxes could never exceed 1 percent of the "real cash value" of the property, and reassessments for taxing purposes could occur only when property changed hands. Furthermore, Proposition 13's rules were placed outside the control of the state legislature: they could be altered only by another referendum. The measure mandated a two-thirds vote for all future state tax increases and a two-thirds vote for local increases as well. Finally, the measure did not include a provision prescribing how the state and local governments were to replace lost revenue: the hope was that they would simply cut.[50]

Pre-election studies and warnings began to appear in the winter of 1978 and mushroomed in the spring months leading up to the June election. Most came from local and state agencies, county governments, and nonprofit organizations opposed to Proposition 13. A typical example was the May 1978 report issued by the Committee on Local Government and Taxation of the State Assembly. It projected a loss of $7 billion in property tax revenue across the state and predicted massive reductions in all government services, including "property-related" services. The latter issue stood out, because Proposition 13's supporters contended that the measure would leave local governments with sufficient revenues to fund essential property-related services—fire and police, sewers, parks, street maintenance, and the like. The state legislature disagreed, arguing that some of the sharpest cuts would come from just these areas, in addition to education. The Oakland City Council declared its opposition to Proposition 13 in a resolution asserting that the measure "will severely limit the services available to the citizens of Oakland, it will create substantial unemployment, and it will cause confusion in local government." As the battle of studies and projections played out through the months of the early spring, and as the public culture became glutted with statistics and percentages, both sides boiled their rhetoric down to familiar colloquial platitudes. Opponents argued that tax reform was necessary, but that Proposition 13 went too far, too fast, and would have too many unintended consequences. Proponents of the measure responded that their adversaries used "scare tactics" to frighten the public and that, in the words of the *Milpitas Post*, "after waiting so long and being promised tax reform so often, nothing seems too fast."[51]

The reactions to Proposition 13 in Alameda County's official circles ran parallel to the statewide response. In a letter to the County Board of Supervisors, county administrators predicted that the Jarvis initiative would cut $115.5 million from annual property tax revenues: total revenues would fall from $162.5 million to $47 million. "So many imponderables," the letter admitted, made it difficult to estimate losses accurately, but officials believed that placing the worst-case scenario before the voters—county layoffs in excess of five thousand employees, for instance—was both a political necessity and their responsibility as public servants. Union City's city manager estimated that their municipal operating budget would be cut by as much as 65 percent, and every other city in the East Bay prepared "Jarvis initiative budgets" in the pre-election months that predicted unprecedented cutbacks in education and basic governmental services. Ironically, given how much of the pro–Proposition 13 support evolved from resentments of the state's growing social insurance burden, county AFDC budgets would remain the least affected, because state and federal rules mandated minimum payments.[52]

The Proposition 13 debate in Fremont offers a window on the political currents contending over tax reform. The Fremont chapter of the Alameda YES on Proposition 13 Committee was led by a local apartment building owner and a developer. They cast themselves and Proposition 13 as victims of a relentless campaign waged by government employees, cities, and school districts. "People who don't have time [for such a campaign] pay the taxes," Bob Reeder, vice chairman of the YES on 13 Committee told the *Fremont Argus*. The Fremont city manager, projecting budget cuts of up to $4 million, proposed to raise taxes on local businesses to compensate partially for such losses. Before the city council, and an audience of hundreds of the city's business representatives, the city manager explained that while homeowner property valuation had increased by 129 percent, business property valuation had done so by only 8 percent. Increasing business taxes was simply a way to correct these dramatic imbalances. The council was not swayed, nor were those business interests who testified, many of whom attacked the city for "wasteful spending." When the council turned back the tax increase, the city manager lamented that "there doesn't seem to be any distinction in the public mind between this government and any other."[53]

The 1978 campaign was contested principally in two arenas: local ones like Fremont and statewide, primarily through vast media coverage. Many opponents of Proposition 13 insisted that Californians were not prepared to reject the welfare state or liberalism outright but were encouraged into a voting frenzy by the extraordinary media coverage of Proposition 13 and its most vocal supporters. "The meanness and ugliness presently emerging throughout the State of California has largely been encouraged by television and radio," wrote one commentator on "the morning after" Proposition 13. Indeed, Jarvis and Gann proved to be adept, if duplicitous, strategists who forced political opponents onto their terrain. Jarvis frequently made outlandish accusations, as when he claimed that property taxes paid for politicians to travel to Paris and London. Gann would then counter with homilies that softened Jarvis's sharp edge. Proposition 13 will "let us dream the American dream of being safe and secure in our homes," Gann told a television audience during a debate in June. Jarvis's and Gann's greatest success came in placing legislators on the defensive. The California Legislature had done little to reform the state's tax structure. Democratic Governor Jerry Brown had allowed the state to run unprecedented surpluses, largely a product of inflation. And Jarvis and Gann camouflaged Proposition 13 with broad populist, antiwaste political strokes. In this context, legislators often came across exactly as Jarvis and Gann hoped they would, as speaking in bureaucratic language about budget numbers and feasibility studies, while Proposition 13 proponents spoke in easy populist tones.[54]

California voters passed Proposition 13 by a margin of two to one, despite the opposition of nearly the entire state political establishment, both Democrat and Republican. In Alameda County, only the vote in Oakland and Berkeley kept the tallies close. In San Leandro, Fremont, and the Castro Valley, voters approved Proposition 13 by more than 70 percent

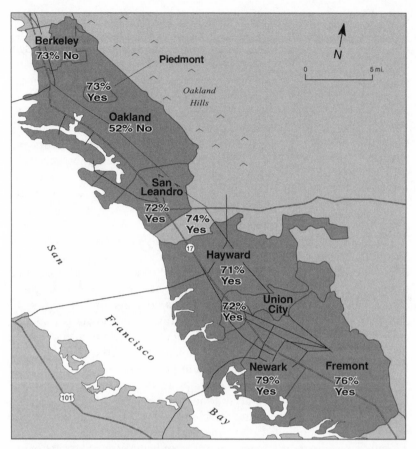

Map 8.1. Proposition 13 voting results in Alameda County, 1978. Suburban-ites in South County voted overwhelmingly in favor of property tax limitation. Only Berkeley, by 1978 one of the most liberal cities in the nation, and Oakland, in a close return, rejected the so-called tax revolt. Cartography Lab, University of Wisconsin.

(map 8.1). South County as a whole represented a Proposition 13 strong-hold. The tax revolt was engineered and led by political forces primarily from Southern California—Los Angeles and Orange County in particu-lar. But voters in southern Alameda County responded aggressively and with near unanimity. Alameda County residents made much less rhetori-cal noise in the months leading up to the election, but their votes spoke volumes in June. In Oakland proper, the vote reflected the broad class di-visions that had persisted in the city for decades. The hill regions voted with the rest of the state, approving Proposition 13 by nearly two to one.

In flatlands neighborhoods, overwhelmingly working-class African American and ethnic Mexican, voters rejected the measure by two to one.[55]

One of the most important contexts in which to understand Proposition 13 and the tax revolt, however, is not the *little* capital of homeownership but the *big* capital of California's corporate business sector. Over the decade preceding the June 1978 election, the share of California's total tax burden borne by individuals in the state had increased, while the share borne by business and industry had declined. This was not solely a product of the property tax legislation (A.B. 80) of the late 1960s, which reduced most business property taxes. It was equally a product of the evolution of other tax structures. The personal income tax, for instance, increased dramatically in California between 1950 and 1975, at a pace far ahead of increases in any comparable corporate taxes. Indeed, the per capita tax in the state increased ahead of income growth, placing individuals on a cycle of adjustment their corporate counterparts largely escaped. Proposition 13 accelerated this overall shift in the state's tax burden, despite the populist rhetoric employed by Jarvis and others. Nearly two-thirds of the property tax relief mandated by Proposition 13 went to businesses and landlords. In Fremont, for instance, Proposition 13 resulted in the reduction of the annual property tax load paid by General Motors from $3.8 million to 1.1 million, an astonishing loss of revenue for the city and a massive corporate subsidy. Between 1967 and 1979 the share of all state taxes borne by individuals increased from 54% to 72%; the share borne by businesses decreased from 46% to 28%. Thus, not only did Proposition 13 help to accelerate a shift in the distribution of public resources away from older, poorer cities like Oakland, it subsidized and masked a larger social redistribution of the tax burden, from corporate and business capital to people.[56]

This moment in late 1970s California revealed a crucial turn in the evolution of postwar political economy and popular politics in the nation. In the 1940s homeowners in California had entered into an epochal bargain with the federal state, industrial capital, and local officials, in which low taxes were promised in exchange for support of industrial growth. Industry "pays your taxes," as San Leandro boosters bragged in the 1950s. In cases like San Leandro, Fremont, and Milpitas, there was in the 1940s a populist sense that industry could be held responsible for paying a "fair share" of local taxes. When that bargain broke down, however, in part because of capitalist restructuring, homeowners rarely sought to hold corporate capital responsible. Instead, they responded to the shift in the state's tax burden onto their shoulders by staging a counterrevolution against the liberal state, its perceived "waste," and one segment of its beneficiaries, mostly poor and low-income people with historically minimal access to public social resources like education and health care.

Rather than turn their attention toward the immense private corporate and business economic sector, they participated in a revanchist politics defined by a withdrawal from civic and financial connections to older, troubled communities like Oakland.

A generation of homeowners who were among the most privileged in the history of the nation—and who, despite increases in property taxes in the 1970s, continued to benefit enormously from additions to their real wealth, embodied in their homes—engineered the political counterrevolution. Proposition 13 was a major turning point in the political narrative of California and the nation and a bookend to the story of this book—the other being the politics of the late 1940s. The tax revolt anticipated and laid the groundwork for the Reagan era in the national political culture and signaled a fundamental shift in the public's relationship to liberalism and the long legacy of the New Deal. In 1979, the year after Proposition 13, more than twenty other states passed property tax reform legislation or measures, as the tax revolt swept east. More than twenty states also passed income tax reductions. Ronald Reagan would make tax reductions at the federal level part of his broad indictment of government spending and the welfare state. The outcome of tax reform politics in 1978 underscores the centrality of class and racial segregation in the shaping of political interest and ideology in postwar California. Proposition 13 was made possible by more than an ideological turn in the state's electorate. It was made possible because postwar metropolitan development had subsidized segregation.

In Babylon, there was always the possibility of deliverance and rebirth. Yet African American radical and nationalist politics in the 1960s and 1970s were strongest at the level of the U.S. state system, municipal government, where mechanisms for political realization remained the weakest. Despite the Black Panther Party's enthusiasm for intercommunalism and its ambitious plans for socialism in one city, municipalities like Oakland are poor instruments for either revolutionary or social-democratic projects. The property tax can never act as the primary leverage for redistribution because the very survival of the city's institutions depends on it—overtaxed employers and industries simply flee to cities that will not burden them with high taxes. Moreover, the post–Proposition 13 environment in California rendered the property tax an even more unwieldy mechanism for progressive redistribution. Furthermore, the large-scale withdrawal of federal support for urban programs specifically and the welfare state generally in the 1970s and 1980s weakened cities' leverage in the national political economy even more. Black power had no real chance of instantiation at the city level other than in the limited nationalist actions—black capitalism, boycotts, and electing African American mayors and city councilmembers—that emerged as dominant strategies in the 1970s. These were not inconsequential—indeed, for many they were epochal in importance—but neither were they capable of forcing the sorts of transformations that people like Paul Cobb and Elaine Brown believed places like Oakland needed. The colonial analogy of urban black America, no matter its analytic utility, could thus only take its adherents so far in practical political economic terms.

The year between Lionel Wilson's election in 1977 and the Proposition 13 election in 1978 embodied the muted enthusiasms, complex ironies, and unanswered questions that mark historical transitions. The city's political regime had been overturned, and for the first time in two generations black Oaklanders and their allies had access to real municipal power. But Wilson did not look like the kind of leader who would emerge as the champion of a dramatically new politics—certainly not the sort of new politics that neighborhood activists had been articulating for a decade. Was his Panther support merely symbolic—a reflection of the capacity of middle-class black political leaders to capitalize on the rhetoric of black power radicalism without pursuing its substance—or the signal of progressivism? Other questions pressed with even greater intensity on veterans of black Oakland's political struggles. What did it mean for an African American–led municipal administration to be coming to power at exactly the historical moment when urban resources were approaching a postwar nadir—and when hostility to spending on cities in California was not merely a vague tendency but part of a major political movement, quite soon a national one? These questions lay not very far below the surface as Wilson completed his first year in office. Both the possibilities and the limitations seemed so real, so palpable to observes across the political spectrum that the entire situation seemed suspended, held in sort of liminal rest. Oaklanders who wanted to make a new city—indeed, a new history— struck out into this world with tentative apprehension, heirs to the social and political legacy of three decades of struggle over the fate of the East Bay metropolis.

Conclusion _____

THE STORY of this book ends at a poignant but ambivalent moment. The enormous costs of postwar metropolitan growth in the East Bay had become undeniable. "Those who govern American cities today face such terrible problems that no solutions seem achievable," wrote Paul Jacobs with more than a hint of defeatism.[1] But a new generation of political movements, from both the liberal left and the conservative right, sought to revive and reinvent the promise of California as a place of economic security and upward mobility. As they did so, they moved ever more explicitly into contention, framing a contest that took place not just across a political divide, but literally across the spaces produced by the postwar metropolis, the spaces of the nation. The story of that ongoing struggle after 1978 is another history. In what follows, I reflect back on the history I tell here and in doing so underscore the importance of the period between 1945 and the late 1970s as a coherent moment in twentieth-century America. Those three decades, the long postwar period, were defined by three major developments: the emergence, flowering, and retreat, under considerable opposition, of the century's major struggle for racial equality; the articulation of the New Deal welfare state into the fabric of urban life, economy, and politics; and a thirty-year suburban economic boom linked to a white middle-class-centered federal urban policy. As I have argued here, these three developments overlapped and shaped one another. They gave contour and definition to the period.[2]

What I have done in this book is to join these complicated narratives together on the terrain of political culture. The period's most compelling historical developments and lessons lie at that conjuncture. More specifically, the story of Oakland and the East Bay explored here opens onto four critical historical and historiographical issues in postwar U.S. history. In each case, my hope is that this book has helped to push our understandings and conceptions modestly in new directions.

The first issue is liberalism and the American welfare state. In the last decade and a half a scholarship has emerged that focuses on, in the words of one volume of essays, the "rise and fall of the New Deal order." This scholarship brackets the period between the late 1930s and the 1970s as the moment of the national welfare state's instantiation and subsequent erosion under a combination of attack from the right and the weight of its own programmatic and political limitations. The best of this scholarship has taken up the analytic task of asking how committed working- and middle-class whites, the New Deal state's principal beneficiaries, were to racial equality. The answer invariably is not very or not at all.

Continued work on this question is important, but new scholarship on the New Deal, the welfare state, and midcentury liberalism generally would also benefit from a more explicit engagement with African American history. As Dona Hamilton and Charles Hamilton have recently argued, national civil rights organizations maintained a "dual agenda" in the postwar decades: they fought for racial equality and consistently sought expansion of the welfare state and the social wage for all workers. Indeed, African Americans since the 1930s have been among the most vocal supporters of broad, multiracial social programs: from full employment and national health insurance to antipoverty programs, child care, and unemployment benefits. Black political leaders have maintained this dual agenda in part because black Americans have remained the group most excluded from the welfare state's protections and support.[3]

My work complements the Hamiltons' argument and proposes a modified framework for conceiving of the relationship between black-led political movements and the liberal welfare state of the three postwar decades. That welfare state needs to be understood expansively. Welfare, as contemporary political debates have defined it, suffers from a reductionism fueled by two decades of attacks on impoverished African Americans. "Welfare" has been reduced in this assault to a mere handful of programs, such as Aid to Families with Dependent Children, that involve direct transfer payments to poor people. Meanwhile, one of the largest federal welfare transfers in the nation remains the home mortgage deduction, an enormous subsidy to middle-class homeowners, the vast majority of whom are suburban and white. Historically, the national welfare state that emerged after World War II included social insurance programs (which included the precursor to AFDC), but also the massive federal housing program; labor law and its attendant collective bargaining apparatus; highway construction; urban renewal programs; the War on Poverty and other antipoverty efforts; and a variety of additional programs aimed at urban labor, housing, and property markets. These dimensions of the welfare state profoundly shaped postwar cities and suburbs, both structurally and politically. It would be hard to imagine postwar metropolitanization proceeding as it did without the national welfare state.[4]

Once we engage a broader, more historical view of the shape of this New Deal welfare state and its political coalition, two developments become clear. First, the long postwar African American struggle for racial equality represented in large part an engagement with and challenge to the deep racial inequities built into the welfare state and the political coalitions behind it. Black leaders pushed for fair employment and fair housing; for desegregation of the labor movement; for public housing; for an unbiased urban renewal program; for antipoverty efforts far more extensive than the Great Society's; and, ultimately, for federal investment in urban

America on a massive scale, what the National Urban League called a "Domestic Marshall Plan." All of these efforts were either responses to black exclusion from state programs or calls for shifts in the middle-class bias of the state's supports and subsidies. It is understandable that historical attention has focused on the civil rights struggle against legalized Jim Crow in education, public accommodation, and voting, and that research has concentrated on the principal national organizations, individuals, and places that carried that struggle forward. However, in doing so we have undertheorized and understudied an entire dimension of the postwar black struggle for racial equality—its complex, long-term, militant engagement with the national welfare state and the expression of that state on the ground in local urban and suburban places like Oakland and the East Bay. In the end, the American civil rights movement as a whole represented one of the world's most sustained political confrontations with the modern state apparatus.[5]

An additional point is clear as well. An urban political economy and welfare state framework for studying African American political struggle helps to explain shifts in ideology and strategy within the broad civil rights movement. The failure of fair employment laws, for instance, explains the shift to affirmative action. The failure of fair housing explains the shift to urban investment schemes. The failure of War on Poverty programs explains the shift to community empowerment and liberation as both practical and ideological positions. The spectacular growth of segregated suburbs under federal subsidy helps to explain the adoption of a colonial analogy of metropolitan America. In general, the failure of the liberal state, and liberalism as a political orientation, to secure black equality and to lift impoverished African Americans into a stable working class helps to explain the rise of self-determination and liberation politics among large sectors of the black population in the 1960s and 1970s. Urban political economy and welfare state deficiencies do not explain every dimension of postwar African American political movements, of course. However, that context is far more important to the evolution of black political movements than historians have to date suggested. We need more research on these dimensions, and more attention to theorizing these developments, as historical research on this period progresses.[6]

The second major issue has to do with how the 1960s are represented and conceived in American historiography, as well as within the national imagination. Dominant historiographical constructions of the 1960s persist in bifurcating the decade and either explicitly or implicitly treating the second half as a retreat from the legitimate reforms advanced in the first half. The second half of the 1960s represents in this view a period of chaos, violence, and withdrawal from the spirited liberal politics ascendant earlier in the decade. According to this interpretation, a descent into violence and the revolutionary turn of movement activism called forth state repression and marginalized the left within a decidedly liberal national civic culture. While not entirely inaccurate, this dominant interpretation is seriously flawed, in large part because it rests on the trajectory of two groups—Students for a Democratic Society and the Student Nonviolent Coordinating Committee—that stand for a more complex array of movements and politics. There is little argument that the fracturing of SDS made it a far less effective organization later in the decade. But to allow an SDS narrative to stand for movement activism in the period is to adopt uncritically the subjectivity of a small handful of white, middle-class, disillusioned male radicals. For its part, SNCC helped to win both local desegregation struggles as well as enormous legislative victories in 1964 and 1965 that are among the signal achievements of the postwar period. But to define the long civil rights movement in terms of SNCC objectives is to miss entirely the political trajectory of black-led urban reform and radical movements across the whole of the decade.[7]

Both the SDS and SNCC stories have encouraged an "optimism to disillusionment" paradigm for the decade. That there was enormous optimism among both the white new left and civil rights leaders in the early 1960s is without dispute. That many grew disillusioned between 1965 and 1968 is also undeniable. But to allow those facts to determine our critical purchase on movement activism or the period as a whole is to put on historical blinders. In particular, the "optimism to disillusionment" paradigm implicitly dismisses the enormous flowering of black political movements after 1965 across the nation and ignores the fundamental urban story of the period between 1965 and the middle 1970s: the rise of African American urban political power in dozens of American cities. Indeed, one could argue that despite the costly, destructive, and disheartening urban violence between 1964 and 1968, African American leaders and their urban constituents were *more* optimistic during and after that brief period than they had been in 1962 or 1963. They may have lost faith in the liberal promises and platitudes of early 1960s activism, but many reinvested that faith in the political rise of new urban coalitions led by African Americans. In addition, the rise of the black studies movement on college campuses, the emergence of internationalism among both black and white activists, and the extraordinary grassroots work that went into implementing the Voting Rights Act of 1965—post-1965 developments all—cannot be understood or accurately represented within our dominant conceptions of the decade.[8]

Oakland helps us to see the weaknesses of understanding the civil rights movement strictly in terms of a national narrative. That narrative traditionally begins with *Brown v. Board of Education* in 1954 and ends with passage of the Voting Rights Act of 1965. But such a narrative, however powerful and illustrative it may be of critical and defining moments in American politics and racial struggle, is incomplete. In the urban North and West, African American and white voters, activists, and politicians had been engaged in contests over property, housing, redevelopment, taxes, employment, and antipoverty programs since World War II. They continued to do so long after 1965. For Oaklanders, the Civil Rights Act of 1964 was profoundly important, but it did not mark a turning point—either a great victory after long struggle or a point when the movement fractured. Oaklanders in 1964 were far more concerned with fighting Proposition 14, with implementing the state's five-year-old fair employment law, with securing jobs on BART construction, and with building institutions and coalitions to attack poverty. It makes little sense to use either 1964 or 1965 to delineate their story, especially if that delineation is intended to mark one period as implicitly productive and pregnant with possibility and the other as implicitly a fall or a retreat.

A third interpretive issue follows closely on the one discussed above. The dichotomies that have traditionally divided the long postwar black liberation movement—civil rights versus black power, nonviolence versus violence, integration versus separatism—have proven so limiting as to be unhelpful in thorough understandings of the period. This is not to suggest that certain distinctions—as between Black Panther Party armed resistance and SNCC lunch-counter protests, for instance—are unimportant. Rather, it is to argue that raw dichotomies never, at virtually any moment, defined the actual philosophical choices activists and their constituencies faced or made. The political and ideological milieu of black struggle in the three decades after World War II was far more fluid and included far more complex and subtle choices than between supposed polar opposites. An essentially liberal bourgeois organization like the East Bay Democratic Club, for instance, entered into coalitions with whites based on power and organizing in all-black institutions and communities. A strict integration versus separation model or civil rights versus black power paradigm can hardly capture this organization's history. The Black Panther Party believed that black Americans constituted a nation, that international solidarity with a multiracial colonized world was essential, and that strategic alliances with anticolonial and even liberal whites were an appropriate, even necessary, step toward achieving their goals. None of these positions, and their simultaneity, can be understood if we deploy traditional dualist formulas.[9]

What is needed is a framework that emphasizes the interplay of region, ideology, and strategy. It is clear that regional and local political economies with their own cultural, political, and structural constraints presented unique and specific versions of segregation and discrimination. The postwar civil rights movement emerged within these regional and local contexts across the country. In each, leaders and constituencies responded to both the obstacles and opportunities those conditions presented. Certainly there were national strategies: calls for full employment and fair housing and fair employment laws at the national and state levels immediately after World War II; calls for antidiscrimination in the federal government's housing program; calls for massive urban investment and antipoverty programs in the 1960s; and so on. But the differences from city to city and from political context to political context are striking. Think of Detroit and the mobilizations by black radicals within UAW locals; Chicago with its disparate grassroots struggles for open housing in the context of a machine politics with large-scale black incorporation; New York City with its strong labor movement, influential left, and complicated interethnic and interborough politics; and Oakland with its War on Poverty mobilizations, the Black Panther Party, and the East Bay Democratic Club. The trajectories of struggle in each of these cases, and dozens of others, varied with the location of black strength within highly differentiated urban political economies. Their successes and failures, too, were largely (though not entirely) matters of local opportunities and barriers. In the end, my intention is not to suggest that the movement is too differentiated to produce a historical synthesis. Rather, it is to argue that we need more subtle regional and urban-centered paradigms to fill out a useful and accurate historical synthesis. And, we need to pay more attention to specific political ideologies and their relationship to practical political strategies.

A fourth and final issue centers on suburban growth and politics. More than a decade ago Kenneth Jackson's seminal work of suburban history argued that suburbanization should be understood as a consolidated form of consumption driven by two impulses. The first was the broad subsidizing of the American middle class by the federal government in the post-World War II decades. The second was the privatization of the public sphere in which suburban landscape architecture, detached single-family homes, and property-centered politics together accelerated the demise of public culture and a democratic commitment to communal responsibility. Like much of the recent new work on suburban history, this book stands in the shadow of Jackson's. As with civil rights, however, the history of postwar suburbanization must increasingly yield to approaches that judiciously combine local, regional, and national frameworks. But historians have to date understudied and undertheorized local municipal governments as important state actors. As I have noted here, "white flight" was less a flight than the complex and ideological process of state building within discrete spatial boundaries. Suburban Americans came to understand their interests, political obligations, and especially the limits of their social responsibility within those spatially bounded communities.

Race, rights, and taxes did not "emerge" in the 1960s in reaction to the fight for racial equality—they were always present as constitutive elements in the decades-long midcentury project of erecting suburban places as racially homogeneous property markets and arenas of conspicuous consumption.[10]

It is now commonplace to talk about the postwar United States in terms of urban decline and crisis. We possess an extensive popular and academic vocabulary to describe the features of post-1945 urban transformation: the racialization and deindustrialization of cities, suburban growth, urban decline, the weakening of unions and working-class consciousness, the increasing mobility of capital, and the rise of a politics focused on private property. That these processes victimized African American communities in the North and West more than white communities has been established. But there is a pressing need to move beyond the trope of the black ghetto and the paradigm of crisis and to theorize how African American communities responded—in creative, productive, and at times even halting and unsuccessful ways—to the structural changes brought on by migration and metropolitan reorganization. Further, we historians need to assess more thoroughly the enormous opposition these attempts encountered from the political right. In short, there is a pressing need to place the dynamics of African American political organizing and political ideology between the 1940s and the 1970s in the broader context of American urban and political history. At the same time, there is an equally pressing need to move beyond the trope of white flight to examine the process of suburban city-building and the instantiation of segregation in specific places. Looking at how the various spaces and political cultures of urban America were produced in the postwar decades in places like Oakland is one way to do this.

Appendix

Population, Housing, and Taxes

TABLE A.1
African American Population of Oakland, Berkeley, and Selected Cities in Southern
Alameda County, 1950–1980

	1940	1950	1960	1970	1980
Oakland	8,462	47,562	83,616	124,710	159,351
Berkeley	3,395	13,289	21,840	27,421	20,671
Alameda	249	5,312	3,127	1,869	2,663
San Leandro	5	20	17	84	907
Hayward	13	32	86	1,688	5,270
Union City	N/A	N/A	16	152	3,331
Fremont	N/A	N/A	18	397	3,384
Newark	N/A	N/A	1	185	1,147
Milpitas (Santa Clara Co.)	N/A	N/A	277	1,411	2,751

Sources: Calculated from U.S. Department of Commerce, Bureau of the Census, Census of Population, 1940, vol. 2, part 1 (Washington, DC, 1943); Census of Population, 1950, vol. 2, part 5 (Washington, DC, 1952); Census of the Population, 1960, vol. 1, part 6 (Washington, DC, 1963); Census of Population, 1970, vol. 1, part 6 (Washington, DC, 1972); Census of Population, 1980, vol. 1, part 6 (Washington, DC, 1982).

TABLE A.2
Population of Selected Alameda County Cities, 1950–1980

	1940	1950	1960	1970	1980
Oakland	302,163	384,575	367,548	361,607	339,337
Berkeley	85,547	113,805	111,268	116,691	103,328
Alameda	36,256	64,430	63,855	70,952	63,852
Fremont	N/A	N/A	43,790	100,875	131,945
Hayward	N/A	14,272	72,700	93,165	94,167
Newark	N/A	N/A	9,884	27,125	32,167
San Leandro	14,601	27,542	65,962	68,698	63,952
Union City	N/A	N/A	6,618	14,724	39,406

Sources: See table A.1.

TABLE A.3
Spanish Surname Population of Selected Cities in Alameda
County

	1970	1980
Oakland	35,372	32,133
Berkeley	6,429	5,177
Alameda	6,972	5,202
Fremont	16,566	18,364
Hayward	18,925	19,160
Newark	6,069	6,631
San Leandro	12,811	8,307
Union City	6,708	10,908

Sources: Census of Population, 1970, vol. 1, part 6; Census
of Population, 1980, vol. 1, part 6.

TABLE A.4
Property Taxes and Revenue in San Leandro, 1949–1972 (in 1972 dollars)

Fiscal Year	Net Assessed Value (in millions)	Tax Rate per $100	Tax Revenue (in millions)
1949–1950	$46.1	$1.86	$0.857
1951–1952	$48.7	$1.75	$0.853
1953–1954	$65.8	$1.68	$1.10
1955–1956	$115.3	$1.39	$1.60
1957–1958	$138.7	$1.27	$1.75
1959–1960	$173.6	$1.22	$2.11
1961–1962	$195.7	$1.18	$2.30
1963–1964	$213.1	$1.15	$2.44
1965–1966	$243.1	$1.07	$2.60
1967–1968	$260.0	$0.99	$2.60
1969–1970	$298.0	$0.95	$2.83
1971–1972	$275.7	$0.86	$2.37

Source: Adapted from Philip J. Bona, Residential Development Analysis of Seventeen
Acres in the City of San Leandro, California (San Leandro, 1977).

TABLE A.5
Municipal Property Tax Levies (per $100 of assessed value)

Fiscal Year	Oakland	San Leandro	Fremont
1957–1958	2.35	1.27	0.73
1959–1960	2.91	1.18	0.83
1961–1962	2.86	1.14	0.98
1963–1964	3.15	1.11	1.01
1965–1966	3.07	1.05	1.24
1967–1968	3.07	0.97	1.20
1969–1970	2.77	0.93	1.27
1971–1972	2.74	0.86	1.30

Source: Alameda Country, "California Tax Rates, Fiscal Year," papers of the Auditor of Alameda County, Bancroft Library, University of California, Berkeley.

TABLE A.6
Combined Tax Rates: Includes City, County, School, District Levies (per $100 of assessed value)

Fiscal Year	Oakland	Berkeley	San Leandro	Fremont	Hayward
1958–1959	8.09	7.63	7.50	7.26	9.50
1962–1963	10.05	9.94	8.06	8.80	9.90
1966–1967	11.78	13.38	9.24	12.07	11.65
1968–1969	12.23	14.40	9.51	12.30	12.26
1969–1970	11.80	13.46	8.74	11.59	11.52
1970–1971	12.76	15.49	9.62	12.81	12.53

Source: See table A.5.

TABLE A.7
Median Home Values, 1950–1980 (in 1980 dollars), and Percent Increase over
Previous Decade

City	1950	1960	1970	1980
Alameda	n/a	$41,900	$55,600 (33%)	$99,600 (79%)
Berkeley	$42,000	46,200 (10%)	56,467 (22%)	96,400 (71%)
Castro Valley[a]	n/a	47,300	57,900 (22%)	94,700 (63%)
Fremont	n/a	43,700	52,000 (19%)	93,000 (79%)
Hayward	n/a	43,100	48,000 (11%)	77,400 (61%)
Milpitas	n/a	40,000	49,700 (24%)	91,500 (84%)
Newark	n/a	37,800	49,000 (30%)	86,800 (77%)
Oakland	35,900	39,500 (10%)	45,200 (14%)	66,600 (47%)
San Leandro	40,000	42,500 (6%)	50,500 (19%)	96,400 (91%)
San Lorenzo[a]	n/a	41,500	48,600 (17%)	77,600 (60%)
Union City	n/a	n/a	51,600	90,100 (75%)

Sources: *Census of Housing, 1950*, vol. 1, part 2; *Census of Housing, 1960*, vol. 1, part
2; *Census of Housing, 1970*, vol. 1, part 6; *Census of Detailed Housing Characteristics,
1980*, vol. 1, part 6.
[a] Unincorporated

TABLE A.8
Homeownership Rate, 1950–1980 (as percent of total housing units)

	1950	1960	1970	1980
California	54	58	55	56
Alameda	39	44	38	41
Berkeley	48	44	35	38
Castro Valley[a]	n/a	81	70	69
Fremont	n/a	82	75	66
Hayward	65	75	56	55
Milpitas	n/a	n/a	79	72
Newark	n/a	n/a	76	77
Oakland	49	47	42	43
San Leandro	76	77	66	62
San Lorenzo[a]	n/a	92	86	82
Union City	n/a	n/a	74	68

Sources: See table A.7.
[a] Unincorporated

Notes

Manuscript Collection Abbreviations

California Federation for Civic Unity Records, 1945–1956, Bancroft Library, University of California, Berkeley (CFCU)

Central Labor Council of Alameda County Collection, Labor Archives and Research Center, San Francisco State University (CLCAC/LARC)

C. L. Dellums Papers, Bancroft Library, University of California, Berkeley (Dellums Papers)

Cyprus Freeway Oral History Project, Anthropological Studies Center, Sonoma State University (ASC Oral History)

Institute of Governmental Studies, University of California, Berkeley (IGS)

Oakland Chamber of Commerce, held at the Institute of Governmental Studies, University of California, Berkeley (OCC/IGS)

United Autoworkers Collection, Fair Practices Section, Archives of Labor and Urban Affairs, Wayne State University (UAW/ALUA)

William Byron Rumford Papers, 1950–1966, Bancroft Library, University of California, Berkeley (Rumford Papers)

William F. Knowland Collection, Bancroft Library, University of California, Berkeley (WFK)

Newspaper Abbreviations

Black Panther (BP)
California Voice (CV)
East Bay Labor Journal (EBLJ)
East Oakland Times (EOT)
Fremont Argus (FA)
Fremont News Register (FNR)
Hayward Daily Review (HDR)
Labor Herald, San Francisco (LH)
Milpitas Post (MP)
Montclarion, Oakland (MT)
New York Times (NYT)
Oakland Post (OP)
Oakland Tribune (OT)
People's World, San Francisco (PW)
San Francisco Chronicle (SFC)
San Francisco Examiner (SFE)
San Jose Mercury News (SJMN)
San Leandro Morning News (SLMN)
San Leandro News-Observer (SLNO)
San Leandro Reporter (SLR)
Union City Leader (UCL)
Wall Street Journal (WSJ)

Introduction

1. Few historical studies have examined urban and suburban political movements together. On the Black Panther Party, see Charles E. Jones, ed., *The Black Panther Party Reconsidered* (Baltimore, 1998); Kathleen Cleaver and George Katsiaficas, eds., *Liberation, Imagination, and the Black Panther Party: A New Look at the Panthers and Their Legacy* (New York, 2001). For recent work on California suburban politics, see Lisa McGirr, *Suburban Warriors: The Origins of the New American Right* (Princeton, 2001); Becky Nicolaides, *My Blue Heaven: Life and Politics in the Working Class Suburbs of Los Angeles, 1920–1965* (Chicago, 2002). Neither deals with the tax revolt of 1978. For that, see David O. Sears and Jack Citrin, *Tax Revolt: Something for Nothing in California* (Cambridge, MA, 1982).

2. On ghetto formation, see Kenneth L. Kusmer, *A Ghetto Takes Shape: Black Cleveland, 1870–1930*; Arnold Hirsch, *Making the Second Ghetto: Race and Housing in Chicago, 1940–1960* (New York, 1983).

3. On the processes of metropolitanization, see Kenneth Jackson, *Crabgrass Frontier: The Suburbanization of the United States* (New York, 1985); Carl Abbott, *The Metropolitan Frontier: Cities in the Modern American West* (Tucson, 1993); Greg Hise, *Magnetic Los Angeles: Planning the Twentieth-Century Metropolis* (Baltimore, 1997). On the break with liberalism among African Americans, see Robert L. Allen, *Black Awakening in Capitalist America: An Analytic History* (New York, 1969); Stokeley Carmichael and Charles V. Hamilton, *Black Power: The Politics of Liberation in America* (New York, 1967).

4. For a related political struggle, see Joshua B. Freeman, *Working-Class New York: Life and Labor since World War II* (New York, 2000).

5. Mark Gelfand, *A Nation of Cities: The Federal Government and Urban America, 1933–1965* (New York, 1975); Barry Bluestone and Bennett Harrison, *The Deindustrialization of America: Plant Closings, Community Abandonment, and the Dismantling of Basic Industry* (New York, 1982); Susan S. Fainstein and Norman I. Fainstein, "Economic Change, National Policy, and the System of Cities," in Susan S. Fainstein et al., eds., *Restructuring the City: The Political Economy of Urban Redevelopment* (New York, 1987); Robert O. Self and Thomas J. Sugrue, "The Power of Place: Race, Political Economy, and Identity in the Postwar Metropolis," in Roy Rosenzweig and Jean-Christophe Agnew, eds., *A Companion to Post-1945 America* (Cambridge, MA, 2002).

6. For comparisons with other midcentury African American communities and political cultures, see Robin D. G. Kelley, *Race Rebels: Culture, Politics, and the Black Working Class* (New York, 1994); Wendell Pritchett, *Brownsville, Brooklyn: Blacks, Jews, and the Changing Face of the Ghetto* (Chicago, 2002); Martha Biondi, *To Stand and Fight: The Civil Rights Movement in Postwar New York City* (Cambridge, MA, 2003).

7. "It's an Amazing New West," 1946, 2–3, Oakland Chamber of Commerce, held at the Institute for Governmental Studies, University of California, Berkeley (hereafter OCC/IGS).

8. *Oakland Cultural Heritage Survey: Fruitvale Neighborhood Revitalization Area Survey*, vol. 34A (Oakland, 1993), 8–18.

9. *The Metropolitan Oakland Area* (Oakland, c. 1935).

10. Ebenezer Howard, *Garden Cities of To-morrow* (London, 1898); Hise, *Magnetic Los Angeles*, 6; Robert Fishman, *Urban Utopias in the Twentieth Century* (New York, 1977).

11. American Social History Project, *Who Built America? Working People and the Nation's Economy, Politics, Culture, and Society* (New York, 1992); Jonathan Birnbaum and Clarence Taylor, *Civil Rights since 1787: A Reader on the Black Struggle* (New York, 2000). See, among many others, Harvard Sitkoff, *The Struggle for Black Equality, 1954–1980* (New York, 1981); Aldon D. Morris, *The Origins of the Civil Rights Movement: Black Communities Organizing for Change* (New York, 1984); Jack M. Bloom, *Class, Race, and the Civil Rights Movement* (Bloomington, 1987); John Dittmer, *Local People: The Struggle for Civil Rights in Mississippi* (Urbana, 1994); Patricia Sullivan, *Days of Hope: Race and Democracy in the New Deal Era* (Chapel Hill, 1996). For narratives of the civil rights movement, see Clayborne Carson, *In Struggle: SNCC and the Black Awakening of the 1960s* (Cambridge, MA, 1981); Bloom, *Class, Race, and the Civil Rights Movement*; Taylor Branch, *Pillar of Fire: America in the King Years, 1963–65* (New York, 1998).

12. For examples of recent work, see William J. Grimshaw, *Bitter Fruit: Black Politics and the Chicago Machine, 1931–1991* (Chicago, 1992); Gretchen Lemke-Santangelo, *Abiding Courage: African American Migrant Women and the East Bay Community* (Chapel Hill, 1996); Kenneth Goings and Raymond A. Mohl, eds., *The New African American Urban History* (Thousand Oaks, CA, 1996); Gerald Horne, *The Fire This Time: The Watts Uprising and the 1960s* (New York, 1997); Komozi Woodard, *A Nation within a Nation: Amiri Baraka (LeRois Jones) and Black Power Politics* (Chapel Hill, 1999); Robin D. G. Kelley and Betsy Esch, "Black Like Mao: Red China and Black Revolution," *Souls* (Fall 1999): 6–41; Yohuru Williams, *Black Politics/White Power: Civil Rights, Black Power, and the Black Panthers in New Haven* (New York, 2000); Eric Arnesen, *Brotherhoods of Color: Black Railroad Workers and the Struggle for Equality* (Cambridge, MA, 2001); Peniel Joseph, "Black Liberation without Apology: Reconceptualizing the Black Power Movement," *The Black Scholar: Journal of Black Studies and Research* 31 (Fall/Winter 2001): 3–20; Kevin Gaines, "The Historiography of the Struggle for Black Equality since 1945," in Rosenzweig and Agnew, eds., *A Companion to Post-1945 America*.

13. Rob Kling, Spencer Olin, and Mark Poster, eds., *Postsuburban California: The Transformation of Orange County since World War II* (Berkeley, 1991); Bruce Schulman, *From Cotton Belt to Sunbelt: Federal Policy, Economic Development and the Transformation of the South, 1938–1980* (New York, 1990); Roger Lotchin, *Fortress California, 1910–1961: From Warfare to Welfare* (New York, 1992); Fraser and Gary Gerstle, eds., *The Rise and Fall of the New Deal Order* (Princeton, 1989); John H. Mollenkopf, *The Contested City* (Princeton, 1983).

14. Allen, *Black Awakening in Capitalist America*; Bayard Rustin, *Down the Line: The Collected Writings of Bayard Rustin* (Chicago, 1971); Timothy Tyson, *Radio Free Dixie: Robert F. Williams and the Roots of Black Power* (Chapel Hill, 1999).

15. Thomas J. Sugrue, *The Origins of the Urban Crisis: Race and Inequality in Postwar Detroit* (Princeton, 1996); Hirsch, *Making the Second Ghetto*.

16. For guides to African American engagement with urban social inequality, see Martin Luther King, Jr., *Where Do We Go from Here?* (New York, 1967); Whitney Young, *Beyond Racism: Building an Open Society* (New York, 1969); Floyd Barbour, *The Black Seventies* (Boston, 1970); Theodore Cross, *The Black Power Imperative: Racial Inequality and the Politics of Nonviolence* (New York, 1987); Thomas F. Jackson, "Recasting the Dream: Martin Luther King, Jr., African American Political Thought and the Third Reconstruction, 1955–1968" (Ph.D. diss., Stanford University, 1995); Dona Cooper Hamilton and Charles V. Hamilton, *The Dual Agenda: The African American Struggle for Civil and Economic Equality* (New York, 1997).

17. On urban liberalism, see Freeman, *Working-Class New York*; Mollenkopf, *The Contested City*; Harriet Nath and Stanley Scott, eds., *Experiment and Change in Berkeley: Essay on City Politics, 1950–1975* (Berkeley, 1978); Ira Katznelson, *City Trenches: Urban Politics and the Patterning of Class in the United States* (Chicago, 1981); Chester Hartman, *The Transformation of San Francisco* (New York, 1984).

18. *BP*, 6 April 1969.

19. On Babylon as a metaphor and political referent, see Cleaver and Katsiaficas, eds., *Liberation, Imagination, and the Black Panther Party*; William L. Van DeBurg, *New Day in Babylon: The Black Power Movement and American Culture, 1965–1975* (Chicago, 1992).

20. AnnaLee Saxenian, *Regional Advantage: Culture and Competition in Silicon Valley and Route 128* (Cambridge, MA, 1994); John Findlay, *Magic Lands: Western Cityscapes and American Culture after 1940* (Berkeley, 1992); Richard A. Walker, "The Playground of U.S. Capitalism? The Political Economy of the San Francisco Bay Area in the 1980s," in Mike Davis et al., eds., *Fire in the Hearth* (London, 1990), 3–82; Charles Wollenberg, *Golden Gate Metropolis: Perspectives on Bay Area History* (Berkeley, 1985).

21. On twentieth-century suburban forms, see Nicolaides, *My Blue Heaven*; Hise, *Magnetic Los Angeles*; Jon C. Teaford, *City and Suburb: The Political Fragmentation of Metropolitan America, 1850–1970* (Baltimore, 1979); Robert Fishman, *Bourgeois Utopias: The Rise and Fall of Suburbia* (New York, 1987); Evan McKenzie, *Privatopia: Homeowners Associations and the Rise of Residential Private Government* (New Haven, 1994); Richard Longstreth, *City Center to Regional Mall: Architecture, the Automobile, and Retailing in Los Angeles, 1920–1950* (Cambridge, MA, 1997).

22. On maximizing markets, see Sharon Zukin, *Landscapes of Power: From Detroit to Disney World* (Berkeley, 1991); Paul E. Peterson, *City Limits* (Chicago, 1981); David Harvey, *The Urban Experience* (London, 1982); Ira Katznelson, *Marxism and the City* (New York, 1993).

23. Mark Gottendiener, *The Social Production of Urban Space* (Austin, 1985); Marshall Berman, *All That Is Solid Melts into Air: The Experience of Modernity* (New York, 1981).

24. David Harvey, *Justice, Nature, and the Geography of Difference* (Cambridge, MA, 1997).

25. I am not endorsing an older, Chicago School spatial functionalism. Rather, I am interested in preserving the notion that people's cognitive spatial maps of place are important to how they conceive of political interest and ideology. There are few good studies of this, but none is better than George Chauncey, *Gay New York: Gender, Urban Culture, and the Making of the Gay Male World, 1890–1940* (New York, 1994). See also Jane Jacobs, *The Death and Life of Great American Cities* (New York, 1961); St. Clair Drake and Horace A. Cayton, *Black Metropolis: A Study of Negro Life in a Northern City* (New York, 1945); Michael, J. Dear, ed., *From Chicago to L.A.: Making Sense of Urban Theory* (Thousand Oaks, CA, 2002).

Chapter 1
Industrial Garden

1. Thomas J. McCormick, *America's Half-Century: United States Foreign Policy in the Cold War* (Baltimore, 1989); Eric Johnston, *America Unlimited* (Garden City, NJ, 1944).

2. On social processes and politics mediating between markets and place, see Karl Polanyi, *The Great Transformation* (Boston, 1957); Joseph Schumpeter, *Capitalism, Socialism, and Democracy* (New York, 1942).

3. Robert A. Beauregard, *Voices of Decline: The Postwar Fate of U.S. Cities* (Cambridge, MA, 1993); Robert M. Fogelson, *Downtown: Its Rise and Fall, 1880–1950* (New Haven, 2001). A biracial model is inadequate as a guide to the full range of racial politics in California. For studies that compare the axes of discrimination of African Americans, ethnic Mexicans, and Asian Americans, see George Sánchez, *Becoming Mexican American: Ethnicity, Culture, and Identity in Chicano Los Angeles, 1900–1945* (New York, 1993); David Gutiérrez, *Walls and Mirrors: Mexican Americans, Mexican Immigrants, and the Politics of Ethnicity* (Berkeley, 1995); Henry Yu, *Thinking Orientals: Migration, Contact, and Exoticism in Modern America* (New York, 2001); Stephen Pitti, *The Devil in Silicon Valley: Northern California, Race, and Mexican Americans* (Princeton, 2003); Mae Ngai, *Impossible Subjects: Illegal Aliens and the Making of Modern America* (Princeton, 2003).

4. These ideas are informed by Leo Marx, *The Machine in the Garden: Technology and the Pastoral Ideal in America* (New York, 1964). See also Roger Lotchin, *Fortress California, 1910–1961: From Warfare to Welfare* (New York, 1992), 3–8; Mel Scott, *The San Francisco Bay Area: A Metropolis in Perspective* (Berkeley, 1959), 224–25. For earlier promotional efforts in Southern California, see Tom Sitton and William Deverell, eds., *Metropolis in the Making: Los Angeles in the 1920s* (Berkeley, 2001); Oakland Chamber of Commerce, "Industrial Facts about Oakland and Alameda County California," 1935, 11, IGS (hereafter OCC/IGS); "The Natural Industrial Center of the West," 1937, OCC/IGS, "Fame of Industrial and Residential Oakland Told to Nation," *Oakland Tribune 1926 Year Book* (hereafter *OT/1926/YB*), 71; "Oakland and Eastbay Area Gain National Recognition," *OT/1927/YB*, 8–10; Oakland Postwar Planning Committee, "Oakland's Formula for the Future," 1945, IGS; "Ad Campaign Is Metropolitan Oakland Plan," *OT*, 29 October 1936; "Greater Oakland Luncheon Theme,"

OT, 18 August 1945; "Oakland Trade Growth Shown," *OT*, 17 October 1946; "Oakland Chamber of Commerce Important Factor in Coordinating Progressive Forces of City and Eastbay," in *OT/1928/YB*, 143; "Important Facts Concerning the Eastbay's Matchless Climate," in *OT/1933/YB*, 16.

5. Fogelson, *Downtown*, 218–48; Paul F. Wendt, *The Dynamics of Central City Land Values: Oakland and San Francisco, 1950–1960* (Berkeley, 1961).

6. Marilynn S. Johnson, *The Second Gold Rush: Oakland and the East Bay in World War II* (Berkeley, 1993), 13–29; Edgard J. Hinkel and William E. McCann, eds., *Oakland, California, 1852–1938: Some Phases of the Social, Political, and Economic History*, 2 vols. (Oakland, 1939); Beth Bagwell, *Oakland: The Story of a City* (Novato, CA, 1982), 38–39, 56, 80–83, 156; "Industrial Empire," in *OT/1946/YB*, 7–13; "Industry Has Growing Pains," in *OT/1945/YB*, 17–20.

7. "Help Us Build a Bigger, Better Oakland" and "At Your Service," *OT/1945/YB*, 53–54. See Johnson, *The Second Gold Rush*, 30–34, 60–67; Bagwell, *Oakland*, 80–83; Gerald Nash, *World War II and the West: Reshaping the Economy* (Lincoln, NE, 1990), 41–66; Charles Wollenberg, *Marinship at War: Shipbuilding and Social Change in Wartime Sausalito* (Berkeley, 1990); Hise, *Magnetic Los Angeles*.

8. Jackson, *Crabgrass Frontier*; Gayle Montgomery, interview with author, 2 September 1997, Walnut Creek, CA; "Industry Has Growing Pains," 17–20; Postwar Development Department, Oakland Chamber of Commerce, "Help Us Build a Bigger, Better Oakland"; *1943 Oakland City Directory*.

9. David Harvey, *The Urban Experience* (Baltimore, 1985); Marc Weiss, *The Rise of the Community Builders: The American Real Estate Industry and Land Planning* (New York, 1987).

10. "It's an Amazing New West," 1946, 2–3, OCC/IGS. For a discussion of the cultural foundations of the industrial garden, see Lewis Mumford, *The City in History: Its Origins, Its Transformations, and Its Prospects* (New York, 1961).

11. "How to Win the Markets of the New West," 1948, 39–43, OCC/IGS; "It's an Amazing New West," 29; John Rennie Short, "Urban Imagineers: Boosterism and the Representation of Cities," in Andrew E. G. Jonas and David Wilson, eds., *The Urban Growth Machine: Critical Perspectives Two Decades Later* (Albany, 1999).

12. "It's an Amazing New West," 43; "Industrial Empire of the West," in *OT/1948/YB*, 19–25; "How to Win the Markets of the New West," 5; "Why They Chose the Metropolitan Oakland Area of California: Facts That Led National Industries to Locate Branch Plants in Alameda County, California," 1951, 9, OCC/IGS; *Oakland Cultural Heritage Survey: Fruitvale Neighborhood Commercial Revitalization Area Survey* (Oakland, 1993) 9, IGS.

13. Elaine Tyler May, *Homeward Bound: American Families in the Cold War Era* (New York, 1988); Joanne Meyerwitz, ed., *Not June Cleaver: Women and Gender in Postwar America, 1945–1960* (Philadelphia, 1994).

14. Hise, *Magnetic Los Angeles*; Joseph Arnold, *The New Deal and the Suburbs: A History of the Greenbelt Town Program, 1935–1954* (Columbus, 1971); Christine M. Boyer, *Dreaming the Rational City: The Myth of American City Planning* (Cambridge, 1983).

15. See the excellent description of the prewar arguments for a new kind of housing market in Adam Rome, *The Bulldozer in the Countryside: Suburban Sprawl and the Rise of American Environmentalism* (New York, 2001), 15–43, and Hise, *Magnetic Los Angeles*, 14–55.

16. See Scott, *The San Francisco Bay Area*; Jon C. Teaford, *The Rough Road to Renaissance: Urban Revitalization in America, 1940–1985* (Baltimore, 1990). For San Francisco's postwar plans, see Hartman, *The Transformation of San Francisco*. For the deeper Silicon Valley story, see Findlay, *Magic Lands*; Saxenian, *Regional Advantage*.

17. Oakland City Planning Commission, "The Oakland Civic Center and Lake Merritt Improvement: A Unit of the Oakland Master Plan," 1947, 12; "Land Use Inventory of the Light and Heavy Industrial Zones, Oakland, California," 1945, 1; "Oakland General Plan," 1959, IGS. See also "3 Groups Back Bond Issue Plan," *OT*, 28 March 1945; *Oakland Outlook*, 26 April 1947.

18. William Issel, "New Deal and World War II Origins of San Francisco's Postwar Political Culture," in Roger Lotchin, ed., *The Way We Really Were: Everyday Life in California during World War II* (Urbana, 1999); "Industrial Facts about Oakland and Alameda County, California," 1935, and "The Natural Industrial Center of the West," 1937, OCC/IGS; *LH*, 28 August 1951.

19. Gwendolyn Wright, *Building the Dream: A Social History of Housing in America* (Cambridge, MA, 1981); Harvey Molotch, *The Contested City* (Princeton, 1983). For discussions of Keynesianism as it relates to industrial economic growth, see Barry Bluestone and Bennett Harrison, *The Deindustrialization of America: Plant Closings, Community Abandonment, and the Dismantling of Basic Industry* (New York, 1982), 133.

20. *SFE*, 6 December 1946; *Contra Costa Labor Journal*, 6 December 1946.

21. Wolman, "The Oakland General Strike of 1946," 150; *EBLJ*, 2 November 1945; 1 February, 29 March, 6 September 1946; Moody, *An Injury to All*, 1–40. See Arthur F. McClure, *The Truman Administration and the Problems of Postwar Labor, 1945–1948* (Rutherford, NJ, 1969), and Elizabeth Fones-Wolf, *Selling Free Enterprise: The Business Assault on Labor and Liberalism, 1945–1960* (Urbana, 1994).

22. Chris Rhomberg, "Collective Actors and Urban Regimes: Class Formation and the 1946 Oakland General Strike," *Theory and Society* 24 (1995): 578–80; *EBLJ*, 12 and 15 March 1946, 19 April 1946, 26 April 1946.

23. *EBLJ*, 15 and 29 November 1946; *SFC*, 16 August 1969; Wolman, "The Oakland General Strike of 1946"; Frank Douma, "The Oakland General Strike" (master's thesis, University of California, 1951); Stan Weir, "American Labor on the Defensive: A 1940s Odyssey," *Radical America* (July–August 1975): 163–186; George Lipsitz, *Rainbow at Midnight: Labor and Culture in the 1940s* (Urbana, 1994); Rhomberg, "Collective Action and Urban Regimes," 567–94.

24. Johnson, "Mobilizing the Homefront," 357; Rhomberg, "Collective Action and Urban Regimes," 580–82; Wolman, "The Oakland General Strike of 1946," 154.

25. "The Oakland General Strike of 1946: Interviews with Participants," Pacific Radio Archives, North Hollywood, California, tape reference number AZ0049.

26. Worker quoted by Philip J. Wolman, "The Oakland General Strike of 1946," *Historical Society of Southern California* 57 (1975): 167.

27. Wolman, "The Oakland General Strike of 1946," 152–53; Gayle Montgomery and James W. Johnson, *One Step from the White House: The Rise and Fall of Senator William F. Knowland* (Berkeley, 1998).

28. For labor's embrace of postwar growth liberalism, see Kevin Boyle, *The UAW and the Heyday of American Liberalism, 1945–1968* (Ithaca, 1995).

29. Fred Stripp, "The Treatment of Negro-American Workers by the AFL and the CIO in the San Francisco Bay Area," *Social Forces* 28 (March 1950): 330–32; Louise Berman, "The Central Labor Council of Alameda County, AFL-CIO" (Berkeley, 1964, mimeographed); Johnson, *The Second Gold Rush*, 60–82; Johnson, "Mobilizing the Homefront," 347–50.

30. Katznelson, *City Trenches*.

31. Hinkel and McCann, eds., *Oakland, California*, 368.

32. Interviews with Ben Albanese, Angela Albanese Cosy, Dewey Bargiacchi, and Glenn King conducted by Sonoma State University Anthropological Studies Center (ASC) for the Cypress Freeway Replacement Project, CALTRANS, District 4, transcript held by Anthropological Studies Center (hereafter ASC Oral History); interviews with Manuel Fernandez and Nick Petris, in Bill Jersey, ed., *West Oakland Oral History Interviews: Index to and Partial Transcripts of Interview on Videotape* (Oakland, 1995), Oakland History Room, Oakland Public Library (hereafter WO Oral History).

33. Interview with Manuel Fernandez, p. 54; interview #36-B, 18 July 1969, Oakland Project Interviews, IGS; "Citizens Look at Their City," 7.

34. For a sampling of the literature and debate around whiteness in this and earlier periods, see the special issue, "Scholarly Controversy: Whiteness and the Historians' Imagination," *International Labor and Working Class History* 60 (October 2001): 1–92.

35. Interview #39-C, 21 July 1969, Oakland Project Interviews, IGS.

36. For the significance of "Okie" subculture in Depression-era California, see James N. Gregory, *American Exodus: The Dust Bowl Migration and Okie Culture in California* (New York, 1989).

37. Bureau of the Census, *Sixteenth Census of the United States, 1940* (Washington, DC, 1943), vol. 3, part 2; Bureau of the Census, *Seventeenth Census of the United States, 1950* (Washington, DC, 1952), vol. 2, part 5.

38. Bureau of the Census, *Sixteenth Census of the United States, 1940*, vol. 3, part 2; Bureau of the Census, *Seventeenth Census of the United States, 1950*, vol. 2, part 5.

39. Bureau of the Census, *Special Reports, Characteristics of the Population, Labor Force, Families, and Housing: San Francisco Bay Congested Production Area* (Washington, DC, April 1944), 14; Johnson *The Second Gold Rush*, 42–43.

40. On working-class populism in this era, see Lizabeth Cohen, *Making a New Deal: Industrial Workers in Chicago, 1919–1939* (New York, 1990); and Michael Kazin, *The Populist Persuasion: An American History* (New York, 1995). On the racialized dimensions of this white working-class populism, see Kelley, *Race Rebels: Culture, Politics, and the Black Working Class* (New York, 1994).

41. Cy Record, "Willie Stokes at the Golden Gate," *Crisis* (June 1949): 175–79.

42. Bureau of the Census, *Characteristics of the Population*, 8; Bureau of the Census, *Census of Population: 1950*, 262; Edward Everett France, "Some Aspects of the Migration of the Negro to the San Francisco Bay Area Since 1940" (Ph.D. diss., University of California, Berkeley, 1962).

43. C. L. Dellums, *International President of the Brotherhood of Sleeping Car Porters and Civil Rights Leader: Oral History Transcript* (Berkeley, 1973), 101 (hereafter Dellums/OH); President's Fair Employment Practice Committee, *Key System and Division 192, Amalgamated Association of Street, Electric Railway and Motor Coach Employees of America, Hearings Held in Oakland, California* (Washington, DC, 1945), 115 (hereafter FEPC Hearings).

44. FEPC Hearings, 276; Dellums/OH, 101–3.

45. Interview with Royal Towns, ASC Oral History, 4.

46. Dellums quoted in letter to A. Philip Randolph, 13 May 1940, Carton 4, Dellums Papers; interviews with Royal Towns and Arthur Patterson, ASC Oral History. See also Paul Cobb, interview with author, 20 August 1997, Oakland; Joe Johnson, interview with author, 21 August 1997, Oakland; Johnson, *The Second Gold Rush*, 97–103.

47. Dellums quoted in Joyce Henderson, comp., *Transcript of Interview with Cottrell Lawrence Dellums, International President of the Brotherhood of Sleeping Car Porters and Civil Rights Leader* (Berkeley: Earl Warren Oral History Project, Bancroft Library, 1973); interview with Arthur Patterson; author interview with Norvel Smith.

48. Interview with Royal Towns, ASC Oral History, 4; interview with Robert Edwards, ASC Oral History; interview with Tippy Alexander Jones, WO Oral History, 424.

49. Interviews with Royal Towns, Arthur Patterson, Cleophus Williams, Clarence Oldwine, Norman Joseph Bradley, and Willie B. Jackson, ASC Oral History.

50. Richard Dalfiume, *Fighting on Two Fronts: Desegregation of the Armed Forces, 1939–1953* (Columbia, MO, 1969); Beth Bailey and David Farber, "The 'Double-V Campaign and World War II Hawaii: African Americans, Racial Ideology, and Federal Power," *Journal of Social History* 26 (Summer 1993); Kevin Gaines, *Uplifting the Race: Black Leadership, Politics, and Culture in the Twentieth Century* (Chapel Hill, 1996).

51. Stripp, "The Treatment of Negro-American Workers"; Broussard, *Black San Francisco*, 156–57; Joe Johnson, interview with author; Paul Cobb, interview with author; interview with Royal Towns, ASC Oral History.

52. Johnson, *The Second Gold Rush*, 83–111; Lemke-Santangelo, *Abiding Courage*; *West Oakland Oral History*, 224–32, 261–63, 394–98, 431–40. See Record, "Willie Stokes at the Golden Gate"; Charles Johnson, *Negro War Workers in San Francisco, a Local Self-Survey* (San Francisco, 1944); Joseph James, "Profiles, San Francisco," *Journal of Educational Sociology* (November, 1945): 166–78; Xiaojian Zhao, "Women and Defense Workers in World War II" (Ph.D. diss., University of California, Berkeley, 1993).

53. FEPC Hearings, 8.

54. James won an important, but belated, decision in the California Supreme Court, *James vs. Marinship* (1945). See Albert S. Broussard, *Black San Francisco: The Struggle for Racial Equality in the West, 1900–1954* (Lawrence, 1993),

143–65; Charles Wollenberg, "*James vs. Marinship*: Trouble on the New Black Frontier," *California History* 60 (Fall 1981): 262–79.

55. *CV*, 3 August, 7 December 1951; FEPC Hearings, "The Findings," 1–2; FEPC Hearings, 18, 142; Statement of Marcia Lee Eckford, Box 23, "Key System" Folder, Dellums Papers; *OT*, 24 March 1945, 4; C. L. Dellums letter to A. Bruce Hunt, 26 April 1945, "Key System" Folder, Box 23, Dellums Papers.

56. C. L. Dellums letter to A. Bruce Hunt, 26 April 1945, and A. Bruce Hunt letters to C. L. Dellums, 23 and 24 April 1945, "Key System" Folder, Box 23, Dellums Papers.

57. Stripp, "The Treatment of Negro-American Workers," and Stripp, "The Relationships of the San Francisco Bay Area Negro-American Workers with the Labor Unions Affiliated with the American Federation of Labor and the Congress of Industrial Organizations" (Ph.D. diss., Pacific School of Religion, Berkeley, 1948). See also Bruce Nelson, *Divided We Stand: American Workers and the Struggle for Black Equality* (Princeton, 2001).

58. Lemke-Santangelo, *Abiding Courage*; Jacqueline Jones, *Labor and Love, Labor of Sorrow: Black Women, Work, and the Family from Slavery to the Present* (New York, 1985); Elizabeth Clark-Lewis, *Living In, Living Out: African American Domestics and the Great Migration* (New York, 1994).

59. Broussard, *Black San Francisco*, 207; interview with Cleophus Williams, ASC Oral History.

60. "What Tensions Exist between Groups in the Local Community?; "What Courses of Action Are Needed to Achieve the Essentials of Good Human Relations in the Local Community?"; "Are the Rights of All Secure in the Local Community?" (Oakland Institute on Human Relations, Seminar Reports, 13 November 1946, mimeographed); East Bay Conference on Human Relations, 27 August 1949, California Federation of Civic Unity Collection, Carton 1, Bancroft Library, University of California, Berkeley.

Chapter 2
Working Class

1. Julie Meyer, "Trade Union Plans for Postwar Reconstruction in the United States," *Social Research* 11 (1944): 491–505; Fraser and Gerstle, eds., *The Rise and Fall of the New Deal Order*; Hamilton and Hamilton, *The Dual Agenda*; Michael K. Brown, *Race, Money, and the American Welfare State* (Ithaca, 1999). For accounts of the emergence of a multiracial popular front in World War II New York and Los Angeles, see Biondi, *To Stand and Fight*; and Scott Kurashige, "Transforming Los Angeles: Black and Japanese American Struggles for Racial Equality in the 20th Century" (Ph.D. diss., UCLA, 2000).

2. Other instances of the contradictions within liberal coalitions at the local level in the 1940s can be found in Michael Honey, *Southern Labor and Black Civil Rights: Organizing Memphis Workers* (Urbana, 1993); Lipsitz, *Rainbow at Midnight*; Sugrue, *The Origins of the Urban Crisis*.

3. Manuel Castells, *The City and the Grassroots: A Cross-Cultural Theory of Urban Social Movements* (Berkeley, 1983); Katznelson, *Marxism and the City*.

4. Johnson, "Mobilizing the Homefront," 344–68.

5. Alan Brinkley, "The New Deal and the Idea of the State"; Nelson Lichtenstein, "From Corporatism to Collective Bargaining: Organized Labor and the Eclipse of Social Democracy in the Postwar Era," in Fraser and Gerstle, eds., *The Rise and Fall of the New Deal Order*; James C. Foster, *The Union Politic: The CIO Political Action Committee* (Columbia, MO, 1975).

6. Gayle Montgomery, interviewed by the author, 2 September 1997, Walnut Creek, CA; Eugene C. Lee, *California Votes, 1928–1960: A Review and Analysis of Registration and Voting* (Berkeley, 1963), A–91; John A. Gothberg, "The Local Influence of J. R. Knowland's *Oakland Tribune*," *Journalism Quarterly* (Autumn 1968): 487–95; Edward C. Hayes, *Power Structure and Urban Policy: Who Rules in Oakland?* (New York, 1972), 14–17; Bagwell, *Oakland: The Story of a City*, 229–30.

7. *LH*, 9 March 1945; *EBLJ*, 23 November, 16 March, 13 April 1945.

8. For a guide to left and Popular Front politics in other places, see Biondi, *To Stand and Fight*; Freeman, *Working-Class New York*; Michael Denning, *The Cultural Front: The Laboring of American Culture in the Twentieth Century* (London, 1996).

9. *PW*, 9 April 1945; *EBLJ*, 6 April 1945.

10. *LH*, 2 and 16 March 1945; *EBLJ*, 13 April 1945. The UOC candidates for city council were Robert Ash; Herman Bittman, a CIO machinist; Frank Youell, former president of an AFL Painter's local; and John L. Stegge, an insurance broker.

11. Johnson, "Mobilizing the Homefront," 353–55; *LH*, 9 March 1945.

12. "Election Results, Oakland Municipal, 1931–1959," IGS; Johnson, "Mobilizing the Homefront," 355.

13. *LH*, 10 and 17 May 1946, 14 March 1947; *EBLJ*, 16 April 1946. On taxes, see Fones-Wolf, *Selling Free Enterprise*.

14. Galliano quoted in the *LH*, 9 April 1947. See also *LH*, 10 22 January, 29 April, 6 May 1947; *OT*), 7 February, 4 August 1947; *EBLJ*, 3 and 10 January 1947; Oakland Voters League Circular, Oakland Politics File, Oakland Public Library; Hayes, *Power Structure and Urban Policy*, 21–22. For Ash's comments, see *Labor Leaders View the Warren Era: Interviews*, conducted by Miriam Feingold Stein and Amelia R. Fry (Berkeley, 1976), 34 (hereafter Ash Oral History).

15. U.S. Congress, *Hearings Before the Joint Committee on Housing, Eighteenth Congress* (Washington, DC, 1948), 4059–64; Housing Authority of the City of Oakland, *Annual Report, 1948–1949*, 7; Helen Smith Alancraig, "Cordonices Village: A Study of Non-Segregated Public Housing" (M.A. thesis, University of California, Berkeley, 1953), 138; Johnson, *The Second Gold Rush*, 213–14.

16. *MT*, 24 April and 8 May 1947. The existing city charter mandated that the mayor was a council member chosen by a majority vote of the council. The city was run by a city manager.

17. *PW*, 17 April 1947 (emphasis mine); *LH*, 15 July 1947.

18. *OT*, 19, 23, 25 September 1946; 12 May, 7 November 1947; Dellums quoted in letter to Mayor Clifford Richell and the City Council, Carton 20, "Political Material 1949" folder, Dellums Papers; *MT*, 24 April 1947; *LH*, 28 March 1947, 26 August 1947; Johnson, "Mobilizing the Homefront," 358–59; Hayes, *Power Structure and Urban Policy*, 22–23.

19. Jessica Mitford, *A Fine Old Conflict* (New York, 1977), 100; Gregory, *American Exodus; LH*, 2 September 1947.

20. *EOT*, 10 October, 12 November 1947; 2 January, 13 February 13, 30 April, 5 November, and 17 December, 1948.

21. *EOT*, 5 and 19 November, 17 December, 1948; 21 January, 11 February, 4 and 25 March 1949.

22. *EOT*, 5 and 19 November, 17 December 1948; 21 January, 11 February, 4 and 25 March 1949; *OT*, 17, 19, and 20 April 1949.

23. *OT*, 11, 17, 19, 20, and 22 April 1949; 25 January, 16, 23, and 27 February, 1950; *MT*, 23 February 1950; *CV*), 27 January 1950; Johnson, "Mobilizing the Homefront," 360. Precinct-level voting returns for city council elections in Oakland have been destroyed. Reporting in the *Tribune* was spotty. It is thus impossible to reconstruct a detailed spatial map of the crucial elections of 1947, 1948, and 1950.

24. *OT*, 27 and 28 February, 1 March 1950; *MT*, 23 February 1950; *CV*, 27 January 1950; Johnson, "Mobilizing the Homefront," 360.

25. Katznelson, *City Trenches*, 6. Also important in this regard is Peterson, *City Limits*.

26. *LH*, 20 May 1947; *PW*, 10 May 1947.

27. E. Franklin Frazier, *On Race Relations: Selected Writings*, ed., G. Franklin Edwards (Chicago, 1968); W.E.B. DuBois, *Black Reconstruction in America* (New York, 1935); Arnesen, *Brotherhoods of Color*.

28. Dellums/OH; "A Recollection from the Past by C. L. Dellums," n.d., Box 4, "Race Problems—Civil Rights" Folder, Rumford Papers.

29. *LH*, 1 August 1950; *CV*, 27 January 1950; Mitford, *A Fine Old Conflict*, 118–38; Gerald Horne, *Communist Front? The Civil Rights Congress, 1946–1956* (London, 1988), 320–47; *LH*, 21 October 1947; 11 January, 5 April 1949; 27 March, 1 August 1950; author interview with Tom Berkley, Oakland.

30. *CV*, 4 April 1952, 27 May 1955.

31. Lawrence P. Crouchett, *William Byron Rumford: The Life and Public Service of a California Legislator* (El Cerrito, CA, 1984), 27–37; *William Byron Rumford, Legislator for Fair Employment, Fair Housing, and Public Health: An Interview*, conducted by Joyce A. Henderson, Amelia Fry, and Edward France (Berkeley, 1973), 27–33 (hereafter Rumford Oral History).

32. Brown quoted in "D. G. Gibson: A Black Who Led the People and Built the Democratic Party in the East Bay," in Harriet Nathan and Stanley Scott, eds., *Experiment and Change in Berkeley: Essays on City Politics, 1950–1975* (Berkeley, 1978), 24. See also Crouchett, *William Byron Rumford*, 28–32; *OT*, 10 November 1973; Rumford Oral History, 31–32; *A. Wayne Amerson: Northern California and Its Challenges to a Negro in the Mid 1900s* (Berkeley, 1974).

33. Bill Patterson, interviewed by the author, 3 September 1997, Oakland, California; Tom Berkley, interviewed by the author, Oakland; Paul Cobb, interviewed by the author, 20 August 1997, Oakland.

34. This is not to mention the substantial African American community in Richmond. See Shirley Ann Wilson Moore, *To Place Our Deeds: The African American Community in Richmond, California, 1910–1963* (Berkeley, 2000). For reminiscences of Gibson as well as comments by former Berkeley and Oakland

civic and political leaders, see Nathan and Scott, eds., *Experiment and Change in Berkeley.*

35. The California state government, unlike those in the South, had the potential to become a lever for racial equality. The analogy is thus not perfect.

36. East Bay Conference on Human Relations, Carton 1, CFCU; "A Recollection from the Past by C. L. Dellums," Carton 4, Rumford Papers; *Alameda County Branch NAACP Bulletin,* June 1948; *The Black Worker,* September 1944.

37. "Postwar Status of Negro Workers in San Francisco Area," *Monthly Labor Review* (June 1950): 612–17; Bureau of the Census, *Census of Population: 1950,* vol. 2, *Characteristics of the Population,* part 5, 262.

38. Bureau of the Census, *Census of Population: 1950,* vol. 2, *Characteristics of the Population,* part 5. For comparisons, see Joe William Trotter, *Black Milwaukee: The Making of an Industrial Proletariat, 1915–1945* (Urbana, 1985), 226–30.

39. Minutes, East Bay Conference on Human Relations, 27 August 1949, Carton 1, CFCU; Dettering Report on East Bay (n.d.), Carton 3, CFCU; Dellums Oral History, 103. For comparisons and precedents, see St. Clair Drake and Horace R. Cayton, *Black Metropolis: A Study of Negro Life in a Northern City* (New York, 1945).

40. Stripp, "The Treatment of Negro-American Workers," 330–32.

41. *LH,* 14 September 1948, 6 June 1950; Bruce Nelson, "Class, Race, and Democracy in the CIO: The 'New' Labor History Meets the 'Wages of Whiteness,'" *International Review of Social History* 41 (1996): 351–74; Bruce Nelson, "Harry Bridges, the ILWU, and Race Relations in the CIO Era," Working Paper no. 2, Occasional Paper Series, Center for Labor Studies, University of Washington (Seattle, 1995); Nancy Quam-Wickham, "Who Controls the Hiring Hall? The Struggle for Job Control in the ILWU during World War II," in Steve Rosswurm, ed., *The CIO's Left-Led Unions* (New Brunswick, 1992), 47–67.

42. *CV,* 1 June 1951, 15 and 29 August 1952, 6 February 1953, 23 October 1953, 19 March 1954, 8 April 1955, 27 May 1955, 16 December 1955; Civil Rights File, Box 22, CLCAC/LARC; East Bay Employment Organizations Committee File (letters and memberships lists), Box 21, CLCAC/LARC. For the statewide story, see Mark Brilliant, *Color Lines: Struggles for Civil Rights on America's "Racial Frontier," 1945–1975* (Oxford, forthcoming).

43. Dellums/OH, 115–29; Delores Nason McBroome, *Parallel Communities: African Americans in California's East Bay, 1850–1963* (New York, 1993), 137–43.

44. Dellums/OH, 115–29; McBroome, *Parallel Communities,* 137–43; Minutes, East Bay Local Offices Advisory Committee on Minority Group Employment, 14 September 1955, Box 21, Dellums Papers; *CV,* 17 April 1959.

45. See issues of *The Black Worker,* Carton 19, Dellums Papers.

46. *OT,* 7 November 1958; Alan Ware, *The Breakdown of Democratic Party Organizations, 1940–1980* (New York, 1985), 55–58.

47. "Keep Mississippi Out of California," NAACP Pamphlet, Clipping File, Box 162, WFK.

48. Totton J. Anderson, "The 1958 Election in California," *The Western Political Quarterly* (March 1959): 276–300; Houston I. Flournoy, "The 1958 Knowland Campaign in California—Design for Defeat," *The Western Political*

Quarterly (June 1959): 571–72; *OT*, 7 September 1958; NAACP campaign material, Box 162, WFK.

49. Flournoy, "The 1958 Knowland Campaign"; *SFE*, 3 January 1961; *The Washington Teamster*, 18 August 1950; *San Francisco News* (n.d.), clipping file, WFK; *U.S. News and World Report*, 14 January 1959; *San Francisco News*, 4 June 1952; *Los Angeles Times*, 31 January 1954; *New York Daily News*, 4 May 1954.

50. Daniel Flanagan, "Big Fight in California," *AFL-CIO American Federationist* (June 1958): 6–9; Philip Taft, *Labor Politics American Style: The California State Federation of Labor* (Cambridge, MA, 1968), 231–46; Knowland campaign material, Box 35, CLCAC/LARC; Helen Knowland quoted in the *Los Angeles Examiner*, 26 October 1958. See also Anderson, "The 1958 Election in California"; *OT*, 11 May 1958; *San Francisco Call-Bulletin*, 1 August 1958.

51. Bay Area Council, *Guide to Industrial Locations in the San Francisco Bay Area* (San Francisco, 1964).

52. Citizens Committee Against Proposition 18 memorandum, Box 33, File 10, CLCAC/LARC; Minutes, Joint Committee Meeting, CLCAC/LARC.

53. Anderson, "The 1958 Election in California"; William Harris, "A. Philip Randolph, Black Workers, and the Labor Movement," in Melvyn Dubofsky and Warren Van Tine, eds., *Labor Leaders in America* (Urbana, 1987); Robin D. G. Kelley, *Hammer and Hoe: Alabama Communists during the Great Depression* (Chapel Hill, 1990); Joe William Trotter, *Coal, Class, and Color: Blacks in Southern West Virginia, 1915–1932* (Urbana, 1990).

54. Eugene C. Lee, *The Politics of Nonpartisanship: A Study of California City Elections* (Berkeley, 1960); Knight quoted in the *Sacramento Bee*, 10 May 1958; *San Francisco Call-Bulletin*, 1 August 1958; Anderson, "The 1958 Election in California"; Montgomery and Johnson, *One Step from the White House*. See also Eugene C. Lee, *California Votes, 1928–1960* (Berkeley, 1963), 80–81, A-75; Ware, *The Breakdown of Democratic Party Organization*, 51–59, 131–35; James Q. Wilson, *The Amateur Democrat* (Chicago, 1962).

55. Peter Schrag, *Paradise Lost: California's Experience, America's Future* (Berkeley, 1999); Jewelle Taylor Gibbs and Teiahsha Bankhead, *Preserving Privilege: California Politics, Propositions, and People of Color* (Westport, CT, 2001).

56. Gutiérrez, *Walls and Mirrors*; Pitti, *The Devil in Silicon Valley*; Brilliant, *Color Lines*. The notion of "reasoning by analogy" comes from Brilliant's excellent forthcoming book on the multiple axes of racial discrimination in postwar California.

57. On anticommunism's affect on postwar liberal and radical politics, see Manning Marable, *Race, Reform, and Rebellion: The Second Reconstruction in Black America, 1945–1990* (Jackson, MI, 1991); Penny Von Eschen, *Race against Empire: Black Americans and Anticolonialism, 1937–1957* (Ithaca, 1997); Ellen Schrecker, *Many Are the Crimes: McCarthyism in America* (Boston, 1998).

58. Peterson, *City Limits*.

59. Kurt Schuparra, *Triumph of the Right: The Rise of the California Conservative Movement, 1945–1966* (New York, 1998); McGirr, *Suburban Warriors*.

Chapter 3
Tax Dollar

1. For other examples of this kind of suburban city building, see Hise, *Magnetic Los Angeles*; Nicolaides, *My Blue Heaven*.

2. Cox quoted in *Hayward Daily Review*, 3 January 1950.

3. U.S. Commission on Civil Rights, *1961 Report, Book 4: Housing* (Washington, DC, 1961), 1–26; Charles Abrams, *Forbidden Neighbors: A Study of Prejudice in Housing* (New York, 1955); Jackson, *Crabgrass Frontier*; Hamilton and Hamilton, *The Dual Agenda*; Arnold R. Hirsch, "With or Without Jim Crow: Black Residential Segregation in the United States," in Arnold R. Hirsch and Raymond Mohl, eds., *Urban Policy in Twentieth-Century America* (New Brunswick, NJ, 1993); Stephen Grant Meyer, *As Long as They Don't Move Next Door: Segregation and Racial Conflict in American Neighborhoods* (New York, 2000); David Freund, "Making It Home: Race, Development, and the Politics of Place in Suburban Detroit, 1940–1967" (Ph.D. diss., University of Michigan, 1999).

4. Edward P. Eichler and Marshall Kaplan, *The Community Builders* (Berkeley, 1967). The interaction between national economic restructuring and local political projects has been studied primarily for the places that capital *left*. See, for example, Sugrue, *The Origins of the Urban Crisis*; Bluestone and Harrison, *The Deindustrialization of America*.

5. Bruce Palmer, *"Man Over Money": The Southern Populist Critique of American Capitalism* (Chapel Hill, 1980); John R. Logan and Harvey L. Molotch, *Urban Fortunes: The Political Economy of Place* (Berkeley, 1987); Kazin, *The Populist Persuasion*.

6. Ronald Tobey, Charles Wetherell, and Jay Brigham, "Moving Out and Settling In: Residential Mobility, Home Owning, and the Public Enframing of Citizenship, 1921–1950," *American Historical Review* 95 (December 1990); Nicolaides, *My Blue Heaven*, 185–237; U.S. Civil Rights Commission, *1961 Report*, 4.

7. David Harvey, *The Limits to Capital* (London, 1982); Katznelson, *Marxism and the City*.

8. *WSJ*, 4 March 1966; *SLNO*, 27 August 1948; "San Leandro California: Land of Sunshine and Flowers" pamphlet in "Historical Scrapbook of San Leandro," vol. 1, Local History Room, San Leandro Public Library; "Your Success Story—Annual Report 1951, San Leandro Chamber of Commerce, San Leandro Public Library; Alameda County Taxpayers Association, "News and Facts," 1955–1970, IGS.

9. Thompson quoted in *SLNO*, 28 February and 11 April 1947. Also, see *SLNO*, 17 and 31 January, 2 May, 25 July 1947; Wes McClure, interviewed by the author, San Leandro, 16 February 1999.

10. Robert Dworak, *Taxpayers, Taxes, and Government Spending: Perspectives on the Taxpayer Revolt* (New York, 1980); Steven Hahn, *The Roots of Southern Populism: Yeoman Farmers and the Transformation of the Georgian Upcountry, 1850–1890* (New York, 1983).

354   NOTES TO CHAPTER THREE

11. Barbara Burbank quoted in *SLR*, 13 February 1948 (italics in original). See also *SLNO*, 27 June, 4 and 18 July, 28 November 1947; Jack Maltester, interviewed by the author, San Leandro, 1 March 1999; Wes McClure, interviewed by the author.

12. *SLR*, 5 and 12 March 1948; *SLNO*, 26 March, 2, 9, and 16 April 1948; Jack Maltester, interviewed by the author; Wes McClure, interviewed by the author.

13. On San Leandro's industrial strategy, see "Industrial Locations of the West: San Leandro," *Pacific Factory* (January 1957), and the collection of pamphlets and flyers in "Historical Scrapbook of San Leandro," vols. 1 and 3, Local History Room, San Leandro Public Library.

14. *SLNO*, 12 September 1947, 9 January 1948; August Mark Vaz, "The Portuguese: A Study in Immigration Patterns" (San Leandro, 1971). See Matthew Frye Jacobson, *Whiteness of a Different Color: European Immigrants and the Alchemy of Race* (Cambridge, MA, 1998), and Tomás Almaguer, *Racial Fault Lines: The Historical Origins of White Supremacy in California* (Berkeley, 1994).

15. John Denton, *Apartheid American Style* (Berkeley, 1967); Douglas Massey and Nancy Denton, *American Apartheid: Segregation and the Making of the Underclass* (Cambridge, MA, 1993); Melvin L. Oliver and Thomas M. Shapiro, *Black Wealth/White Wealth: A New Perspective on Racial Inequality* (New York, 1995). U.S. Commission on Civil Rights, *1961 Report, Book 4: Housing* (Washington, DC, 1961); *SLMN*, 14 and 15 May 1971; *FNR*, 1 September 1971.

16. *SLNO*, 12 September 1947, 9 January 1948; *SFC*, 4 January 1948. For the use of racial covenants to restrict and contain Oakland's Chinese community, see Willard T. Chow, *The Reemergence of an Inner City: The Pivot of Chinese Settlement in the East Bay Region of the San Francisco Bay Area* (San Francisco, 1977); for San Francisco, see, among others, Judy Yung, *Unbound Feet: A Social History of Chinese Women in San Francisco* (Berkeley, 1995).

17. *SLNO*, 21 May 1948; *SFC*, 4 January 1948; letter from C. L. Dellums to Baptist Ministers Union, 1950 NAACP outgoing folder, Box 9, Dellums Papers; County of Alameda Human Relations Commission, minutes, IGS.

18. Luigi Laurenti, "Effects of Nonwhite Purchase and Occupancy on Market Prices of Residences in San Francisco, Oakland, and Philadelphia" (Ph.D. diss., University of California, Berkeley, 1957). I take issue with the "backlash" thesis because it distracts attention from these early, aggressive white segregationist strategies that were in place before any black protests were made. The onus of historical responsibility should be placed where it belongs: on white exclusionary tactics.

19. *WSJ*, 4 March 1966; *SLNO*, 17 and 27 August 1948; "San Leandro California: Land of Sunshine and Flowers" pamphlet in "Historical Scrapbook of San Leandro," vol. 1, Local History Room, San Leandro Public Library; "Your Success Story—Annual Report 1951, "San Leandro Chamber of Commerce, San Leandro Public Library; Alameda County Taxpayers Association, "News and Facts," 1955–1970, IGS; Philip J. Bona, *Residential Development Analysis on Seventeen Acres in the City of San Leandro, California* (San Leandro, CA, 1977). In 1950 Democrats outnumbered Republicans among registered voters in San Leandro, 8,177 to 5,100. See *SLNO*, 5 May 1950.

20. Marion Clawson, *Suburban Land Conversion in the United States: An Economic and Governmental Analysis* (Baltimore, 1971).

21. For housing statistics, see Kenneth T. Jackson, "The Spatial Dimensions of Social Control: Race, Ethnicity, and Government Housing Policy in the United States, 1918–1968," in Bruce M. Stave, ed., *Modern Industrial Cities: History, Policy, and Survival* (Beverly Hills, 1981), 94, and Henry J. Aaron, *Shelter and Subsidies: Who Benefits from Federal Housing Politics?* (Washington, DC, 1972), 77–80.

22. "Standard Market Data for San Leandro, California," Historical Scrapbook of San Leandro, vol. 3; *Official Statement of the City of San Leandro, Alameda County, California: City of San Leandro 1958 Library Bond, Series A* (San Leandro, 1958); "Nationally Known Manufacturers Having Head Offices, Branch Manufacturing, or Distribution Plants in Alameda County, California" (photocopy, IGS, n.d.); *Industrial and Distribution Firms in San Leandro* (San Leandro, 1977); *WSJ*, March 4, 1966. Figures are adjusted for inflation.

23. *SLNO*, 17 December 1948. For pamphlets and other materials related to the program to sell industry to San Leandro residents, see Historical Scrapbook of San Leandro, vols. 1–7, Local History Room, San Leandro Public Library. See also Fones-Wolf, *Selling Free Enterprise*.

24. See *SLNO*, 9 June 1959; 30 October 1959.

25. *SLNO*, 23 September 1949, 3 March 1950.

26. "Standard Market Data for San Leandro, California," Historical Scrapbook of San Leandro, vol. 3; *Official Statement of the City of San Leandro, Alameda County, California: City of San Leandro 1958 Library Bond, Series A* (San Leandro, 1958); *WSJ*, 4 March 1966.

27. Mort Levine, interviewed by the author, Milpitas, June 9, 1999; Ernesto Galarza, *Alviso: The Crisis of a Barrio* (San Jose, 1973); William Alfred Whiteside, "An Economic History of the Milpitas Area," (masters' thesis, Stanford University, 1955); *Milpitas: An Arrested Community Meets the Twentieth Century* (Santa Clara County, 1954); *History of Milpitas* (Milpitas, 1976); Patricia Loomis, *Milpitas: The Century of "Little Cornfields," 1852–1952* (Cupertino, CA, 1986). On the use of the term "ethnic Mexican" to refer to the total Mexican-origin population within the nation or a region, see *Walls and Mirrors*.

28. *SJMN* 9 and 14 July, 8 September 1953. For an earlier interpretation of Milpitas, see Bennett Berger, *Working Class Suburb* (Berkeley, 1960).

29. On the ethnic Mexican communities of San Jose's Eastside, see Pitti, *The Devil in Silicon Valley*.

30. Gross quoted in *Plant Slants*, December 1954.

31. Ibid.; *Frontier*, January 1956; letter from William Oliver to Walter Reuther, 6 February 1957, Box 65, Folder 10, UAW/ALUA; "Annual Report, San Lorenzo Homes Association, 1954–55" (photocopy, IGS). Also see Stanley S. Jacobs, "The Awakening of Milpitas," unpublished manuscript, Box 66, Folder 3, UAW/ALUA; Eunice and George Grier, "Case Studies in Racially Mixed Housing: Sunnyhills, Milpitas, California," Princeton Conference on Equal Opportunity in Housing, 16–18 October 1962, Box 66, Folder 3, UAW/ALUA; G. W. Sherman, "Democracy in Action: UAW's Interracial Housing Project in California," *Frontier* (January 1956): 10–11.

32. Letter from Oliver to Reuther, 6 February 1957, UAW/ALUA; Sherman, "Democracy in Action."

33. Denton, *Apartheid American Style*, 57.

34. See issues of *UAW Solidarity* in Box 65, Folders 12 and 21, UAW/ALUA; Sherman, "Democracy in Action."

35. Eunice and George Grier, "Case Studies in Racially Mixed Housing."

36. Whiteside, "An Economic Survey of the Milpitas Area"; Eunice and George Grier, "Case Studies in Racially Mixed Housing."

37. Drake and Cayton, *Black Metropolis*; Abrams, *Forbidden Neighbors*; Oliver and Shapiro, *Black Wealth/White Wealth*.

38. Mort Levine, interviewed by the author.

39. *MP*, 17 June, 29 July, 12 August, 12 September, 4 November, 2 December 1960; 18 and 27 January, 1 February 1961; *SJMN*, 2 and 3 August, 8 September, 19 and 30 January 1960; 1 February 1961.

40. *MP*, 3 and 23 January, 21 and 28 February, 4 and 11 April 1962; 24 January 1964; *Plant Slants*, 25 January 1961; 9 April 1962; *SJMN*, 5 March 1959.

41. Del Green Associates, "San Leandro Freedom of Choice in Housing Project," distributed by U.S. Dept. of Commerce, 1974; William Bowser Gray, "Residential Patterns and Associated Socioeconomic Characteristics of Black Populations of Varying City-Suburban Locations within the San Francisco Bay Area," (Ph.D. diss., University of California, Berkeley, 1975); *Fremont Community Profile, 1975* (Fremont, CA, 1975).

42. *FNR*, 18 February 1966, 3 April 1967, 22 and 23 February 1971.

43. Eden Writers, *Hayward: The First 100 Years* (Hayward, 1975); *Information Directory of the Hayward Area California* (Hayward, 1950); *A Master Plan for Future Development* (Hayward, 1953).

44. Ronald Bartels, "The Incorporation of the City of Fremont: An Experiment in Municipal Government" (masters' thesis, University of California, Berkeley, 1959), 12–14, 20, 31–38; Stanley Weir, *Separate Efforts, Similar Goals and Results: A Study of the New Public City of Fremont, California, for Comparison with Private New Communities* (Berkeley, 1965), 10–15; Patricia O'Rourke, "Trend Surface Analysis of Urban Development: A Study of the Growth of the City of Fremont, California, 1956–1970" (masters' thesis, California State University, Hayward, 1973); Oral History Associates, *City of Fremont: The First Thirty Years, A History of Growth* (Sausalito, 1989), 33; Jack Parry, interviewed by the author, Fremont, 5 May 1999.

45. *FNR*, 2 June, 10 November 1955; 3 May 1956; Weir, *Separate Efforts, Similar Goals and Results*, 10–12; Oral History Associates, *City of Fremont*, 34–37; Jack Parry, interviewed by the author.

46. *FNR*, 2 June, 10 November 1955; 3 May 1956; Weir, *Separate Efforts, Similar Goals and Results*, 10–12; Oral History Associates, *City of Fremont*, 34–37; Jack Parry, interviewed by the author. For an account of zoning as a dimension of urban planning, see Nigel Taylor, *Urban Planning Theory since 1945* (Thousand Oaks, CA, 1998).

47. Weir, *Separate Efforts, Similar Goals and Results*, 13–14; Bartels, "The Incorporation of the City of Fremont," 98–106; Jack Parry, interviewed by the author; *Fremont: the Planned City* (Fremont, December 1963); *Preliminary General Plan, Fremont, California* (Fremont, 1956, photocopy in author's possession).

48. Oral History Associates, *City of Fremont*, 52; Weir, *Separate Efforts, Similar Goals and Results*, 13–14; *Preliminary General Plan, Fremont, California*.

49. Weir, *Separate Efforts, Similar Goals and Results*, 45–48.

50. *FNR*, 14 June 1956, 31 October 1957, 27 March 1958, 21 December 1960, 19 March 1964; *Preliminary General Plan, Fremont, California*, General Motors file, Fremont Public Library.

51. *FNR*, 14 June 1956, 31 October 1957, 27 March 1958, 21 December 1960, 18 and 19 March 1964; General Motors file, Fremont Public Library.

52. Catherine Bauer Wurster, *Housing and the Future of the San Francisco Bay Area* (Berkeley, 1963), 32; Weir, *Separate Efforts, Similar Goals and Results*, 45–48; *FNR*, 3 April 1967; Bureau of the Census, *1970 Census of Population and Housing, San Francisco-Oakland, California* (Washington, DC, 1973).

53. *FMN*, 3 October 1957, 5 March 1964.

54. *FNR*, 18 and 28 February, 1, 2, 9, and 21 March, 1, 3, 7, and 12 April, 6 and 14 June 1966.

55. Bureau of the Census, *U.S. Census of Housing and Population: 1960, San Francisco-Oakland, California* (Washington, DC, 1961); Bureau of the Census, *1970 Census of Population and Housing, San Francisco-Oakland, California* (Washington, DC, 1973); "News/Facts: Property Tax Rates," Alameda County Taxpayers Association, IGS; Alameda County Tax Rates, Fiscal Year, Auditor of Alameda County, Bancroft Library, University of California, Berkeley; Tax Rates, County of Alameda, Fiscal Year, Auditor-Controller of Alameda County, Bancroft Library, University of California, Berkeley.

56. Freund, "Making it Home."

57. See Sabina Deitrick, *The Rise of the Gunbelt: The Military Remapping of Industrial America* (New York, 1991). On the importance of grassroots politics to conservatism in the second half of the twentieth century, see McGirr, *Suburban Warriors;* Richard Riddle, "The Rise of the 'Reagan Democrats' in Warren, Michigan: 1964–1984" (Ph.D. diss., Wayne State University, 1998).

Chapter 4
Redistribution

1. "A Report on Current Activities," Oakland Redevelopment Agency, 21 April 1965, IGS; John Fugard, "The Office Building of Today and Tomorrow," *Proceedings of the Thirty-First Annual Convention of the National Association of Building Owners and Managers*, 1938, 144.

2. Stephen Weicker, "Behind the Building Boom," *San Francisco Business* (April 1978): 7–8.

3. These consequences of redevelopment were common nationwide. See John F. Bauman, *Public Housing, Race, and Renewal: Urban Planning in Philadelphia* (Philadelphia, 1987); Teaford, *The Rough Road to Renaissance;* June Manning Thomas, *Redevelopment and Race: Planning a Finer City in Detroit* (Baltimore, 1997).

4. "A Country of Crowded Clusters," *Newsweek*, 54 (14 December 1959), 44. There are no definitive demographic or ethnographic histories of either the postwar African American southern diaspora or white suburbanization. For works that deal with one or the other in local or regional contexts, see Lemke-Santangelo, *Abiding Courage;* Lawrence B. de Graaf, Kevin Mulroy, and Quintard Taylor,

eds., *Seeking El Dorado: African Americans in California* (Seattle, 2001); Moore, *To Place Our Deeds*. On industrial restructuring, see Bluestone Harrison, *The Deindustrialization of America*; Schulman, *From Cotton Belt to Sunbelt*.

5. Lola Bell Sims to Harry Truman, 30 August 1949, File 650, Box 30, Files of the Housing and Home Finance Agency, National Archives, Record Group 207. The 1949 housing legislation was known as the Wagner-Ellender-Taft Act. See Bauman, *Public Housing, Race, and Renewal*, 83, 93.

6. Lola Bell Sims to Harry Truman, 30 August 1949. On concern over the mid-century decline of American cities, see Teaford, *The Rough Road to Renaissance*; Robert A. Beauregard, *Voices of Decline: The Postwar Fate of U.S. Cities* (Cambridge, MA, 1993); Fogelson, *Downtown*. On the destruction of African American communities, see Howard Gilette, *Between Justice and Beauty: Race, Planning, and the Failure of Urban Policy in Washington, D.C.* (Philadelphia, 1995); Larry Keating, *Atlanta: Race, Class, and Urban Expansion* (Philadelphia, 2001).

7. For the story of downtown property values, see Paul F. Wendt, *The Dynamics of Central City Land Values: San Francisco and Oakland, 1950–1960* (Berkeley, 1961); Donald Livingston, "The Logical Place Is Oakland: The Potential of the Oakland Central District as Viewed by Selected Business Leaders," report prepared by the Coro Foundation and the Oakland City Planning Department, Oakland, 1961, 5; Oakland City Planning Department, "Retail Trade in the Oakland Central District: Analyses and Projections, 1962 to 1980," report of the Central Business District Plan Advisory Committee, 1965, 9; *Redevelopment in Oakland: A Part of the Master Plan* (Oakland, 1949); "OUR Program," report by Oakland Urban Renewal (1956), IGS.

8. Teaford, *The Rough Road to Renaissance*; "OUR Program": *Redevelopment in Oakland*, 15–16.

9. Oakland's Future (Oakland, 1957), 2; *Redevelopment: Annual Report, 1966* (Oakland, 1966); *The Clinton Park Story* (Oakland, n.d.); Livingston, "The Logical Place Is Oakland"; Oakland City Planning Department, "Retail Trade in the Oakland Central District."

10. CV, 16 January, 10 July 1959; *Oakland's Formula for the Future* (Oakland, 1957), 18; *Redevelopment in Oakland: A Part of the Master Plan* (Oakland, 1949), 1–20; "General Neighborhood Renewal Plan Study" (Oakland, 1958), 4; "Citizens Make Oakland a Wonderful Place," Oakland's application for designation as an "All-American City" in 1956, Box 36, Joseph R. Knowland Collection, Bancroft Library, University of California, Berkeley (hereafter, J. R. Knowland Collection); Michael Marans, "Relocation in Acorn: A Focal Point for the Study of the Transition in Urban Renewal Policy and Politics in Oakland," manuscript, IGS.

11. CV, 20 October 1961; Katherine Wurster, "Draft Report to the Governor's Advisory Commission on Housing Problems," manuscript, Box 7, Katherine Wurster Collection, Bancroft Library, University of California, Berkeley.

12. John H. Mollenkopf, *The Contested City* (Princeton, 1983), 47–115; John R. Logan, Rachel Bridges Whaley, and Kyle Crowder, "The Character and Consequences of Growth Regimes: An Assessment of Twenty Years of Research; Allan Cochrane, "Redefining Urban Politics for the Twenty-First Century," in Andrew E. G. Jones and David Wilson, eds., *The Urban Growth Machine: Critical Perspectives Two Decades Later* (Albany, 1999), 73–93, 109–124.

13. Letter about OCCUR (then called OUR) to Robert Ash from Norris Nash, OCCUR chairman, 24 September 1956, Box 16, Folder 18, CLCAC/LARC.

14. "Report Given for the NAACP before the Oakland City Council's Special Meeting on Housing and Slum Clearance," 29 July 1949, NAACP 1949 Folder, Box 9, Dellums Papers; Hayes, *Power Structure and Urban Policy*; 113–15; "General Neighborhood Renewal Plan Study" (Oakland, 1958), 1–3; CV, 15 June 1956, 16 January 1959.

15. Among the best guides to this issue remains James Baldwin. See *Nobody Knows My Name* (New York, 1961); *Another Country* (New York, 1962); *The Fire Next Time* (New York, 1963).

16. CV, 11 and 25 December 1959.

17. CV, 22 January 1960.

18. Johnson, *The Second Gold Rush*: 213, 228–31; Helen Smith Alancraig, "Cordonices Village: A Study of Non-Segregated Public Housing" (Master's thesis, University of California, Berkeley, 1953); CV, 20 October 1961.

19. CV, 22 June 1962, 12 and 19 April 1963.

20. Rose Edith Hightower Sherman, "A Diary on How This Was Done in Oak Center," manuscript, n.d., IGS; "Oak Center News," manuscript, n.d., IGS; Redevelopment Agency of the City of Oakland, "Oak Center Project Redevelopment Plan," 28 August 1965, IGS; interview with Vivian Bowie, Caltrans Oral Histories, 225–36. Love quoted in U.S. Commission on Civil Rights, *Hearing before the U.S. Commission on Civil Rights*, Oakland, California, 4–6 May 1967, 469.

21. *Hearing before the U.S. Commission on Civil Rights*, 468–69.

22. *Hearing before the U.S. Commission on Civil Rights*, 470, 493–96; Redevelopment Agency of the City of Oakland, "A Report on Current Activities" (Oakland, 1965); *OT*, 14 December 1966, 10 July 1967.

23. Redevelopment Agency of the City of Oakland, "A Report on Current Activities."

24. "Changes in the Housing Inventory in Oakland, California" (Oakland, 1966).

25. "General Neighborhood Renewal Plan Study"; Richard Zettel and Paul Shuldiner, "Highway Location Conflicts in California," Institute of Transportation and Traffic Engineering Report no. 29, University of California, Berkeley, 1959; *The California Highway System: A Report to the Joint Interim Committee on Highway Problems of the California Legislature* (Sacramento, 1958); "A Summary Statement by the Alameda County Highway Advisory Committee to the Joint Fact-Finding Committee on Highways" (Oakland, 16 January 1953, mimeographed).

26. Melvin M. Webber, "The BART Experience—What Have We Learned?" Institute of Urban and Regional Development and Institute of Transportation Studies, Monograph no. 26, University of California, Berkeley, 1976; Stephen Zwerling, *Mass Transit and the Politics of Technology: A Study of BART and the San Francisco Bay Area* (New York, 1974); Daniel Jack Chasan, "Bay Area Subway: A Catastrophe or an Urban Triumph?" *Smithsonian* (June 1972): 34–41; Weicker, "Behind the Building Boom."

27. Oakland Board of Port Commissioners, *The Port of Oakland, Sixty Years: A Chronicle of Progress* (Oakland, 1987); Port of Oakland, "Development of

Containerization at the Port of Oakland," 28 January 1975; Tim Reagan, "A Brief History of the Oakland Harbor," *East Bay Express*, 25 April 1986; David Olson and Michael Denning, "Comparative Analysis of West Coast Ports," November 1988, manuscript in author's possession.

28. Jeffrey L. Pressman and Aaron B. Wildavsky, *Implementation: How Great Expectations in Washington are Dashed in Oakland* (Berkeley, 1973), 67–70; Amory Bradford, *Oakland's Not for Burning* (New York, 1968), 2, 123; Ben Nutter, *The Port of Oakland: Modernization and Expansion of Shipping, Airport, and Real Estate Operations, 1957–1977* (Berkeley, 1991); David J. Olson, "Public Port Accountability: A Framework for Evaluation," in Marc J. Hershman, ed., *Urban Ports and Harbor Management: Responding to Change Along U.S. Waterfronts* (New York, 1988).

29. Oakland Board of Port Commissioners, *The Port of Oakland 1957 Revenue Bonds* (Oakland, 1970).

30. Mari Malvey and Aaron Wildavsky, "The Citizens of Oakland Look at Their City," manuscript, IGS, n.d., 32; Hayes, *Power Structure and Urban Policy*, 78; William L. Nicholls and Earl R. Babbie, *Oakland in Transition: A Summary of the 701 Household Survey* (Berkeley, 1969), 16; "Changes in the Housing Inventory in Oakland, California"; California State Advisory Committee to the United States Commission on Civil Rights, *Civil Rights in Oakland, California*, (San Francisco, August 1967), 12. See also Hirsch, *Making the Second Ghetto;* Jackson, "The State, the Movement, and the Urban Poor."

31. Lionel Wilson, *Lionel Wilson: Attorney, Judge, and Oakland Mayor* (Regional Oral History Office, Berkeley, 1992), hereafter Wilson Oral History; on Don McCullum, see *OT*, 16 August 1968; interview with Paul Cobb; interview with Tom Nash, WO Oral History, 183; interview with Landon Williams, WO Oral History.

32. Interview with Audrey Robinson, ASC Oral History, 1; Dellums/OH, 74; interview with Vivian Bowie, WO Oral History, 226; Survey Research Center, *Housing and Population Tabulations from the 701 Household Survey of Oakland* (Berkeley, 1968).

33. Interview with Vernon Sappers in *West Oakland: A Place to Start From*, 171; interview with Gregg Kosmos, ASC Oral History, 16.

34. Interview with Tom Nash, WO Oral History, 184; interview with Landon Williams, WO Oral History, 273.

35. Interview with Landon Williams, WO Oral History, 281; interview with Vivian Bowie, WO Oral History, 229; interview with Tom Nash, WO Oral History, 184; interview with Josie de la Cruz, WO Oral History, 520.

36. Floyd Hunter, *Housing Discrimination in Oakland, California: A Study Prepared for the Oakland Mayor's Committee on Full Opportunity and the Council of Social Planning, Alameda County* (Berkeley, 1963–1964), 44–56, 70. For the San Francisco–Oakland metropolitan statistical area the indices of dissimilarity were 80.1 (1970), 71.7 (1980), and 66.8 (1990). See Massey and Denton, *American Apartheid;* U.S. Commission on Race and Housing, *Report of the Commission on Race and Housing: Where Shall we Live?* (Washington, DC, 1958), 27.

37. Survey Research Center, *Housing and Population Tabulations*.

38. Interview with Landon Williams, WO Oral History, 272; Dellums/OH, 74; interview with Norvel Smith.

39. Area Description and Residential Survey Map of Oakland, Box 145, record Group 195, Home Owners Loan Corporation City Files, National Archives, Washington, DC. I thank Andy Wiese for bringing this to my attention.

40. Hunter, *Housing Discrimination in Oakland*, 24, 33.

41. Ibid., 39.

42. Nicholls and Babbie, *Oakland in Transition*, 57–58, 62–65; Survey Research Center, *Housing and Population Tabulations;* anonymous interview by Jeff Pressman, 18 June 1969, Oakland Project Public Interviews, Part 4, Institute of Governmental Studies, University of California, Berkeley.

43. Osborne quoted in the CV, 29 March 1963.

44. *NYT*, 10 May 1964; *California Real Estate Magazine*, May, June, July, August 1964; CV, 17 May and 9 August 1963; Clare Short, "What Are the Obligations of the Housing Industry to Resolve Such Conflicts as Exist in This Area?" speech manuscript, University of California, Berkeley, Library; Raymond Wolfinger and Fred Greenstein, "The Repeal of Fair Housing in California: An Analysis of Referendum Voting," *The American Political Science Review* 62 (September 1968): 753–69; Thomas W. Casstevens, *Politics, Housing and Race Relations: California's Rumford Act and Proposition 14* (Berkeley, 1967).

45. California Secretary of State, "Statement of Canvass of All Votes Cast, General Election, November 3, 1964" (Sacramento, 1964); Casstevens, Politics, Housing and Race Relations, 68.

46. Nicholls and Babbie, *Oakland in Transition*, 57–58, 62–65; Survey Research Center, *Housing and Population Tabulations*, 72–73.

47. Regal, "Oakland's Partnership for Change," 16; Nicholls and Babbie, *Oakland in Transition*, v.

48. Regal, "Oakland's Partnership for Change," 16; Nicholls and Babbie, *Oakland in Transition*, v; "Industry Goes Places in MOAP," Alameda County New Industries Committee, Oakland Chamber of Commerce, IGS; "Statistical Summary of Industrial Growth in Alameda County, 1951–1960," Alameda County New Industries Committee, Oakland Chamber of Commerce, 1961; Wayne Thompson, "Oakland—East: A Laboratory City for the Solution of Urban Problems" City of Oakland, 17 December 1964; Hise, *Magnetic Los Angeles;* Nicholls and Babbie, *Oakland in Transition*, 5, 129; *Oakland's Economy: Background and Projections* (Oakland, 1976), 29; *Hearing Before the U.S. Commission on Civil Rights*, 461, 587; Bureau of the Census, *United States Census of Manufactures, Area Statistics: California*, (Washington, DC, 1958, 1963, 1967, 1972); Oakland Chamber of Commerce, "Fifty Largest Employers in Alameda County," April 1970.

49. CV, 21 January 1966; U.S. Department of Labor, "Income, Education, and Unemployment in Neighborhoods: Oakland, California" (Washington, DC, 1961), table B-3; Nicholls and Babbie, *Oakland in Transition*, 123.

50. *Oakland's Economy: Background and Projections*, 28; "Fifty Largest Employers in Alameda County"; Oakland Chamber of Commerce, "Fifteen Largest Federal and Public Employers," April 1970.

51. William H. Harris, *The Harder We Run: Black Workers since the Civil War* (New York, 1982).

52. Nicholls and Babbie, *Oakland in Transition*, 102; "Civil Rights in Oakland, California," 5.

53. Nadasen, "The Welfare Rights Movement in the United States, 1960–1975."

54. Nicholls and Babbie, *Oakland in Transition*, 120, 181.

55. May, *Homeward Bound*, 152.

Chapter 5
Opportunity Politics

1. Press release, East Bay Advisory Committee on Minority Group Employment, 1958, Box 21, Dellums Papers.

2. Clinton White quoted in "Conditions in the Oakland Ghetto," KPFA broadcast, Pacific Radio Archives, North Hollywood, California, tape reference number BB1309.

3. American Social History Project, *Who Built America?*, Birnbaum and Taylor, *Civil Rights since 1787*. See, among many others, Sitkoff, *The Struggle for Black Equality, 1954–1980*; Carson, *In Struggle*; Morris, *The Origins of the Civil Rights Movement*; Bloom, *Class, Race, and the Civil Rights Movement*; Charles M. Payne, *I've Got the Light of Freedom: The Organizing Tradition and the Mississippi Freedom Struggle* (Berkeley, 1995).

4. Allen, *Black Awakening in Capitalist America*; Hamilton and Hamilton, *The Dual Agenda*.

5. Robert Plotnick and Felecity Skidmore, *Progress against Poverty: A Review of the 1964–1974 Decade* (New York, 1975); Alice O'Connor, *Poverty Knowledge: Social Science, Social Policy, and the Poor in Twentieth-Century U.S. History* (Princeton, 2001).

6. See, for instance, Floyd Barber, ed. *The Black Power Revolt* (Boston, 1968); Young, *Beyond Racism*.

7. Louis Lomax, *The Negro Revolt* (New York, 1962); Stephen Lawson, *Running for Freedom: Civil Rights and Black Politics in America since 1941* (New York, 1991); Hamilton and Hamilton, *The Dual Agenda*.

8. Philip S. Foner, *Organized Labor and the Black Worker, 1619–1981* (New York, 1981), 323–39; *CV*, 6 April, 15, 22 June 1962; 7 May 1965.

9. *CV*, 6 April, 15, 22, June 1962; 7 May 1965.

10. *OT*, 7 August 1963. The emphasis is mine.

11. *OT*, 7, 17, 21 August 1963. On affirmative Action's history in the 1940s, see Biondi, *To Stand and Fight*.

12. "Proceedings of the Preliminary Meeting between the Ad Hoc Committee to End Discrimination and the *Oakland Tribune*," 4 May 1964, unpublished minutes, CLCAC/LARC; letter from Michael Meyerson to Richard Groulx, 20 July 1964, CLCAC/LARC; letter from Robert Ash to Michael Meyerson, 30 July 1964, CLAC/LARC; *OT*, 13 December 1964, 13 March 1965.

13. *OT*, 12 and 13 December 1964, 13 March 1965; *SFC*, 29 November 1964; "Proceedings of the Second Meeting between the Ad Hoc Committee to End Discrimination and the *Oakland Tribune*," 12 May 1964, 26, 29.

14. *OT*, 12 and 13 December 1964, 13 March 1965; *SFC*, 29 November 1964; "Proceedings of the Second Meeting," 12 May 1964, 26, 29.

15. *CV*, 16 February, 30 March 1962, 31 May 1963, 5 March 1965; CORE letter to AFL-CIO Central Labor Council, 21 March 1965, CLCAC/LARC, Box 93/6; Joint statement of labor and management, Box 93/6, CLCAC/LARC.

16. *CV*, 16 February, 30 March 1962, 31 May 1963, 5 March 1965; CORE letter to AFL-CIO Central Labor Council, 21 March 1965, CLCAC/LARC, Box 93/6; Joint statement of labor and management, Box 93/6, CLCAC/LARC; *San Francisco Labor*, 6 December 1966, 13 January 1967; "Official Bulletin," San Francisco Labor Council, 20 January 1967, San Francisco Labor Council Collection, LARC; author interview with James Gay, San Francisco, 9 August 1995.

17. California Department of Industrial Relations, Division of Labor Statistics and Research, "Labor Gain in California Union Membership," 5 February 1965, and "New 5-County Bay Area Statistics Reveal Record Employment and Earnings," Box 17, San Francisco Labor Council Collection, LARC; Press Release, Advisory Committee on Minority Group Employment, 1958.

18. Brown quoted in the *CV*, 17 April 1959. Dellums quoted in a speech before the California State Senate Committee on Labor, Carton 8, "FEPC Letters" folder, Dellums Papers.

19. Stephen Yabroff, "An Evaluation of California's FEPC and Its Affirmative Action Program" (master's thesis, University of California, Berkeley, 1966); Philip F. Rubio, *A History of Affirmative Action, 1619–2000* (Jackson, MS, 2001).

20. Yabroff, "An Evaluation of California's FEPC," 16; *Hearings on S. 773, S. 1210, S. 1211 and S. 1937 Before the Subcommittee on Employment and Manpower of the Senate Committee on Labor and Public Welfare*, 88th Congress, 1st Session (1963), 229; letter from California Chapters of CORE to Mrs. Carmen Warschaw, Chair, California FEPC, Appendix E, "Bank of America Employment Practices—First Report by California FEPC" (San Francisco, 1964) (hereafter Warschaw Letter); Thomas J. Sugrue, "The Tangled Roots of Affirmative Action," *American Behavioral Scientist* 41 (April 1998): 886–97.

21. Warschaw Letter; "Memo of Understanding: Full Text of Agreement between California State Fair Employment Practice Commission and the Bank of America National Trust and Savings Association," 1 June 1964; Appendix A, "Bank of America Employment Practices—First Report by California FEPC"; *CV*, 4 September 1964.

22. Warschaw Letter; "Memo of Understanding"; Appendix A, "Bank of America Employment Practices"; *CV*, 4 September 1964.

23. Herbert Hill, "Is the Past Prologue? The Law and Employment Discrimination," *The Crisis* (February 1975): 56–61.

24. Barbour, *The Black Seventies*; Gertrude Ezorsky, *Racism and Justice: The Case for Affirmative Action* (Ithaca, 1991); Michael C. Dawson, *Black Visions: The Roots of Contemporary African American Political Ideologies* (Chicago, 2001).

25. Allen, *Black Awakening* in capitalist America.

26. *SFC*, 15 March, 28, 29 April, 27 May 1966; JOBART press release, 28 September 1966, NAACP Collection, Box 39.

27. Joseph Rodriguez, "Rapid Transit and Community Power: West Oakland Residents Confront BART," *Antipode* (April 1999): 212–28.

28. *SFC*, 8, 10 February, 11 March 1966; "Community Groups Press for BART Job Training, Minority Hiring"; letter from JOBART, n.d., Box 39, NAACP

Collection; Gene Bernardi, "Evaluation of the Council of Social Planning's Neighborhood Organization Program" (Oakland, 1966), 42; *Flatlands*, 12 March and 18 June–1 July 1966; 15–28 June 1967.

29. *SFC*, 8, 10 February, 11 March 1966; "Community Groups Press for BART Job Training, Minority Hiring," Box 39, NAACP Collection; letter from JOBART, n.d., Box 39, NAACP Collection; Bernardi, "Evaluation of the Council of Social Planning's Neighborhood Organization Program," 42.

30. JOBART Newsletter, July 1966, "JOBART Demands to BART."

31. See Bay Area Rapid Transit District, 1969, *BART and the Ghettos: A Report Prepared by BART Community Services*, 1–4; Papers of A. Falk, Bancroft Library, University of California, Berkeley, Box 8; *San Francisco Examiner*, 9 November 1962.

32. "JOBART Demands to BART." Jackson quoted on KPFA radio, Pacific Radio Archive, tape reference number BB1309.

33. *SFC*, 15 March, 28 and 29 April, 27 May 1966; California, Fair Employment Practice Commission, "Bank of America Employment Practices"; Yabroff, "An Evaluation of California's FEPC and Its Affirmative Action Program."

34. *SFC*, 15 March, 28 and 29 April, 27 May 1966; *CV*, 13 January 1967.

35. *CV*, 21 and 28 July 1967; "Statement of Ms. Leonard Carter, NAACP West Coast Regional Director, to the Board of Directors of the BART System, January 25, 1968," NAACP Collection, Box 39.

36. Wilson and Smith quoted in *California Voice*, 26 March 1965; McCullum quoted in U.S. Commission on Civil Rights, *Hearing Before the U.S. Commission on Civil Rights*, Oakland, California, 4–6 May 1967, 442; Nicholls and Babbie, Oakland in Transition, 125; William Nicholls, *Poverty and Poverty Programs in Oakland* (Oakland, 1966), 157.

37. Walter Lippman quoted in the *New York Herald Tribune*, 17 March 1964. For a more complete discussion of the War on Poverty's programs, philosophy, and origins, see James T. Patterson, *America's Struggle against Poverty* (1981; reprint, Cambridge, MA, 1986); Michael B. Katz, *In the Shadow of the Poorhouse: A Social History of Welfare in America* (New York, 1986); Jackson, "The State, the Movement, and the Urban Poor."

38. For classic studies of the War on Poverty, and especially its political context, see Frances Fox Piven and Richard A. Cloward, *Poor People's Movements: Why They Succeed, How They Fail* (New York, 1977); Norman I. Fainstein and Susan S. Fainstein, *Urban Political Movements: The Search for Power by Minority Groups in American Cities* (Englewood Cliffs, NJ, 1974).

39. "Oakland's War on Poverty," Oakland Economic Development Council, 1966.

40. Nicholls, *Poverty and Poverty Programs in Oakland*.

41. Ibid., 117–20; *CV*, 26 March 1965; Regal, "Oakland's Partnership for Change," 99; Max Awner, "Oakland Labor Backs Up Youth," *The American Federationist*, 12 April 1966; untitled report on the Central Labor Council Summer Youth Employment Project, n.d., Box 95, Folder 1, CLCAC/LARC.

42. *CV*, 2 July 1965; Eldridge Cleaver, *Post-Prison Writings and Speeches*, ed. Robert Scheer (New York, 1969), 22. King is quoted in Thomas Powers, *The War at Home: Vietnam and the American People, 1964–1968* (New York, 1973), 152.

For Whitney Young's "Marshall Plan for the Negro," see Nancy J. Weiss, *Whitney Young, Jr., and the Struggle for Civil Rights* (Princeton, 1989); for A. Philip Randolph's "Freedom Budget for All Americans," see U.S. Senate Committee on Government Operations, *Federal Role in Urban Affairs*, 1853–2013.

43. Schultze quoted in a 1965 memo to Johnson, cited in Gareth Davies, *From Opportunity to Entitlement: The Transformation and Decline of Great Society Liberalism* (Lawrence, 1996), 91.

44. Judith May, "Struggle for Authority: A Comparison of Four Social Change Programs in Oakland, California" (Ph.D. diss., University of California, Berkeley, 1975), 294–315; Regal, "Oakland's Partnership for Change," 93–96; CV, 30 July, 1 October, 5 November 1965; Bernardi, *Evaluation Analysis of the Council of Social Planning's Neighborhood Organization Program*, 3.

45. Smith quoted in James V. Cunningham, "The Struggle of the American Indigent for Freedom and Power," manuscript prepared for the Ford Foundation, August 1967.

46. CV, 2 August 1963, 13 May 1966; Judith May, "Little Summit Conference Sponsored by the NAACP," unpublished report, 17 August 1967, Oakland Project Interviews, vol. 3, IGS; May, "Struggle for Authority," 314, 311–18; CV, 15 July 1971.

47. WSJ, 25 April 1966; Louise Resnikoff, "The EDA in Oakland: An Evaluation" (Berkeley: University of California Oakland Project, October 1969, mimeographed); Bradford, *Oakland's Not for Burning*, 123.

48. Bradford, *Oakland's Not for Burning*, 3–21, 123; WSJ, 5 January, 25 April 1966.

49. WSJ, 5 January, 25 April 1966; Owen McShane, "Toward a Transitional Economic: A Reappraisal of Urban Development Economics Based on the Experience of the Economic Development Administration in Oakland" (Berkeley, 1970, mimeographed), 1–23; Pressman and Wildavsky, *Implementation*, 1–6; Resnikoff, "The EDA in Oakland," 20–21.

50. OT, 11, 18 December 1965; CV, 17, 31 December 1965; Bradford, *Oakland's Not for Burning*, 151.

51. "East Bay Skills Center," 7 April 1966, Box 102, Folder 4, CLCAC/LARC; letter from Norman Amundson to Secretary of Labor Willard Wirtz, 13 June 1966, Box 102, Folder 3, CLCAC/LARC; CV, 30 September 1966.

52. Pressman and Wildavsky, *Implementation*, 149–51; Resnikoff, "The EDA in Oakland," 20–21.

53. OT, 28 March 1968; Hearings, Manpower Development and Training Program, Senate Committee on Labor and Public Welfare, 91st Congress, 1970, 2063.

54. *Flatlands*, 15–28 June 1967.

55. Donald K. Tamaki, "Oakland Politics and Powerless Pressure Groups," September 1970, 8, IGS; BP, 23 December 1972; Cleaver, *Post-Prison Writings and Speeches*, 67.

56. Song lyrics quoted (with permission) in Robin D. G. Kelley, *Yo' Mama's Disfunctional: Fighting the Culture Wars in Urban America* (Boston, 1997), 6; *Hearing Before the U.S. Commission on Civil Rights*, 443.

57. *Hearing Before the U.S. Commission on Civil Rights*, 451, 455–56.

58. *OT*, 12 January 1967.

59. Alan A. Altshuler, *Community Control: The Black Demand for Participation in Large American Cities* (New York, 1969); David Greenstone and Paul E. Peterson, *Race and Authority in Urban Politics* (Chicago, 1976); Barbour, *The Black Seventies*.

Chapter 6
Black Power

1. Cobb quoted in *OT*, 20 June, 2 and 3 July 1968; Eldridge Cleaver, *Post-Prison Writings and Speeches*, ed. Robert Scheer (New York, 1968), 57. On the emerging languages of black power and black liberation in this period, see Allen, *Black Awakening in Capitalist America*; Woodard, *A Nation within a Nation*; Kelley and Esch, "Black Like Mao"; Williams, *Black Politics/White Power*; Joseph, "Black Liberation without Apology."

2. Carmichael and Hamilton, *Black Power*. The received wisdom about civil rights and black power is slowly changing, but it is still reflected in both scholarly and popular accounts of the period. See, for instance, Birnbaum and Taylor, *Civil Rights since 1787*; Charles Kaiser, *1968 in America: Music, Chaos, Counterculture, and the Shaping of a Generation* (New York, 1988).

3. Bayard Rustin, "From Protest to Politics: The Future of the Civil Rights Movement," *Commentary* (February 1964): 25–31; Joseph, "Black Liberation without Apology"; Floyd Barbour, *The Black Seventies* (Boston, 1970).

4. *BP*, 11 April 1970; Allen, *Black Awakening in Capitalist America*; Rustin, *Down the Line*, 154–55.

5. When I use the term *ghetto*, I do so self-consciously in the way black activists in the period used it: as a way of drawing attention to urban segregation and the white institutions that created it.

6. "In Defense of Self-Defense I: June 20, 1967," in Toni Morrison, ed. *To Die for the People: The Writings of Huey P. Newton* (New York, 1972), 85–86. For an introduction to the literature on the Black Panther Party, see Hugh Pearson, *The Shadow of the Panther: Huey Newton and the Price of Black Power in America* (New York, 1994); Jones, ed., *The Black Panther Party Reconsidered*; Cleaver and Katsiaficas, eds., *Liberation, Imagination, and the Black Panther Party*. For Panther memoirs, see Bobby Seale, *Seize the Time: The Story of the Black Panther Party and Huey P. Newton* (New York, 1991); Elaine Brown, *A Taste of Power: A Black Woman's Story* (New York, 1992); David Hilliard and Lewis Cole, *This Side of Glory: The Autobiography of David Hilliard and the Black Panther Party* (Boston, 1993). Robyn Spencer, "Repression Breeds Resistance: The Rise and the Fall of the Black Panther Party in Oakland, 1966–1982" (PhD diss., Columbia University, 2001).

7. Letter to Huey Newton from Dee Dee Parks, 22 January 1976, Huey P. Newton Collection, Series 2, Box 41, Folder 5 (emphasis in original).

8. Judith May, "Black Panther Party for Self Defense," unpublished report, 3 May 1968, Oakland Project Interviews, vol. 4, IGS; letter to Huey Newton from Norvel Smith, 16 October 1970, Newton Papers, Series 1, Box 37, Folder 5; Paul Cobb, interview with author, 20 August 1997, Oakland; Seale quoted in *Seize the*

Time, 14, see also 6–15; Warden quoted in Judith May, "Little Summit Conference, Sponsored by the NAACP," unpublished report, 17 August 1967, Oakland Project Interviews, vol. 3, IGS; Warden quoted in *OT*, 11 September 1963; Bobby Seale, *A Lonely Rage: The Autobiography of Bobby Seale* (New York, 1978), 129–30; Pearson, *Shadow of the Panther*, 45–47.

9. Lemke-Santangelo, *Abiding Courage*; William J. Rorabaugh, *Berkeley at War: The 1960s* (Berkeley, 1989). Even a cursory reading of the following newspapers during this era will underscore this geography: *The Black Panther, Flatlands, California Voice, California Post*.

10. Newton, *Revolutionary Suicide*, 73–74; Judith May, "Black Panthers," unpublished report, 8 May 1968, Oakland Project Interviews, vol. 4, IGS; Seale quoted from *Seize the Time*, 34; "'All Power to the People': The Political Thought of Huey P. Newton and the Black Panther Party," in Jones, ed., *The Black Panther Party Reconsidered*.

11. Newton, *Revolutionary Suicide*, 73–74; May, "Black Panthers"; Kelley and Esch, "Black Like Mao: Red China and Black Revolution"; Allen, *Black Awakening in Capitalist America*.

12. Judith May, "Black Panther Party for Self Defense," unpublished report, 3 May 1968, Oakland Project Interviews, vol. 4, IGS; Paul Cobb, interview with author; Seale, *Seize the Time*, 6–10, 35–36. See also Pearson, *The Shadow of the Panther*.

13. Ronald Steel, "Letter from Oakland: The Panthers," Newton Collection, Series 2, Box 4, File 4; Nikhil Pal Singh, "The Black Panther and the 'Undeveloped Country' of the Left," in Jones, ed., *The Black Panther Party Reconsidered*, 57–108. See Harold Cruse, *The Crisis of the Negro Intellectual* (New York, 1967); V. I. Lenin, *The Rights of Nations to Self-Determination* (New York, 1951).

14. *BP*, 20 July 1967; Seale, *Seize the Time*, 67–69, 93; May, "Black Panther Party for Self Defense"; White quoted in *Riots, Civil, and Criminal Disorders, Hearings of the Senate Subcommittee on Government Operations*, 18, 24, 25 June 1969, 3826; Moore quoted in *OT*, 26 January 1969.

15. Von Eschen, *Race against Empire*; Biondi, *To Stand and Fight*.

16. Pearson, *The Shadow of the Panther*, 93–110; McKee quoted in *SFC*, 26 September 1971.

17. Hoover quoted in U.S. Congress, *Book III: Final Report of the Select Committee to Study Government Operations with Respect to Intelligence Activities*, S.R. no. 94-755, 94th Congress, 2d Sess. (Washington, DC, 1976), 188. The literature on police and FBI repression of the Black Panther Party is extensive. See Ward Churchill and Jim Vander Wall, *Agents of Repression: The FBI's Secret War against the Black Panther Party and the American Indian Movement* (Boston, 1988); Charles E. Jones, "The Political Repression of the Black Panther Party, 1966–1971: The Case of the Oakland Bay Area," *Journal of Black Studies* (June 1988): 415–21; Roy Wilkins and Ramsey Clark, *Search and Destroy: A Report by the Commission of Inquiry into the Black Panthers and the Police* (New York, 1973); Winston A. Grady-Willis, "The Black Panther Party: State Repression and Political Prisoners," in Jones, ed., *The Black Panther Party Reconsidered*, 363–90.

18. JoNina Abron, " 'Serving the People': The Survival Programs of the Black Panther Party," in Jones, ed., *The Black Panther Party Reconsidered*, 177–92.

368 NOTES TO CHAPTER SIX

19. Abron, "'Serving the People.'"

20. Seale, *Seize the Time*, 86; *BP*, 3 January 1970; Pearson, *The Shadow of the Panther*, 197–200; Hilliard, *This Side of Glory*, 182; Brown, *A Taste of Power*. On Survival Programs in New Haven, see Williams, *Black Politics/White Power*. On the Survival Programs and gender in the party, see essays by JoNina M. Abron, Regina Jennings, Tracye Matthews, and Angela LeBlanc-Ernest in Jones, ed., *The Black Panther Party Reconsidered*; Adolph Reed, Jr., "Response to Eric Arneson," *International Labor and Working-Class History* (Fall 2001): 69–80.

21. Stokeley Carmichael, *Black Power: The Politics of Liberation in America* (New York, 1992); Cleaver quoted in *Guardian*, 13 April 1968; Allen, *Black Awakening in Capitalist America*.

22. CV, 2 August 1963, 13 May 1966; May, "Little Summit Conference Sponsored by the NAACP." The quotations are drawn from the *Community Action Workbook*, published by the Community Action Program in 1965, and quoted in Allen J. Matusow, *The Unraveling of America: A History of Liberalism in the 1960s* (New York, 1986), 247. On the federal OEO and the War on Poverty, see Jeremy Larner and Irving Howe, eds., *Poverty: Views from the Left* (New York, 1968); James T. Patterson, *America's Struggle against Poverty, 1900–1985* (1981; reprint; Cambridge, MA, 1986); Katz, *The Undeserving Poor*.

23. Thomas F. Jackson, "The State, the Movement, and the Urban Poor: The War on Poverty and Political Mobilization in the 1960s," in Katz, ed. *The "Underclass" Debate*, 403–39; *OT*, 13 March 1966.

24. *OT*, 17 January 1964; 11 January, 22 July 1965; 30 May 1968. The history of the Spanish Speaking Unity Council and Mexican American involvement in the city's antipoverty programs is more extensive than I have space here to relate. For the beginning of the fuller story, see Ernesto Galarza, *Economic Development by Mexican Americans, Oakland, California* (Oakland, 1966); "Overall Economic Development Plan, 1978–1983," Spanish Speaking Unity Council, 1978, Ethnic Studies Library, University of California, Berkeley; "Balancing Economic and Human Development: A Case Study of the Spanish Speaking Unity Council, the Peralta Service Corporation, and the Employment and Training System in Oakland," prepared by Philip Shapira, March 1982, Ethnic Studies Library. See also issues of Oakland's *Mundo Hispano* and the *OEDCI Reporter* from the late 1960s and early 1970s.

25. Letter from Jack Ortega, 6 April 1966, Box 14, Folder 8, Ernesto Galarza Papers, Stanford University Archives.

26. *OT*, 22 August 1967; May, "Little Summit Conference," 8; McCullum quoted in "Human Relations News," September 1967, Alameda County Human Relations Commission, IGS.

27. *OT*, 9 June, 23 August 1967, 29 October 1968; Jeffrey L. Pressman, *Federal Programs and City Politics: The Dynamics of the Aid Process in Oakland* (Berkeley, 1975), 63; Judith May, "City Council Meeting," 14 September 1967, unpublished report, Oakland Project Interviews, vol. 3, IGS. Smith went on to head the regional OEO before becoming president of Merritt College.

28. *SFE*, 28 July 1968.

29. *OT*, 28 March 1968; 24 September 1970; Pressman, *Federal Programs and City Politics*, 64–65; Nicholls and Babbie, *Oakland in Transition*, 99; Norvel

Smith quoted on Pacific Radio, KPFA, 14 November 1968, Pacific Radio Archives, Tape BB2469.

30. *OT*, 9 October 1970.

31. OECDI, "Discover Oakland—The Friendly City" (Oakland, 1970); *OT*, 11 August 1970.

32. *OT*, 10 January, 22 March, 13 April 1971; Pressman, *Federal Programs and City Politics*, 65.

33. *OP*, 27 March, 4 September 1969; *OT*, 29 October, 16 and 29 August 1968, 30 January 1969.

34. *CV*, 22 and 29 July, 5 and 12 August 1971; *OT*, 26 January 1969.

35. See, for instance, Whitney Young's *Beyond Racism*; Allen, *Black Awakening in Capitalist America*.

36. June Manning Thomas, "Model Cities Revisited: Issues of Race and Empowerment," in June Manning Thomas and Marsha Ritzdorf, ed., *Urban Planning and the African American Community: In the Shadows*, (Thousand Oaks, CA, 1997), 143–66; Bernard J. Frieden and Marshall Kaplan, *The Politics of Neglect: Urban Aid from Model Cities to Revenue Sharing* (Cambridge, 1975).

37. WOPC memo quoted in May, "Model Cities," unpublished meeting minutes and notes, 27 February–23 April 1968, Oakland Project Interviews, vol. 4, IGS; Reading quoted in May, "Model Cities," meeting minutes and notes, 24 April 1968, Oakland Project Interviews, vol. 4, IGS. See also *OT* April 3 and 15, 1968; May, "Model Cities," meeting minutes and notes, 25 and 26 April 1968, Oakland Project Interviews, vol. 4, IGS.

38. Redevelopment Agency of the City of Oakland, "City Center: Linking Federal Programs for Job Opportunities and Economic Development," May 1967, IGS; *OP*, 14 February 1968.

39. May, "Model Cities," 27 February–23 April 1968, 24 April 1968, 25 and 26 April 1968; *OT* 3 and 15 April 1968; Judith May, "Police-Community Relations: Black Panthers and the Black Strike for Justice Committee, April–June, 1968," sections 1 and 2, and "Black Panthers," 8 May 1968, Oakland Project Interviews, vol. 4, IGS. Judith May, "Black Strike for Justice," 9 May 1968, 2–6.

40. May, "Police-Community Relations," Section 1, 28–29; Section 2, 15–17, 30, 44–54; May, "Black Panthers"; "Black Strike for Justice"; *OT*, 8 May 1968, 1.

41. Judith May, "The Politics of Growth Versus the Politics of Redistribution: Negotiations over the Model Cities Program in Oakland," paper delivered at the meeting of the American Orthopsychiatric Association, San Francisco, 24 March 1970, Oakland Project files, IGS; May, "Two Model Cities: Negotiations in Oakland," in George Frederickson, ed., *Neighborhood Control in the 1970s: Politics, Administration, and Citizen Participation* (New York, 1973), 217–46; *OT*, 9 February 1968; *SFE*, 28 July 1968; *OT*, 20 June 1968.

42. *OT*, 2 and 3 July 1968.

43. *OT*, 21 June 1968; May, "Police-Community Relations," 43.

44. *CV*, 2 and 9 August 1968; Paul Cobb, interview with author.

45. *OT*, 11 June 1969, 22 January 1970; *CV*, 24 October 1969; *OP*, 3 April 1969.

46. *OT*, 7 February, 27 November 1969.

47. Hayes, *Power Structure and Urban Policy*, 99, 111.

48. David M. Gordon, "An Impressionistic Report about Minority Unemployment in Oakland, California," The Ford Foundation, October 1966, Oakland Collection, Ford Foundation Archives; Warren Hinckle, "Metropoly: The Story of Oakland," *Ramparts* (February 1966): 25.

49. U.S. Commission on Civil Rights, *Hearing Before the U.S. Commission on Civil Rights*, Oakland, 4–6 May 1967, 705; *OT*, 21 April 1966.

50. *OP*, 31 July 1968.

51. *OT*, 3 October, 26 and 28 November 1969; *CV*, 27 June 1969.

52. *OT*, 23 March, 18 December 1970; 10 January 1971; *CV*, 28 August, 18 December 1970; Judith May, "Percy Moore," notes, 7 May 1968, Oakland Project Interviews, vol. 4, IGS.

53. *OT*, 31 January, 18 April 1971; *CV*, 18 December 1970; *PW*, 17 April 1971.

54. *OT*, 31 January, 18 April 1971; *CV*, 18 December 1970; *PW*, 17 April 1971.

55. Wiley quoted in Nick Klotz and Mary Lynn Kotz, *A Passion for Equality: George Wiley and the Movement* (New York, 1977).

56. Cleaver, *Post-Prison Writings and Speeches*, 169.

Chapter 7
White Noose

1. As a description of suburbanization, "white noose" gained popular attention in 1961, when it appeared in *Volume 4: Housing, 1961 United States Commission on Civil Rights Report* (Washington, DC, 1961). By the late 1960s it was in common usage across the country.

2. U.S. Department of Commerce, *Census of Population: 1950, Characteristics of the Population, California* (Washington, DC, 1951); *1970 Census of the Population, Characteristics of the Population, California* (Washington, DC, 1973).

3. For distinct, but similar, political stories in Southern California, see Nicolaides, *My Blue Heaven*; McGirr, *Suburban Warriors*.

4. See newspaper clippings and other material in "Fair Housing—1963" and "Fair Housing Bill" folders, Box 1, Rumford Papers. See also Casstevens, *Politics, Housing, and Race Relations*; Denton, *Apartheid American Style*.

5. *California Real Estate Magazine*, May, June, July, August, and December 1964; *NYT*, 10 May 1964; *CV*, 17 May and 9 August 1963; state senator quoted in *California Real Estate Magazine*, February 1964, 5; Rumford quoted in Regional Oral History Office, *William Byron Rumford: Legislator for Fair Employment, Fair Housing, and Public Health* (Berkeley, 1973), 120, 124.

6. *California Real Estate Magazine*, May, June, July, August, and December 1964; *NYT*, 10 May 1964; *CV*, 17 May and 9 August 1963; California Committee for Fair Practices, "Public Education and the CREA—Control by the Subsidized," manuscript, Box 2 Rumford Papers; Clare Short, "What Are the Obligations of the Housing Industry to Resolve Such Conflicts as Exist in This Area?" speech manuscript, University of California, Berkeley Library; Raymond Wolfinger and Fred Greenstein, "The Repeal of Fair Housing in California: An Analysis of Referendum Voting," *American Political Science Review* 62 (September 1968): 753–69.

7. *William Byron Rumford*, 120, 124; California Secretary of State, "Statement of All Votes Cast, General Election, November 3, 1964" (Sacramento, 1964); Wolfinger and Greenstein, "The Repeal of Fair Housing in California."

8. *Ramparts*, April 1966, 7; Denton, *Apartheid American Style*; "Remarks on the Rumford Act and the Housing initiative," by State Senator Albert S. Rodda, and "California's New Fair Housing Law," by Carmen H. Warschaw, Box 7, Rumford Papers.

9. *Ramparts*, April 1966, 7; *FNR*, 23 July, 10 September, 26 October 1964; Alameda County Committee Against Proposition 14, *News*, Central Labor Council of Alameda County Collection, Box 88, Folder 7, CLCAC/LARC; *California Real Estate Magazine*, April 1964, 5; "Proposition 14—Campaign Flyers," Box 7, Rumford Papers.

10. Denton, *Apartheid American Style*, 30, 32–37.

11. For evidence of these practices and the real estate industry's investment in control of racial segregation in California, see ibid. For the nation as a whole, see Massey and Denton, *American Apartheid*; Bruce D. Haynes, *Red Lines, Black Spaces: The Politics of Race and Space in a Black Middle Class Suburb* (New Haven, 2001). See also any volume of the *Hearings Before the National Commission on Urban Problems* (Washington, DC, 1968), where these issues received an open hearing in cities across the country.

12. *SLMN*, 27 March, 26 July, 8 August 1963; *FNR*, 25 June, 26 August, 5 and 6 September 1963.

13. I owe these last observations to Martha Biondi and Matthew Lassiter.

14. *SLMN*, 9, 23, 24, 26, and 27 July, 1,17, 29, and 31 August, 17 September, 21 November 1963; 10 January, 1 May 1964.

15. Transcript of a debate on Proposition 14 and the Rumford Act, 19 September 1964, KNXT TV, Box 2, Rumford Papers.

16. *SLMN*, 14 and 15 May 1971; *FNR*, 1 September 1971.

17. *OT*, 5 January 1969; Wilson Record, "Minority Groups and Intergroup Relations in the San Francisco Bay Area," 1963, 22–23, IGS; "Draft Report to the Governor's Advisory Committee on Housing Problems," ms., 1962, Box 7, Catherine Bauer Wurster Collection, Bancroft Library, 4; Young, *Beyond Racism*, 6.

18. *Hearings Before the U.S. Commission on Civil Rights*, 587, 687, 1036; *FNR*, 25 June, 5 and 6 September 1963.

19. Oakland Chamber of Commerce, Research Department, "Fifty Largest Private Employers in Alameda County," April 1970; Bay Area Council, "A Guide to Industrial Locations in the San Francisco Bay Area," 1964. For a discussion of the relative weight historians should place on union versus employer discrimination in labor markets, see the set of essays in *International Review of Social History* 41 (1996): 351–406.

20. Harold H. Martin, "Our Urban Revolution, Part I: Are We Building a City 600 Miles Long?" *Saturday Evening Post* 232 (January 2, 1960): 15.

21. Gerald Horne, *Fire This Time: The Watts Uprising and the 1960s* (New York, 1995).

22. Jerry Schimmel, *Union City, California, Part II: A Community Study Extended*, ms., Union City Public Library; *SLMN*, 21 July 1964; 26 January 1965; *FNR*, 29 August 1963; "Progress Edition," 1964.

23. Galarza quoted in *Action Research in Defense of the Barrio: Interviews with Ernesto Galarza, Guillermo Flores and Rosalio Muñoz*, collected and edited by Mario Barrera and Geralda Vialpando (Los Angeles, n.d.), 14. See also Ernesto Galarza, "Alviso: The Crisis of a Barrio," sponsored by the Mexican American Community Services Organization, San José, California, 15 August 1973. For other colonias, see *HDR*, 16 and 23 August 1950; 14 April 1954; 13 January 1962; *SLMN*, 23 and 28 January, 27 March 1963. In 1970 the "Spanish language" and "Spanish surname" population in Alameda County was over 130,000, more than 10 percent of the county's total residents. Some of these individuals were of Filipino, Central American, and Puerto Rican background, but the overwhelming majority were ethnic Mexican.

24. *U.S. Census of Population and Housing: 1960, San Francisco-Oakland* (Washington, DC, 1961), 14–17; *1970 Census of Population and Housing, Census Tracts, San Francisco-Oakland* (Washington, DC, 1972), 73–80.

25. Galarza, *The Crisis of a Barrio*; *1970 Census of Population and Housing: Census Tracts, San Jose, California* (Washington, DC, 1973).

26. Galarza, *The Crisis of a Barrio*; Mario Barrera and Geraldo Vialpando, eds., *Action Research In Defense of the Barrio: Interviews with Ernesto Galarza, Guillermo Flores and Rosalio Muñoz* (Los Angeles, n.d.); *1970 Census of Population and Housing: Census Tracts, San Jose, California; Californians of Spanish Surname: Population, Employment, Income, Education* (San Francisco, 1964). The *Milpitas Post* reprinted several of its features in Spanish during its first few years of publication. See, for example, the issues of 31 March and 9 June 1955.

27. Schimmel, *Union City, California*.

28. *UCL*, 9 April 1970, and 22 April 1971; *Southern Alameda County Spanish Speaking Organization (SASSO)* v. *City of Union City, California, et al.*, appeal from the U.S. District Court for the Northern District of California, 16 March 1970.

29. Pitti, *The Devil in Silicon Valley*.

30. Doty quoted in *UCL*, July 1969 (article on file, Union City Public Library); *SASSO* v. *City of Union City*.

31. *FNR*, 22 September 1969, and 22 April 1971. The other ground-breaking case in suburban housing was in Mt. Laurel, New Jersey. See David L. Kirp, John P. Dwyer, and Larry A. Rosenthal, *Our Town: Race, Housing, and the Soul of Suburbia* (New Brunswick, 1995).

32. *UCL*, 9 April 1970, 22 April 1971; *SFC*, 31 May 1970; *FNR*, 22 April 1971; *SASSO* v. *City of Union City*; Kirp, Dwyer, and Rosenthal, *Our Town*.

33. *SLNO*, 26 January and 26 March 1965.

34. *SLNO*, 9 August 1968, 22 August 1969; *FNR*, 3 December 1963, 14 March 1969, 4 January 1971; letter from Citizens' Committee for Low-Rent Housing to Governor Edmund G. Brown, Box 82, Folder 6, ACLC Collection, LARC; Weir, *Separate Efforts—Similar Goals and Results*.

35. *1970 Census of Population and Housing, Census Tracts, San Francisco-Oakland*.

36. *SLNO*, 22 July 1964, 26 January 1965.

37. "Draft Report to the Governor's Advisory Committee on Housing Problems," ms., 1962, Box 7, Catherine Bauer Wurster Collection, Bancroft Library, 19.

38. *FNR*, 28 June 1967; *SLMN*, 9 June 1959; 4, 10, and 11 May 1960; 27 August 1963.

39. *SLNO*, 7 September 1962; "Draft Report to the Governor's Advisory Committee on Housing Problems," 4.

40. *FNR*, 18 March 1964.

41. *SLMN*, 16 August 1966, 23 August 1969;

42. *WSJ*, 4 March 1966; *SLMN*, 27 August 1965; *City of San Leandro 1958 Library Bonds, Series A* (San Leandro, 1958).

43. *Growth: An Analysis of the Effects of Severe Growth Curtailment Policies Upon the City of Fremont* (Fremont, 1973), 2; *FNR*, 1 March and 6 June 1966; *MP*, 6 April 1966; *SFC*, 10 May 1963.

44. *SLMN*, 1 and 2 July 1960.

45. *SLMN*, 2 April 1964, 31 August 1966, 9 July 1967; *SFC*, 10 May 1963, 16 July 1967.

46. On the trial of Wolden and the scandal in San Francisco, see *SFC*, 12, 17 May, 16 November, 28 December 1966; see also Sears and Citrin, *Tax Revolt*; Schrag, *Paradise Lost*.

47. *SFC*, 12 and 17 May, 16 November, 28 December 1966; Sears and Citrin, *Tax Revolt*, 19–21.

48. *SLMN*, 17 and 18 July 1967; *SFC*, 28 May 1968; *Fremont Argus*, 17 September, 7 November 1968, 11 April 1969.

49. *SLMN*, 17 and 18 July 1967; *SFC*, 28 May 1968.

50. *Fremont Argus*, 17 September, 7 November 1968, 11 April 1969; Sears and Citrin, *Tax Revolt*, 19–21.

51. Phil Ethington, "Mapping the Local State," *Journal of Urban History* (July 2001): 686–702.

Chapter 8
Babylon

1. Cleaver, *Post-Prison Writings and Speeches*, 145.

2. Mollenkopf, *The Contested City*; Todd Swanstrom, *The Crisis of Growth Politics: Cleveland, Kucinich, and the Challenge of Urban Populism* (Philadelphia, 1985).

3. David R. Colburn and Jeffrey S. Adler, *African American Mayors: Race, Politics, and the American City* (Urbana, 2001).

4. For a critique of the co-optation of radical black politics, see Adolph Reed, Jr., *Stirrings in the Jug: Black Politics in the Post-Segregation Era* (Minneapolis, 1999). See also Woodard, *A Nation within a Nation*; Heather Ann Thompson, *Whose Detroit? Politics, Labor, and Race in a Modern American City* (Ithaca, 2001); Robin D. G. Kelley, *Freedom Dreams: The Black Radical Tradition* (Boston, 2002).

5. *CV*, 22 April 1971; Cleaver, *Post-Prison Writings and Speeches*, 117; "Oakland Election Results," ms., n.d., IGS; Jeffrey L. Pressman, "Preconditions of Mayoral Leadership," *The American Political Science Review* 66 (June 1972): 511–24; William Lunch, "Carpentier's the One, or, Who's This Guy Knowland? A Political History of Oakland, California" ms., 1 September 1969, IGS; Kristen

Johnson, "Elections and Representation in Oakland," ms., 7 March 1969, IGS; Edward C. Hayes, *Power Structure and Urban Policy: Who Rules in Oakland?* (New York, 1972), 30–37.

6. Johnson, "Elections and Representation in Oakland," 4. See also William Lunch, "Carpentier's the One"; Pressman, "Preconditions of Mayoral Leadership."

7. *OT*, 24 July, 17 October, 1 November 1968; Pickus, "A Study and Analysis of the Campaign for Proposition M,"ms., 5 November 1968, IGS, 12–15.

8. *OT*, 6 and 26 October 1968; Pickus, "Campaign for Proposition M"; Bill Cavala, "Inside Oakland: The Story of the Campaign for Proposition J," ms., n.d., IGS; Lorna Jones, interview with author, Oakland, 3 September 1997.

9. Donald R. Hopkins, "Development of Black Political Organization in Berkeley since 1960," in Nathan Scott, eds., *Experiment and Change in Berkeley*, 105–36. In the same volume, see Ronald V. Dellums, "Statement," 22–23; William Byron Rumford, Jr., "Reflections on My Relationship With D. G. Gibson," 35–37; T. J. Kent, Jr., "Berkeley's First Democratic Regime, 1961–1970: The Postwar Awakening of Berkeley's Liberal Conscience," 73–104.

10. *OP*, 24 and 31 January, 29 May 1968.

11. *OP*, 11 June, 22 October 1970; Dellums 1970 campaign material, Dellums Miscellaneous Material, IGS.

12. Lorna Jones, interview with author; Dellums, "Statement"; *OP*, 5 November 1970.

13. Lorna Jones, interview with author; *Experiment and Change in Berkeley*, 105–35, 231–68; Rorabaugh, *Berkeley at War*.

14. Pearson, *The Shadow of the Panther*, 217–24; Hilliard and Cole, *This Side of Glory*, 295–300. Hilliard quoted in *BP*, 17 February 1970.

15. Hilliard, *This Side of Glory*, 182; Brown, *A Taste of Power*. See essays by JoNina M. Abron, Regina Jennings, Tracye Matthews, and Angela LeBlanc-Ernest in Jones, ed., *The Black Panther Party Reconsidered*; Craig Martin Peck, "'Educate to Liberate': The Black Panther Party and Political Education" (Ph.D. diss., Stanford University, 2001); *BP*, 17 January 1970.

16. *BP*, 29 July 1972; Pearson, *The Shadow of the Panther*, 230–41; Brown, *A Taste of Power*, 310–16; Hilliard, *This Side of Glory*, 318–21.

17. *BP* 29 July 1972; Pearson, *The Shadow of the Panther*, 247.

18. *BP*, 29 July 1972; HPN, Series 1, Box 38, Folder 13, Huey Newton, "Oakland: An All-American Example," ms., 1974.

19. *BP*, 9 September 1972; 13 January 1973. The Panthers, of course, were not alone in turning to colonial analogies for urban America. A group of radical social scientists and scholars did so as well. See William K. Tabb, *The Political Economy of the Black Ghetto* (New York, 1970); Wildred L. David, "Black America in Development Perspective, Part I," *Review of Black Political Economy* (Winter 1973): 89–104; "Part II" (Summer 1973): 79–112; Robert Blauner, *Racial Oppression in America* (New York, 1972). For a discussion of this school of urban theory, see Katz, *The Undeserving Poor*, 52–65.

20. Huey P. Newton, "Uniting against a Common Enemy," 23 October 1971, in David Hilliard and Donald Weise, eds., *The Huey P. Newton Reader* (New York, 2001).

21. Peck, "'Educate to Liberate.'"

22. *BP*, 9 September 1972, 13 January 1973. See David J. Olson, "Public Port Accountability: A Framework for Evaluation," in Marc J. Hershman, ed., *Urban Ports and Harbor Management: Responding to Change along U.S. Water-fronts* (New York, 1988), 307–33; and *Port of Oakland 1957 Revenue Bonds, $8,500,000 Series J.*

23. *BP*, 23 December 1972.

24. *BP*, 5 and 12 August, 2, 16, 23, and 30 September, 14 and 28 October, 30 November, 16 December 1972.

25. *BP*, 20 and 27 January, 3 February, 10 and 31 March 1973.

26. Party worker quoted in memo to Newton, Friday, 16 March, HPN, Series 2, Box 5.

27. *MT*, 14 February, 28 March 1973; *BP*, 7 and 14 April 1973.

28. *MT*, 7, 21, and 28 March 1973.

29. *MT*, 7 March, 4 April 1973.

30. *MT*, 25 April, 23 May 1973; *BP*, 21 April, 5, 12, and 19 May 1973.

31. Brown quoted in *BP*, 10 August 1974. See Brown, *A Taste of Power*, 400–50; Angela D. LeBlanc-Ernest, " 'The Most Qualified Person to Handle the Job': Black Panther Party Women, 1966–1982," in *The Black Panther Party Reconsidered*, 305–34. On Brown's direct involvement in Oakland politics, see *CV*, 28 February 1974; *BP*, 30 November, 28 December 1974.

32. *BP*, 28 December 1974; 11 and 18 January 1975.

33. *BP*, 4 January, 15 February, 1 March 1975; Brown, *A Taste of Power*, 365–81.

34. Reed, *Stirrings in the Jug*.

35. *BP*, 15 February 1975.

36. For comparisons, see David R. Colburn, "Running for Office: African American Mayors from 1967 to 1996," in Colburn and Adler, eds., *African American Mayors*, 23–56; in the same volume, see James B. Lane, "Black Political Power and Its Limits: Gary Mayor Richard G. Hatcher's Administration, 1968–1987," 57–79; Ronald H. Bayor, "African American Mayors and Governance in Atlanta," 178–99.

37. *CV*, 16 April 1977. On Harold Washington and Chicago politics, see Manning Marable, "How Washington Won: The Political Economy of Race in Chicago," *The Journal of Intergroup Relations* 11 (Summer 1983): 56–81.

38. *BP*, 15 January, 12 March, 2 April 1977; *MT*, 13 April 1977; *CV*, 26 March, 16 April 1977; *OP*, 17 April 1977.

39. *OP*, 18 May 1977; *CV*, 21 May 1977; *MT*, 11 May 1977; *BP*, 14 May 1977.

40. Heather Ann Thompson, "Rethinking the Collapse of Postwar Liberalism: The Rise of Mayor Coleman Young and the Politics of Race in Detroit," in Colburn and Adler, eds., *African American Mayors*, 227–48.

41. See Fred Bloch, et al., *The Mean Season: The Attack on the Welfare State* (New York, 1987).

42. Steele and Cobb quoted in *Proposition 13 Impact on Minorities: Proceedings of a Workshop* (Davis, CA, 1979), 87, 96.

43. Schrag, *Paradise Lost*, 132; John Rennie Short, "Urban Imagineers: Boosters and the Representation of Cities," in Jonas and Wilson, ed., *The Urban Growth Machine*, 37–54.

44. W. Eliot Brownlee, "California Taxes: Historical Roots" and "The Property Tax: Will It Survive?"; Perry Shapiro, "California's Hidden Tax: Inflation," in *Taxation: A California Perspective* (Sacramento, 1978).

45. Legislative Analyst, "An Analysis of Proposition 13: The Jarvis-Gann Property Tax Initiative" (Sacramento, 1978).

46. The most comprehensive treatment of the tax revolt is Sears and Citrin, *Tax Revolt.* See also George G. Kaufman and Kenneth T. Rosen, *The Property Tax Revolt: The Case of Proposition 13* (Cambridge, MA, 1982); Jaffrey Chapman, *Proposition 13 and Land Use: A Case Study of Fiscal Limits in California* (Lexington, MA, 1982).

47. Howard Jarvis with Robert Pack, *I'm Mad as Hell: The Exclusive Story of the Tax Revolt and Its Leader* (New York, 1979), 12.

48. Brownlee, "California Taxes: Historical Roots" and "The Property Tax: Will It Survive?"; brief on Proposition 13 prepared by Assembly Committees on Local Government and Revenue and Taxation, IGS.

49. *SLDR,* 1 and 2 June 1978; *FA,* 28 May 1978.

50. Arthur Slaustein, "Proposition 13: The Morning After," *New Spirit* (February 1979): 6–9; Eric Smith and Jack Citrin, "The Building of a Majority for Tax Limitation in California: 1968–1978," ms., IGS; "Jarvis-Gann vs. SB 1 (Proposition 8), A Summary Report," *San Francisco Business* (June 1978): 20–23; Richard P. Simpson, "Spotlight on Proposition 13," *Western City* (April 1978): 9–12.

51. *MP,* 14 March 1978; Roger Lark Kemp, "Coping with Proposition 13: A Case Study of Oakland, California" (Ph.D. diss., Golden Gate University, 1979), 92.

52. Letter, 8 February 1978, IGS; Percy Steele speech, 88.

53. *Fremont Argus,* 24 and 25 May 1978.

54. *FA,* 28 May 1978; *HDR,* 2 June 1978; Slaustein, "Proposition 13," 7.

55. Kemp, "Coping with Proposition 13," 172.

56. James M. Wessel and Roy H. Gesley, "Behind the Tax Revolt: The Shifting Tax Burden in California," in *Proposition 13 Impact on Minorities: Proceedings of a Workshop* (Davis, CA, 1979), 102–5; *FA,* 24 May 1978.

Conclusion

1. Paul Jacobs, *Prelude to a Riot: A View of Urban America From the Bottom* (New York, 1967), 6.

2. Internationalists would have a good argument with this assertion, because the Cold War, emerging U.S. neo-imperialism, and the extension of American global economic hegemony under Bretton Woods also help to define this long postwar period. I make no claim that these are unimportant. Indeed, the domestic sociopolitical developments that I emphasize are linked with these international events in enormously consequential ways. But I leave to other historians the drawing out of the specifics of those connections and the making of that argument.

3. Fraser and Gerstle, eds., *The Rise and Fall of the New Deal Order;* Hirsch, *Making the Second Ghetto;* Sugrue, *Origins of the Urban Crisis;* Nicolaides, *My Blue Heaven;* Hamilton and Hamilton, *The Dual Agenda.* See also many relevant essays in Henry Louis Taylor, Jr., and Walter Hill, eds., *Historical Roots of the*

Urban Crisis: African Americans in the Industrial City, 1900–1950 (New York, 2000).

4. This broad view of the national welfare state has yet to receive a thorough and synthetic treatment by a historian. For good beginnings, see Gelfand, *A Nation of Cities*; Adolph Reed, Jr., ed., *Without Justice for All: The New Liberalism and Our Retreat from Racial Equality* (Boulder, 1999); Michael B. Katz, *The Price of Citizenship: Redefining America's Welfare State* (New York, 2001); Self and Sugrue, "The Power of Place."

5. Brown, *Race, Money, and the American Welfare State*; Hamilton and Hamilton, *The Dual Agenda*.

6. For examples of works that do this, see Doug McAdam, *Political Process and the Development of Black Insurgency, 1930–1970* (Chicago, 1999), and Biondi, *To Stand and Fight*.

7. On the SDS narrative, see Todd Gitlin, *The Sixties: Days of Hope, Days of Rage* (New York, 1987), and James Miller, *"Democracy in the Streets": From Port Huron to the Siege of Chicago* (New York, 1987). Even the otherwise wonderful new collection of material on the 1960s by David Farber and Beth Bailey reproduces some of this periodization. See Farber and Bailey, *The Columbia Guide to the 1960s* (New York, 2001). For more helpful syntheses, see Maurice Isserman and Michael Kazin, *America Divided: The Civil War of the 1960s* (New York, 2000). For the SNCC narrative, see Sitkoff, *The Struggle for Black Equality, 1954–1980* Carson, *In Struggle*; David Garrow, *Bearing the Cross: Martin Luther King, Jr., and the Southern Christian Leadership Conference, 1955–1968* (New York, 1986). A generation of work on the local context of the southern civil rights movement has thoroughly complicated the dominant narrative, but this work has only begun to change how civil rights is represented in broad, synthetic treatments of period's history. See, for instance, the still problematic syntheses by Matusow, *The Unraveling of America*; Birnbaum and Taylor, *Civil Rights since 1787*; Thomas Borstelmann, *The Cold War and the Color Line: American Race Relations in the Global Arena* (Cambridge, MA, 2001).

8. Historians are beginning to reinterpret the decade and to push the historiography away from the dominant narrative of disillusionment. See Steven Lawson, *In Pursuit of Power: Southern Blacks and the Electoral Politics, 1965–1982* (New York, 1985); Terry Anderson, *The Movement and the Sixties: Protest in America From Greensboro to Wounded Knee* (New York, 1995); Woodard, *A Nation within a Nation*; Williams, *Black Politics White Power*; Isserman and Kazin, *America Divided*; Max Elbaum, *Revolution in the Air: Sixties Radicals Turn to Lenin, Mao, and Che* (London, 2002); and Van Gosse, "A Movement of Movements: The Definition and Periodization of the New Left," in Rosenzweig and Agnew, ed., *A Companion to Post-1945 America*, (Cambridge, MA, 2002). Gosse's essay, in particular, charts a productive way out of stagnant historiographical waters.

9. The monographic literature is full of studies that are moving the historiography away from a reliance on dichotomies. See William Sales, Jr., *From Civil Rights to Black Liberation: Malcolm X and the Organization of Afro-American Unity* (Boston, 1994); Jones, ed., *The Black Panther Party Reconsidered*; Tyson, *Radio Free Dixie*; Nikhil Singh, *Black Is a Country: Politics and Theory in the*

Long Civil Rights Era (Cambridge, MA, 2003). Most black intellectuals writing at the time did not trust the dichotomies either. See, for instance, Allen, *Black Awakening in Capitalist America*; Young, *Beyond Racism*; Rustin, *Down the Line*.

10. Jackson, *Crabgrass Frontier*. For excellent new histories of suburbanization, see Pitti, *The Devil in Silicon Valley*; Andrew Wiese, *Places of Our Own: African American Suburbanization since 1916* (Chicago, 2003); Nicolaides, *My Blue Heaven*; McGirr, *Suburban Warriors*.

Index

POLITICS AND SOCIETY IN TWENTIETH-CENTURY AMERICA